CHORA: Intervals in the Philosophy of Architecture
Managing Editor: Alberto Pérez-Gómez
Edited by Alberto Pérez-Gómez and Stephen Parcell

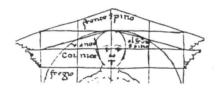

Chora 7: Intervals in the Philosophy of Architecture

Intervals in the Philosophy of Architecture

C H O R A

V O L U M E   S E V E N

Edited by Alberto Pérez-Gómez and Stephen Parcell

McGill-Queen's University Press

Montreal & Kingston · London · Chicago

CHORA is a publication of the History and Theory of Architecture
graduate program at McGill University, Montréal, Canada.

MANAGING EDITOR
Alberto Pérez-Gómez, *McGill University*

EDITORS
Alberto Pérez-Gómez, *McGill University*
Stephen Parcell, *Dalhousie University*

ASSISTANT EDITOR
Ron Jelaco, *McGill University*

ADVISORY BOARD
Ricardo L. Castro, *McGill University*
Agostino De Rosa, *Università IUAV di Venezia*
Donald Kunze, *Pennsylvania State University*
Phyllis Lambert, *Canadian Centre for Architecture*
David Michael Levin, *Northwestern University*
Katsuhiko Muramoto, *Pennsylvania State University*
Stephen Parcell, *Dalhousie University*
Louise Pelletier, *Université de Québec à Montréal*

For author information, please contact
www.mcgill.ca/architecture-theory/chora/

Legal deposit first quarter 2016
Bibliothèque nationale du Québec
Printed in Canada on acid-free paper

McGill-Queen's University Press acknowledges the support of the Canada Council for the Arts for
our publishing program. We also acknowledge the financial support of the Government of Canada
through the Canada Book Fund for our publishing activities.

Library and Archives Canada has catalogued this publication as follows:
Chora: intervals in the philosophy of architecture
Each issue also has distinct title.
Irregular.
Vol. 1 (1994)–
ISSN 1198-449X
ISBN 978-0-7735-4701-8 (volume 7) (bnd)
ISBN 978-0-7735-4702-5 (volume 7) (pbk)
ISBN 978-0-7735-9879-9 (volume 7) (ePDF)

1. Architecture—Philosophy—Periodicals. I. McGill University.
History and Theory of Architecture Graduate Program. II. Title.

NA1.C46   720'.1   C94-900762-5

This book was designed and typeset by studio oneonone in Sabon 10/13

Contents

Preface

This final volume of *Chora: Intervals in the Philosophy of Architecture* includes fifteen essays on provocative topics in architecture, its history, and related disciplines.

Four focus on embodied human experience. Diana Cheng leads us through a seductive house, commissioned and governed by an eighteenth-century Parisian courtesan, that slowly builds up erotic fantasies in her clientele as they anticipate arrival in her boudoir. Paul Holmquist revisits the civic brothel at the centre of Claude-Nicolas Ledoux's ideal city of Chaux, using Jean-Jacques Rousseau's *Emile* as an illuminating guide. Angeliki Sioli evokes the spatial qualities and lived experience of Frederick Kiesler's enigmatic Endless House, drawing from descriptions in his writings, drawings, and models. Christos Kakalis describes daily and annual rituals in a 1,600-year-old monastery on Mount Athos in northeastern Greece, focusing on how sound and silence organize the monks, pilgrims, and visitors.

Theatre, one of the ancient roots of architecture, is pursued in three other essays. Lisa Landrum distills meanings of *chōra* from ordinary human situations and dramatic performances in ancient Greece, before *chōra* was recast philosophically by Plato in *Timaeus*. Negin Djavaherian describes the origins, staging, and experience of Peter Brook's 1971 theatrical production of *Orghast* at the ruins of ancient Persepolis in Iran, manifesting his concept of Immediate Theatre. Marc Neveu presents a previously unpublished project by Douglas Darden for an unfinished graphic novel entitled *The Laughing Girls*, set in Troy, New York; Troy, Greece; and a future Troy.

Architectural creation, a topic of interest to everyone who is architecturally active, is approached differently in four of the essays. Alberto Pérez-Gómez examines Filarete's ideal city of Sforzinda, in which the political seed from a benevolent prince gestates in the architect's imagination for nine months before emerging as a fully formed urban design. Paul Emmons considers the role of the Renaissance frontispiece in three analogous locations: the illustrated title page of a book, the pedimented front of a building, and the human forehead. Anne Bordeleau elucidates different concepts of time that underlie compelling projects by filmmaker Andrei Tarkovsky, sculptor Andy Goldsworthy, and architect Peter Zumthor. Stephen Wischer takes us on a journey through the labyrinthine constructions and installations in the private studio and compound of German artist Anselm Kiefer at La Ribaute in southern France.

Historical origins of architecture are probed in four more essays. Nikolaos-Ion Terzoglou unpacks significant words and concepts in Leon Battista Alberti's *De re aedificatoria*, recognizing an underlying structure from principles of law that distinguish between the universal and the particular. Ron Jelaco assembles clues at the origins of modern architecture in seventeenth-century France to dispute the prevalent belief that Claude Perrault was the architect of the Paris Observatory. Robert Nelson takes us on a historical and etymological stroll through different concepts of "street" and the urban principles with which streets around the world have been created and represented. Yoonchun Jung highlights Japan's attempt to construct a new Western tradition for itself, represented in the buildings and historical narrative of an industrial exhibition at the former Gyeongbok Palace in Seoul in 1915, when Korea was a colony under Japanese rule.

Along with the four themes mentioned above, the essays could be categorized in other ways: different scales (from a forehead to a city), different types of subjects (books, buildings, drawings, exhibitions, and performances), different locations (France, Greece, Iran, Italy, Korea, United States, and the world at large), and various historical eras (antiquity, Renaissance Italy, early modern France, and the past hundred years). Topics in architectural history and theory are multifaceted rather than hierarchical, so many paratactic links can be made throughout *Chora 7*, as well as our discipline.

The authors have brought different intentions and motivations to their work: righting a wrong, solving a puzzle, piecing together fragments, presenting a discovery, building an argument, evoking experience, and illuminating a familiar subject in a new way. Some of them spent years – not just nine months – conceiving their topic, nourishing it, exercising it, and polishing it to a brilliant shine. Now it's time to give it a name and send it out into the world. Some of them are trying something new. "Essay" is not just a stuffy academic assignment; it comes from the French *essayer*, to try. We believe that the world – or at least the architectural discipline –

will be a better place after these essays have been disseminated, savoured, internalized, and externalized.

The order of essays in *Chora* 7 is alphabetical by author, so there's no real beginning or end. There is one exception: this volume ends with Lisa Landrum's study of pre-philosophical *chōra*, a solid bookend that loops back to the very first essay in *Chora* 1, by Alberto Pérez-Gómez, also on *chōra* and its significance for architecture.

Architects who build things can observe the finished products and witness others inhabiting and interpreting them. Architects who write may feel like they're speaking into the void. If an essay inspires you, we encourage you to check "About the Authors" and send the author an email; ask a question or deliver a compliment. Keep the ball rolling by citing the essay in your own essay, your blog, your tweets, whatever.

On this occasion, the final book in the *Chora* series, the editors would like to congratulate everyone who participated in this venture throughout its 25 years, 7 volumes, 78 authors, 87 essays, and 2,305 pages. Most, but not all, have been associated with the doctoral program in architectural history and theory at McGill University: as faculty, students, visitors, or distant acquaintances. Because McGill has offered the only architectural PhD program in Canada, it has been a hotbed of academic activity for decades, especially in history and theory. In cosmopolitan Montreal, with the bottomless collection of the Canadian Centre for Architecture nearby, and with so many excellent students and visitors from around the world, *Chora* has enjoyed an abundance of riches.

Monumentality and Contemporaneity in the Work of Tarkovsky, Goldsworthy, and Zumthor

Anne Bordeleau

Chora

SPEED, INNOVATION, AND CHANGE are the catchwords of our modern world, and the appeal of the ephemeral over the durable affects our conception of architecture. In projects such as *Uchronia* by Arne Quinze, in the celebration of the ephemeral surface, and in the growing fascination with responsive systems, architects approach the contemporary by identifying it with what resides within time's flow. Embracing this shift from the monumental to the contemporary, architects today have a propensity to acclaim the timely over the timeless – and yet, to use the words of Paul Ricoeur, architecture always materializes as a "temporary victory over the ephemeral."[1] Because the construction and duration of architecture traditionally extended beyond a single lifetime, its temporal scale encouraged humans to come to terms with our mortality. Now, architects tend to pursue an elusive contemporaneity by reifying architectural production, accepting the imperatives of technological innovation and economic consumption, and negating architecture's monumentality as a materialization in time and in the public realm. "No real writer ever wanted to be contemporary," wrote Jorge Luis Borges.[2] Shouldn't this apply also to architects?

The aspiration to contemporaneity in architecture is the desire to be "of one's time," seamless within this incessant flow of time that has come to characterize modernity. If contemporaneity is narrowly defined as that which is of its time, the monumental is regarded negatively as that which cannot progress along time's arrow. But both contemporaneity and monumentality have greater depth. Paradoxically, they may not be mutually exclusive and perhaps may represent two apparently contradictory but parallel ambitions of architecture. As Baudelaire described the quest of modernity to find the eternal in the transitory, could we also conceive of an architecture that is both "of its day" and "of all times"?[3]

Although architects may not recognize this explicitly, the architecture they construct always conveys an implicit position with respect to time. For example, Peter Zumthor's Protective Housing for Roman Archaeological Excavations carefully stages the relation between the Roman ruins and the modern visitor, the contemporary city, and the sediments of history. The architecture of this museum – especially its elevated entrance and suspended bridges – operates as a threshold between the life of the contemporary city and the stratification of rock and ruins that were formed and deposited in time and are now embedded in layers of earth.

Epistemologically, Zumthor positions the project within a larger concept of history and selectively constructs relations between the new building and the existing traces on site, foregrounding certain histories and alluding to others. In turn, these staged temporalities are experienced by the visitors as they move through the building. In their phenomenal experience of the building, new meanings arise in time. Considering architecture as an epistemological quest that monumentalizes a certain perspective on time, and its communicative power as a phenomenological experience that unfolds in time, my contention is that the role of today's architecture in the development of the ideas and values of culture lies precisely in its capacity to express a figure of durability in the face of incessant movement. Reflecting on the cinematographic work of Andrei Tarkovsky, the artistic work of Andy Goldsworthy, and the architectural work of Peter Zumthor, this essay considers the complex relation between monumentality and contemporaneity: two conditions that tread a shadowy line between the temporal and the eternal.

Fig. 1.1 Peter Zumthor, Protective Housing for Roman Archaeological Excavations, Chur, Switzerland (1985–86). © Hélène Binet.

ANDREI TARKOVSKY: SCULPTING IN TIME

> Keep awake, keep awake, artist,
> Do not give in to sleep ...
> You are eternity's hostage
> And prisoner of time.
> –Boris Pasternak[4]

Andrei Rublev, or *The Passion According to Andrei* (1966), is Tarkovsky's film on the famous monk and icon painter who lived in Russia between 1360 and 1430. Rublev is best known as the author of *Trinity*, painted circa 1410. In this icon, three figures are gathered around a table, each dressed in a different colour and conveying a different attribute that hints at a particular realm: heaven, earth, or sky. Their tripartite organization is broken in the lower centre by a table at which guests, viewers from all times, are invited to sit and join the trinity. Typical of medieval icon paintings, Rublev's *Trinity* brings the figures of God, Christ, and the Holy Spirit right to the surface of the representational plane. At the front, the two pedestals flanking the composition recede in different directions, thereby implying a similarly inverted perspective for the central table upon which a cup rests. As suggested by the eighth-century monk Saint John of Damascus, the icon is conceived as a threshold between the mortal and eternal.[5] One does not look *at* the icon, but *through* the icon, from time to eternity, and the "image is expressive of something in the future, mystically shadowing forth what is to happen."[6] In the *Trinity*, one is drawn into the spiritual space of the painting rather than its material construct, invited to dwell on the eternal rather than the earthly and the temporal.[7]

Tarkovsky's cinematic rendition of Rublev's *Trinity* can be considered an icon that enables the viewer to glimpse the eternal. The film opens with a scene of a man being lifted up into the air, a scene in which Tarkovsky anachronistically uses a hot air balloon, departing from both a typical human viewpoint and a typical human experience of time (fig. 1.3). Up in the air, the protagonist sees not the limited horizontal view that is granted to mortals, but an approximation of an all-encompassing divine view from above. As our spatial perception is skewed, so is our experience of time. The flying man embarks on a short and fatal journey in which his death is juxtaposed to the image of a fallen horse. Nothing below can match the movement of the balloon above, yet the aerial views

Fig. 1.2 Andrei Rublev, *Trinity* (ca 1410). Tretyakov Gallery, Moscow.
Image in the public domain.

convey a sense of stability, as though in its acceleration and elevation the perspective of the flying man could approximate the eternity of God's gaze on the temporal world.

The dramatic opening scene sets the tone for the film: from the fundamental movement of life, through slowness and speed, the film offers continual reflections on movement and questions what is temporal, mortal, and eternal. As a prologue to the film, this scene also introduces Tarkovsky's concept of cinema as an imprint of time: "Time, printed in its factual forms and manifestations: such is the supreme idea of cinema as an art ... What is the essence of the director's work? We could define it as sculpting in time."[8] Upholding that cinema had an unprecedented ability to *sculpt* in time, Tarkovsky believed that directors ought to be

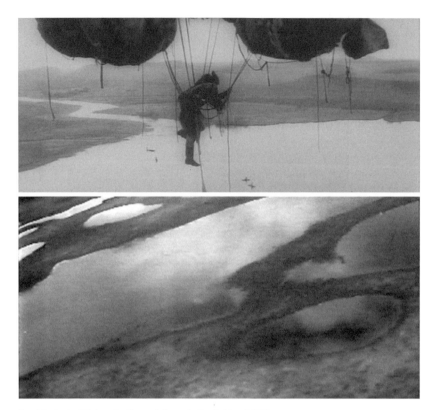

Fig. 1.3 Andrei Tarkovsky, film still from *Andrei Rublev* (1966).
By kind permission of Andrey A. Tarkovsky.

sensitive to the temporality that is embedded in a scene: in the movement of water flowing down a river, or in movement around an old wooden table: "No 'dead' object – table, chair, glass – taken in a frame in isolation from everything else, can be presented as [if] it were outside passing time, as if from the point of view of an absence of time."[9] As through an icon, it was in the thickness of time that the filmmaker sought meaning – of object, nature, or a lifetime.

Tarkovsky was fascinated by the idea that a ninety-minute film could hint at the meaning of a lifetime:

So the film-maker, from a "lump of time" made up of an enormous, solid cluster of living facts, cuts off and discards whatever he does not need, leaving

only what is to be an element of the finished film, what will prove to be integral to the cinematic image ... This is how I conceive an ideal piece of filming:
the author takes millions of meters of film, on which systematically, second by
second, day by day and year by year, a man's life, for instance, from birth to
death, is followed and recorded, and out of all that come two and a half thousand meters, or an hour and a half of screen time ... The point is to pick out
and join together the bits of sequential fact, knowing, seeing and hearing precisely what lies between them and what kind of chain holds them together.
That is cinema.[10]

In *Andrei Rublev*, this task was complicated by the need to communicate a fifteenth-century reality to a twentieth-century audience. Relin-
quishing an archaeological approach, Tarkovsky presented that period as
Walter Benjamin's historical materialist might have done, blasting "a specific era out of the homogeneous course of history – blasting a specific
life out of the era or a specific work out of the lifework. As a result of this
method, the lifework is preserved in this work and at the same time cancelled; in the lifework, the era; and in the era, the entire course of history."[11] Tarkovsky's work is contemporary because it both embraces and
denies time; it stands neither in this time nor in the other. According to
Tarkovsky, "This distancing, that view from the outside, from a certain
moral and spiritual height is what enables a work of art to live in historical time, its impact ever renewed and ever changing."[12] Refusing to present the icon as a museum piece that speaks of a bygone time, Tarkovsky
considered what it could hold in both the past and the present, foregrounding its human and spiritual meaning, "alive and understandable
for us who live in the second half of the twentieth century."[13]

At the centre of Tarkovsky's *Andrei Rublev* lies a specific work: the
depiction of the *Trinity* by Rublev. Appearing only in the final minutes of
this three-hour film, the icon acts as a threshold. Cancelling as it preserves,
the work is a nomad encapsulating a lifetime, an era, and the entire course
of history. The icon, offered as a potential hinge between time and eternity, bridges the works of both Andreis. Slowly travelling the surface of the
fifteenth-century painting, Tarkovsky hints at the reciprocity of time's flow
and time's stillness. Like this image that encapsulates a lifelong quest for
meaning, it is also as an icon that the film achieves monumentality. A construction of many novellas, the film accumulates layers of temporal
imprints that hint at wholeness when brought together in a sequence that

Fig. 1.4 Andrei Tarkovsky, film sequence from *Andrei Rublev* (1966). By kind permission of Andrey A. Tarkovsky.

follows their own rhythms. As a harmonious mosaic of different temporalities, undeniably rooted *in* time, the film monumentalizes Rublev's quest for eternity in the world. Only in the final sequence does Tarkovsky use colour, as his camera moves across Rublev's *Trinity* (fig. 1.4). Horses reappear, literally emerging from the image, as if the icon had given both life and eternity, a double-sided mirror that reflects both what is and what becomes: eternal trinity on one side and perpetual cycles of nature on the other. While horses represent life for Tarkovsky, the horses that stand proud in the rain by a small body of water in the meadow also convey cycles of time in nature. Throughout the film, nature is continually moving, but is also a frame that tricks the eye, oscillating between fragment and totality. A close-up view of mud with water trickling across it may appear either as a vast landscape or simply as a small patch of mud. Nature is a mirror between perpetual cycles that might be traces of eternity and fleeting presences of life that can be read against those cycles. The horses in the final scene carry us back to the first scene, approximating an effect suggested by Paul Virilio in one of his essays on time: "We can hardly hope to grasp [God's] atemporal perspective, in which before and after coexist, unless we see it as a film. Only, a film in which the sequence shot would constantly keep the beginning and the end in view."[14]

ANDY GOLDSWORTHY: SCULPTING WITH TIME

It is not God's eternity but the temporality of nature and its cycles that are central to the work of Andy Goldsworthy. Like Tarkovsky, Goldsworthy places time at the very centre of his artistic quest. His work engages natural phenomena that are brief, daily, seasonal, or continuous, such as an afternoon storm, a sunset, a thaw, or the flow of a stream. Nature may be Goldsworthy's eternity or, at the very least, its shadow. Against this reference, the artist measures more fleeting presences: his own passage against the perpetuity of nature. Goldsworthy navigates between what is controlled and unexpected through the traces of natural as well as unnatural interventions, whether the random cracks in the inevitable drying process of a wet clay wall, or their modulation through the subtle alteration in the depth of clay he applies.

Goldsworthy works with various materials – stones, leaves, clay, ice, water – but the works in which he creates a recognizable trace of his own presence are particularly relevant to our discussion. In a series of works involving frost, he stood in one place as the sun rose, so that his frozen shadow would remain on the ground after he moved away. In another series, he lay down on public squares, sidewalks, or roads as rain fell, leaving behind a pale figure where his body masked the ground. In another instance, he held his hand against a thin sheet of ice, leaving a recognizable imprint that became distorted as the ice continued to melt. In all of these works, human temporality is measured against unforgiving cycles of nature. While the traces of the human body are bound to disappear, the beauty of the art lies in the quasi-reverential bow that nature – whether rain, ice, sun, or frost – makes briefly to the body that was present. As Goldsworthy notes, these imprints express "a concern about the broader human condition."[15]

Goldsworthy's shadows are situated at a threshold between the perpetuity of natural cycles and the linearity of a human life. When these different trajectories intersect, their encounter has a slight effect on the processes of the natural world, as well as a slight effect on the human life – a memory of lying in the rain or standing in the cold. Goldsworthy's

Fig. 1.5 Andy Goldsworthy, *Rain Shadow*, Illinois, USA (1991).
© Andy Goldsworthy. Courtesy Galerie Lelong, New York.

works are imbued with time, but a time that is never clock time. It is "time between freeze and thaw," time between "cold night and warm day," time of a sky clouding over, or "best times, [in] autumn and spring, when the sun rises warmer, higher and more rapidly than in midwinter,"[16] thereby producing a sharper shadow in the frost. For Goldsworthy, the figure, "standing still in an empty field, is almost a sculpture in itself." Indeed, the figure is a sculpture, and its shadow is sculpted by time. Here again is a reversal: the monumental, the moment of eternity cast onto the perpetual cycles of nature, is expressed in a living figure standing still. This stillness and its resulting traces monumentalize a certain relation to time, a play between mortality and perpetuity, a play between linearity and circularity, a play between the linear trajectory of human beings and their "universe where everything, if it moves at all, moves in cyclical order."[17]

Goldsworthy's work gives greater depth to the definition of contemporaneity, implying not simply the ability to move seamlessly within time's flow, but encompassing also the ability to stand beside time. In this respect, it embraces the contemporary as defined by Giorgio Agamben: "Those who are truly contemporary, who truly belong to their time, are those who neither perfectly coincide with it nor adjust themselves to its demands."[18] Elsewhere, Agamben describes the contemporary as the ability "to return to a present where we have never been," explaining that in order to do so, one must accept the "dishomogeneity of time," thereby

Fig. 1.6 Andy Goldsworthy, *Stone Shadow Fold*, Yorkshire Sculpture Park, Wakefield, UK (2007). Film still. © Andy Goldsworthy. Courtesy Galerie Lelong, New York.

accepting a break in the continuity of time that enables different times to be placed in a special relationship.[19] This special relationship is particularly vivid in some of Goldsworthy's shadow casts. In one instance, the artist describes how he made a shadow in the garden of his parents' home on a day when his father was in hospital, very ill. It was cold and he had to borrow his father's coat: "I stood on the lawn newly exposed to the sun and watched as the frost slowly burnt off – a time to think."[20] Here, both the time to think and the time to thaw parallel the time of the illness, the time when one is in the hospital, and the time when one isn't. Passages of time are marked and referenced to a multiplicity of meanings that coexist when the shadow is cast. Thus, contemporariness is not in one's progressive time, but in the fragmentation, the embedded plurality, and the realization that to stand in one time is often to stand out of another.

Tarkovsky sculpts in time; Goldsworthy sculpts with time. The first records, listens, and tries to do justice to the flow; the second acts and waits, controlling the "throw but not the outcome."[21] Both endeavours are rooted intrinsically in time, searching for what inevitably flows and what invariably remains. Tarkovsky tracks the speed of one mortal, slowing down or speeding up along the thin line between birth and death to measure the inescapable tension between time and eternity. Goldsworthy tracks the finitude and momentaneity of human temporality against the cycles of nature's perpetuity. In modernity the project of architecture also treads the line between humanity and its multiple histories, inscribing the work within a hoped-for continuity, if only to forsake our ability to actually annihilate ourselves. Perhaps continuity today is the only trace of eternity we have left.

PETER ZUMTHOR: SCULPTING IN TIME, SCULPTING WITH TIME

The search for meaning and wholeness in the here and now, but also beyond it, grounds the practice of Peter Zumthor: "Personally, I still believe in the self-sufficient, corporeal wholeness of an architectural object, even if not as a natural or given fact but as the essential if difficult aim of my work. Yet, how are we to achieve this wholeness in architecture at a time when the divine, which once gave things a meaning, and reality itself, seem to be dissolving in the endless flux of transitory signs and images?"²² Zumthor's unwillingness to do away with the quest of eternity translates as a reluctance to do away with history:

I have a passionate desire to design such buildings, buildings which, in time, grow naturally into being a part of the form and history of their place. Every new work of architecture intervenes in a specific historical situation. It is essential to the quality of the intervention that the new building should embrace qualities which can enter into a meaningful dialogue with the existing situation. For if the intervention is to find its place, it must make us see what already exists in a new light. We throw a stone into the water. Sand swirls up and settles again. The stir was necessary. The stone has found its place. But the pond is no longer the same.²³

The stone is architecture; the water is history – or the episteme in which the architectural project is now rooted. Zumthor aspires to an architecture that works with history – and affects the pond – but is also worked *by* history, slowly finding a place in its environment and, to use Doreen Massey's words, in the multiplicity and "simultaneity of its stories so far."²⁴ Referring to Tarkovsky and Goldsworthy, we could say that Zumthor is attempting to sculpt both in time and with time.

Hiroshi Nakao suggests that some of Zumthor's buildings, such as the Sogn Benedetg Chapel in Sumvitg, Switzerland, suddenly bring their whole surroundings into focus.²⁵ The localized intervention engages a larger world – not by standing as an isolated monument, but by monumentalizing a new relationship to the locality. The building's play with the surrounding environment – whether landscape, city, or ruin – becomes embedded in its materials, forms, and details. The monumentality of the building can be deciphered in the most fundamental joint. In his addition to the Gugalun House in Versam, Switzerland, the meeting of the existing building and the new construction expresses both the fluidity of time and the arrest of time. Embedding fluidity, the contrast between the weathered wood and the new planks already withholds expectations of a quasi-seamless joint in a remote future. Yet, at each specific moment, a precise relationship is captured in the contrast between the more or less weathered wood of the addition and the aged greyness of the original building. Zumthor believes that "details express what the basic idea of the design requires at the relevant point in the object: belonging or separation,

Fig. 1.7 Top Peter Zumthor, Sogn Benedetg Chapel, Sumvitg, Switzerland (1985–88).
© Anne Bordeleau.

Fig. 1.8 Bottom Peter Zumthor, Gugalun House, Versam, Switzerland (1990–94).
© Hélène Binet.

tension and lightness, friction, solidity, fragility."[26] In this instance, the detail expresses both belonging and separation, holding the old and the new, fixity and continuity.

"Monument," from the Latin *monumentum*, can designate a commemorative statue or building, a tomb, a reminder, a written record, or a literary work. Its roots are *monere*, "to remind," and *mentum*, "mind." Beside the root *men-*, "to think," the word oscillates between monument and *munimentum*, which means "a defensive wall or protection."[27] Leaving aside the monumentality associated with petrifaction and commemoration, we must foreground *munimentality*, architecture's capacity to materialize protection from the inessential. In a global world, the essential might refer to the ability of Zumthor's chapel to redefine a locality, or his shelter for archaeological ruins to open a new window onto the contemporary city. The monumental role of architecture thus could be twofold: as a form of protection and resistance, and as a materialized record or trace of this very resistance. In Zumthor's Kolumba Museum, the monumentality of architecture is not an end in itself, but a means through which temporality may be made visible against the shadow of eternity, the continuity of humanity's multiple histories. Zumthor's twenty-first-century intervention claims its own temporality by standing against, between, over, and within the layers of architectural traces already in place. Conversely, the resulting monumentality of the ensemble hinges on the multiple temporalities displayed by the palimpsestic building. In this respect, the monumental presupposes the contemporary.

Likewise, for the Protective Housing for Roman Archaeological Excavations in Chur, Zumthor builds a threshold between history and the present. Looking at the relation between the specific program, the site, and the pre-existing histories, he conceives the raised steel footbridge as an "a-historical observation level" (fig. 1.10). The ahistorical belongs to no time; it stands beside time. The rest of the building measures and bridges time: advancing, turning, ascending, descending, and pausing, even when visitors are absent. The architecture, like that of Zumthor's Bregenz and Kolumba museums, is static, materially durable, and stable, but like an icon, it is located at the threshold of time and eternity, outlining a gap between now and continuity. Zumthor's architecture monumentalizes the shadow that we, as mortals, cast onto the melting frost of time when illuminated by the rays of multiple histories. While this conception of architecture embraces time, it celebrates not only the ephemeral but also the

Fig. 1.9 Peter Zumthor, Kolumba Art Museum, Cologne, Germany (1997–2007). © Hélène Binet.

durable, materializing a threshold between time passed and lives yet to be lived. Architecture is "an envelope and background for life which goes on in and around it, a sensitive container for the rhythm of footsteps on the floor, for the concentration of work, for the silence of sleep."[28]

BETWEEN MONUMENTALITY AND CONTEMPORANEITY

Sculpted *in* time, architecture epistemologically engages existing layers of history. Through the temporal positioning of their constructions, architects constantly redefine what it means to build and create against this given historical ground. Architecture's monumentality results from this act of sculpting in time, providing an expression of the eternal against theological, natural, or historical epistemological frameworks. Sculpted *with* time, architecture accrues cultural meaning and the patina of time through historical, natural, and phenomenal weathering. It is not fixed in time and does not respond to one single time, but is able to bear its multiple traces. As it casts the moving shadow of the sun and accepts continuous appropriation by humans, as it engages the daily and weekly

Fig. 1.10 Peter Zumthor, Protective Housing for Roman Archaeological Excavations, Chur, Switzerland (1985–86). © Peter Zumthor Studio.

cycles of the city and the various cycles of nature, architecture is truly contemporary when it is able to gather and celebrate disparate rhythms that otherwise might have remained imperceptible.

In the past century, monumentality acquired a bad name due to its association with reductive and universalizing narratives. For thousands of years, architecture's cultural role relied on durability and continuity, but in a modern world that seeks progress, change, and novelty, this very durability has threatened architecture's relevance. First used to denote stability, then embracing fluidity, the definition of monumentality further shifted to match the experience of an accelerated time-space. When Sigfried Giedion turned to the question of monumentality in a world in flux, he defined what he considered to be a New Monumentality, an approach to architecture that sided with the work of the Cubists and Futurists as they embraced this incessant flow and sought to represent time. Around the same time, Henri Bergson opened new avenues for understanding time and duration, but also contributed to the modern emphasis on novelty over eternity. Building on Bergson's theory, Sanford Kwinter assessed the past hundred years by praising novelty and uncompromised forms.[29] But the denial of anything but the incessant flow of time is not a celebration of time. Novelty for its own sake is a negation of time that distracts architecture from its cultural role. The quest for novelty and progress occludes the richer meanings of contemporaneity, including its anachronistic underpinnings and its necessary distancing. In Agamben's words, "Contemporariness is, then, a singular relationship with one's own time, which adheres to it and, at the same time, keeps a distance from it. More precisely, it is *that relationship with time that adheres to it through a disjunction and an anachronism.* Those who coincide too well with the epoch, those who are perfectly tied to it in every respect, are not contemporaries, precisely because they do not manage to see it; they are not able to firmly hold their gaze on it."[30]

Current references to "contemporary" buildings typically regard them as fixed moments in time, rather than as buildings that may continue to gather time, like Zumthor's chapel in the alpine landscape. Likewise, when Borges suggests that no real writer ever wanted to be contemporary, he is defining contemporaneity as a seamless insertion in time. However, the work of Tarkovsky, Goldsworthy, and Zumthor suggests a different type of contemporaneity: a willingness to stand beside time, or between times. If architectural monumentality can make time momentarily tangible, architectural contemporaneity can permit a slippage in time, an anachronistic positioning that does not align with any single moment.

NOTES

1 Paul Ricoeur, "Architecture and Narrative," in *Identity and Difference: Integration and Plurality in Today's Forms* (catalogue, Milan Triennale), ed. Pietro Derossi (Milan: Electa, 1996), 69.

2 Quoted in Marc Treib, ed., *Spatial Recall: Memory in Architecture and Landscape* (London: Routledge, 2009), 39.

3 Charles Baudelaire, *Le peintre de la vie moderne* (Clamecy, France: Éd. Mille et une nuits, 2010), 26.

4 Boris Pasternak, quoted in Andrei Tarkovsky, *Sculpting in Time*, trans. Kitty Hunter-Blair (Austin: University of Texas Press, 2006), 181.

5 St John of Damascus, *St. John of Damascene on Holy Images* (London: Thomas Barker, 1898), http://www.ccel.org/ccel/damascus/icons.html.

6 Ibid., 12.

7 Pavel Florensky, a priest, philosopher, and polymath who coined the term "inverted perspective," provides perhaps the strongest interpretation of the significance of Russian medieval icons when he contextualizes the icon painters' attempt to address the eye of the soul and portray "'the lofty peace' of the celestial world" in the prevailing conditions of the times: "the discords, the local wars, the general savagery." Similarly, Tarkovsky offers his poetic film in a troubled Soviet Union. P. Florensky, "The Trinity-St. Sergius Monastery and Russia," *The Trinity-St. Serguis Monastery* (Sergiyev Posad, 1919), 19–20, quoted in Alexander V. Voloshinov, "'The Old Testament Trinity' of Andrey Rublyov: Geometry and Philosophy," *Leonardo* 32, no. 2 (1999): 103–12.

8 Tarkovsky, *Sculpting in Time*, 63.

9 Ibid., 68.

10 Ibid., 64–5.

11 Walter Benjamin, "Theses on the Philosophy of History," thesis XVII, in *Illuminations*, ed. Hannah Arendt, trans. Harry Zohn (New York: Schocken, 1985), 262–3.

12 Tarkovsky, *Sculpting in Time*, 166.

13 Ibid., 79.

14 Paul Virilio, *A Landscape of Events*, trans. Julie Rose (Cambridge, MA: MIT Press, 2000), x.

15 Andy Goldsworthy, *Time* (Moffat, UK: Cameron Books, 2000), 21.

16 Ibid., 16.

17 Hannah Arendt, *The Human Condition* (Chicago: University of Chicago Press, 1998), 42.

18 Giorgio Agamben, "What Is the Contemporary?" in *What Is an Apparatus and Other Essays,* trans. David Kishik and Stefan Pedatella (Stanford, CA: Stanford University Press, 2009), 40.

19 Ibid., 51–2.

20 Goldsworthy, *Time,* 16.

21 Ibid., 23.

22 Peter Zumthor, *Thinking Architecture* (Basel: Birkhäuser, 2006), 30.

23 Ibid., 18.

24 Doreen Massey, "Some Times of Space," in *Olafur Eliasson: The Weather Project*, ed. Susan May (exhibition catalogue) (London: Tate Publishing, 2003), 117.

25 Hiroshi Nakao, "No Ideas but in Things," in *Peter Zumthor,* 221.

26 Peter Zumthor quoted in Nobuyuki Yoshida, ed., *Peter Zumthor* (Tokyo: A+U, 1998), 220.

27 *Dictionnaire historique de la langue française*, ed. Alain Rey (Paris: Dictionnaires Le Robert 2006), s.v. "monument."

28 Zumthor, *Thinking Architecture,* 12.

29 See Sanford Kwinter, *Architectures of Time: Toward a Theory of the Event in Modernist Culture* (Cambridge, MA: MIT Press, 2002), esp. 2–100.

30 Agamben, "What Is the Contemporary?" 41, emphasis original.

The Public Boudoir of an Actress:
The *Petite Maison* of
Mademoiselle Dervieux

Diana Cheng

Chora

IN JEAN-FRANÇOIS DE BASTIDE's tale of architectural seduction from 1758, the *petite maison* is an exemplary site of erotic affect. In this novelette, an aristocrat wagers with a young, beautiful woman that his little house can convince her to fall in love with him.[1] Not merely fictional licence, this little house was based on contemporary petites maisons where love affairs and libertinage were conducted. Gaillard de la Boissière's pavilion (1751), designed by Antoine-Mathieu Le Carpentier and considered by Jacques-François Blondel to be one of the best architectural examples of its kind, was the real-life inspiration for Bastide's setting.[2] Although the owners of petites maisons were men,[3] female courtesans also commissioned these small houses devoted to love. Starting with the Temple of Terpsichore, designed in 1769 by Claude-Nicolas Ledoux for Opéra dancer and courtesan Marie-Madeleine Guimard,[4] the courtesan's petite maison had an enormous pull on the eighteenth-century public. Following her rival Guimard, the singer and dancer Anne Victoire Dervieux (1752–1826) also had a petite maison built for her, and it became equally notorious. Designed by Alexandre-Théodore Brongniart in 1777, her two-storied pavilion and attached garden were located on the rue Chantereine, in the Chaussée-d'Antin quarter near the Maison Guimard.[5] Mademoiselle Dervieux's petite maison disregarded Blondel's recommendation that buildings should not promote corruption in the manners of citizens, hurt honest people, or authorize debauchery.[6] Maison Dervieux featured a boudoir where erotic fantasies played out, conjuring images of oriental exoticism, sex, and luxury for paying customers and the public.

This type of house displayed Dervieux's social status as a sought-after and celebrated courtesan. A petite maison was a freestanding square building surrounded by a garden. As Blondel explains, a *maison de plaisance*[7] generally was a country retreat for pleasurable aristocratic pursuits such as musical entertainment and suppers, whereas a petite maison referred more specifically to its clientele and their activities. A petite maison typically was frequented by the wealthy, by elite *hommes du monde*: nobles of the sword, magistrates, the upper bourgeoisie, and financiers (who usually commissioned the building of these petites maisons).[8] In the suburban areas around Paris, particularly in Bercy, Passy, Clichy, and Montrouge, these men conducted love affairs and, as Blondel hints, practiced indecencies that might have offended the modesty of visitors.[9] According to writer and academician Charles Duclos, at a petite maison one could meet for a discreet rendezvous or "hold orgies which people would have been scared to have in brothels, which were considered dangerous, and ashamed to hold in their own house."[10] His assessment of the dual purpose of the petite maison is supported by contemporary police reports on the activities, proprietors, and users of *petites maisons galantes*, noting that the *demoiselles* were invited for suppers, overnights, or afternoons. For instance, it was recorded that on 2 August 1762, M. de la Boissière brought a girl by the name of Alexandrien to his petite maison, where he played all afternoon; on 1 September, he brought another girl, Julie, for a few hours.[11]

Everyone – even wives – knew what transpired in petites maisons, according to Charles-Jean-François Hénault's play *La petite maison* (1742).[12] Madame d'Épinay, for instance, complained in her memoirs about the scandal that her husband had brought to the family by installing two girls from the Comédie-Française under assumed names in a petite maison in the village near the family estate.[13] The pursuits inside the petite maison became so well known in Duclos's high society that they were no longer secret and were something to boast about. Some would even pretend to have an affair merely by spending time alone in a petite maison.[14] Of course, not all affairs happened there. The petite maison was reserved for sexual trysts that had to be hidden from public view.[15] Liaisons with a certain class of *demoiselles* – *filles à parties*, *filles galantes*, *filles d'Opéra*, bourgeois women, and "public" women – took place at petites maisons since, as the court painter Élisabeth Louise Vigée-Le Brun noted, a man usually was not seen in public with a kept woman.[16]

Anne Victoire Dervieux was one of these *filles d'Opéra*. Groomed for the stage by her mother, she was not expected to become a pious, modest, and dutiful Christian woman under the protection of church and family. As a stage performer, she would have been denied Catholic sanctions such as marriage and burial in consecrated ground; instead, she was expected to acquire protection, money, and career advancement from male admirers, in exchange for sexual favours. Despite being socially ostracized, a girl from the lower ranks of society who wished to become an actress, dancer, or singer could gain riches and fame as the mistress of an elderly great lord who would cover her in diamonds.[17]

Anne Victoire's career aspirations began to materialize when she became a dancer in the Académie royale de musique, usually referred to as the Opéra.[18] Admittance to the troupe depended on the authorization of individuals such as the Gentlemen of the Bedchamber and the Master of the Ballet. Anne Victoire likely won their good favour in the same way as many other fourteen-year-old girls: through luck, socializing, and especially nights with the right gentlemen. Taking advantage of the protection given to the king's performers, Anne Victoire moved from her parents' house into rooms near the theatre and supported herself through prostitution.[19] Compared to the two other royal theatres, the Comédie-Italienne and the Comédie-Française, the Opéra was more prestigious and was patronized more by the aristocracy, so a performer at the Opéra was very likely to become a sought-after courtesan.[20] Anne Victoire's success would depend on her association with these influential aristocrats, together with her own assets: her fresh face, figure, light spirit, and quick wit.[21]

Anne Victoire's career took off in the summer of 1767, when she caught the attention of the Prince de Conti by singing at a series of private theatrical performances. Later that year she made her debut at the Opéra.[22] Her appearances in various ballets at the Opéra, as well as in private performances at royal residences, brought her into the social elite. Within three years, Anne Victoire, now known as Mademoiselle Dervieux, became a celebrated performer, as described by Grimm.[23] Even after retiring from the Opéra in 1774, she continued to be known as a famous courtesan. Indeed, the *Mémoires secrets* described the involvement of a trio of courtesans – Mesdemoiselles Guimard, Duthé,[24] and Dervieux – in a libertine celebration that was planned at the Temple of Terpsichore. Entry to the party, which was to include supper and theatrical performances in which each *fille* demonstrated her assets, would cost five *louis* per person.[25] Although this scandalous event at the Temple of Terpsichore was prevented, it highlights the commodified role of the courtesan as a provider of pleasure and entertainment to a paying audience. Courtesans, certainly, were nothing new. Their lineage can be traced back to the *megalomisthoi* of ancient Greece, "big fee" *hetaerai* who provided conversation, entertainment, drinking companionship, and sex for men gathered at symposia.[26]

Having amassed a fortune from her admirers, Mademoiselle Dervieux decided to build a showcase for herself, advertising the sexual promiscuity that was a privilege of the French elite.[27] The magnificence of the decor of this petite maison would enable her male guests to display their virility as an integral element of their grandeur.[28] As a playground for both aristocrats and the wealthy, Mademoiselle Dervieux's petite maison attracted the courtiers of Versailles, Parisians, and tourists such as the

Baroness d'Oberkirch, who described it as a "délicieuse bonbonnière" with furnishings worth a king's ransom.[29] They came to observe, to gamble, or to receive custom services. According to the gossip in the *Correspondance secrète*, the magistrate class – the "robins" of the highest rank – played in Mademoiselle Dervieux's elegant apartments, where the best cuisine in Paris was offered, and where high stakes were played at cards and dice. Her casino, with a reported annual income of fifty thousand *livres*, was successful in attracting and retaining happy customers.[30]

Mademoiselle Dervieux's petite maison was financially lucrative for her; however, she was not satisfied with its luxury, compared to her rival's Temple of Terpsichore. Around 1785, Mademoiselle Dervieux increased the size of her property by buying the adjoining lot. In 1787, the Comte d'Artois's architect, Joseph-François Bélanger (who was one of her lovers and eventually became her husband), began redesigning both the garden and the buildings.[31] By 1789, the house and the English and Italian gardens were completed. The interior was entirely redecorated and the main pavilion now included two new wings: one for a dining room and one for a bathing room and boudoir.

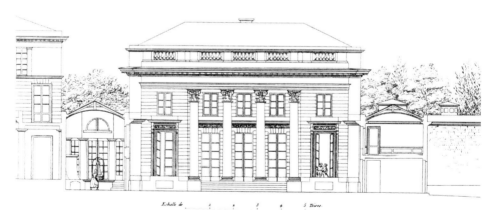

Fig. 2.1 House of Mademoiselle Dervieux, rue Chantereine, Paris. Court elevation, showing the central building by Alexandre-Théodore Brongniart (1777) and the two side wings by François-Joseph Bélanger (1789). Johann Karl Krafft and Nicolas Ransonette, *Plans, coupes, élévations des plus belles maisons et des hôtels construits à Paris et dans les environs* (1801–03; Paris: Librairie d'art décoratif et industriel G. Hue 1909), plate 7. Rare Books and Special Collections, McGill University Library.

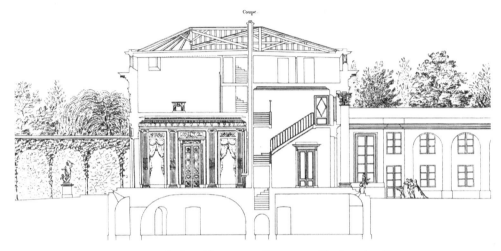

Fig. 2.2 Section through the house. Krafft and Ransonette, *Plans, coupes, élévations*, plate 7.

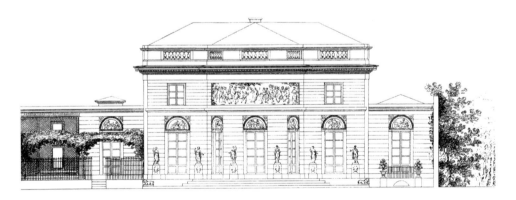

Fig. 2.3 Garden elevation. Krafft and Ransonette, *Plans, coupes, élévations*, plate 66, no. 1.

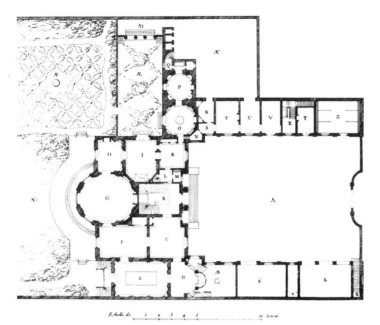

Fig. 2.4 Ground floor plan. Krafft and Ransonette, *Plans, coupes, élévations*, plate 7.

Legend:
A Court; B Vestibule; C Antechamber; D Buffet; E Dining room; F Music room; G Salon; H Cabinet; I Bedchamber; K Cabinet de toilette; L Stair and private passage; M Water closet; N Private passage; O Bathing room; P Boudoir; Q Private passage; R Cabinet; S Second cabinet; T Chamber; U Passage; V Store room; X Service stairs to first floor; Y Porter's lodge; Z Stable for six horses, coach house, and workshops; AB Pump; AC Court; AD Stairs to Italian garden and vineyard; AE Italian garden and vineyard; AF Arbour; AG English garden

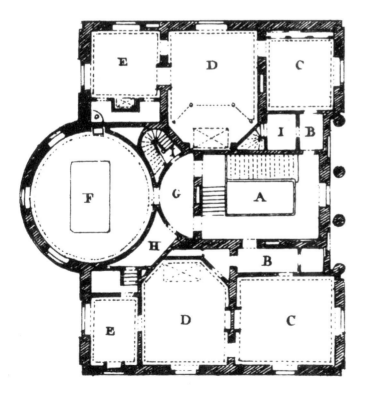

Fig. 2.5 First floor plan. Krafft and Ransonette, *Plans, coupes, élévations*, plate 7.

Legend:
A Staircase; B Private passage; C Cabinet; D Bedchamber; E Cabinet; F Billiard room; G Private passage; H Dressing room; I Staircase

Even though Bélanger changed the house to suit himself, most likely installing his apartment on the first floor, next to Dervieux's apartment,[32] the redesigned interior presented erotic narratives in which the courtesan played a leading role. The house epitomized the joys of sensuous living and continued to be an attraction for visitors such as the eighteenth-century traveller Nikolaï Mikhaïlovich Karamzin, who described the newly redecorated temple:

The former actress Dervieux, a mediocre actress but famous enchantress, after labouring for twenty years at her lucrative art and accumulating millions, decided to erect a house that would attract the admiration of Paris. Such was her wish, and so it was done: this edifice is regarded as a miracle ... What rooms! What decor! Painting, bronzes, marble, wood, everything shines, everything attracts the gaze. The house is not large; but reason sketched out the plans, art was the architect, profligacy the decorator, and wealth gave the money. Here there is nothing unbeautiful; and comfort and ease of use are added to beauty of look.[33]

Karamzin most likely arrived at the house on foot, proceeded through the ornate wrought-iron front gates, and entered a landscaped courtyard (fig. 2.4, A) with a pavilion house fronted by four Corinthian columns. Passing through French doors, he would have entered the ground floor of the building to encounter a double-height vestibule containing the main staircase (fig. 2.4, B). The vestibule was sparsely furnished, containing a dresser with a Flemish marble top, a lamp decorated with silk cords, and two firewood chests, each covered with a green rug. A frequent visitor to *maisons de compagnes* would expect to be ushered into the oval salon (fig. 2.4, G), which usually was connected axially to the vestibule.[34] At the Maison Dervieux, the visitor instead was led to the left, into a large antechamber of almost five and a half by six metres (fig. 2.4, C). In this waiting room, with twelve padded chairs covered in green tapestry, the visitor could admire the multi-basined fountain with gold gilt fixtures.[35]

Continuing straight ahead, he entered Bélanger's addition: the buffet (fig. 2.4, D) and the dining room (fig. 2.4, E), approximately eight by five metres. At one end of the dining room was an arched window over-looking the garden; at the other end, *enfilade*, was the buffet (fig. 2.4, D), with a large mahogany-framed window overlooking the courtyard. These two windows, the only sources of daylight in the dining room,

Fig. 2.6 Dining room, designed by François-Joseph Bélanger; plate rendered by Detournelle. Frédéric Contet, *Intérieurs directoire et empire* (Paris: F. Contet 1932). Rare Books and Special Collections, McGill University Library.

emphasized the length of the room and visually balanced the nearly four-and-a-half-metre-high ceiling. The ceiling itself was extremely elaborate with sculpted ornaments, giving a heavy visual impression. Despite being a long space enclosed on both sides, the dining room was animated with light, thanks to two full-height framed mirrors along the side walls that replicated the shape of the French window looking out over the garden (fig. 2.6). Light bounced off the cool silver of the picture frames, the arabesques on the warm sienna yellow stucco walls, the medallions and panels in yellow wood, and the white architrave and stucco cornices. Their shimmering surfaces were replicated by the ceiling's predominant colours of blue and yellow, together creating a vibrant green in the eye of the beholder.[36] In the evening, when the room was illuminated by four English crystal chandeliers, two bronze and crystal lanterns, four-branched sconces with gilded copper holders, and a suspended English

Fig. 2.7 Ceiling of the dining room. Krafft and Ransonette, *Plans, coupes, élévations*, plate 97.

crystal garland,[37] the effect was even more dramatic against the dark background of the ceiling: like stars in the night sky.

Warm images decorated the dining room, contrasting the cool colour palette (yellow, grey, white, silver, and blue) and the cold materiality of the marble floor and column bases. Yellow medallions on the mahogany doors and pilasters depicted Cupid and Psyche with Leda and the Swan. The theme of sinful pleasures, portrayed by serpents above the arches, continued onto the ceiling (fig. 2.7). A swan devouring a serpent was repeated in a frieze around a central image of courtesans entertaining men at a symposium[38] (fig. 2.8). Flanking this central panel were two others depicting Bacchus playing the lute in a vineyard, apparently serenading a sphinx-like creature feeding grapes to a lion (fig. 2.9). Also flanking this central image were two triangles depicting a lyre, associated with Erato, the muse of erotic poetry.[39] At the corners of the ceiling, four light yellow medallions with white stucco frames portrayed loving couples (fig. 2.10).

Echoing Bélanger's Italian arbour on the opposite side of the garden, the dining room interior was like a verdant arcade. The mirrors in the

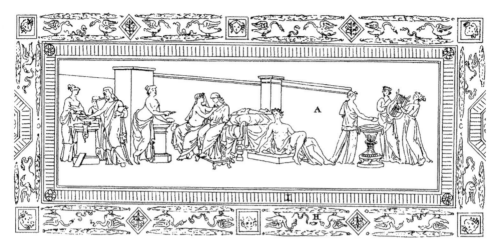

Fig. 2.8 Central panel and frieze on the ceiling of the dining room. Krafft and Ransonette, *Plans, coupes, élévations*, plate 97.

Fig. 2.9 Flanking panel on the ceiling of the dining room. Krafft and Ransonette, *Plans, coupes, élévations*, plate 97.

Fig. 2.10 Medallions on the ceiling of the dining room. Krafft and Ransonette, *Plans, coupes, élévations*, plate 97.

arches behind their mahogany balustrades opened up visual spaces beyond the wall, merging interior and exterior. Surrounded by a decor that portrayed an abundant nature and half-man, half-animal creatures such as Pegasus and gryphons, a visitor could imagine himself dining *al fresco* with sixteen other guests at the long mahogany table, made of a single large plank with two extensions.[40]

From the dining room, the visitor entered the music room (fig. 2.4, F), with similar dimensions. Its double-height window looked out over the English garden and was decorated with two 3.7-metre-long cotton curtains and draped with a blue window valence ornamented with fringes and silk cords. Eight mahogany chairs, four armchairs, and two stools, all with petit-point upholstery edged in silk fabric and decorated with grey cushions edged with embroidered yellow roses, surrounded a bronze and gold gilded harp. There was also a glass Bohemian lantern with brass branches gilded in gold. The visitor then walked across the Aubusson carpet and into the oval salon (G), the largest gathering space in the house.[41]

Like the previous room, the entire floor of the grand salon was covered with a carpet. In the middle of the room was an English crystal chandelier with sixteen candle rings: eight made of crystal and the other eight with pearls embedded in a gold gilded crown. There were various seats: six large gilded armchairs *à la reine*, each covered in puce Beauvais tapestry decorated with arabesques and populated with Etruscan-style bird people; four loveseats and two *voyeuses*[42] in the same style; eight gilded chairs with cherry-coloured velour coverings; and eight mahogany chairs covered with blue petit-point upholstery. The grand salon had an impressive fireplace with a brass lion and lioness gilded in gold. Its accessories – a spade, pincer, and poker – had same material and finish. Above the fireplace was a "superb" mirror; on either side, there were two niches, each lined with a mirror.[43] Opposite the fireplace, three French windows, decorated with white and rose stripped-taffeta curtains and window valences of the same material as the armchairs, opened out into a picturesque English garden (AG) where, according to Karamzin, "all paths are covered in flowers; where all the trees give off fragrances as they cast shade" and where little roads wove in and out of meadows, small cliffs, and groves, leading to a "wild grotto, where you read the inscription: *Art leads to nature; it extends its hand in friendship*. And in another spot: *here I take pleasure in thoughtfulness.*"[44]

On the other side of the grand salon was the ceremonial apartment: a series of rooms in aristocratic houses where guests were formally received. Mademoiselle's ceremonial apartment was comprised of a *cabinet* used as a trictrac[45] salon, a bedchamber, and a *cabinet de toilette* (fig. 2.11, H, I, K). The trictrac room, an intimate cabinet of five by four metres, was a soothing place to calm the excitement from games of chance played in the grand salon. Its furnishings had a luminous tone and texture: a green satin damask fabric upholstered four mahogany chairs, two gilded love-seats, and two armchairs, with borders of yellow silk, white taffeta, or a garland of roses. The French window was draped with a valence of the same material and curtains made of stripped chiffon edged with violet satin brocade. On either side of the door to the bedchamber were two

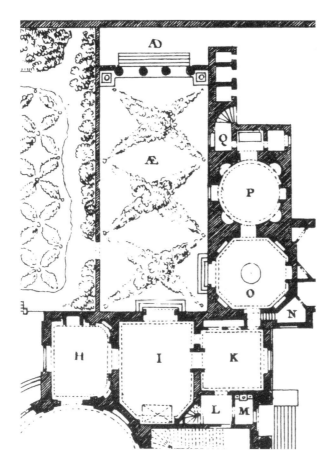

Fig. 2.11 Detail of ground floor plan, showing Mademoiselle Dervieux's apartment after the 1789 renovations by Bélanger. Krafft and Ransonette, *Plans, coupes, élévations*, plate 7.

Legend:
H Cabinet; I Bedchamber ;
K Cabinet de toilette;
L Stair and private passage;
M Water closet;
N Private passage;
O Bathing room; P Boudoir;
Q Private passage;
AD Stairs to Italian garden and vineyard
AE Italian garden and vineyard

niches, each with a heating stove with a white marble table and a varnished metal front decorated with bronze gilt.[46] Above the stoves were mirrors covered with rising steam, anticipating a warm environment behind the bedchamber door.

Upon entering the bedchamber (I), the visitor was presented with a fully carpeted room and a fireplace, accessorized with two gilded brass fire dogs, a bronze poker, shovel, and pincer, a gilded iron fender, and a brass grill. Over the fireplace were two "beautiful" mirrors: one 2 by 1.3 metres, the other 0.7 by 1.3. There were two mahogany loveseats, four chairs, and a *bergère* (a fashionable lounging chair), all upholstered in blue damask, patterned with rose-coloured flowers and trimmed with white satin. Over the window was a valence of the same fabric. The curtains were made of a stripped chiffon trimmed with a white satin brocade of rose flowers and an assortment of fringes. Two crystal globes stacked in the Japanese style and decorated with tassels hung from the ceiling. These furnishings were impressive but the bed ensemble *à la turque* at the far end was the main feature of the room. The bed was partitioned from the rest of the room by a mahogany balustrade. On each pilaster were two small antique green tables topped with a bronze and gold gilt candelabra. The back of the bed was decorated with mirrors across its width and up to the ceiling. The mahogany bed had two backrests and four columns. On the base of the bed were four mattresses: three filled with wool and one filled with horse hair, covered with fustian.[47] On the bed there were two bolsters and a twill cover. The bed was surrounded on all sides by blue- and rose-coloured damask tapestry. From an ebony trestle, ornamented with red and white ivory, decorative brackets, fringes, and feathers, eight banners embroidered with gold and silk were suspended *à la tartare*.[48]

Imitating French kings, Mademoiselle Dervieux would receive guests and petitioners on the bed. In Karamzin's eyes, her oriental bedchamber became a shrine "where a painting on the walls depicted Hercules on his knees before Omphale, five or six Erotes riding on his chariot; Armida who gazes into the mirror, far more intrigued by her beauty than by the adoration of Rinaldo who sits alongside her; Venus, who after removing her girdle gives it to … you can't see to whom, but presumably it is the mistress of the house. Your eyes search for … guess what for. The bed of pleasures, smothering in unfading – that is, artificial – roses without thorns, rises on several steps; here without doubt every Adonis must bend the knee."[49]

On axis with the bed, a French window opened onto a covered Italian garden and a vineyard fenced on one side. Looking back from the far end of the Italian garden (fig. 2.11, AD) was a series of steps in front of a colonnade, suggesting the classical temple façade of the sanctuary of Venus, with the garden as the *cella*, her bedchamber as the *adytum*, and her bed as the altar.

Next to the bedchamber was the *cabinet de toilette* (K) where guests were invited to partake in the aristocratic social practice of honouring a lady by assisting her in grooming, makeup, and dressing before she went out in public. Here, a small, select group could sit on one of the four chairs and witness Mademoiselle on a yellow Moroccan leather armchair, preparing her courtesan's costume in front of the floor-to-ceiling mirror.[50]

Beyond the *cabinet de toilette* was Bélanger's 1789 addition to the main pavilion. The first room (fig. 2.11, O; fig. 2.12) was the octagonal bathing room. At the centre of this room was a sunken circular pool surrounded by four mahogany chairs and two loveseats, all decorated with chiffon fabric. In two of the niches were large mahogany chiffoniers, one of which was a writing desk. There was a polished crystal and gilded bronze lantern decorated with garlands of crystal cords and counterweights. Directly above the pool was a circular opening to a gallery with a mahogany balustrade onto which were fixed two mahogany music stands, one covered in green Moroccan leather, the other with a mirror. Up there, surrounded by a library, musicians played "so that the beauty can splash to the rhythm as she listens to their harmonious playing."[51] Accompanying the music, birdsong emanated from the birdcage in the natural history conservatory located at the end of this gallery, opposite the entrance.[52] From the circular opening, daylight illuminated the room through an overhead skylight. Light was provided also through the glass French doors that opened out to the Italian garden. Reflected in the mirror above the fireplace were the Italian garden and the arbour outside. This visual overlap of interior and exterior was repeated in the central motif of the four niches in the bathing room: Venus, flanked by swans,[53] atop a quincunx that framed a circular portal with a painted landscape where one could imagine the incarnation of sexual love (fig. 2.13). This wall decoration suggests that the main activity in the room was the

Fig. 2.12 Circular bathing room, designed by Bélanger, with a view into the boudoir of Mademoiselle Dervieux; plate rendered by Detournelle. Contet, *Intérieurs directoire et empire*.

voyeuristic gaze at the naked Mademoiselle Dervieux, undressing on a sofa or bathing in the circular pool.

This theme of voyeurism was extended from the bathing room to the next room, the circular boudoir (fig. 2.11, P). At its centre, a single chair on a Beauvais carpet was illuminated by an overhead lantern window. Under the domed ceiling, the empty chair (fig. 2.12) marked the site of a privileged view that was shared by the guests who waited their turn on the four mahogany chairs, two loveseats, and a *bergère*.[54] An additional voyeur on a bench under a trellis in the Italian garden outside (fig. 2.14) could look through the window and watch the privileged guests in the boudoir, with his own image reflected in the mirror over the fireplace. Four niches around the edge of the boudoir displayed valuable porcelains. In a fifth niche, on axis with the bathing room and recessed almost two metres beyond the wall of the boudoir, was a daybed, a *lit de repos*, furnished with two mattresses and five down-filled pillows, all decorated with damask, with a Peking grey border and garlands of embroidered roses. Outside, the voyeur could hear and imagine the ecstasy of Mademoiselle Dervieux.

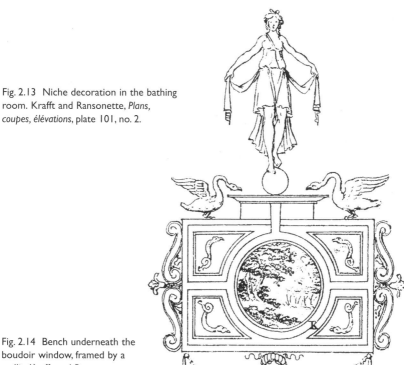

Fig. 2.13 Niche decoration in the bathing room. Krafft and Ransonette, *Plans, coupes, élévations*, plate 101, no. 2.

Fig. 2.14 Bench underneath the boudoir window, framed by a trellis. Krafft and Ransonette, *Plans, coupes, élévations*, plate 7.

Mademoiselle's boudoir, the site of sexual arousal, corresponded to Nicolas Le Camus de Mézières's ideal description, in which furniture anticipates the possibility of sexual orgasm, with *jouissance* nearly at hand.[55] As a stage for the voyeur's sexual fantasies, the boudoir provides an erotic tableau where he is simultaneously actor and spectator, both near and far from his object of desire, suspended between promise and sexual gratification. This is evoked in Jean Jacques Lequeu's *Dessin d'un boudoir, côté du canapé*, where the voyeur at the edge of the boudoir is invited onto the *lit de repos* by a small footstool that seems to project in front of the picture plane. It links the space inside the picture to the foreground space of the voyeur, whose looming shadow falls across the left side of the painting. The sultan, about to step onto the footstool to partake in unchristian pleasures, is poised to bed "Scheherazade on a raised dais in the style of oriental monarchs."[56]

Fig. 2.15 Jean Jacques Lequeu, *Dessin d'un boudoir, côté du canapé* (1779–95). Bibliothèque nationale de France.

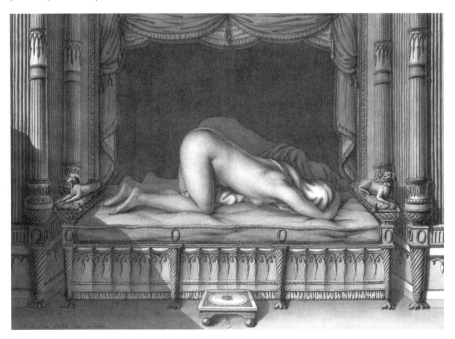

As the Baroness d'Oberkirch observed, the boudoir was like a setting from *The Arabian Nights*,[57] not just because the bed resembled a Turkish bed, but because the boudoir enabled the voyeur to occupy the space and role of a sultan. This was recognized earlier by another visitor, Antoine Caillot, who had toured the house in 1788, prior to Bélanger's 1789 addition, and commented that the boudoir was lined with mirrors on all sides, including the floor and ceiling. On the floor of this little temple of Venus were pillows on which embracing lovers could see themselves from many different points of view. Unfortunately, Caillot's fantasy was shattered when the concierge informed him that this boudoir was the preserve of a man of taste, an aristocrat of the greatest quality, implying that Caillot was merely a paying tourist.[58]

Ticket-holding visitors, immersed in the fantasy of a privileged viewer, reveled in the courtesan's possessions. A visitor such as Karamzin could observe small details in the boudoir and imagine the presence of the courtesan: "The lady of the house lives on the second floor, which we also viewed and where the rooms, whilst decorated with taste, nonetheless do not have the charm of the first floor. I was curious to see the nymph; but it suited her to play the role of a hostess. On the sofa there lay her corset, proof of her slender figure, a little bonnet with rose ribbons and a tortoise comb."[59]

Viewing her personal effects encouraged an intimate fantasy. Her nightcap, corset, pink ribbons, and tortoise-shell comb, placed with apparent negligence, made the visitor feel as if he had just missed her. Mademoiselle Dervieux's absence made her even more desirable, as he anticipated seeing the actress in person, knowing that only a "green taffeta curtain separated the famous enchantress from us; but we did not dare pull it away."[60] As the visitors Karamzin, Caillot, and the Baroness d'Oberkirch attest, Mademoiselle Dervieux was seldom present, and at times would vanish from her boudoir by retreating into a secret room through a small door skilfully concealed in a crystal rose window. The Baroness d'Oberkirch recounted the effect of the empty boudoir on the Duchess of ***, a malicious, ugly, and promiscuous woman who had been brought to see this fabulous house by one of her admirers, also a follower of Mademoiselle Dervieux. The duchess was mesmerized by the luxurious decor but was inflamed into jealous anger by being compared to the actress. Believing she was alone with her lover, the duchess vented her indignation with disparaging words about the house and the lady of the house – but on entering the boudoir with her companion, the duchess exclaimed that this room exceeded even her own *coquette* imagination. As if on cue, the actress suddenly emerged through the hidden doorway and retorted that the duchess was correct in her assessment but probably could not offer anything half as charming.[61]

The entire house fuelled the erotic expectations of its visitors by being conflated with the boudoir as a site for illicit pleasures. As the visitor promenaded through the petite maison, the sequence of successively intimate spaces seduced the visitor into becoming a voyeur to his own erotic fantasies about her eating, her singing, her gambling, her reception to his tribute, her dressing, her bathing, and finally her sexual enjoyment. The house was an exemplary expression of an appropriate character "in using correctly all the means by which no other sensations may be created in the beholder's mind but those that are required by the theme of the building."[62]

Mademoiselle Dervieux's petite maison displayed the aura of the courtesan – the ultimate desirable object – beyond the limits of a closed aristocratic culture to a larger public. It excited the public's fascination in what Grimm characterized as "the era of her celebrity."[63] Unlike the common *fille* who remained a discreet object of male sexual promiscuity behind the walls of his love nest, Mademoiselle Dervieux celebrated her sexuality with her petite maison, living like her clients who displayed their excess wealth and libertine habits. Her public expression of her sexuality greatly influenced other women.[64] When the eighteenth-century writer Madame de Genlis remarked after the Revolution that young women of quality and of the upper bourgeoisie now use the word *boudoir*, she was noting a change in how female sexuality was becoming part of their public identity.[65] Previously, *boudoir* had been used only by courtesans to refer to their *cabinet*. Under the old regime, the sex of a woman belonged to the patriarch of the family and was not discussed openly, except for women whose sexuality was their own and therefore could be exchanged.

In return for this exchange, Mademoiselle Dervieux became one of the rare women to commission a building. Her house excited the curiosity of Parisians and foreigners alike and had a great influence on contemporary fashion. However, as a stage for various fantasies, its design presumed that the house of a courtesan is where a woman is paid to give customers corporeal pleasure. In expressing this intended use, Mademoiselle Dervieux's petite maison, a house of a high-class prostitute to the Parisian elite, revealed the limits of self-construction for a public woman of the late eighteenth century.

NOTES

1 Jean-François de Bastide, *The Little House: An Architectural Seduction*, trans. Rodolphe el-Khoury (New York: Princeton Architectural Press, 1995); and Anthony Vidler, *Claude-Nicolas Ledoux: Architecture and Social Reform at the End of the Ancien Régime* (Cambridge, MA: MIT Press, 1990), 50–4.

2 Jacques-François Blondel, *Cours d'architecture, ou, Traité de la décoration, distribution & construction des bâtiments contenant les leçons données en 1750 & les années suivantes* (Paris: Desaint, 1771–77), 2:251–2; and Bastide, *The Little House*, xv.

3 Bruno Pons, "Le théâtre des cinq sens," in Jean-François de Bastide, *La petite maison* (Paris: Éditions Gallimard/Le Promeneur, 1993), 80.

4 It was built in 1770–72 in the new suburban Chaussée-d'Antin quarter, located in the northwest part of Paris. Maison Guimard is described in Jacques-François Blondel, *L'Homme du monde éclairé par les arts* (Amsterdam: Monory, 1774), 2:109–11. Reprinted in the gossip journal *Correspondance secrète, politique & littéraire: Ou mémoires pour servir à l'histoire des cours, des sociétés & de la littérature en France, depuis la mort de Louis XV* (London: John Adamson, 1787), 8:404–5.

5 Jean Stern, *À l'ombre de Sophie Arnould, François-Joseph Bélanger: Architecte des menus plaisirs, premier architecte du Comte d'Artois* (Paris: Plon, 1930), 1:172.

6 Jacques-François Blondel, *L'architecture françoise* (Paris: Jombert, 1752–56), 1:22, note a.

7 Jacques-François Blondel, *De la distribution des maisons de plaisance, et de la décoration des édifices en général* (Paris: Chez Charles-Antoine Jombert, 1737), 7; and Augustin-Charles d'Aviler, *Dictionnaire d'architecture, ou Explication de tous les termes, dont on se sert dans l'architecture* (Paris: Chez Nicolas Langlois, 1693), 269.

8 Blondel, *Cours d'architecture*, 2:251–2; *Dictionnaire de l'Académie française*, 4th ed. (1762); ARTFL Project, http://artflx.uchicago.edu/; and Pons, "Le théâtre des cinq sens," 80.

9 Blondel, *Cours d'architecture*, 2:251–2.

10 Charles Duclos, *The Confessions of the Comte de ****, in *Two French Libertine Novels*, trans. Douglas Parmée (Brooklyn, NY: AMS Press, 2006), 120; originally published as *Les confessions du Comte de **** (1747). Duclos was elected to the Académie française in 1747 and became its secretary until his death in 1772.

11 Jean Hervez, *Le parc aux cerfs et les petites maisons galantes, d'après les mémoires, le rapport de police, les libelles, les pamphlets, les satires, chanson du temps* (Paris: Bibliothèque des curieux, 1925), 179–80, 219–20. Police spy reports on the activities of these petites maisons were ordered by the lieutenants general of police, Berryer de Renouville (lieutenant general from 1747 to 1757) and Sartine (from 1759 to 1774). Originally stored at the Bastille from 1716 to 1789, the manuscripts are currently located at the Bibliothèque de l'Arsenal, Mss. de l'Arsenal, 10.252. See Frantz Funck-Brentano, *Catalogue des mss. de la bibliothèque de l'Arsenal, tome IX: Archives de la Bastille* (Paris, 1892); and Pons, "Le théâtre des cinq sens," 74.

12 Charles-Jean-François Hénault, *La petite maison*, in *Pièces de théâtre en vers et en prose* (1770), 5. Hénault's play was performed by amateurs in 1742; see *Mémoires du Président Hénault* (Geneva: Slatkine, 1971), 189.

13 *Mémoires de Madame d'Epinay* (Paris: G. Charpentier, 1865), 1:371.

14 Duclos, *Confessions of the Comte de ****, 120.

15 Hénault, *La petite maison*, 5.

16 In the seventeenth century, love affairs were conducted mainly between married ladies and gentlemen. Around the turn of the century, between 1680 and 1720, theatre women became the primary object of these affairs. Lenard R. Berlanstein, *Daughters of Eve: A Cultural History of French Theater Women from the Old Regime to the Fin-de-Siècle* (Cambridge, MA: Harvard University Press, 2001), 39; Erica-Marie Benabou, *La prostitution et la police des moeurs au XVIIIe siècle* (Paris: Perrin, 1987), 362–83; and Marie Louise-Élisabeth Vigée-Le Brun, *Souvenirs de Mme Louise-Élisabeth Vigée-Le Brun, 1755–1789* (Paris: Arthème Fayard, 1909), 28.

17 Giacomo Casanova, *Histoire de ma vie* (Paris: Laffont, 1993), 1:616–20, cited in Maurice Lever, *Théâtre et lumières: Les spectacles de Paris au XVIIIe siècle* (Paris: Fayard, 2001), 196.

18 Martine Rougemont, *La vie théâtrale en France au XVIIIe siècle* (Paris: Champion, 1988), 193–212.

19 A *fille d'Opéra* did not receive a salary from the Académie royale de musique. Pamela Cheek, "The 'Mémoires secrets' and the Actress: Tribadism, Performance and Property," in *The Mémoires Secrets and the Culture of Publicity in Eighteenth-Century France*, ed. Jeremy D. Popkin and Bernadette Fort (Oxford: Voltaire Foundation, 1998), 109–11; and Lever, *Théâtre et lumières*, 191–214.

20 James H. Johnson, "Musical Experience and the Formation of a French Musical Public," *Journal of Modern History* 64, no. 2 (1992): 194, http://www.jstor.org/stable/2124630.

21 Friedrich Melchior Grimm, *Correspondance littéraire, philosophique et critique* (Paris: Garnier, 1877–82), 9:129; and Henriette Louise von Waldner Oberkirch, *Mémoires sur la cour de Louis XVI et la société française* (Brussels: Meline, Cans et Compagnie, 1854), 1:192.

22 Lever, *Théâtre et lumières*, 191–4; Stern, *À l'ombre de Sophie Arnould, François-Joseph Bélanger*, 1:172–87; and Barbara Scott, "A Delightful Bonbonnière: Mlle Dervieux's Hôtel, Paris," *Country Life* (Nov. 20, 1980): 1902–3.

23 Grimm, *Correspondance littéraire*, 9:129.

24 Marie-Madeleine Guimard (1743–1816); Rosalie Duthé (1748–1830).

25 Louis Petit de Bachaumont, *Mémoires secrets pour servir à l'histoire de la république des lettres en France* (London: John Adamson, 1783–88), 9:52–3; and Grimm, *Correspondance littéraire*, 11:212.

26 Katie Hickman, *Courtesans: Money, Sex and Fame in the Nineteenth Century* (New York: HarperCollins, 2003), 12.

27 She purchased parcels of land from Antoine-Guillaume de La Chaude, Bouret de Vézelay, and Denis Lemaître and his wife Madeleine Ligné in February, March, and September 1777. Archives nationale de France Seine C⁶ 12² (Étude de M. La Roche), cited in Jacques Silvestre de Sacy, *Alexandre-Théodore Brongniart, 1739–1813* (Paris: Plon, 1940), 26n2.

28 Berlanstein, *Daughters of Eve*, 46.

29 Oberkirch, *Mémoires*, 1:192. The baroness, in the company of the Crown Prince and Princess of Russia, who were styled as the Comte et Comtesse du Nord, toured the house on 31 May 1782.

30 Dervieux was on good terms with the lieutenant of police, M. Antoine Gabriel de Sartine, and his successor, M. Jean Charles Lenoir. Rumours

circulated in the latter half of the eighteenth century that the owner of a gambling house would have to pay thirty thousand *livres* per year to the lieutenant of police. Alan Williams, *The Police of Paris, 1718–1789* (Baton Rouge: Louisiana State University Press, 1979), 56; Stern, *À l'ombre de Sophie Arnould, François-Joseph Bélanger*, 1:191; Scott, "A Delightful Bonbonnière," 1903; and *Correspondance secrète, politique & littéraire, ou mémoires pour servir à littérature en France, depuis la mort de Louis XV* (London: John Adamson, 1790), 18:408, Eighteenth Century Collections Online, http://galenet.galegroup.com/servlet/ECCO.

31 While he wanted to keep his liaison with Dervieux secret, Bélanger considered her house his abode. During the Revolution, they were both arrested and sent to Saint-Lazare. They subsequently married on 5 September 1794. Stern, *À l'ombre de Sophie Arnould, François-Joseph Bélanger*, 1:195–201; 2:58, 81; and *Alexandre-Théodore Brongniart, 1739–1813, Musée Carnavalet* (Paris: Musées de la ville de Paris, 1986), 52.

32 The contents of these rooms were not included in the sale of Dervieux's furnishings, suggesting that Bélanger occupied this apartment. Acte de vente de la maison de la rue Chantereine et des meubles à Vilain XIV, 21 mai 1793 (Étude de M. Aleaume, M. Thion de la Chaume, succ.), Archives nationales de France, ET/LXXVI/886.

33 Nikolaï Mikhaïlovich Karamzin, *Letters of a Russian Traveller: A Translation of Pis'ma russkogo Puteshestvennika* (Oxford: Voltaire Foundation, 2003), 296–7.

34 The typical plan can be seen in the 1758 Grand Prix Competition for a *pavillon* project. Jean-Marie Pérouse de Montclos, *"Les prix de Rome": Concours de l'Académie royale d'architecture au XVIIIe siècle: Inventaire général des monuments et richesses artistiques de la France* (Paris: Berger-Levrault, 1984), 17; Henry Lemonnier, *Procès-verbaux de l'Académie royale d'architecture, 1671–1793; publiés pour la Société de l'histoire de l'art français sous le patronage de l'Académie des beaux arts* (Paris: Edouard Champion, 1911–29); and Helen Rosenau, "The Engravings of the Grand Prix of the French Academy of Architecture," *Architectural History* 3 (1960): 19, http://www.jstor.org/stable/1568211. Also see Blondel, *De la distribution des maisons de plaisance*, 19.

35 Archives nationales de France, ET/LXXVI/886.

36 The dining room and bathing room surface decorating schemes are outli-

ned in Johann Karl Krafft and Nicolas Ransonette, *Plans, coupes, éléva-tions des plus belles maisons et des hôtels construits à Paris et dans les environs* (1801–03; Paris: Librairie d'art décoratif et industriel G. Hue, 1909), 96, 101n2.

37 Archives nationales de France, ET/LXXVI/886.

38 Hickman, *Courtesans*, 12.

39 Robert E. Bell, *Dictionary of Classical Mythology: Symbols, Attributes & Associations* (Oxford: Clio Press, 1982), 154.

40 Archives nationales de France, ET/LXXVI/886.

41 Ibid.

42 A *voyeuse* is a backward chair used while watching a card game. Resembling a *prie-dieu*, it was designed for kneeling on or sitting astride, with a padded top for resting one's arms. Henri Havard, *Dictionnaire de l'ameublement et de la décoration: Depuis le XIIe siècle jusqu'à nos jours* (Paris: Maison Quantin, 1894), 4:1735.

43 Archives nationales de France, ET/LXXVI/886.

44 Karamzin, *Letters of a Russian Traveller*, 297 [May 1790].

45 Trictrac is a board game, similar to backgammon.

46 Archives nationales de France, ET/LXXVI/886.

47 Fustian is a thick, durable twilled cloth with a short nap.

48 Archives nationales de France, ET/LXXVI/886.

49 Karamzin, *Letters of a Russian Traveller*, 297.

50 Archives nationales de France, ET/LXXVI/886.

51 Karamzin, *Letters of a Russian Traveller*, 297.

52 Archives nationales de France, ET/LXXVI/886.

53 The swans are usually associated with Venus. Bell, *Dictionary of Classical Mythology*, 354–5.

54 Archives nationales de France, ET/LXXVI/886.

55 Nicolas Le Camus de Mézières, *Le génie de l'architecture: ou, L'analogie de cet art avec nos sensations* (Paris: Benoît Morin, 1780), 123.

56 Antoine Galland, *Les mille et une nuits, contes arabes, traduits en français par Galland* (Paris: J.A.S. Collin de Plancy, 1822), 1:37. According to the Christian fathers, sodomy, as well as sexual positions other than missionary, was ungodly. Jean-Louis Flandrin, *Sex in the Western World: The Development of Attitudes and Behaviour*, trans. Sue Collins (Berkshire, UK: Harwood, 1991), 119–20.

57 Oberkirch, *Mémoires*, 1:192–3.

58 Antoine Caillot, *Mémoires pour servir à l'histoire des moeurs et usages des français* (Paris: Dauvin, 1827), vol. 2; (Geneva: Slatkine, 1976), 99–101.

59 Karamzin, *Letters of a Russian Traveller*, 297.

60 Ibid.

61 Oberkirch, *Mémoires*, 1:192–3.

62 Etienne-Louis Boullée, *Architecture. Essai sur l'art* (Paris: Hermann, 1968), 73.

63 Grimm, *Correspondance littéraire*, 9:129; Caillot, *Mémoires*, 2:99–101.

64 On the influence of courtesans on generating a pre-celebrity interest for glamour at the end of the eighteenth century, see Berlanstein, *Daughters of Eve*, 56–7.

65 Stéphanie Félicité, Comtesse de Genlis, *Dictionnaire critique et raisonné des étiquettes de la cour ou l'esprit des étiquettes et des usages anciens* (Paris: Mongie, 1818), 1:210.

Peter Brook's "Empty Space": *Orghast* at Persepolis

Negin Djavaherian

> Within us at every moment, like a giant musical instrument
> ready to be played, are strings whose tones and harmonies
> are our capacity to respond to vibrations from the invisible
> spiritual world which we often ignore, yet which we
> connect with every new breath.[1]
> –Peter Brook, *There Are No Secrets: Thoughts
> on Acting and Theatre*

IN *THE EMPTY SPACE*, Peter Brook (1925–), one of the most influential
directors in modern theatre, describes his concept of Immediate Theatre
by bringing together two others: Holy Theatre, which deals with the
"invisible" and its hidden impulses, and Rough Theatre, which focuses on
the actions of human beings.[2] In Brook's view, Immediate Theatre is able
to "slide" us between our "ordinary level and the hidden level of myth."
It awakens in us a sudden insight into hidden folds of the "fabric of reality."[3] This is achieved through what he calls "empty space." Emptiness
allows our imagination to fill the gap[4] that has been opened up between
Rough and Holy.

This essay interprets Brook's 1971 production of *Orghast* at the ruins
of Persepolis in Iran as one instance of this "empty space." Architecture
and theatre have been closely related since before the time of Vitruvius.[5]
As a paradigmatic ritual for public involvement and cultural revelation,
theatre has always inspired architects. My intention is to show how theatre can continue to suggest possibilities for architectural creation. In
modern times, Brook's *Orghast* achieved this by inducing in its audience
a sense of emptiness that liberated them from convention and opened up
a primordial "space of human creation and participation" that situated
them in the world.[6]

Orghast was produced for the 1971 Shiraz Arts Festival, the fifth in a
series of annual festivals held from 1967 to 1977. The festival was an
ongoing encounter between East and West that highlighted recent experimental and avant-garde creations. Considered one of the world's leading
theatre festivals of its kind, the Shiraz Arts Festival provoked enthusiastic and critical discourse on "the development of cultural communication
among nations,"[7] beyond racial, national, cultural, and geographical
boundaries. Recognizing its power to create change in music, theatre, and
dance, the festival encouraged fearless innovation and experimentation.

Besides Brook, directors such as Jerzy Grotowski (1933–1999), Arby Ovanessian (1942–), Robert Wilson (1941–), Tadeusz Kantor (1915–1990), and Victor Garcia (1934–1982) participated in the festival.

Arby Ovanessian has pioneered new directions that shaped the outlook of modern Iranian theatre. His productions at the Shiraz Arts Festival include *A Modern Profound and Important Research in the Fossils of the 25th Geological Era, 14th, 20th, makes no difference* (1968) and *Vis and Ramin* (1970). Asked why he staged *Vis and Ramin* at the ruins of Persepolis, Ovanessian responded, "At Persepolis, I have employed the elements of real time. The play moves ahead in step with real time and when the sun sets at Persepolis the actors appear like shadows. Furthermore, Persepolis helps us evoke historical memories. Thus the historical existence of the characters can be better felt."[8] In a review of *Vis and Ramin*, Irving Wardle notes, "Visually the production is utterly eclipsed by its setting … Evidently his aim was to draw spectators into the myth by blending living performers with bas-reliefs of the ancient palace. And in this way, he did achieve some haunting effects … Persepolis at twilight, with the setting sun burning like doomsday over the dusty plain, is one of the most awesome prospects in the world."[9] Brook saw both of Ovanessian's productions at the Shiraz Arts Festival and later declared that "Arby [Ovanessian] is exceptional … He is both a man of the East and of the West, open equally to the visible and invisible worlds."[10] He invited Ovanessian to collaborate with him in establishing the International Centre of Theatre Research (ICTR) in Paris. Ovanessian's ideas and contributions helped in shaping *Orghast* for the fifth Shiraz Arts Festival (1971).[11] The theme for that year was "Today's Art," seeking new possibilities for a "free discourse."

The following study of Brook's production of *Orghast* considers three related aspects. First, I will examine its experimental work on sound and language – the most essential features of *Orghast* – and introduce the unconventional setting for the performance at the tombs of ancient Persian kings. Second, I will consider how *Orghast* engaged both the performers and the audience through both the setting and the unfolding action of the play. Finally, I will touch on correlations between *Orghast* and the ancient Greek *chora*, highlighting the participatory ground for creation that *Orghast* brought into being.

THE FLESH OF SOUND

Orghast was a theatrical experiment that developed from explorations of the structure of sound and non-verbal communication by Brook's ICTR. ICTR pursued "a form of research much closer to that of the scientists in an experimental laboratory: the search for processes, combinations, causes and effects hitherto unknown."[12] Preliminary sound studies for *Orghast* were based on ancient writings by Seneca in Latin and Aeschylus in Greek. Various passages without spaces between words provided a seemingly random string of letters for the actors; for example: *EIELEUELELEUUPOMAUSFAKELOSKAIFREENOPLEGEIS*. Brook compared the actors to archaeologists whose role was to discover fragments within each series of letters. Guided by their emotions and senses, the actors explored the rhythms in the "flow of letters" and attempted to enunciate them with a deep, embodied meaning.[13] The actors worked "for a long time with a dozen or so set syllables that had no fixed meaning, and therefore infinitely variable potential meaning."[14] In "The Flesh of Language," David Abram makes a similar observation, noting that Maurice Merleau-Ponty "distinguishes sharply between genuine, expressive speech and speech that merely repeats established formulas and treats the language as 'a finished institution'";[15] however, "wild, living speech takes up, from within, the interconnected matrix of the language and gestures with it, subjecting the whole structure to a coherent deformation."[16] This understanding of the innate power of language aligns with Brook's experimental work on sound, which deconstructed conventional syntax and grammar to uncover the "sensorial and sentient" properties of language.[17] Brook explained that his main goal was "to discover more fully what constitutes living expression" by eliminating common words and signs that are part of the "shared cultural and sub-cultural imagery."[18] The program of the fifth Shiraz Arts Festival asked the audience, "What is the relation between verbal and non-verbal theatre? What happens when gesture and sound turn into word? What is the exact place of the word in theatrical expression? As vibration? Concept? Music? Is any evidence buried in the sound structure of certain ancient languages?"[19]

Besides ancient Greek and Latin, two other languages provided material for *Orghast*. One was the long-forgotten language of ancient Persepolis: Avesta, the ceremonial language of ancient Persia, used by the Zoroastrians. One characteristic of Avesta had special significance for

Brook: the qualities of its sounds were very close to their meanings. As he points out, the meaning of the words in Avesta came from the act of speaking them.[20] Its letters "were diagrams of the inner paths the breath has to make to make the sounds vibrate."[21] Avesta had "powerful dignity and beauty, and promised a new sort of theatrical vibration."[22]

But the primary tongue in *Orghast*'s excavation of sound and meaning was the newly invented language from which the play took its name. The language of Orghast was developed by the English poet Ted Hughes (1930–1998). Its name derived from two roots: *org*, the sound for life, and *ghast*, the flame. The word *orghast* thus means the "fire of being," with the fire symbolizing the sun. (In Zoroastrianism, Zoroaster was "the fire prophet.") With faith in the "magical properties of sound,"[23] Hughes sought "a language of tones and sounds, without specific conceptual or perceptual meaning,"[24] hoping to discover sounds that could communicate directly through the emotions and senses. As linguistic meaning is "primarily expressive, gestural, and poetic,"[25] *Orghast* was exploring precisely these qualities of language, where meaning and sound are inseparable. There were no meanings independent of the sounds. Within the dramatic action, language played an essential theatrical role in communicating sound to the senses ("sense" as in meaning, but also "sense" as in lived and felt experience).

Asked if the language of Orghast has a dictionary, Hughes replied with another question: whether music has a dictionary. For both music and Orghast, the dictionary is within our minds and bodies. Hughes likened Orghast to music that is unearthed and heard for the first time in thousands of years, yet still conveys recognizable qualities, like those of a poem.[26] It lacks "the complexities of civilization, but belongs to human beings at a basic level of experience." This is the ideal of Orghast.[27] Orghast invites us to experience the splendid music of language itself: the forgotten music of words.[28] It was based on a series of rhythmic syllables that sought to convey meanings of light, darkness, life, and death. Without a "system of fixed, semantic/symbolic references, reflections ... each word of it c[ould] shift as a poetic image, modifiable by setting."[29] Brook asks in *The Empty Space*, "Is there a language of actions, a language of sounds – a language of word-as-part-of-movement, of word-as-lie, of word-as-parody, of word-as-rubbish, of word-as-contradiction, of word-shock or word-cry?"[30] He points out that the sound language of Orghast, together with ancient Greek, Latin, and Avesta, "could penetrate directly to the sub-conscious."[31] The reverberating power of ancient languages and the new language of Orghast sought sound qualities with which the actors could express meanings and emotions.

The script of *Orghast* was based largely on the story of Prometheus and was performed in two parts. Part I, at the ruins of Persepolis, started before sunset and continued late into the night. The performance took place at the tomb of Artaxerxes (II or III), where a sizable portion of the sloping mountain had been removed, creating a space sheltered by a back wall and triangular side walls of solid rock (fig. 3.1). The fourth side was open, with views of the ruins of ancient Persepolis. The tomb carved into the mountain was located high above the ground on a man-made ledge protruding from the back wall. This platform served as the performance area. The public was seated on the platform, next to the side walls, leaving an open space in the middle. The place was "intense" and "vibrant to the rock it was cut in,"[32] concentrating the energy in the play (fig. 3.2).

Part II started in the middle of the night and ended at sunrise. It was performed at a different location, Naqsh-e-Rustam, five kilometres from the main historical site at Persepolis. Naqsh-e-Rustam is an area about four hundred metres by one hundred metres, backed by a mountain cliff about a hundred metres high. It is the final resting place of four ancient Achaemenian kings: Darius I (Darius the Great), Darius II, Xerxes I, and Artaxerxes I (fig. 3.3). High above the ground, in the face of the cliff, a deep tomb for each revered king had been hollowed out of the rock. In the ground below the cliff was an excavated pit, in the middle of which stood a cubic structure built of large stone blocks: the ancient Zoroastrian Fire Temple.

These two locations were chosen for *Orghast* after a meticulous search that considered both the visible and invisible qualities of the sites. Many criteria were considered, including how the sound was "retained" or "amplified" by the stone walls when passages from Avesta and phrases from *Orghast* were recited; how the rock influenced sound propagation and attenuation; how the actors appeared as silhouettes against the sky at twilight; and how the light at sunrise illuminated the tombs (fig. 3.4). The site studies during the preparation of *Orghast* marked an important point in Brook's career, one that permeated throughout his subsequent work in quarries and other unconventional settings. The empathic endeavour to detect hidden theatrical qualities of a site – what one might call

Fig. 3.1 Top The tomb of Artaxerxes (II or III) at Persepolis, *Orghast*, Part I. Photograph by Malie Létrange.

Fig. 3.2 Bottom Actors and audience at the tomb of Artaxerxes (II or III) at Persepolis, *Orghast*, Part I. Photograph by Malie Létrange.

Fig. 3.3 General view of Achaemenid tombs at Naqsh-e-Rustam.
Photograph by Nicol Faridani; copyright Monavar Mola Soltani Sohi.

Fig. 3.4 Preparation for *Orghast*, Part II at Naqsh-e-Rustam. Photograph by Malie Létrange.

its "persona" – is akin to an architect's careful assessment of the qualities of a site: its visible and formal features, its acoustic and aural characteristics, the slope of the ground, its potential for spatial propositions, its character at sunrise and sunset, the shadows of elements at various hours, and so forth (fig. 3.5).

Orghast, which is concerned with man as myth-maker, offers an imaginative arena – an empty space – for exposing myth to the modern world.[33] *Orghast* was not intended to present a story, line by line. Its plot loosely followed "basic myths – the gift of fire, the massacre of the innocents, the imprisonment of the son by the father, the search for liberation through revenge, the tyrant's destruction of his children: and the search for liberation through knowledge – as reflected in the hymns of Zoroaster, the stories of Prometheus and Hercules, Calderón's *Life's a Dream*, Persian legends, and other parallel sources."[34] One play in particular, *The Chained One* by Levon Shant,[35] greatly influenced the creation of

Fig. 3.5 Testing the qualities of the site at Naqsh-e-Rustam, *Orghast*, Part II.
Photograph by Malie Létrange.

Orghast. Brook recalls, "Arby [Ovanessian] at once introduced us to the great Armenian writer Levon Shant and his play *The Chained One* which linked thematically with Calderón's *Life Is a Dream*. Hearing the Armenian's words inspired the English poet Ted Hughes who was developing a sound language of his own which together with ancient Greek and Avesta could penetrate directly to the sub-conscious."[36] In *Orghast* the theme of darkness imprisoning light and the composition of consonants and vowels were borrowed from *The Chained One*.[37] *Orghast* "was created from a poet's dream world, with a poet's tools: metaphor, image, symbol and sound."[38] Although it improvised on a "tight sound structure," the play offered something "much looser" and "much freer," centred on a series of "key images and relationships."[39]

The script of *Orghast* was a "non-referential" and "non-intellectual" expression of emotional states rather than a story.[40] What was seen and, most importantly, heard "was riveting, beautiful and disturbing; but what it meant, precisely, was elusive and still is; … it worked on first encounter, as music, spectacle and (in part) as ritual, emotionally apprehended but half-understood."⁴¹ Seeking a theatrical experience that would be truly participatory, rather than merely literary or visual, *Orghast* created conditions in which the audience could observe the play as a "religious experience" or as "listen[ing] to music."⁴² Its various ambiguities enabled a secular audience at an ancient architectural site in Iran to experience a modern play that could convey a sense of sacred and spiritual awareness connected to ancient Persian mythology. Insights by the audience relied on their immediate experience of the play, resonating like a poem; "its 'meaning' is inseparable from the experience of the poem itself."⁴³

SPACE, TIME, HISTORY, AND ENGAGEMENT

From the very beginning, *Orghast* was freed from conventional frames of reference, purging the memory and opening the senses to the invisible. For the performers, the creative process commenced with a period of intensive preparation that included training during dry, hot summer days, with lengthy acoustic tests at different times of day and at different heights on the cliff. For the audience, the journey began with a long, expectant walk up a steep, tortuous road of rock, gravel, and sand to the tombs of ancient Persian kings. The "stage" in front of the tombs shattered modern preconceptions about theatre buildings and performances. It denied the audience their normal habits and provoked them into an awareness of the temporality of the world.

The play precluded the audience from associating sounds with known words, verbal rules, or recognizable language. A resonating sound was the first experience for the audience. At sunset, "chanting, rumbling voices broke out from different places – beneath the ledge, on the heights, [and] inside the tomb."⁴⁴ "Silhouetted on the skyline of the western sidewall, a woman (Light) s[ang] a long, tremulous note over the silent ruins. From the distance, Man answer[ed] with a guttural *gaveh*.⁴⁵ Light crie[d] again, Man's response [was] closer. The chorus, earth's creatures, beg[an] with throaty, staccato murmurs and swells, not in unison."⁴⁶ *Orghast* revealed the enigma of language as the sounds "echoe[d] and 'prolong[ed] unto the invisible' the wild, interpenetrating, interdependent nature of the sensible landscape itself."⁴⁷ It liberated the audience from preconceived rules and images by offering primordial experiences. Ovanessian emphasizes the role of "vibration of pure sounds."⁴⁸ Arriving from near and far, from low and high, and from inside and outside, the sounds engaged the emotions and senses of the audience, exploring the depths of human and spatial experience.

Sudden, immediate actions during the play created moments of lucid emptiness. In Part I, when tortured Prometheus was chained to the cliff, far above the burial chamber, a luminous ball of fire suddenly appeared in the dark sky and descended towards the audience. In Part II, during the darkness of the night, a ring of fire suddenly encircled the Cube of Zoroaster, introducing moments of astonishment and suspense. *Orghast* created new rapports with the history of those ancient places. The unexpected fireball and fire ring invoked the Zoroastrian religion, in which fire was the most sacred symbol. Engravings on the tombs portray the kings worshipping the sun, that blazing ball of fire that symbolizes the spirit and power of Ahura Mazda, the Zoroastrian god. The setting for *Orghast* was imbued with Zoroastrian reverence for the sacred fire and the struggle to preserve it. The radiating light and "non-physicality" of the fire symbolized the spiritual radiance and power of Ahura Mazda. Beyond these specific references to Zoroastrian history, *Orghast* recognized that fire is an archetypal symbol of life in many cultures (fig. 3.6).

Orghast also challenged conventional linear narrative. The vibrating sounds of the actors were accompanied by scenes with deeply beautiful imagery: a surreal silhouette of a woman on top of the cliff; Prometheus chained to the mountain; a woman at the entrance to the burial chamber. The performance was permeated by "cries, screams, howls and writhing bodies"[49] springing to life from the crags and tombs of the cliff. Using the full height of the rock face and the side walls gave spatial depth to the performance, with the actors positioned at different locations and heights. Languages were also distributed spatially, with chanting, murmuring, reverberating voices, and other sounds emanating from the ground, walls, ledges, and crags, and from inside the burial chamber. This array of sounds was perceived by the audience in an immediate way "as vectors," "not as finished chunks of matter given once and for all, but as dynamic ways of engaging the senses and modulating the body."[50] David Williams has observed that Brook's theatre activates the imagination by presenting incomplete, relational, and elliptical information.[51] The performance of *Orghast* dispersed visual and auditory stimuli both spatially and temporally, disrupting the audience's expectations by immersing them in a tangled array of sounds and actions.

As the play proceeded, the action became increasingly decentralized. Members of the audience became aware of separate events in different locations, including sounds from unseen sources. As alert observers with their own individual focus, they became involved in particular parts of the play, selected from the concurrent array. Especially in Part II, with its harsh, frenetic events transgressing and interfering with one another, each scene was woven with others to become part of a non-linear narrative tapestry in which the audience was fully engaged. The audience were cajoled into assembling disparate events into their own composite inter-pretation of the play, like a collage. In turn, a larger whole was formed

Fig. 3.6 The presence of fire during the performance of *Orghast*, Part I, the tomb of Artaxerxes (II or III) at Persepolis. Photograph by Malie Létrange.

through the audience's collective experience (fig. 3.7). Ovanessian pointed out that "*Orghast* resembled a dream without any linear story; when you wake up we perceive something else, uncertain of the reality and whereabouts. It is full of abstraction through which one may understand wholeness out of it. I had called it a magic circus."[52]

Time was manipulated provocatively in *Orghast* to disrupt the audience's expectations, sharpen their senses, and demand their participation. The audience arrived for the play at peculiar times of day: before sunset and before sunrise. They were placed amidst ancient tombs dating back to 550–330 BCE. They were inundated with harsh "pre-words," sound vibrations, and a melee of ancient, defunct, and invented languages. The non-linear structure of the play confronted them with various historical events. In one scene, the ghost of Darius the Great (550–486 BCE) appeared at the entrance of his own tomb, twenty metres above the ground and flanked by torch-bearers, to address the audience below in ancient Avesta, as though they were his soldiers. This event was not only dramatic, but literally dreadful and threatening.[53] The voice of Darius echoed throughout the space, bringing life to the tombs carved into the stoic mountain cliffs. The rebirth of Avesta itself demonstrated how "time-lessness and myth c[ould] come into the present and become part of the direct experience."[54] The chants and murmurs in this ancient Zoroastrian language resonated between the solemn mountain walls once again, after a hiatus of more than two thousand years. At another point in the play, remnants of the Persian army were revived to move freely across this site, known as the City of Dead.

While *Orghast* revived actions, languages, and images from the ancient past, its existence in the present moment was critical. The audience was acutely aware of the here and now, due to the screams, cries, and chants that surrounded them, the dramatic scenes with fire, and the dazzling movements of actors. Members of the audience also moved from place to place to follow the play's energetic yet fleeting scenes, absorbed in the present moment of the performance. The audience recognized that the architecture and the history of the site were not rooted in a single epoch, the Persian Empire. Both the artists and the audience at Persepolis, which in its entirety served as a staging-ground for myth, established together new meanings and relationships in the present moment in this "theatre of creation," which was, ultimately, also a place

Fig. 3.7 Actors on scaffolding next to the Zoroastrian Fire Temple (The Cube of Zoroaster) during the performance of *Orghast*, Part II at Naqsh-e-Rustam. Photograph by Malie Létrange.

of architectural creation. As an architectural repository with traces of many mythologies and narratives about the world,[55] the site was understood during the performance as a living, animated present with multiple histories. The performance of *Orghast* provoked a discourse between the very distant past and the very present moment. Ovanessian refers to this quality of time when he points out that it cannot be measured with a clock. It enables the time of Persepolis, two-and-a-half millennia ago, and the time of twentieth-century *Orghast* to became one. It is a vertical time that can be perceived through myth. It is a time through which the cosmos can be felt within one's body in space.[56] *Orghast* generated an elusive quality of time for the participants: touching them, awakening them, and steering them toward engagement in the exploration and revelation of what Brook deems to be the core narratives and "structures of feeling" of the universe.[57]

ORGHAST: SPACE OF POTENTIALITY

For architecture, the most significant characteristic of *Orghast* is the creation of a "space" that encourages profound human involvement and interaction. This space of action in *Orghast* aligns closely with the qualities of *chora* that Plato describes in *Timaeus* as the "third form of reality," "the receptacle of becoming."[58] Alberto Pérez-Gómez describes *chora* as "Plato's space of ontological continuity, the ground that makes it possible for Being and beings to relate and to share a name, in language and in human action."[59] In *Built upon Love*, Pérez-Gómez emphasizes that *chora* "is properly *human* space. It is the space of human communication that is *inherently* bounded and ambiguous."[60] This resonates with the space created in *Orghast*: a space that brings audience and actors together in wordless communion and encourages a deep, shared human experience.

Orghast opened up an "empty space" between the ordinary world (Rough Theatre) and a historical or mythical world (Holy Theatre). This concept of emptiness is fundamentally different from modern notions of "absence," "nothingness," and "the void." As Williams points out, it is an empty space of potentiality, attunedness, readiness, availability – like *ma* in Japanese aesthetics – and it has potential for "fullness." Brook's "free space" engages "our complicity and participation in our imagination, inviting us to experience spectatorship as a celebratory and empowering action." Williams refers to the quarries in Brook's later projects as a "free space" that "operates as interactive microcosm, perhaps even the temporary eco-system, places of contact and meeting, places of both individual and communal experience."[61] In my view, the emptiness of the stone walls and cliff faces at Persepolis and Naqsh-e-Rustam became *chora*-like places of human engagement during the performance of *Orghast*. Unlike conventional theatre buildings, these locations heightened the audience's alertness and involvement during the free-ranging performance.

The experience of time in *Orghast* also aligns with qualities of *chora*. The "empty space" of the performance heightened the audience's awareness of the present. Brook believes that "the real present moment isn't a moment. It's when you come through the movement of time into something which is where there is no time"; it is time-less. This is the present moment: a threshold into an empty space and into eternity. Eternity lies in neither the future nor the past; it is just an empty space. "The real present moment," as experienced in *chora*, has a quality of suspension. Brook believes that one of the crucial aims of theatre is to lead one gradually through different stages, steps, and levels to a point where there is "non-form" and "non-time."[62] In a similar way, architecture would lead one gradually through different phases, states, and conditions to a point beyond form and time.

Within Brook's empty space, any action is possible. The events in *Orghast* could not be dissected or analyzed rationally; they were unpredictable, wet, and messy. It is from this condition that the alchemical magic of Brook's theatre emerges.[63] It resembles Plato's *chora* as a "neutral plastic material on which changing impressions are stamped by the things which enter it." It receives all things – including sound, fire, and dramatic action – but, like *chora*, never accepts a permanent imprint of any kind.[64] Their traces linger only briefly before vanishing. *Chora* is not simply a space, but a space for communal action: "an empty gap that is not nothingness, assumed by common sense to be the exclusive space of action, is the meaning of architecture."[65]

In *Orghast*, the formless "empty space," impregnated with potentialities, offers a ground for constant events and happenings. In its emptiness lie infinite possibilities for extension of the imagination and experiencing the invisible. The audience was in an occult relationship with the actors and the action. Unlike a conventional performance in a proscenium-framed theatre, *Orghast* provoked the audience's involvement. In Brook's empty space, the distance between the audience and the actors can approach zero. Like the space between two lovers, it is fluid and elastic, both full and empty at the same time: a space of participation, momentarily and eternally bridged with sound and movement.

The interpretation of Brook's empty space as *chora* is reinforced by Yoshi Oida's observation that *Orghast* restored ancient Greek theatre. He says that the human actions playing out on its stage resembled a small world, a microcosm, within the immensity of the universe. He adds that Brook's theatre is like a bridge between two worlds: If we look up, we see an expanded cosmos; if we look down, we see the realities of daily life, full of social, political, and economic problems.[66] Brook's actors and audience occupy a threshold between these two worlds, slipping back and forth from one to the other. The same dichotomy is bridged by *chora*: between the transcendent cosmos and the human condition; between Being and being. The same threshold exists in architecture: "touching, moving, and recollecting, opening for the spectator a gap to catch a furtive glimpse of Being in the vivid present of experience."[67]

The various theatrical explorations that led to *Orghast* show that, contrary to Cartesian philosophy, meanings are not created in the mind of a "subjective genius," but are "out there." They can be discovered not only through visual means but through all of our senses, as well as our embodied experience of places and actions. In this "empty space" that theatre shares with architecture, Brook's creative process reminds us of the vital yet nebulous realities of the world and our capacity to engage them.

NOTES

1 Peter Brook, *There Are No Secrets: Thoughts on Acting and Theatre* (London: Methuen Drama, 1993), 81–2.

2 Peter Brook defines his concepts of Deadly, Holy, Rough, and Immediate Theatre in *The Empty Space: A Book about the Theatre* (London: Granada Publishing, 1977). See also Brook, *There Are No Secrets*.

3 Brook, *There Are No Secrets*, 86.

4 Ibid., 27.

5 See Alberto Pérez-Gómez, "Chora: The Space of Architectural Representation," in *Chora: Intervals in the Philosophy of Architecture*, vol. 1, ed. Alberto Pérez-Gómez and Stephen Parcell (Montreal and Kingston: McGill-Queen's University Press, 1994), 1–34. See also Lisa Landrum, "Architectural Acts: Architect-Figures in Athenian Drama and Their Prefigurations" (PhD diss., McGill University, 2010).

6 Alberto Pérez-Gómez, *Built upon Love: Architectural Longing after Ethics and Aesthetics* (Cambridge, MA: MIT Press, 2006), 46.

7 "Meeting of Two Worlds," in *Catalogue of the Fifth Festival of Arts*, ed. Iradj Gorguin (Shiraz-Persepolis: Public Relation of the Festival of Arts, 1971).

8 See "Nader Ebrahimi Talks to Arby Ovanessian about 'Vis and Ramin,'"

in *Catalogue of the Fourth Festival of Arts*, ed. Iradj Gorguin (Shiraz-Persepolis: Public Relations Bureau of the Festival of Arts, 1970).

9 Irving Wardle, "Rituals in the Desert: The Shiraz Festival," *International Theatre Review* 5, no. 18–19 (1970): 150.

10 Peter Brook, Preface to *Teātr va Sinamāye Arby Ovanessian – Az Varāye Gofteh-hā, Nevešteh-hā va Aks-hā* [The Theatre and Cinema of Arby Ovanessian: Through Writings, Conversations, and Images], vol. 1, researched, compiled, and edited by Majid Lashkari (Tehran: Rowzaneh Publications and Majid Lashkari, 2014), 25–6.

11 *Orghast* was presented at the Shiraz Arts Festival as a "work in progress" in a collaboration of four directors: Peter Brook, Arby Ovanessian, Geoffrey Reeves, and Andrei Serban. See Anthony Charles H. Smith, *Orghast at Persepolis: An Account of the Experiment in Theatre Directed by Peter Brook and Written by Ted Hughes* (London: Eyre Methuen, 1972); see also "A Programme Note for the Production of 'Orghast,'" Fifth Shiraz Arts Festival, Shiraz-Persepolis, 1971. *Orghast* was never presented to the public anywhere else. See also Richard Helfer and Glenn Loney, eds., *Peter Brook: Oxford to Orghast* (Amsterdam: Harwood, 1998), 158.

12 Anthony Charles H. Smith, *Orghast at Persepolis: An Account of the Experiment in Theatre Directed by Peter Brook and Written by Ted Hughes* (London: Eyre Methuen, 1972).

13 Peter Brook, *The Shifting Point: Theatre, Film, Opera, 1946–1987* (New York: Harper & Row, 1989), 108.

14 Tom Stoppard, "Orghast," *Times Literary Supplement* (London) 1174 (1 Oct. 1971).

15 David Abram, *The Spell of the Sensuous: Perception and Language in a More-than-Human World* (New York: Vintage Books, 1997), 83.

16 Ibid., 84.

17 Ibid.

18 Brook, *The Shifting Point*, 108.

19 Ibid., 110. See "A Programme Note for the Production of 'Orghast,'" Fifth Shiraz Arts Festival, Shiraz-Persepolis, 1971.

20 Brook, *The Shifting Point*, 110.

21 Brook, Preface to *Teātr va Sinamāye Arby Ovanessian*, 25.

22 David Williams, ed., *Peter Brook: A Theatrical Casebook* (London: Methuen Drama, 1988), 179.

23 Stoppard, "Orghast."

24 Albert Hunt and Geoffrey Reeves, *Peter Brook* (Cambridge: Cambridge University Press, 1995), 157.

25 Abram, *Spell of the Sensuous*, 80.

26 "Tajrobeh Tāzeh Mā, Bedur Afkandan Teātr Qarārdādi Ast" [Brook: Our New Experiment is Getting away from Conventional Theatre], *Eṭelā'āt* 13585 (31 Aug. 1971).

27 Peter Wilson, "Interview with Ted Hughes, Author of Orghast," *Tamāšā* 7, special daily edition for Fifth Festival of Arts, Shiraz-Persepolis (1 Sept. 1971).

28 "En'ekās Jahāni Panjomin Jašn Honar, Širāz - Takt-e-Jamšid: Peter Brook va Zabāni Tāzeh: Orghast" [World Reflection on the Arts Festival, Shiraz-Persepolis: Peter Brook and a New Language: Orghast], *Tamāšā* 26 (17 Sept. 1971).

29 Peter Wilson, "A Survey of the Work of I.C.T.R. in Iran from June to September 1971," 1971, Peter Brook private collection. See also Wilson, "Interview with Ted Hughes, Author of Orghast."

30 Brook, *The Empty Space*, 49.

31 Brook, Preface to *Teātr va Sinamāye Arby Ovanessian*, 25.

32 Smith, *Orghast at Persepolis*, 104.

33 "Orghast," *Tamāšā* 3 (28 Aug. 1971), special daily edition for the Fifth Festival of Arts, Shiraz-Persepolis.

34 "A Programme Note for the Production of 'Orghast.'"

35 Levon Shant, *The Chained One* [1918], unpublished typescript (1970), trans. Mischa Kudian, commissioned by Galoust Goulbenkian Foundation, ICTR archive and Arby Ovanessian private collection.

36 Brook, Preface to *Teātr va Sinamāye Arby Ovanessian*, 25.

37 Arby Ovanessian, communication with author, Dec. 2011.

38 Margaret Croyden, "The Center" (May 1980), Peter Brook private collection.

39 Geoffrey Reeves, "The Persepolis Follies of 1971," *Performance* 1, no. 1 (1971): 59.

40 Dennis Kennedy, "Review of the Book *Orghast at Persepolis: An Account of the Experiment in Theatre Directed by Peter Brook and Written by Ted Hughes*," *Educational Theatre Journal* 25, no. 4 (1973): 525.

41 Richard Findlater, "Myth and Magic among the Persians," *Observer* (London), 12 Sept. 1971.

42 Margaret Croyden, *Conversation with Peter Brook, 1970–2000* (New York: Faber & Faber, 2003), 46.

43 Alberto Pérez-Gómez, "Hermeneutics as Architectural Discourse," in *FOLIO 05: Documents on Nus Architecture*, ed. Li Shiqiao (Singapore: Department of Architecture, National University of Singapore, 2003), 20.

44 Hunt and Reeves, *Peter Brook*, 166.

45 *Gaveh* is a word used in Orghast language. In Avesta, *gaveh* connotes soul and cow. In Persian, *gav* means a cow. In Avesta, a cow is a poetic image for the soul of creation. See Smith, *Orghast at Persepolis*, 183.

46 Ibid., 201.

47 Abram, *Spell of the Sensuous*, 85.

48 Arby Ovanessian, unpublished interview by the author, Paris, 23 May 2011.

49 Croyden, *Conversation with Peter Brook*, 51.

50 Abram, *Spell of the Sensuous*, 81.

51 David Williams, communication with author, 23 Feb. 2010.

52 Arby Ovanessian, unpublished interview by author, Paris, 23 May 2011.

53 Andrew Porter, "En'ekās Jahāni Panjomin Jašn Honar, Širāz - Takt-e-Jamšid: Orghast 2" [World reflection on the Arts Festival, Shiraz-Persepolis: Orghast 2], *Tamāšā* 29 (7 Oct. 1972), 63.

54 Peter Brook, *Threads of Time: Recollections* (Washington, DC: Counterpoint Press, 1998), 155–6.

55 David Williams, communication with author, 9 Nov. 2010.

56 Arby Ovanessian, communication with author, 1 Apr. 2012.

57 Brook talks about the role of theatre in relation to the meaning of the cosmos, excerpts from Peter Brook's speech at Epson Awards, Oslo, Norway, 1 Sept. 2008, CD, Peter Brook private collection.

58 Plato, *Timaeus and Critias*, trans. Desmond Lee (Harmondsworth, UK: Penguin, 1977), 67, 71.

59 See Alberto Pérez-Gómez and Louise Pelletier, *Architectural Representation and the Perspective Hinge* (Cambridge, MA: MIT Press, 1997), 10–11.

60 Pérez-Gómez, *Built upon Love*, 46.

61 Williams, communication with author, Jan. 2012. See also David Williams, "A Free Space Frees: The Mahabharata in Australia," 1993, reposted *Skywritings* (blog), 29 Aug. 2008, http://sky-writings.blogspot.ca/2008/08/free-space-frees.html.

62 Peter Brook, interview by the author, Paris, 7 Dec. 2009, in Negin Djavaherian, "Not Nothingness: Peter Brook's 'Empty Space' and Its Architecture" (PhD diss., McGill University, 2012), 37.

63 Qāsem Hāšemi Nežād, "Orghast: Yek Katar Ju'iye Qahremāni" [Orghast: A Heroic Adventure Seeking], *Āyandegān* (Tehran), 11 Sept. 1971.

64 Plato, *Timaeus and Critias*, 69.

65 Pérez-Gómez, "Chora: The Space of Architectural Representation," 32.

66 Yoshi Oida, "Namāyeš Orghast dar Jašn Honar Širāz" [Play 'Orghast' in Shiraz Arts Festival], trans. Nāser Ḥosayni, *Gardun* (Tehran) 50 (1996): 41.

67 Alberto Pérez-Gómez, "The Modern City: Context, Site or Place For Architecture?" in *Constancy and Change in Architecture*, ed. Malcolm Quantrill and Bruce Webb (College Station: Texas A&M University Press, 1991), 88.

Bodies, Books, and Buildings: Encountering the Renaissance Frontispiece

Paul Emmons

Chora

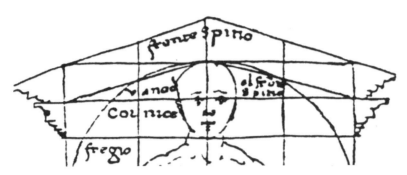

Fig. 4.1 Detail of the *frontispicio* of a youth measured to a temple elevation; from Francesco di Giorgio Martini, *Trattato di architettura, ingegneria e arte militare* (ca 1475–90), MS II.I.141, 36; Biblioteca Nazionale, Florence.

In the brow the heart is read.

–Petrarch[1]

THE FRONTISPIECE IS AN encounter between reader and book, inhabitant and building, as well as self and other. With the increasing use of personal devices and impresas in the Renaissance, close relationships were reinforced among clothing, books, and buildings.[2] The word *frontispiece* was used in Renaissance England to triply name the human forehead, the illustrated title page of a book, and the pedimented front of a building. Deriving from the Latin *frontispicium*, it means literally "looking at the forehead." In Latin, *frōns* is the forehead and *specere* is "to look," later corrupted into English as "piece."[3] *Frontispicium*, as looking at the forehead, references metoposcopy, a form of divination analyzing the lines on a person's brow to read their character and foretell their destiny.[4] From metoposcopy, *frontispiece* was extended by analogy to the façade of a building. Of architecture, Roger North wrote in 1695, "The middle is most considerable in every building; and ought to be set off with a large and massy frontone, that *speaks*."[5] "Fronton" was a variation for both forehead and pediment, which, according to North, presents meaning. In each of these three situations – body, book, and building – an outer, visible appearance suggests an inner, invisible state.

The story of the frontispiece begins in the ancient world, when the Romans associated the forehead with a person's "genius," the spirit that was situated in the head but separate from the conscious mind. As the nearest body part, the forehead was believed to present this genius most clearly.[6] To honour his genius, a Roman would touch his hand to his forehead (*venerantes deum tangmus frontem*). The genius was manifest through unwilled acts such as sneezing, sexual arousal, or the reddening of the face due to embarrassment or rage. This may account for the Roman custom of rubbing the forehead when blushing or when angry, to propitiate the genius.[7] When Roman generals left for battle, departing from the Temple of Jupiter, their faces were painted red, called "gleaming face." This echoed the god Jupiter Optimus Maximus, who resided in the Capitoline temple and whose cult statue was periodically adorned with red cinnabar.[8] In Greece, Pheidias's sculpture of Zeus – one of the seven ancient wonders – was reportedly based on Homer's description of him "nodding his dark brow." Strabo's famous quip – that the seated statue of Zeus in his Temple at Olympia is so large that his head would "unroof the temple" if he stood up – suggests a deeper resonance between genius and divinity through the conjunction and concussion of forehead and pediment.[9]

Not unlike the human forehead, the classical temple pediment or *fastigium* was closely identified with the gods. Cicero asserted that even in heaven, where no rain falls and where pitched roofs would be unnecessary for shedding water, temples would still require pediments for dignity.[10] Sculptures above and in front of the smooth triangular stone wall of the tympanum presented divinities to the populace. In Greek drama, Euripides's *Ion* begins and ends with references to temple pediments, called *aetos* (eagle) in ancient Greek. This name probably references the sweep of a bird's extended wings and its role in connecting earth and sky.[11] The play opens in the morning with "a beautifully-shaded [literally 'eye-lidded'] light of twinned faces," anthropomorphizing the two pediments and their projecting cornices. The eyes in archaic Greek statues were rendered in a triangular, pediment-like shape and Aristotle compares eyebrows to the eaves of a house, protecting the eyes from fluids running down the head.[12] At the end of the play, Ion has an epiphany of the goddess Athena appearing on the *aetos*.[13] Similarly, in ancient Rome, Ovid's *Fasti* describes the god Mars descending from the heavens onto the *fastigia* of his new temple in the Forum of Augustus.[14] Because the gods could choose to inhabit their stone likenesses, these sculptures were finished on all sides even though the back was not visible. Sometimes they were also chained to prevent the gods from being

Fig. 4.2 A statue of Apollo inside a temple; fragment of a calyx krater from Taranto, first quarter of fourth century BCE; courtesy Allard Pierson Museum, Amsterdam.

lured away. The confinement of images occurred in ancient Greece and continued into postclassical times.[15] Some ancient temples had tympana with doorways or windows, perhaps derived from early structures, as seen in the archaic votive models that had openings in their gable ends to release smoke (which is the part of the sacrifice given to the gods). Although the purpose of these later temple openings is unclear, their ornamentation suggests cult rituals.[16] The pediment doorways could have provided a heavenly gate for performing ritual divine epiphanies. Ancient temple tympana were often painted a particular bright blue to evoke not the moist sky of the mortal realm but the burning sky of the heavens above the clouds, which Lucretius describes as "purest blue, the air is almost laughter in its radiance."[17] Doric temples were often dedicated to gods of war and sometimes had tympana painted red, perhaps to symbolize the forehead's life-soul.[18] The temple's frontispiece, the pedimented entry, projected the genius or character of the building. Colour transformed the tympanum's smooth, solid stone into a thin membrane, like an animal skin stretched taut for a drum (*tympanon*), the pediment vibrating with divine presence and echoing the music of worshipers. In the opening of one of his poems, Pindar compared the beginning of his writing to an architect designing a building: "The fore-head of every work begun must shine from afar."[19] This may well have been inspired by a temple's high *fastigium*, gleaming as it welcomes the rising sun. In the English Renaissance, Pindar's ode was translated in an epigram explaining the frontispiece of a book on heraldry:

> The noble *Pindare* doth compare somewhere,
> Writing with Building, and instructs us there,
> That every great and goodly *Edifice*,
> Doth aske to have a comely *Frontispice*.[20]

Both the face of the wall and the face of the book were edifying con-structions. The frontispiece in buildings had long been a site of significa-tion when its idea was extended to printed books in the Renaissance.

The architectural frontispiece of books developed along with printing technology in the late fifteenth century.[21] During the Renaissance, pages of a book were printed individually and sold loose, then taken by the owner to a separate artisan who would sew the binding and the leather-work of the cover. A cover represented primarily the book's owner and often was embossed with his or her initials or devices. This explains why

Fig. 4.3 Temple of Diana at Ephesos, with three openings in its *tympanon*; silver coin reverse (42–41 BCE); from Münzkabinett, Staatliche Museen zu Berlin, Object no. 18213943, image by R. Saczewski.

more than one unrelated book might be combined into a single binding.[22] After printing the pages, the stationer over time added a blank top sheet to protect the completed work. To distinguish these stacks of paper, information such as the title and the author eventually were added to the formerly blank top sheet, thus becoming a title page.[23] Rather than the cover, it was the first page that represented the early modern book. Historian Margery Corbett traces the origins of the illustrated frontispiece to late fifteenth-century humanists and artists in the Veneto. Inscriptions on classical ruins attracted both architects and scribes, who drew letter forms with the architectural remains in sketchbooks while visiting the ruins. Early illustrated title pages probably grew out of these studies. Veronese printer Alvise's 1479 edition of Aesop's *Fables*, for example, displays its title on what appears to be a Roman funerary monument, probably from a drawing of an actual tomb.[24] In a short time, these illustrated title pages developed into full frontispieces with architectural elements, figures, and inscriptions. The ideas within the pages of a book were translated into a single, synoptic architectural image.

Renaissance book frontispieces often include a portrait of the author, sometimes looking out at the reader. Dominating the frontispiece of Vignola's 1562 treatise, *Regola delli cinque ordini d'architettura*, is his self-portrait in a melancholic pose, with pronounced lines on his forehead.[25] He leans forward through the imaginary space of a window, as if into the realm of the reader. Representational techniques such as this questioned the apparently clear division between author and reader or, more broadly, between imagination and world.[26] Renaissance portraits increasingly represented the sitter's outer physical appearance, but also were used physiognomically to portray inner character traits of the individual and his or her office.[27] Girolamo Cardano (1501–1576), a physician, mathematician, and astrologist, explained that metoposcopy, like medicine, cannot "always foresee things that will really happen," yet "as in every other art, we can predict things that for the most part will happen, actually quite reliably from the point of view of the emotions of the soul."[28] He also describes how some experts in this art use portraits for divination. The similar practice of portraying authors in libraries where their books are collected was described at the time in a letter to Federico Borromeo, founder of the Ambrosiana library in Milan: "To judge at the same time the spirit of the authors by their books and bodies, face and physiognomy ... excites a generous soul."[29] Giambattista della

Fig. 4.4 Frontispiece from Iacomo Barozzi da Vignola, *Regola delli cinque ordini d'architettura* (1562).

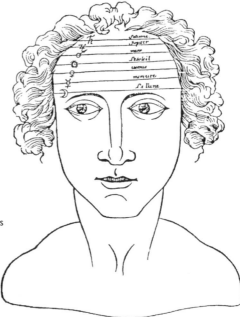

Fig. 4.5 Lines with different characteristics appearing on the foreheads of men and women; from Girolamo Cardano, *Lettura della fronte: Metoposcopia* (1560).

Porta's 1586 treatise on physiognomy compares human and animal faces, then predicts the character of humans according to the traits of the animals they resemble. One desirable type is described as leonine. In addition to genius, the lion is associated with audacity, so the pronounced scowl of its forehead is a key sign of an audacious person. Della Porta, following (pseudo-)Aristotle, describes this kind of forehead as a "cloudy brow." Michelangelo's *David* is a famous example of a leonine cloudy brow.[30] Architects were characterized as standing between the twin (but opposed) virtues of audacity and prudence.[31] Cesare Cesariano, in his 1521 translation and commentary on Vitruvius, created a quasi-frontispiece that describes his personal architectural journey. He reaches out to "touch the forehead of Fortuna" while Prudentia cautions him and Audacia encourages him across the chiasm from earthly "poverty" to the heavenly realm where fame awaits.[32] The exaggerated forehead of Vignola's clowdy brow in this frontispiece portrays him as an audacious architect endowed with genius. The portrait of Vincenzo Scamozzi in the frontispiece of his 1615 treatise, *L'Idea della architettura universale*, includes a rather pronounced brow and is encircled by the inscription, "Here the outward image of the author's body is revealed. Inside is shown the image of his genius."[33] This

Fig. 4.6 Leonine cloudy forehead, from Giambattista della Porta, *De humana physiognomonia libri IIII* (Vici Aequensis: Apud Iosephum Cacchium, 1586); courtesy United States National Library of Medicine.

Fig. 4.7 Frontispiece from Vitruvius, *De architectura*, trans. Cesare Cesariano (Como, 1521), LXXXXIIr.

correspondence between face and mind with frontispiece and text was fairly common among author portraits in book frontispieces during the Renaissance.[34] Whether for a person, a building, or a book, the frontispiece reveals inner character through outer appearance.

A book's frontispiece often includes an architectural structure or scaffolding in the foreground that opens onto a realm beyond and invites readers to step into the depths of the book. This foreground threshold takes various forms: an altarpiece (Palladio), triumphal arch (Barbaro), curtain (Bartoli), window (Vignola), or pedimented gateway (Scamozzi).[35] The architectural frontispiece is both a literal and metaphorical portal, with words and images representing the contents of the book.[36] Inhabiting the architectural structure are allegorical figures as sculptures with attributes to personify certain traits. A common pairing of figures in the frontispieces of architectural treatises, such as Palladio's *Four Books on Architecture* (1570), are the maidens Theory and Practice.[37] Usually they are balanced and opposite. Theory, dressed in blue, gazes aloft and holds her compasses pointing upwards, while Practice, dressed in brown, points her compasses down to the earth. The two figures in the side niches of Vignola's iconographic frontispiece are often identified as Theory (on the left, holding a quadrant and a tablet of geometry) and Practice (on the right, holding a square, rule, and compass); however, the latter figure is lifting both arms and holding the compasses upward, so the pair of figures may both be interpreted as Theory, especially as each is posed under identical polyhedral lamps.[38] Unlike the two female figures, Vignola holds his compasses pointing downward as if at work on the windowsill, concretely demonstrating practice.[39] Opposite the title page, Vignola's dedication describes himself (with an excess of rhetorical humility) as a "mere manual worker."[40] The maidens are crowded in the theatrical space of the box while Vignola is in the "real" space of the window. For Vignola, theory is relegated to the shadowy wings of the stage, while dominating practice is in the world. The architectural structure of a frontispiece defines meaningful spatial relationships.

Books of emblems also appeared during the Renaissance. To present an idea, they juxtaposed words (a motto, title, or poem) and a symbolic, personified image. Andrea Alciati wrote the first published book of emblems, *Emblematum Liber*, in 1531.[41] These books were widely used as sources of iconography by artists, craftsmen, and architects. Emblems appeared on buildings, while buildings appeared in emblems. With so

Fig. 4.8 Frontispiece from Andrea Palladio, *I quattro libri dell'architettura* (Venice, 1570).

much in common, the English translation of Henri Estienne's *L'art de faire les devises* (1645) referred to emblems as "frontispieces."[42] The word *emblem* derives from the Greek *emballein* (ἔμβλημα), an "insertion." In Latin, *emblemata* refers to mosaic inlay work that joins together various elements. Both emblems and frontispieces employed allegorical illustrations to create the "mystical mixture of *body* (image) and *soul* (motto)."[43] The emblem's ambiguity presents the reader with a visual *enigma* that Alciati defined as "a truthful saying wrapped in obscurity," requiring interpretation. This emblematic mode of thought will be illustrated with a reading of one early architectural frontispiece.

AN EMBLEMATIC ARCHITECTURAL FRONTISPIECE

Despite his short life, Walther Hermann Ryff (or Rivius) (ca 1500–1548) was an enormously prolific author of popular scientific works.[44] As historian William Eamon noted, Ryff stressed that his books were for the "common man," not the well-educated nor the "ignorant blockheads whose brains you could make into pig's troughs."[45] Ryff's writing and images were always grounded rather than abstract.[46] By compiling and translating other authors' works from Latin and Italian into German – including Cesariano's publication on Vitruvius – Ryff earned a reputation as an "archplagiarist," though he was fairly typical, if more extreme, for his time. Ryff at least briefly named the "excellent artists ... whose writings I have chiefly used in this enterprise as trustful preceptors."[47] Ryff did not simply copy his sources; he added to, deleted from, and altered foreign works to interpret them for his audience, calling it "Germanization."[48] While residing in Nuremberg, Ryff produced five architectural treatises in five years: most importantly *Der Architectur* (1547), an adaptation and compilation of various Italian treatises, and *Vitruvius Teutsch* (1548), the first German translation of Vitruvius.[49] The frontispiece was the same for both books: a figure standing on a base, surrounded by numerous tools and instruments.[50]

If Ryff had been merely a lazy plagiarist, he could have simply copied the frontispiece from a previous book, from which he had already taken so much. Instead, he adapted and juxtaposed new and existing elements to form a new whole. Like the inlay of *emblemata*, the woodblocks that had been carved for printing images were sometimes cut into parts, reassembled with new elements, and held together with clamps at the press to print a new set of images. Although we assume that printing produces identical copies, early books were created individually and enjoyed substantial variation from one copy to the next.[51] Whoever designed and created Ryff's frontispiece knowingly made a proposition about architecture.[52]

The figure in Ryff's frontispiece is a putto with an unusually tall, gleaming forehead: a spirit of architecture. Putti developed from the ancient idea of genius, which was associated with many different characters. The Renaissance putto was not merely Eros, but a sprite (*spiritello*) associated with the spirit. As pneumatic creatures, putti are usually winged because they have a highly rarified material presence.[53] Ryff's putto, with curly

Viuitur ingenio, cætera mortis erunt.

Aurum probatur igni, ingenium uero Mathematicis.

Fig. 4.9 Frontispiece from Walther Ryff, *Der Architectur* (Nuremberg, 1547).

Fig. 4.10 "Genius Constrained by Poverty," from Andrea Alciato, *Emblematum Libellus* (Paris, 1534).

hair and billowing clothing, expresses vivacity imbued with *spiritus*.[54] Ryff similarly describes architects' "subtle skillfulness" to "put forth and prefigure" designs as "ingenious inventions."[55] This putto, as a personification of architecture, is gazing upward with his raised right hand grasping a pair of wings, while his lowered left hand is open and weighed down by a stone hanging from his wrist.

The immediate source of Ryff's figure is Alciati's emblem "Genius Constrained by Poverty."[56] Despite appearing very similar, there are some important differences that will be discussed below. Unlike today, the Renaissance notion of poverty alluded to the human condition as inherently incomplete.[57] Cesariano's frontispiece similarly locates the architect between shadowy, earth-bound "poverty" and enlightened, heavenly fame.[58] Since the stone is not chained to the putto, as in Alciati, but is only looped over his wrist, any limitations due to the physicality of building are freely accepted by the spirit of architecture.

The emblem of constrained genius was popular throughout the Renaissance, appearing in many guises, but the figure always mediated between opposites.[59] The earliest version of this image is in *Hypnero-*

Fig. 4.11 *Festina lente*, from Francesco Colonna (attr.), *Hypnerotomachia Poliphili* (Venice, 1499).

tomachia Poliphili (1499), another of Ryff's sources.[60] A maiden half-seated and half-standing, holding a wing and a turtle, is an emblem of the motto "hurry slowly" (*festina lente*). The saying "make haste slowly" was attributed to Augustus (to whom Vitruvius dedicated his Ten Books) as a motto for ruling the empire prudently by combining speed with restraint.[61] Similarly, architectural work requires slow, deliberate design in the making of drawings, so that construction can be rapid. Emblematic representations of *festina lente* rightfully became associated with the prudently audacious architect.

The emblem of constrained genius affirms architecture as a *scientia media* (in-between science), applying abstract geometry to practical problems with physical materials. In this way, architecture mediates between the metaphysical and the physical. Rather than having separate figures for theory and practice, Ryff unites them into a single figure, writing, "The mathematician involves himself in fashioning groups and forms of things only mentally; he ignores their material reality: we shall present the subjects we treat as perceptible."[62] This contrasts significantly with Alberti's discussion of architectural lineaments as conceived in the mind.

In the frontispiece, one can grasp Ryff's project as a unification of established craft practice with Vitruvian theory.

The meaning of Ryff's figure is evident in its posture. Unlike other versions of the emblem that show one foot down and one foot raised (such as Alciati and *Poliphili*), Ryff's figure has both feet standing on a cube. Cubes in emblems often symbolized stability and permanence due to their physical properties. Another Alciati emblem shows Fortune balancing on a sphere while Mercury, god of the arts, stands on a cube, suggesting that knowledge of the arts can ameliorate the uncertainty of nature.[63] Ryff's emblem, like others, uses the cube to show the certainty of knowledge. With both of the putto's feet standing on it firmly, this reinforces the importance of study and knowledge for the genius of architecture.

As the putto stands on a cube, the cube in turn rests on an eight-pointed plinth, formed by two intersecting and rotated cubes: a design invented specifically for the frontispiece. Different moldings distinguish the two cubes and emphasize their separate identities. In Dürer's *Melencholia I* and the emerging tradition of German perspective manuals, rotated geometric forms symbolized the architect's genius and the efficacy of the tools. Alchemically, rotated geometric forms represented matter undergoing change, as illustrated in Caporali's architectural treatise from 1536 and Stoer's later alchemic geometry.[64] Ryff's precisely finished plinth contrasts the rough stone in the putto's hand, symbolizing the distinction between art (as *poesis* or knowledgeable making) and nature.

Treatises devoted to a trade often illustrated their professional tools on a title page.[65] More than a catalogue, however, the tools in Ryff's frontispiece suggest the expertise latent within them.[66] Drawing from numerous sources, Ryff includes surveying and leveling tools, finish carpentry tools, alchemical equipment, and drawing materials and instruments. Almost all of the tools are related to geometry, either theoretical or practical. Unlike the figure and its perspectival base, the tools are represented in a more upright projection and appear almost to float on the surface of the paper, emphasizing their availability as equipment ready-to-hand. Perhaps this explains why the putto's open hand is reaching down toward them, whereas the putto's open hand in Alciati's emblem is reaching upward toward God.

Bellows appear from behind the plinth, with the nozzle pointing toward flames engulfing a crucible. Alchemically, a crucible was used to melt and purify a base metal, onto which an elixir was projected to make the final transmutation.[67] Through their strong association with air and spirit, bellows were considered a semi-miraculous, animate object with a force of their own.[68] Tellingly, in Cesariano's frontispiece, Fate is operating bellows with a winged angelic spirit blowing out of the nozzle toward the architect. Bellows are a machine of the spirit.

Amidst the tools in Ryff's frontispiece are four books, indicating the importance of knowledge to architecture. The two books on the wing side of the figure are clasped shut, suggesting that divine knowledge is hidden and requires intuition, while on the stone side they are open, displaying discursive human knowledge of the arts that can be learned. The same contrast between open and closed books occurs in Dürer's *Melencolia I*. The lower open book on Ryff's frontispiece presents images of applied geometry, including a six-pointed star made of two rotated equilateral triangles, widely known in alchemy as the Seal of Solomon. This image represents the joining of elements "so that all is in perfect balance" in a "union of ... spirit and flesh ... that transports heaven to earth."[69] From the two opposing elements, fire (upward triangle) and water (downward triangle), the active/passive and *forma/materia* become a union of opposites. The upward movement of the wings symbolizes the levity of fiery air, while the downward movement of stone is related to the earth. This dual movement is described in the text of Alciati's "constrained genius" emblem's epigram. Many elements in Ryff's frontispiece symbolize the mediating role of architecture between the physical and the metaphysical. The putto is situated at the midpoint, reaching up to the ideal and down to the material. The two arms of Ryff's figure form a diagonal that crosses the vertical axis of its upright posture. This vertical axis is reinforced by the level with plumb lines, directly below the putto.

This partial reading of Ryff's frontispiece suggests that he introduced Vitruvian doctrine to northern Europe not merely to import Italian Renaissance ideas but to present a new vision for architecture north of the Alps. Following Vitruvian theory, he suggested that architecture should be understood as a liberal art along with other mathematical arts, but also must maintain a material orientation toward building.[70] He furthered the *architector doctus* as an educated architect who also requires extensive technical and practical skills. Reversing the hands in Alciati's figure, the closed hand of Ryff's putto grasps the wings, while his open hand is extended toward the stone and tools. In this way, unlike the Neoplatonic rhetoric of Italian *disegno*, Ryff's more Aristotelian idea of design is not unidirectional. By uniting Theory and Practice into a single figure, Ryff suggests that design flows not only from idea to material, but also from material to idea, ascending and descending like the overlapping triangles in the open book. The test of emblematic interpretation is not from surmising an author's intent, but from the internal consistency of the symbolization. A well-designed frontispiece rewards close reading with seemingly inexhaustible signification.

ENCOUNTERING FRONTISPIECES

Today, frontispieces and emblems are often considered superfluous decorations of an idea that could be stated more efficiently and directly without needless ornament. This is due to the modern expectation for signs to provide a transparent, precise, and limited meaning. When architecture is conceived as a technical profession, this expectation for exclusively literal meaning is even more pronounced.

Encountering a frontispiece, as in the examination of Ryff above, begins to demonstrate the rewards and value of a slow process of signification. Its emblematic meanings are not merely metaphorical riddles to solve. Frontispieces are pictorial paradoxes that deliciously expand the space between word and image, signifier and signified. Encountering them

Fig. 4.12 Reconstruction of a terracotta Gorgon's head at the centre of a pediment, Temple C at Selinus (ca mid-sixth century BCE); from Accademia nazionale dei Lincei, *Monumenti antichi*, vol. 35 (Milan: Ulrico Hoepli, 1933–35), plate 34.

slows time through reverie, savouring their extended interpretation. Frontispieces are not obfuscations, but fabulous enigmas with their own original mode of speaking. Giorgio Agamben pointed out that *ainigma* has its root in *ainos* (story, fable).[71] He describes enigmas as apotropaic, a protective power that repels the otherness of the uncanny by attracting it and assuming it within itself, approaching as it distances. It is not a coincidence that the earliest sculpted pediments in ancient Greece were apotropaic Gorgons. The frontispiece is a device for divining the unfathomable, making visible the otherwise invisible.

Encounters with frontispieces – whether human, book, or building – reveal our inevitable inclination to seek meaning in the world. Since encounters are face-to-face meetings, they do not isolate the viewer from the object through a gaze, but are rather an apotropaic discovery of self in another, like the reflection of oneself in the pupil of another person's eye. Although we are cautioned "not to judge a book by its cover," we ought to engage the vivid depth of books, buildings, and bodies through their enigmatic frontispieces.

NOTES

1 "Ma spesso ne la fronte il cor si legge." Francesco Petrarca, *Il Canzoniere*, 4.222.

2 Charles Burroughs, "Hieroglyphs in the Street: Architectural Emblematics and the Idea of the Facade in Early 16th Century Palace Design," in *The Emblem and Architecture*, ed. Hans Boker and Peter Daly (Brepolis: Turnholt, 1999), 59.

3 OED *Online*, s.v. "frontispiece," accessed 1 June 2015, www.oed.com.

4 Aristotle makes numerous physiognomic references, including the forehead. Aristotle, *History of Animals* 1.8; and Pseudo-Aristotle, *Physiognomy*, 811–12.

5 Roger North, *Of Building: Roger North's Writings on Architecture*, ed. Howard Colvin and John Newman (Oxford: Oxford University Press, 1981), 60.

6 Joseph Rykwert, *The Dancing Column: On Order in Architecture* (Cambridge, MA: MIT Press, 1996), 41. The research for this essay began in a 1996 seminar at the University of Pennsylvania, led by Joseph Rykwert.

7 Richard Onians, *The Origins of European Thought about the Body, the*

Mind, the Soul, the World, Time, and Fate (Cambridge: Cambridge University Press, 1951), 129, 146, 227.

8 Physiognomic texts characterized Hellenic complexion as "light mixed with red." Elizabeth Evans, *Physiognomics in the Ancient World* (Philadelphia: American Philosophical Society, 1969), 14–16; and Mary Beard, *The Roman Triumph* (Cambridge, MA: Harvard University Press, 2007), 84, 206.

9 Strabo, *Geography*, 8.3.30; Homer, *Iliad*, 1.528.

10 Cicero, *De oratore*, 3.180. See also Cicero, *Phillipic*, 2.110.

11 Basil Gildersleeve, *Pindar: The Olympian and Pythian Odes* (New York: Arno Press, 1979), 230–1.

12 Aristotle, *Parts of Animals*, 658b.

13 Deborah Steiner, *Images in Mind: Statues in Archaic and Classical Greek Literature and Thought* (Princeton: Princeton University Press, 2001), 169.

14 Ovid, *Fasti*, 5.549–68. Ann Kuttner generously provided this reference.

15 Steiner, *Images in Mind*, 160–8.

16 Temples with pediment openings include the Artemisium at Ephesus, Temple of Concord at Agrigento, Temple of Artemis Leukophryene at Magnesia, Temple at Cyrene in Tripoli, and the Propylaea at Athens. Rykwert, *Dancing Column*, 154–5, 455n48; and A.W. Lawrence, *Greek Architecture* (New Haven, CT: Yale University Press, 1983), 230, 256, 282; and Bluma Trell, *The Temple of Artemis at Ephesos* (New York: American Numismatic Society, 1945).

17 Rykwert, *Dancing Column*, 233; and Arthur B. Cook, *Zeus: A Study in Ancient Religion* (New York: Biblo and Tannen, 1965). Vitruvius's method for creating blue for stucco is described as "strange enough" but seems to integrate many of the associations of fiery blue aether.

18 D.S. Robinson, *Greek and Roman Architecture* (Cambridge: Cambridge University Press, 1969), 50; and Vitruvius, *De architectura*, 1.2.5, 4.1.6.

19 Pindar, *The Odes of Pindar*, trans. Richard Lattimore (Chicago: University of Chicago Press, 1942), 14.

20 John Guillim, *A Display of Heraldrie* (London: William Hall, 1611), verso of frontispiece.

21 Desley Luscombe, "Inscribing the Architect: The Depiction of the Attributes of the Architect in Frontispieces to Sixteenth Century Italian Architectural Treatises" (PhD diss., University of New South Wales, 2004); Margery Corbett and Ronald Lightbrown, *The Comely Frontispiece: The Emblematic Title-Page in England 1550–1660* (London: Routledge, 1979); and Hen-

drik Vervliet, "Les Origines du Frontispice Architectural," *Gutenberg Jahrbuch 1958* (Mainz: Gutenberg-Gesellschaft, 1958), 222–31. For the prior manuscript tradition of the incipit, see Ivan Illich, *In the Vineyard of the Text: A Commentary to Hugh's Didascalicon* (Chicago: University of Chicago Press, 1993), 8.

22 English Renaissance bibliophile Samuel Pepys framed separate frontispieces for display. He also bound wooden stilts under the printed pages of his books so that each book on a shelf was the same height, indicating that the binding was understood as the owner's. David McKitterick, "Introduction," in *Catalogue of the Pepys Library at Magdalene College Cambridge* (Wolfeboro, NH: D.S. Brewer, 1991), 7:xi–xxxv.

23 Margaret Smith, *The Title-Page: Its Early Development, 1460–1510* (London: British Library, 2000), 145.

24 Margery Corbett, "The Architectural Title-page: An Attempt to Trace Its Development from its Humanist Origins up to the Sixteenth and Seventeenth Centuries, the Heyday of the Complex Engraved Title-Page," *Motif* 12 (1964): 50.

25 Giacomo Barozzi da Vignola, *Canon of the Five Orders of Architecture*, trans. Branko Mitrović (New York: Acanthus, 1999), plate 1.

26 Sven Sandström, *Levels of Unreality: Studies in Structure and Construction in Italian Mural Painting during the Renaissance* (Uppsala: Almqvist, 1963).

27 Joanna Woods-Marsden, "Ritratto al naturale: Questions of Realism and Idealism in Early Renaissance Portraits," *Art Journal* 46 (1987): 209–16; and Luke Syson, Introduction to *The Image of the Individual: Portraits in the Renaissance*, ed. Nicholas Mann and Luke Syson (London: British Museum, 1998), 11–12.

28 Girolamo Cardano, *Lettura della fronte: Metoposcopia*, ed. Alberto Arecchi (Milan: Mimesis, 1994), 23. Translation generously provided by Paola Frascari.

29 Johannes Wouvcrius, translated in Pamela Jones, *Federico Borromeo and the Ambrosiana: Art Patronage and Reform in Seventeenth-Century Milan* (Cambridge: Cambridge University Press, 1993), 142.

30 David Summers, "'ARIA II': The Union of Image and Artist as an Aesthetic Ideal in Renaissance Art," *Artibus et Historiae* 10, no. 20 (1989): 15–31; David Summers, "David's Scowl," in *Collaboration in Italian Renaissance Art*, ed. W.S. Sheard and J.T. Paoletti (New Haven, CT: Yale University Press, 1978), 113–24; M. Barasch, "Character and Physiognomy: Bocchi on Donatello's St. George, a Renaissance Text on Expression in Art," *Journal*

of the History of Ideas 36 (1975): 413–30; and Giambattista della Porta, *De humana physiognomonia libri IIII* (Vico Equense, 1586), 60.

31 The ancients associated audacity with Daedalus, the cunning architect of the Cretan labyrinth. Vitruvius's story of the architect Dinocrates, who interrupted Alexander the Great to present his design for a city while dressed as Hercules in a lion skin, shows the architect's leonine audacity literally. Battista Alberti added "Leo" to his name to reflect his audacious nature. Ryff uses "audacity" in describing architecture's significance. Vitruvius, Introduction to *Vitruvius Teutsch*, trans. Gualtherum H. Rivium (Nuremberg: Johann Petreius, 1548). Translation generously provided by Ulrike Altenmüller.

32 "A volere tangere la conmata fronte della Fortuna." Vitruvius, *De architectura*, trans. and commentary by Cesare Cesariano (Como, 1521), LXXXIVv, translated in Luscombe, *Inscribing the Architect*, 45; Carole Krinsky, "Cesare Cesariano and the Como Vitruvius Edition of 1521" (PhD diss., New York University, 1965), 292.

33 "Corporis effigies hic obvia cernitur. Intus ipsius effigies cernitur ingenii." Marco Frascari, "The Mirror Theater of Vincenzo Scamozzi," in *Paper Palaces: The Rise of the Renaissance Architectural Treatise*, ed. Vaughan Hart with Peter Hicks (New Haven, CT: Yale University Press, 1998), 260.

34 Peter Burke, "The Frontispiece Portrait in the Renaissance," in *Bildnis und Image; das Portrait zwischen Intention und Rezeption*, ed. Andreas Köstler and Ernst Seidl (Cologne: Böhlau, 1998), 153; and Summers, "ARIA II," 17.

35 Architects often drew frontispieces not only for their own books but for many others. John Webb designed the frontispiece for Bishop Brian Walton's *Biblia Sacra Polyglotia* (1655). Bernini created a frontispiece for a Jesuit treatise on optics. John Bold, *John Webb: Architectural Theory and Practice in the Seventeenth Century* (Oxford: Clarendon Press, 1989); and William Ashworth, Jr., "Divine Reflections and Profane Refractions: Images of a Scientific Impasse in Seventeenth-Century Italy," in *Gian Lorenzo Bernini: New Aspects of his Art and Thought: A Commemorative Volume*, ed. Irving Lavin (University Park: Pennsylvania State University Press, 1985), 179–95.

36 Desley Luscombe and Jeffrey Mueller, "Architecture and the Narrative Dimension of Two Alberti Frontispieces of the Sixteenth and Eighteenth Centuries," in *The Built Surface*, vol. 1: *Architecture and the Pictorial Arts from Antiquity to the Enlightenment* (Burlington, VT: Ashgate, 2002), 180–202.

37 Marco Frascari, "Maidens 'Theory' and 'Practice' at the Sides of Lady Architecture," *Assemblage* 7 (1988): 15–27.

38 The two twenty-six-sided polyhedra are the same as the hanging glass model in the famous portrait of Fra Luca Pacioli, often attributed to Jacopo de Barbari (ca 1495). Leonardo drew the figure (now called a rhombicuboctahedron) for Pacioli's *De divina proportione* and may have conceived of it. Pacioli asserts the shape will be particularly useful to architects. J.V. Field, "Rediscovering the Archimedean Polyhedra: Piero della Francesca, Luca Pacioli, Leonardo da Vinci, Albrecht Dürer, Daniele Barbaro and Johannes Kepler," *Archive for History of Exact Sciences* 50, no. 3–4 (1997): 241–89; and Luca Pacioli, *De divina proportione* (Venice, 1509), Part 1, Chapter 53, 15v. See also Alberto Pérez-Gómez, "The Glass Architecture of Fra Luca Pacioli," *Chora: Intervals in the Philosophy of Architecture*, vol. 4 (Montreal and Kingston: McGill-Queen's University Press, 2004), 245–86.

39 Christof Thoenes, "Vignola's *Regola delli cinque ordini*," *Römisches Jahrbuch für Kunstgeschichte* 10 (1983): 360. Vignola probably designed the frontispiece's architectural framework, which he used two years later for a fireplace in the Palazzo Farnese.

40 Vignola, *Canon*, plate 2. The three figures could be interpreted also as Aristotle's three modes of thought: theory, practice, and production.

41 Andrea Alciato, *A Book of Emblems: The Emblematum Liber in Latin and English*, trans. John Moffitt (Jefferson, NC: McFarland, 2004); Andreae Alciati, *Emblematum Libellus* (Paris, 1534).

42 Henry Estienne, *The Art of Making Devises* (London, 1650), ed. Stephen Orgel (New York: Garland 1979), 3.

43 Alciato, *Book of Emblems*, 8.

44 Walther Hermann Ryff's name is presented variously as Ruff, Reiff, Riff, Rhyff, Rivius, and Rivium, as well as the pseudonym Q. Apollinarem. On his life, see Josef Benzing, "Walter H. Ryff und sein literarisches Werk," *Philobiblon* 2 (1958): 126–54, 203–26; Carl Lüdtke, "Walter Ryff und seine 'Teütsche Apoteck,'" *Zur Geschichte der Pharmazie* 14, no. 4 (1962): 25–8; and Julian Jachmann, *Die Architekturbücher des Walter Hermann Ryff: Vitruvrezeption im Kontext mathematischer Wissenschaften* (Stuttgart: Ibidem, 2006).

45 Ryff, *Kurtz Handbüchlein und Experiment vieler Artzneien*, preface and translation in William Eamon, *Science and the Secrets of Nature: Books of Secrets in Medieval and Early Modern Culture* (Princeton: Princeton University Press, 1994), 96–105.

46 Ryff's version of Cesariano's image of the ideal Vitruvian city adds northern windmills to illustrate the key idea of city-forming wind.

47 Vesalius called Ryff a "notorious plagiarist." Andreas Vesalius, *De humani corporis fabrica libri septem* (Basel, 1543), III, pref. Ryff, Introduction to *Vitruvius Teutsch*, n.p. Translation generously provided by Ulrike Altenmüller.

48 Ryff, Introduction to *Vitruvius Teutsch*, n.p. Translation generously provided by Ulrike Altenmüller; and Kathleen Crowther, *Adam and Eve in the Protestant Reformation* (Cambridge: Cambridge University Press, 2010), 197–8. Of the 190 woodcuts in *Vitruvius Teutsch*, 115 are based on 102 illustrations from Cesariano, 14 from Serlio, and 8 from *Hypnerotomachia Poliphili*. No model is identified in only 14 cases. Ryff's *Der Architectur* used images primarily from Serlio, Tartaglia, and Orontius Fineus, with a few others from Petrus Apianus and Philandrier's commentary on Vitruvius. Jachmann, *Architekturbücher des Walter Hermann Ryff*.

49 The first edition was published as: Gualtherus Hermenius Rivius, *Der furnembsten notwendigsten der gantzen Architectur* (Nuremberg, 1547). The second edition was changed to: Gualtherum H. Rivium, *Der Architectur furnembsten, notwendigsten, angehören Mathematischen und Mechanischen künst, eygentlicher bericht, und verstendliche unterrichtung …* (Nuremberg, 1558).

50 The frontispiece appears in *Der Architectur* on the verso of the title page, I:LIXv, and III:IVr; and in *Vitruvius Teutsch* on page XI with a different motto. Harry Francis Mallgrave, Gerald Beasley, Claire Baines, et al., *The Mark J. Millard Architectural Collection*, vol. 3: *Northern European Books, Sixteenth to Early Nineteenth Centuries* (Washington: National Gallery of Art, 1998), 329–30.

51 David McKitterick, *Print, Manuscript and the Search for Order, 1450–1830* (Cambridge: Cambridge University Press, 2003), 139, 166. See also (including examples from Ryff) Michael Waters, "A Renaissance without Order: Ornament, Single-sheet Engravings, and the Mutability of Architectural Prints," *Journal of the Society of Architectural Historians* 714 (2012): 488–523.

52 Attribution of the frontispiece is uncertain, though its design may have had some input from Ryff, as authors often provided an iconographic program to artists. The woodcut drawings have been attributed to Peter Flötner (ca 1486 or 1495–1546) and/or to Virgil Solis (1514–1562), with a small number of others thought to be by Georg Penez and Hans Springinklee. Jurgen Zimmer, "Walther Rivius or Ryff, *Vitruvius Teutsch*," in *Architectural The-*

ory from the Renaissance to the Present, trans. Gregory Fauria, Jeremy Gaines, and Michael Shuttleworth (Cologne: Taschen, 2003), 484; Jeffrey Smith, *Nuremberg: A Renaissance City, 1500–1618* (Austin: University of Texas Press, 1983), 233; and Heinrich Röttinger, *Die Holzschnitte zur Architektur und zum Vitruvius Teutsch des Walther Rivius* (Strassburg: Heitz, 1914), 33, 41–51.

53 Charles Dempsey, *Inventing the Renaissance Putto* (Chapel Hill: University of North Carolina Press, 2001), 43, 45.

54 Michael Cole, "The Demonic Arts and the Origin of the Medium," *Art Bulletin* 84, no. 4 (2002): 630; Summers, "ARIA II," 15–31.

55 Ryff, Introduction to *Vitruvius Teutsch*, n.p. Translation generously provided by Ulrike Altenmüller.

56 "Paupertatem summis ingeniis obesse, ne provehantur." Alciato, *Emblematum Liber*, 19. The complete text, translated, reads: "My right hand holds a stone, my other hand bears wings. As the feathers lift me, so the heavy weight drags me down. With my intellect I could be soaring among the highest peaks, if envious poverty did not pull me down." Alciato, *Book of Emblems*.

57 "Modernized poverty" turned "lack" into "economic need." Ivan Illich, *The Right to Useful Unemployment* (New York: Marion Boyars, 1978), 8–11.

58 On Cesariano's back: "At last the man of skill is urged forward away from poverty." Krinsky, "Cesare Cesariano," 297–300; Ill. 79, LXXXXIIr, "Allegory of Cesariano's Life."

59 Another version of the emblem appears in Serlio as the printer's colophon. Myra Nan Rosenfeld, "From Bologna to Venice and Paris: The Evolution and Publication of Sebastiano Serlio's Books I and II, *On Geometry and On Perspective, for Architects*," in *The Treatise on Perspective: Published and Unpublished*, ed. Lyle Massey (Washington, DC: National Gallery of Art, 2003), 305; and "*Physicae ac Metaphysicae differentia*," in Johannes Sambucus, *Emblemata cum aliquot Nummi antiqui operis* (Antwerp: Christopher Plantin, 1564), 74.

60 Francesco Colonna, *Hypnerotomachia Poliphili: The Strife of Love in a Dream*, trans. Joscelyn Godwin (London: Thames & Hudson, 1999), 133.

61 Suetonius, *Lives of Caesar*, 2.25.4; Aulus Gellius, *Attic Nights*, 10.11.

62 Christopher Heuer, *The City Rehearsed: Object, Architecture and Print in the Worlds of Hans Vredeman de Vries* (London: Routledge, 2009),

187n70; and Jeanne Peiffer, "The Construction of Perspective in Nuremberg in the Sixteenth Century," *Les cahiers de la recherche architecturale et urbaine* 17 (2005): 58n26.

63 Emblem 98, Alciato (Venice, 1546); and Barbara Bowen, "Mercury at the Crossroads in Renaissance Emblems," *Journal of the Warburg and Courtauld Institutes* 48 (1985): 225.

64 See the frontispieces in Lorenz Stoer, *Geometria et Perspectiva* (Nuremberg, 1567); Wenzel Jamnitzer, *Perspectiva Corporum Regularium* (Nuremberg, 1568); and David Wade, *Fantastic Geometry: Polyhedra and the Artistic Imagination in the Renaissance* (London: Squeeze, 2012), 88–9. Caporali uses intersecting tetrahedrons and octahedrons as fire and air to illustrate the process of generating steam. Giambattista Caporali, *Marco Vitruvio Pollione, De Architectura, Libri I–V* (Perugia: Iano Bigazzini, 1536), 32.

65 Corbett, "Architectural Title-Page," 58. Ryff describes the compass and straight-edge as "righteous" and cautions that "such instruments will be over-loved (*oberkünstlet*)." Ryff, Introduction to *Vitruvius Teutsch*, n.p. Translation generously provided by Ulrike Altenmüller.

66 Ryff, Introduction to *Vitruvius Teutsch*, n.p. Translation generously provided by Ulrike Altenmüller; and Raymond Klibansky, Erwin Panofsky, and Fritz Saxl, *Saturn and Melancholy: Studies in the History of Natural Philosophy, Religion and Art* (New York: Basic Books, 1964), 310n93.

67 Gareth Roberts, *The Mirror of Alchemy: Alchemical Ideas and Images in Manuscripts and Books from Antiquity to the Seventeenth Century* (Toronto: University of Toronto Press, 1994), 107.

68 Mircea Eliade, *The Forge and the Crucible* (New York: Harper, 1962), 29.

69 Titus Burckhardt, *Alchemy: Science of the Cosmos, Science of the Soul*, trans. William Stoddart (Louisville, KY: Fons Vitae, 1997), 68–9, 201.

70 Werner Oechslin, "Vitruvianismus in Deutschland," in *Architekt und Ingenieur: Baumeister in Krieg und Frieden* (Wolfenbüttel: Herzog August, 1984), 55; Harry Francis Mallgrave, "Introductory Essay," in *Mark J. Millard Architectural Collection*, 3:8.

71 Giorgio Agamben, *Stanzas: Word and Phantasm in Western Culture*, trans. Ronald Martinez (Minneapolis: University of Minnesota Press, 1993), 136–9. Aristotle defined enigma as a putting together of impossible things. *Poetics*, 58a.

"More Powerful than Love":
Imagination and Language in the
Oikéma of Claude-Nicolas Ledoux

Paul Holmquist

Chora

> Here the Architect is more powerful than love.[1]
> –Claude-Nicolas Ledoux, *L'architecture considérée sous*
> *le rapport de l'art, des moeurs et de la législation*

OF ALL THE INSTITUTIONS proposed by Claude-Nicolas Ledoux for the ideal city of Chaux, none has resisted interpretation more than his enigmatic "workshop of corruption," the Oikéma. In his *L'architecture considérée sous le rapport de l'art, des moeurs et de la législation* (1804), the Oikéma appears as a civic brothel for the city that Ledoux imagined around the Royal Saltworks (1779) he had built at Arc-et-Senans. Proclaiming that he had done what no government would dare, Ledoux presents the Oikéma as a temple in which the "boiling and unfaithful youth" of Chaux are free to indulge their sexual appetites to excess and dissolution. Declaring that "the feeling of the degradation of man" and "depravity in its nakedness" would awaken "sleeping virtue,"[2] he envisions that patrons would emerge from the Oikéma in horror and disgust to abandon vice for the true pleasures and joys of love in marriage. Through this experience of vice, Ledoux claims that the Oikéma concludes a pact between Cupid and Hymen, the Roman god of marriage, and thus secures desire and sexuality for the institution of marriage. However, Ledoux places one condition upon the patronage of the Oikéma, stipulating that "the names of those who frequent these tolerated dens be indelibly inscribed on these walls that art, in the secrecy of its operations, has taken pleasure to refine." Triumphantly he exclaims, "Who would want to see his name there? ... Oh! I foresee it; already the door is closed, victory is complete."[3] Ignored by many scholars of Ledoux, this final condition and the self-restraint that it entails have challenged all attempts to account comprehensively for the moral and philosophical status of the Oikéma within Chaux. It appears consigned to be, as Mona Ozouf has written, "a school, emptied of its pupils."[4] Yet, the Oikéma is presented in *L'architecture* as one of the key civic institutions of Chaux, whose ambition as a city is to found a new people and way of life based on the principles of natural order and to establish the conditions for achieving happiness. The Oikéma is also one of the most fully described of Ledoux's invented institutions. Its infamous phallic plan is accompanied by a sensuous and poetic narrative depiction of the users' experience of both pleasure and depravity. Furthermore, as much as Ledoux emphasizes the embrace of virtue, he delights in confronting the reader with the moral ambivalence of sexual desire. How can Ledoux's contradictory and ambivalent presentation of the Oikéma be understood? As an institution that appears to succeed only when it is not used, how can the Oikéma be understood as an institution at all, let alone one that takes the form of an architectural proposition? What is the civic significance of its erotic program? And finally, what is the significance of the Oikéma as architecture, and why is architecture necessary for the efficacy of the Oikéma as an institution?

These questions can be approached only by recognizing the Oikéma as an imaginary project. As an architectural fiction, the Oikéma provides the setting for the reader's imagination to experience sexual desire and pleasure, as well as the moral transformation of that desire in recognizing its potential fulfillment in romantic love within marriage. By Ledoux's use of sensuous and poetic narrative to portray a patron's experience, the Oikéma "tells the story" of how natural, adolescent sexual desire becomes moral and fully human love that secures the institution of marriage, and thereby the civil order of Chaux. To understand the "story" of the Oikéma, it must be situated within the eighteenth-century understanding of nature, human nature, desire, and the origin of society, particularly in the thought of Jean-Jacques Rousseau. The moral and philosophical significance of the Oikéma as an architectural fiction is closely related to that of a crucial episode in Rousseau's *Emile, or On Education* (1762), in which the tutor confronts the awakening of sexual desire in the adolescent Emile. In order to negotiate Emile's dangerous passage to moral self-consciousness, the tutor must use what Rousseau calls the figurative "language of signs" to engage Emile's imagination as he speaks of "women, love, [and] pleasures" and guides Emile's nascent desire towards fulfillment in romantic love within marriage. I will first show how the Oikéma as an architectural fiction engages the imagination of the reader of *L'architecture* through Ledoux's use of narrative and poetic language to evoke the moral transformation of sexual desire. I will then discuss how Rousseau's approach to desire and adolescent sexuality in *Emile* parallels key aspects of Ledoux's presentation of the Oikéma. In drawing out these parallels, I will show how the Oikéma attests to the foundational role of human desire and sexuality in the order of "the city" that Ledoux proposes in Chaux, and the capacity of architecture to "educate" this desire by giving it particular form and orientation.

The Oikéma is an imaginary institution presented as a narrative fiction. Its name evokes a mythico-historical image of antiquity that is accentuated

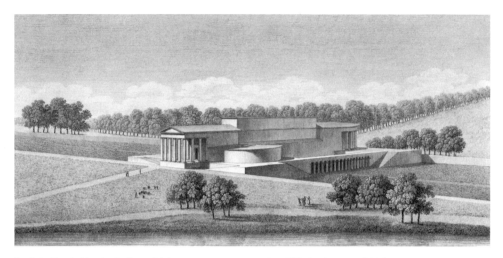

Fig. 5.1 Claude-Nicolas Ledoux, Oikéma, perspective view, plate 103, *L'architecture* (1804), Rare Books and Special Collections, McGill University Library.

by Ledoux's cryptic subtitle, "Fragments of a Greek Monument." Ledoux adopts the term Oikéma from *oikēma*, an ancient Greek word for dwelling place or bedroom that is derived from the word *oikos*, or "household."[5] The term could refer also to a temple or prison, but in particular to a "place of debauchery" or a brothel; this double entendre was certainly intended by Ledoux.[6] His presentation of the Oikéma begins by asking Apollo to show him how to guide those traversing "the inexperienced age" by fixing their "errant imaginations on a monument that awakens the feeling of *pudeur*" or sexual modesty, and whose architectural "combinations" will "destroy tolerated abuses."[7] Ledoux wishes to engage the imagination of the "boiling youth" of Chaux, as well as the reader of *L'architecture*, to encourage the instructive experience that will awaken "sleeping virtue." As Ledoux poetically "retrace[s] this antique abode of the imagination"[8] by describing a patron's sensual and emotional experience, the architecture of the Oikéma appears as both a situational structure and an expressive setting. Ledoux believed in the moral efficacy of architecture, declaring that "the character of monuments, like their nature, serves the propagation and purification of mores [*mœurs*]."[9] The "nature" or program of the Oikéma emerges from the narrative as a tacit "plot" in which the sequence of actions, events, and experiences of the patron cohere, and for which the "character" or expressive qualities of the architecture provide different atmospheres. The precise geometry of the accompanying drawings, and in particular the phallographic organization of the plan that conjoins the temples of Venus and Hymen, confirms the Oikéma as a narrative ordering of the experience of place and time. From the description and the drawings, the reader is able to inhabit and experience the Oikéma imaginatively in time, as a patron would.

Ledoux tells the "story" of the Oikéma as a patron's journey through the institution in a series of episodes that are interspersed with reflections and exhortations on morality and architecture. In each episode, the moral character of the patron's sensual and emotional experience is expressed in poetic descriptions of architectural settings. Ledoux sets the scene under the heading "Emplacement," the physical situation of the building, in which we find ourselves immersed in the natural surroundings of the Loüe River valley, known popularly as the "Vallon de l'Amour."[10] Nature here is passionate, sensuous, and desiring, with a seemingly primeval innocence and goodness: "The valley that supports this edifice is surrounded by seductive fascinations; a sweet wind caresses the atmosphere; the odiferous varieties of the forest, thyme, iris, violet, [and] mint gently breathe their perfumes on these walls; the foliage that shelters them effuses coolness and agitates in murmurs. The loving wave quivers on the shore that confines it; its rubbings sharpen the air, and the echo bursts in delicious sounds."[11] Yet, nature is also voluptuous and erotically charged: "O too fickle fibre! You become inflamed; the artery accelerates its movements and breaks the thread that sustains the principle of life. Where am I? The flash of pleasure takes flight, and the empire of voluptuousness subjugates these places full of charms to the dawn of desire that spreads its rays over a favoured land. Oh! I no longer doubt it, there is where the pleasures promised by Mahomet have made their abode."[12]

Ledoux heightens the perception of all our senses. By anthropomorphizing the natural elements as sensuous, desiring beings, he emphasizes the voluptuousness and pleasure of natural desire in the reader's imagination and, by association, in the youthful initiates for whom the Oikéma awaits. In this blissful and harmonious vision of nature, there is no separation between desire and its satisfaction. Although we encounter no other people, we sense that others would share the immediacy of our desires. Nature here is free from the conflictions of social and moral relationships. The Oikéma promises this blissful freedom, enticing the reader to approach the Temple of Love.

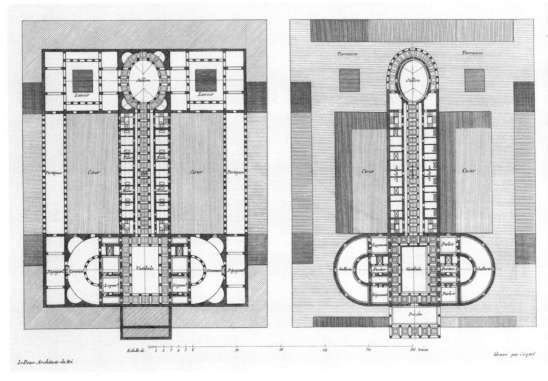

Fig. 5.2 Claude-Nicolas Ledoux, Oikéma, plans, plate 104, *L'architecture*, Rare Books and Special Collections, McGill University Library.

Proceeding to the "Distribution" of the Oikéma, the organization of its plan, we are swept along by the pleasures of natural desire as they swarm into its dark and mysterious interior: "Do you see the vivacious troupe of charms coming down from the forest? It moves forward at an accelerated pace, it arrives; already the Pleasures take hold of the cells destined for mystery; ... disdaining the light of day, in their secret libations, they call down the devouring fires of Prometheus from the sky, and the initiates become familiar with them ... There they assemble and frolic around cold reason to subjugate it; from there the malicious child leads you astray and will be pleased, from a distance, with the arrows he has shot."[13]

Within the Oikéma, erotic desire is no longer immediate as in nature, but mysterious. In "disdaining the light," delightful sensuous pleasures have become the "devouring fires" of knowledge stolen from the gods. Waylaid by Cupid, new desires are awakened in us, confounding our reason. We are initiated by the "hierophants" of Lust into an experience of the Pleasures beyond what we had known in nature. Ledoux lets us imagine the activities taking place in the *cellules* delineated precisely in the plan.

When his narrative resumes under the heading "Basements, Baths, Washing Rooms, Drying Rooms, Dining Rooms," we find ourselves luxuriating beneath the "comforting vaults" that are delicately engraved in the building sections. Proclaiming that "here the Architect is more powerful than love," Ledoux lauds his power to command "the winds of the North to blow through these repeating arches … to strengthen the slackened fibre, and revive the spent forces" and to orchestrate the "impressions" by which we "regain [our] equilibrium."[14] Ledoux then speaks suggestively, if not salaciously, of rekindling our desires in the sensuous, erotic qualities and atmospheres of the rooms: "Do you see these half-naked slaves, the feet, the legs bathing in the waters? How many charms the liquid mirror sends back! Curved arms on linen, beat in harmony one hundred masses that they compress; spouting fountains divert ideas and awaken distraction; some attach on long threads, from portico to portico, shawls of Cashmere that fall in festoons; the others squeeze the weft-fibre of the weaver [*la trame du tisserand*], twist it, and the expression spurts out in pearls of silver on globes hardened by corpulence."[15]

In the "Elevation" of the Oikéma we begin to sense that something is amiss: "These tranquil walls hide the agitations within; it is there where one abandons oneself to the torrent of a false joy that brings with it destruction."[16] In an irony certainly not lost on Ledoux, the elevation signals our descent into depravity and domination by the appetites and senses. As we enter the Oikéma a second time, the interior spaces and decorations express a heightened erotic quality: "What do I see? The pavement of the peristyle is patterned in magnet; its attractive virtue gathers together the lost ones of both poles; in the centre one notices a tripod found in the ruins of the temple of Venus; its flame rises in a pyramid."[17] Declaring that "the painter of nature forgets nothing," Ledoux describes how "winged chimeras of the night"[18] cavort in the flickering light among the moldings and ornaments of the ceilings. The walls display bas-reliefs depicting Perfica, the Roman goddess of sexual performance, and Pertunda, the "goddess of voluptuousness" and the guise by which Juno presided over sexual penetration and the loss of virginity.[19] As Ledoux continues, the atmosphere of the gallery becomes explicitly erotic: "One sees there the moaning young turtledove lurking below the pediment, and

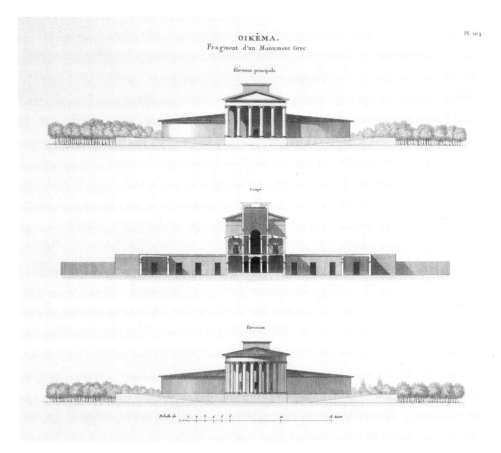

Fig. 5.3 Claude-Nicolas Ledoux, Oikéma, elevations and section, plate 104, *L'architecture*, Rare Books and Special Collections, McGill University Library.

his feathers quivering with desire; children (without doubt ill-intentioned) rekindle the incendiary torches on the repeating shafts of alabaster columns that support the edifice. The images follow each other so powerfully that it seems that the deep nostrils of the bulls of Colchos throw their fire everywhere; everything inspires, everything sets one ablaze."[20]

At this point, having brought the reader from the simple and immediate pleasures of nature to the obscenity of lust within the depths of the Oikéma, Ledoux pauses to tell us why he, as the Architect, has taken us on such a path: "The Architect welcomes the episode, and ... his thoughts extend, even to the centre of disavowed passions. O divine love of art!

Your voluptuousness is pure, your voluptuousness approaches that in which we are portrayed in the world of spirits; it is what inspires affectionate movements of the soul, it is what supports the dignity of man; chagrin, disgust, all cede to your authority. Believe me, have this passion, it will deliver you from all the others."[21]

The "pure" voluptuousness of architecture partakes of the natural, if not divine, voluptuousness that we originally experienced in nature. It is by this voluptuous "passion" of the love of art, rather than the promised sight of human degradation, that Ledoux hopes to awaken us to virtue. While the atmospheres of the Oikéma express our sensuous and emotional experience, the voluptuous character of the architecture "speaks" to our senses, passions, and imagination. Insofar as architecture for Ledoux embodies the principles of nature, this voluptuousness is proportional, beautiful, and in harmonious accord with natural order: in a word, virtuous. Ledoux believed that the "passionate" expression and experience of architecture could shape desire and orient it toward virtue.

Now that our eyes have been opened to what is at stake in the Oikéma, we enter it for the third time and confront an inversion of the natural scene where we began. As "the night commences to lower its immense veils" and "desire stirs" and "swells its forces,"[22] we enter the Temple of Venus no longer as initiates, but as victims. "Seduction was there and guarded the doors. Preceded by languorous sounds of the glass harmonica and an instrument imitating the song of Orpheus of the woods, she opens its casements and conducts the victims who present themselves, in the midst of mysteries, under the soporific escort of the essences of vanilla and of heliotrope. In this way the cunning Circe prepares the dose of her poisons; in this way she profanes the vaults of the heavens to make of them a workshop of tortures."[23] Instead of the gentle murmuring of leaves being caressed by a sweet wind, our senses are insidiously lulled by music played on contrived and dissembling instruments. The scents of thyme, iris, violet, and mint are replaced by artificial narcotic essences used in perfumery. We have not been pierced by Cupid's arrows but, like the crew of Odysseus, poisoned and turned into rutting swine, experiencing our carnal abandon as the agony of our souls. Voluptuousness has been stripped of its naturalness by arts that, unlike architecture, trade on perversions and craven imitations of nature. Reduced to an enslaving appetite and an "epilepsy of blood that deadens the senses,"[24] the virtuous love of voluptuousness is corrupted into a destructive personal and

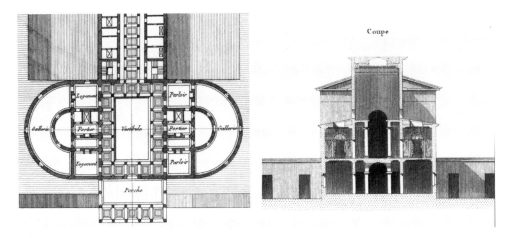

Fig. 5.4 Claude-Nicolas Ledoux, Oikéma, details of plan and section in plate 104, *L'architecture*, Rare Books and Special Collections, McGill University Library.

moral vice that "profanes the vaults of the heavens" by dominating and exploiting others.

Ledoux pauses the narrative again to reflect on the importance of virtue: "Nothing is solid where virtue is missing; emotional attachments, pleasures, all go out of plumb without it; what fatality! Must man be such an enemy of himself that in the spring of his days his future is mutilated by the whims of fate?"[25] Here Ledoux expresses concern for the social consequences of those who would avail themselves of the freedom of the Oikéma, especially the young men of the ascendant bourgeoisie for whom marriageability was essential in establishing a successful emotional, social, and economic life in a family.[26] Ledoux acknowledges that prostitution is an "inevitable evil" in populous cities and that governments have always failed to curtail it. Admitting that the evils of prostitution may produce a good, in that they "foment desires and develop the powers of the population," Ledoux nonetheless proposes that "philosophical sur-veillance converses with them in order to know them, and to favour them even to destroy them."[27] What Ledoux intends to destroy are the abuses of sexual pleasure that the fictional Oikéma ostensibly allows: abuses that prevent the affectionate relations of men and women in romantic love, and in families. "As much as love that follows marriage has charms for sweet paternity, so much it despises the abuses that adorn themselves in false colours that degrade it."[28] Ledoux extols love as the "sweet impulses of our souls, [the] inexhaustible sources of virtues that do us honour."[29] To the extent that "the good" rules in the Oikéma, its ultimate purpose is not only to "purify *mœurs*," but "to neutralize the passions of the head" and prepare for love as "the delicious outbursts of the heart."[30] In love, the pleasures of desire are immeasurably increased when they inspire the affections of the soul. Far from diminishing the pleasures of desire, Ledoux writes that "the economy of pleasure increases it."[31] Romantic love as a moral relationship is fundamentally reciprocal and voluntary. The "mutilation" that Ledoux speaks of above refers to a young man's moral reputation, the public perception of his capacity for and worthiness of reciprocal love. Passionate romantic love traditionally had been a threat to the stability of marriage;[32] however, it increasingly supplanted religious and economic reasons for marriage in the late eighteenth century, especially after marriage was secularized during the French Revolution.[33] The Oikéma was conceived not to control behaviour, but to promote natural desire and voluptuousness in romantic love and to secure the institution of marriage as a civil contract.

As readers, we may agree with Ledoux about the dangers posed to love by sexual depravity, yet nothing compels us to turn away. We may be momentarily disgusted by excess, but are free and naturally inclined to succumb to the corruption of desire. Ledoux knew that reason could not subdue passion, so he had to rely on another passion to "revive the forces that make [virtue] move."[34] He appeals to the reader's *amour propre*, the love of oneself that underlies self-esteem and the desire for the esteem of others, in the form of *pudeur* or modesty, the shame that protected against the loss of self- and public esteem due to sexual behaviour. Writing that he must "put useful *pudeur* in movement," as it does not want to "publicly display the tastes that humiliate it,"[35] Ledoux returns us to the architecture of the Oikéma by asking what, in the end, does *pudeur* demand? "This here; it demands that the names of those who patronize these tolerated dens should be inscribed in indelible letters on these surfaces that art, in the secrecy of its operations, has taken pleasure to refine. Who would want to see his name there? Oh! I hear you; oh! I foresee it; already the door is closed: it is done, victory is complete."[36] By enjoying the Oikéma, one's name and identity would become a permanent and disgraceful part of this public architecture. Ledoux is confident that no one would dare to publicly acknowledge such a fatal corruption of desire due to lust. Furthermore, the civic status of the Oikéma forces the reader, as the patron, to recognize sexual desire as a public concern, and romantic love as a virtue that strengthens the order of civil society. *Pudeur*, the "natural shame" that encourages sexual modesty and chastity, especially for women, was still associated with the upholding of *honnêteté* as "conformity to honour, to probity, [and] to virtue."[37] It was a shame "caused by the apprehension of that which could injure modesty or virtue"[38] or, in the Oikéma, the consciousness of one's worthiness of being loved and therefore one's marriageability. In the stipulation that one's name be inscribed on the walls, the male youth of Chaux are called to an account of their self-esteem, to imagine themselves as worthy of another's love and fit for moral and public responsibilities. Ledoux's intention is not to impose a coercive moral code that is enforced by public disgrace, but for the patrons – and the readers – to account for their own desires and actions. The freedom to patronize the Oikéma is key to the success of Ledoux's "philosophical surveillance," as it preserves the natural autonomy of one's will. One may be seduced by the architecture and the possibilities within, but not coerced by them. In the Oikéma, natural desire is not thwarted, but rather is transformed by the experience of the institution and the voluptuous quality of its architecture. As Ledoux affirms, one chooses freely to "abstain rather than violate a principle."[39]

Immediately following his declaration of victory, Ledoux completes the reader's experience of moral transformation by destroying the architecture of the Oikéma and rendering it as a ruin, the "Fragments of a Greek Monument" foreshadowed by its subtitle. "Hymen, virtuous hymen retakes its rights; the avenging lightning bolt strikes, the cells of the temple are overturned, the galleries are cleared of all that can harm the masses. One reads on the frieze of the frontispiece: "Here one fixes the restless graces to eternalize virtue."[40] The destruction of the Oikéma finally reveals the human degradation promised by Ledoux in the hideous figure of Corruption, as a woman whose body has been destroyed by syphilis. The image that Ledoux portrays of her suffering and death is vivid and horrifying:

What do I see? What picture presents itself to my sight? The colours are dulled in the marshes of the Styx ... It is Corruption ... Despair renders her hideous; she has a cavernous eye and greenish flesh. What! Her hair is gone: the cavity of her teeth betrays the secret of her lungs; her mouth infects the air, and her flanks pant putrefaction. Spread upon the bed of miseries, rent by the troupe of remorses, she begs a pardon for a repentance. Weary from an impure journey, already the inhabitants of her heart breach their enclosure, escape and cover her body with a vermicular leprosy that devours it; already the shadows of death cover her foul eyelids with their funereal nets; weakness weighs her down; her breath escapes and flees from searing reproaches in exhaling. Hymen is thus victorious; but I will be avenged, a life too easy is not lasting, she says, and lets out a final sigh.[41]

We arrive at the image of Corruption only after love has been won for victorious Hymen and enshrined in the ruins of the Oikéma. Perhaps meant as a final warning for those who can understand no other, this graphic portrayal of venereal disease is more blunt than the earlier appeal to *pudeur*. Ledoux closes the narrative of the Oikéma with an admonition to those who would not love: "Such is the nature of man: he dies as he has lived; woe betide him who does not sense the value of a sentimental association!"[42]

The status of the Oikéma as an architectural fiction is essential to its moral and philosophical ambition as a civic institution. Ledoux aspires to guide natural sexual desire by engaging the imagination: not only through expressive language, but also the expressive capacity of the architecture itself. In so doing, he shares Rousseau's understanding of the integral relationship of the imagination to desire, and the capacity of language to guide the passions. For Rousseau, the importance of the imagination to the advent and moral development of human sexual desire is evident in his philosophical novel *Emile, or On Education*, in which he addresses the moral crisis of adolescent sexuality in terms very similar to that of the Oikéma. Rousseau shows how images conjured by figurative language can speak to the heart via the imagination, and why they must be used to give the young Emile an imaginary experience of the pleasures of desire and their relation to the reciprocal nature of romantic love, so that he can choose to preserve this moral principle on his own. By fixing his imagination on an ideal companion soul, in effect making him fall in love, Emile's tutor prepares the conditions in which he can freely choose to preserve the goodness of natural sexual desire and voluptuous pleasure within the reciprocal, moral relationship of romantic love, which is then capable of fulfillment in marriage. For Rousseau, human desire as romantic love is institutionalized in marriage to serve as the foundation of civil and political order.[43] A consideration of the parallels between Ledoux's conception and presentation of the Oikéma and this episode in *Emile* will illuminate his moral and philosophical ambitions for both the Oikéma and his project for the ideal city of Chaux.

Emile, Rousseau's moral and political project of natural education, was published in 1762, the same year as his political treatise, *On the Social Contract*. As opposed to the citizen of the republic and the natural man of the *Discourse on the Origin and Foundation of Inequality among Men* (1755), *Emile* concerns the formation of a "savage made to live in cities,"[44] and certainly would have been known to Ledoux as he developed his vision for Chaux, beginning in the early 1780s. The book is a philosophical thought experiment in which the child Emile, having been removed from his family, is painstakingly raised to adulthood by a tutor, such that he enters society independent of the wills of others and with the natural order of his soul intact. Through a program of natural, moral, and civic education, Emile learns to maintain the balance of his desires and abilities, his natural self-love, and the esteem of others, preserving the independence of his will so that he can lead a reasonably happy life while fulfilling his duties in marriage and society. The tutor carefully manages Emile's childhood experiences such that he meets resistance only in objects, rather than wills. He also prevents the premature development of Emile's imagination, which for Rousseau is the faculty that awakens desires beyond the natural needs that can be satisfied by objects. When the "moment of nature" inevitably arrives, the awakening of Emile's sexual desire provokes a moral crisis that threatens to undo all of the tutor's careful work. Emile's new desire can be satisfied only by another person, which thus implicates another will. For Rousseau, the slightest frustration of desire can provoke the destructive and enslaving passions of anger, jealousy, and vanity, in which Emile would irretrievably lose the independence of his will. Sexual desire for Rousseau is especially disposed to the domination of oneself and others,[45] and is so dangerous to the order of Emile's soul that the tutor must intervene before Emile takes any action. Yet he cannot thwart Emile's desires by making love "a crime," but must allow him to experience the pleasures of desire while making him accountable to himself for his actions. As Ledoux does in the Oikéma, the tutor must now engage Emile's imagination to "instruct him in these dangerous mysteries," which he had "so long hidden from him with so much care,"[46] by "indulg[ing] him in the sweet sentiment for which he has such a thirst" and, in so doing, contrive to make him moderate and chaste by "making him fall in love."[47]

The first thing that the tutor does, however, is the most important: he rescinds the absolute authority he has held over Emile as a child and releases him into the full autonomy of his will. The tutor knows that neither reason nor the warnings of an old man can prevail against the intensity of Emile's nascent passions. Although he has Emile's trust as a friend and guardian, he can no longer compel him to obey: "I have only one reasonable course to take – to make him accountable to himself for his actions, to protect him at least from the surprises of error, and to show him openly the perils by which he is surrounded. Up to now I stopped him by his ignorance; now he has to be stopped by his enlightenment."[48] As with the Oikéma, this enlightenment must proceed through imaginative experience, rather than direct experience that would let him fall into vice, dependency, and domination. For Rousseau, "the senses are awakened by imagination alone,"[49] so Emile's experience of his own desire can be guided only by engaging his imagination. In this way, Emile seeks fulfillment, not by exploiting another person as an object, but in the reciprocal desire of romantic love: "Love, which gives as much as it demands, is in itself a sentiment filled with equity."[50] The essential moral relation of love is based on the voluntary and equal interdependence of wills.[51] Sexual desire in itself is natural and good; its dangers lie in how desire can give rise to passions that lead to domination and exploitation. The tutor's concern is not to proscribe sexual desire and the passions that follow from it, but to prepare Emile for the stronger, moral passion of romantic love that can govern the others. As Rousseau writes later in *Emile*, "A young man must either love or be debauched."[52]

In engaging Emile's desire, the tutor must not "stifle his imagination" but "guide it, lest it engender monsters."[53] As in Ledoux's presentation of the Oikéma through narrative, the tutor guides Emile's imagination through language, which for Rousseau is the spontaneous expression of human desire and passion. To do so, Rousseau must utilize the power of what he calls the "language of signs" to create sensuous images that, in speaking to the imagination, are felt as impressions on the soul. Rousseau writes that only figurative language, which invokes the powerful original human language of object-signs, bodily gestures, and actions, can touch the heart, make one feel, and move one to action.[54] The language of "dry reason" can show only what one must think. By moving Emile's imagination and depicting for him the pleasures of mutual desire and affection, the tutor must make Emile feel, and therefore experience, the shaping of his desire and its attendant passions. For this language to be effective, the tutor, like Ledoux's Architect, must carefully prepare the time and place to speak, such that Emile will be ready to listen and able to remember. Furthermore, the place will serve as both witness and testament to what is spoken and experienced, not unlike the function of the Oikéma as a "monument." Just as Ledoux begins his narrative in the natural surroundings of the Vallon de l'Amour, so the tutor takes Emile out into primeval nature, surrounded by rocks, woods, and mountains. There, by "cloth[ing] reason in forms which will make it loved" and "with an attraction that forces him to listen," the tutor speaks directly to Emile's desire "of love, of women, of pleasures" with "a charm ... which delights his young heart."[55] He depicts to Emile's imagination the pleasures of sexual desire and love, but, as Rousseau stresses, not in any way unchaste. Here, as in Ledoux's sensuous and erotic depiction of nature, pleasure is immediate and innocent. This voluptuous pleasure is what Emile must feel through his imagination, come to love, and wish to preserve within the moral relation of romantic love.

As with Ledoux, the tutor's immediate goal is to persuade Emile, through his own experience and his own will, to embrace chastity for the sake of a moral love that can be fulfilled only within the institution of marriage. The tutor seeks to reconcile the many "contradictions between the rights of nature and our social laws,"[56] such that the goodness that prevails in nature governs the moral order of society. In so doing, he declares that "one must use a great deal of art to prevent social man from being totally artificial."[57] The tutor describes to the reader how, through the artful use of language, he must associate Emile's desire with moral ideas that are wholly new to him, while portraying new images that evoke feelings that accord with his understanding of these ideas.

If in speaking of this inconceivable mystery of generation, one joins to the idea of the allure given to this act by the Author of nature the idea of the exclusive attachment which makes it delicious, and the idea of the duties of fidelity and of modesty which surround it and redouble its charms in fulfilling its object; if, in depicting marriage to him not only as the sweetest of associations but as the most inviolable and holiest of all contracts, one tells him forcefully all the reasons which make so sacred a bond respectable to all men, and which bring hatred and maledictions to whoever dares to stain its purity; if one presents him with a striking and true picture of the horrors of debauchery, of its foolish degradation, of the gradual decline by which a first disorder leads to them all and finally drags to destruction whoever succumbs to it; if, I say, one shows him clearly how the taste for chastity is connected with health, strength, courage, the virtues, love itself, and all the true goods of man, I maintain that one will then render this chastity desirable and dear to him and that his mind will be amenable to the means he will be given for preserving it; for, so long as chastity is preserved, it is respected; it is despised only after having been lost.[58]

Once the tutor prepares Emile to cherish his desire and imagine its fulfillment in mutual affection, he depicts love such that Emile can give himself wholly over to it: "I shall not be afraid to indulge him in the sweet sentiment for which he has such a thirst. I shall depict it to him as the supreme happiness of life, because in fact it is. In depicting it to him, I want him to yield to it. In making him sense how much charm the union of hearts adds to the attraction of the senses, I shall disgust him with libertinism, and I shall make him moderate by making him fall in love."[59]

For Rousseau, love is an original and decisive extension of one's natural being. It can be achieved only by means of the imagination, the faculty by which we exceed ourselves and our given reality.[60] The tutor makes Emile fall in love by portraying to his imagination someone to fall in love with. Again using figurative language, he depicts an ideal companion, Sophie, who would not only deserve his desire and affection, but also demand it in return for hers. Like Emile, Sophie would be educated to recognize that only "the good man, the man of merit"[61] can make her happy. Emile would also know that "one wants to obtain the preference that one grants. Love must be reciprocal. To be loved, one has to make oneself loveable."[62] By falling in love with an ideal companion, Emile in turn imagines himself as worthy of Sophie's esteem and affection, and of being loved. A new self-consciousness emerges for Emile, in which he sees himself in relation to another's desire and esteem. Emile's desire to be worthy of love impels him to embrace chastity and prevents the development of destructive passions. The tutor's reliance on Emile's self-esteem to govern his sexual desire aligns with Ledoux's use of *pudeur* to invoke the self- and public esteem of the patron of the Oikéma.

In this episode of *Emile*, Rousseau essentially re-presents the original human "fall" into the moral order of society that was otherwise described in the *Second Discourse* and *Essay on the Origin of Languages*, written in the late 1750s.[63] In the *Second Discourse*, the birth of properly human sexual desire, which recognizes a reciprocal desire beyond sex as a natural need, represents the decisive extension of human being beyond the state of nature and into the state of society and morality.[64] Here, the fall of one's will into a dependence on the wills of others leads inexorably to social domination and exploitation. In *Essay on the Origin of Languages*, however, another trajectory is proposed in the reciprocal interdependence of desire and wills in romantic love.[65] In love, men and women first enter into a potentially equal interdependence and, by virtue of their complementary natures, come to constitute a single moral person.[66] For Rousseau, romantic love, institutionalized in marriage, is the fundamental moral relationship from which all other moral relationships within the civil order can proceed. Falling in love is the extension of human being into a moral order within which humans can flourish, with the natural order of their souls remaining intact. This is the trajectory that Rousseau addresses in the education of Emile, and the danger of an alternate trajectory is the reason why the awakening of his sexual desire presents a crisis. This critical trajectory is also Ledoux's concern in the Oikéma. As a public institution, it attends to the moral foundation of human desire upon which the ideal city of Chaux can flourish.

Ledoux and Rousseau take similar approaches to the challenge that adolescent sexuality presents to the humanization of sexual desire. Both make use of the expressive capacity of language to evoke an imaginative experience of desire that calls for one's judgment and action. Their immediate objectives are to make the reader of *L'architecture* – as a patron of the Oikéma – and Emile accountable to themselves and to their consciousness of self- and public esteem, by choosing to remain chaste. They come to recognize the virtue of mutual desire in romantic love, and the fulfillment of that desire in marriage, by "fixing" their imaginations upon ideal objects: the imaginary Sophie for Emile, and the monument of the Oikéma for Ledoux's reader. Above all, Ledoux and Rousseau emphasize how the voluptuous quality of desire and pleasure within love is supremely and naturally good and is essential to human happiness. In *Emile*, figurative language engages the imagination and guides the experience of

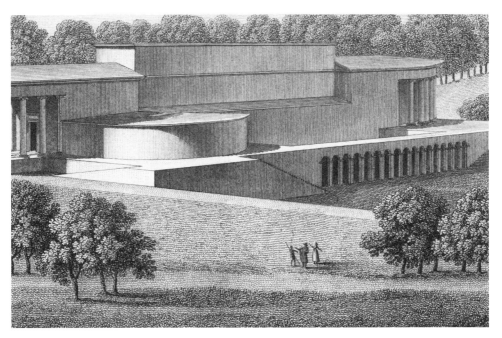

Fig. 5.5 Claude-Nicolas Ledoux, Oikéma, perspective view, detail of plate 103, *L'architecture*, Rare Books and Special Collections, McGill University Library.

desire. The Oikéma, as an architectural fiction, does the same through its poetic narrative. Like the tutor, the Architect prepares the situation in which language can be effective, then crafts the language – both architectural and literary – to speak to the passions of the reader through the imagination and the senses. In this way, architecture, although fictional, is essential for the efficacy of the Oikéma as an institution, insofar as it provides the appropriate temporal and qualitative structure of events, settings, and atmospheres for the experience of desire.

The parallels between Ledoux's presentation of the Oikéma and the episode in Rousseau's *Emile* illuminate the philosophical significance of the Oikéma as a civic institution within the ideal city of Chaux. Rather than simply controlling behaviour, the Oikéma re-enacts the original extension of properly "human" being, in which the moral relation of romantic love is recognized as the highest fulfillment of sexual desire. Institutionalized within marriage, love can serve as the foundation of a moral, civil, and political order in which human happiness might be possible. The meaning of the Oikéma as a double entendre then becomes clear: as the *oikonomia* or "economy" of the wise management of human desire within the order of the city. The Oikéma is far from being a "school, emptied of its pupils" that paradoxically succeeds only when it remains empty. As an architectural fiction, it attests to the foundational role of human desire in the city and the expressive capacity of "voluptuous" architecture to engage this desire as its effective public function. In this respect, the Oikéma is the archetype of Ledoux's understanding of "legislation," in which architecture educates the human desire for "the city" as the moral order within which humans can flourish.

NOTES

1 Claude-Nicolas Ledoux, *L'architecture considérée sous le rapport de l'art, des moeurs et de la législation*, vol. 1 (Paris: Perroneau, 1804), 201. All translations are by the author and are intended to preserve the literal rendering of Ledoux's idiomatic and inventive use of language.

2 Ibid., 2.

3 Ibid., 203.

4 Mona Ozouf, "Architecture et urbanisme: L'image de la ville chez Claude-Nicolas Ledoux," *Annales. Économies, Sociétés, Civilisations* 21, no. 6 (1966): 1301, http://www.persee.fr/web/revues/home/prescript/article/ahess _0395-2649_1966_num_21_6_421483.

5 Allison Glazebrook and Madeleine Mary Henry, *Greek Prostitutes in the Ancient Mediterranean, 800 BCE–200 CE* (Madison: University of Wisconsin Press, 2011), 35.

6 Anthony Vidler, *Claude-Nicolas Ledoux: Architecture and Social Reform at the End of the Ancien Régime* (Cambridge, MA: MIT Press, 1990), 8.

7 Ledoux, *L'architecture*, 199.

8 Ibid., 200.

9 Ibid., 3.

10 Vidler, *Claude-Nicolas Ledoux*, 358. See Ledoux, *L'architecture*, 73.

11 Ledoux, *L'architecture*, 200.

12 Ibid.

13 Ibid., 201.

14 Ibid.

15 Ibid.

16 Ibid., 202.

17 Ibid.

18 Ibid.

19 Andrew Wallace-Hadrill, "The Emperor and His Virtues," *Historia: Zeitschrift für Alte Geschichte* 30, no. 3 (1981): 314, http://www.jstor.org/stable/4435768.

20 Ledoux, *L'architecture*, 202.

21 Ibid.

22 Ibid., 202–3.

23 Ibid., 203.

24 Ibid., 199.

25 Ibid., 203.

26 Allan H. Pasco, *Revolutionary Love in Eighteenth- and Early Nineteenth-Century France* (Surrey, UK: Ashgate, 2009), 66, 156.

27 Ledoux, *L'architecture*, 203.

28 Ibid.

29 Ibid., 200.

30 Ibid.

31 Ibid., 199.

32 Pasco, *Revolutionary Love*, 39.

33 Ibid., 38–9.

34 Ledoux, *L'architecture*, 203.

35 Ibid.

36 Ibid.

37 *Dictionnaire de l'Académie française*, 5th ed. (Paris: J.J. Smits, 1798), s.v. "honnêteté," *Dictionnaires d'autrefois*, ARTFL Project, http://artfl-project.uchicago.edu/node/17.

38 Ibid., s.v. "pudeur."

39 Ledoux, *L'architecture*, 202.

40 Ibid., 203.

41 Ibid., 203–4.

42 Ibid., 204.

43 Joel Schwartz, *The Sexual Politics of Jean-Jacques Rousseau* (Chicago: University of Chicago Press, 1984), 28. See also Allan Bloom, Introduction to Jean-Jacques Rousseau, *Emile, or On Education*, trans. Allan Bloom (New York: Basic Books, 1979), 22.

44 Rousseau, *Emile*, 205.

45 Schwartz, *Sexual Politics*, 79–80.

46 Rousseau, *Emile*, 318.

47 Ibid., 327.

48 Ibid., 318.

49 Ibid., 333.

50 Ibid., 430.

51 Schwartz, *Sexual Politics*, 43.

52 Rousseau, *Emile*, 470.

53 Ibid., 325.

54 Ibid., 323.

55 Ibid., 325.

56 Ibid., 317.

57 Ibid.

58 Ibid., 324.

59 Ibid., 327.

60 Schwartz, *Sexual Politics*, 29.

61 Rousseau, *Emile*, 392.

62 Ibid., 214.

63 *Essay on the Origin of Languages* was published posthumously, in 1781.

64 Schwartz, *Sexual Politics*, 27–32.

65 Ibid.

66 Ibid., 89.

Adrien Auzout and the Origins of the Paris Observatory

Ron Jelaco

Chora

INTRODUCTION: THE PARIS OBSERVATORY AND ITS TWO
DOMAINS OF HISTORY

CLAUDE PERRAULT'S authorship of the east façade of the Louvre has been
debated since its earliest years.[1] Curiously, none of that doubt has ever
spread to his association with the Paris Observatory, even though the two
projects shared nearly every other aspect of their milieu.[2] Only historian
Albert Laprade has ever questioned Perrault's role as the observatory's
architect, dismissing him by lampooning his woeful architectural skills.[3]
Subsequent biographers not only have disregarded Laprade and his critique but have declared that Perrault's design role was inevitable.[4]

This confidence in Perrault's design authorship could be undermined
by the following biographical passage from Harcourt Brown's *Scientific
Organizations in Seventeenth-Century France*: "Adrien Auzout (1622–
1691): Having published little of permanent value, and left few manuscripts to find their way to the great collections of Paris, he has remained
in a comparative obscurity. The biographical dictionaries have almost
nothing to say about him, and his publications are found only in the larger and older libraries ... Auzout was an underdeacon and left a son; and
he is supposed to have drawn the first plans for the Observatoire de Paris,
a supposition which is not at all improbable in view of the mystery that
surrounds the earliest months of its history and the fact that Auzout sent
a sketch of the building to Oldenburg at least six weeks before the wood-
en model was made."[5] Brown expands on this brief description by citing
one of Auzout's acquaintances, who described him as "the son of a clerk
of the court in Rouen. He had an excellent mind, he was a great mathematician and philosopher. He was one of the chief members of the
Académie des Sciences, and it was he who had drawn up the first plans
of it ... He made an exact criticism of Perrault's translation of Vitruvius,
noticing more than three hundred errors in it. He communicated a number of his remarks to me, which I found very good."[6]

For the science historian Brown, these two marginal architectural
exploits – the design of the Paris Observatory and a critique of Perrault's
Vitruvius – must have seemed incidental. Like most who have studied
Auzout, Brown tells his readers that Auzout's primary contribution to
history was the invention of the filar micrometer;[7] however, for those of
us who are curious about these important moments in the history of early
modern architecture, this clear contradiction in the observatory's de facto

Fig. 6.1 Top North façade of the seventeenth-century Paris Observatory.
Photograph by author (2011).

Fig. 6.2 Bottom Plaque on the north façade of the Paris Observatory. For those who use it
daily, the building is referred to as the "Bâtiment Perrault" to differentiate it from the more
modern observatory in the Paris suburbs. Photograph by author (2011).

history encourages us to unravel the full story. Therefore, with the Paris Observatory's two cognate but disconnected histories in mind, my aim here is to add some clarity to its historical place by augmenting one history with the other. In so doing, I also hope to elaborate on the roles that may have been played by these two scientists and *amateurs d'architecture*, Perrault and Auzout.

But first, the mystery that Brown mentioned ought to be explained. The documents describing the origins of the observatory would have been stored in the archives of the Bâtiments du Roi, almost all of which were destroyed in the Tuileries Palace fire in 1871. To reconstruct the observatory's origins, architectural historians have relied primarily on two surviving memoirs. The first are by Claude's younger brother, Charles Perrault. Composed thirty-five years after the events took place, and addressed to his children, his memoirs were not published in full until the twentieth century.[8] Charles praised his brother at every opportunity, portraying him as the creative force behind all the important architectural work of their time. Charles recalled the design of the observatory with a single sentence: "Your uncle was ordered by Monsieur Colbert to make a design for this observatory, which he then approved wholeheartedly."[9] The second memoirs are by the Italian Jean-Dominique Cassini, the astronomer who would eventually occupy the observatory.[10] Upon arriving in Paris in April 1669, Cassini reported finding Perrault "directing" the work.[11] Consequently, the architectural history of the origin of the observatory is founded largely on the personal memories of these two men: Charles positioned his brother at the moment of its inception and Cassini situated him two years later as the architect overseeing the construction phase. With no evidence to the contrary, the work during the two years between these two incidents has been attributed to Claude.

Brown's contribution to this study reminds us that, like many great works of architecture, the Paris Observatory straddles two domains in history. As one of three key architectural works commissioned by Colbert, it became an important building in the history of early modern architecture,[12] yet the construction of the observatory was also a momentous event in early modern science. The Paris Observatory was the realization of a long-anticipated idea: a building that would become the workplace and research centre for a fellowship of savants bent on satisfying an increasing curiosity about nature's secrets. Conceived not only as the first modern astronomical observatory, it was also intended to become the home for what would be known as the Académie des sciences. This idea had been in the imaginations of the savants of Europe since the beginning of the century, following the publication of Francis Bacon's *New Atlantis*, widely read in the seventeenth century.[13]

Fig. 6.3 Sebastien Leclerc, "Louis XIV visiting the Académie des sciences"; frontispiece from Claude Perrault, *Mémoires pour servir à l'histoire naturelle des animaux* (Paris: Imprimerie royale, 1671), Rare Books and Special Collections, McGill University Library. Framed by the window in the background, the Paris Observatory is shown under construction.

AUZOUT'S EPHEMERIS AND THE INVENTION OF THE PROJECT

The historians of early modern science have recorded various incidents that connect Auzout to the observatory. The following event would have been familiar to their readers. In November 1664, Europeans were startled by a spectacular celestial event. A comet appeared over Spain and wandered across the skies of Europe for the next four months. Its unanticipated arrival and unnatural motion caused curiosity and apprehension. In response, France's young king Louis XIV convened a conference for scholars to discuss it. Afterward, Auzout was the first to publish a

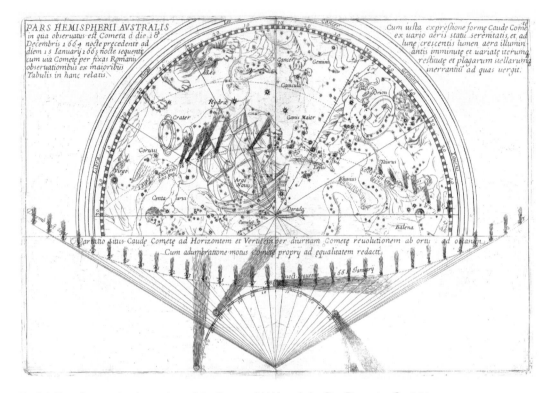

Fig. 6.4 Plate showing the observations of the Comet of 1664 made by Gian Domenico Cassini in Rome as it crossed the southern hemisphere between 18 December 1664 and 15 January 1665. Cassini logged the position of the comet and the orientation and form of its tail. From Cassini, *Theoriae motus cometae anni MDCLXIV* (1665); courtesy Observatoire de Paris.

thesis, in which he asserted that, although the comet's actions may appear erratic, the comet was a natural phenomenon that can be shown to follow predictable rules.[14] He noted that earlier astronomers could merely record the paths that comets had travelled. Auzout's essay was an ephemeris: a precise prediction of the comet's *future* actions. He declared, "No man has been so bold as to venture to foretell the places through which they *should* pass, and where they *should cease to appear*."[15] He then encouraged his colleagues to either confirm or refute his predictions.

The radicalness of Auzout's claims and their cultural and theological implications are now difficult for us to imagine, yet, as bold as his ephemeris must have seemed, it was not the boldest part of Auzout's publication. In an open letter appended to his text, he appealed to his king to build a new observatory. Auzout's letter first described the primitive conditions in which he was obliged to conduct his study of the comet. Without a proper workplace or adequate instruments, he was forced to make his observations from gardens and rooftops, using only "nets, rulers, set squares and sticks."[16] He heralded the many benefits that a new observatory could provide France: "It is up to you, Sire; the glory of Your Majesty and the reputation of France that makes us hope that you will order some place to make in the future all sorts of Celestial Observations, and that you will have it garnished with all the Instruments necessary to that effect."[17]

A new observatory was only part of the larger project that Auzout had in mind. He also encouraged Louis to adopt a plan that had recently been circulating in Paris: to establish a new research academy he called the Compagnie des sciences et des arts.[18] Auzout imagined the observatory as the home and workplace for a new comprehensive academy. He encouraged Louis to imagine it: Celestial observations would be only "one of the principal goals of the Company of the Sciences and the Arts, that waits for nothing other than the protection of Your Majesty to powerfully work at the perfection of all the Sciences and all the useful arts."[19]

Auzout believed it would be a glorious project and would help Louis achieve his larger aims for France: "Your project is so grand and so glorious to the State, and so useful to the Public, it is impossible to not be persuaded that Your Majesty, who has goals so vast and so magnificent, does not approve nor favour it; and I can assure him that all neighbouring Nations are since a short time in an incredible wait for such a beautiful establishment."[20] Fully defined, Auzout's idea was enormous. Its scope could not have been lost on Louis and Colbert, nor on the scientific community who read reports of it in the inaugural volume of the Royal Society's scholarly journal, *Philosophical Transactions*, the first journal devoted to science topics, in March 1665.[21]

Louis must have been quickly persuaded; by the following year, correspondence between interested parties indicate that Colbert was making steady progress on the academy project. Paris insider Henri Justel sent an update in a letter to his London correspondent Henry Oldenburg: "They are laboring here on the establishment of an Academy to be composed of members chosen from all kinds of professions. No one yet knows the details because it is only sketched out. If the matter is taken to heart a considerable establishment will be created and there is good hope of success ... M. Huygens will be a member, and M. Auzout as well, with other very competent men."[22] Henry Oldenburg was the founding secretary of the Royal Society in London, and the creator and editor of *Philosophical Transactions*. As the journal's editor, he became the nexus of scientific communications in the mid-seventeenth century. His promotion of scientific undertakings kept him in contact with the savants in Europe, soliciting and publishing their works and acting as a translator and conduit of their interests. He was a prolific letter writer and a diligent secretary, archiving letters he received along with copies of his own letters. For similar reasons, Henri Justel also played an important role. Justel was a Parisian courtier with an insatiable curiosity for facts and ideas.[23] As one of Louis's personal secretaries, he was ideally situated to provide news from the inner workings of Paris. His irrepressible interest in scientific discovery led to his sponsorship of a circle of savants at his house. He remained a prominent participant in French scientific enterprises for years and was Oldenburg's principal correspondent.

In July 1666, Colbert named the first seven appointees to his academy, and by the end of the year he had completed his roster of about twenty savants.[24] The progress being made in Paris on the academy and observatory was a frequent topic in the correspondence of Europe's savants. For Henry Oldenburg, arguably the world's first scientific journalist and news aggregator, it was a sensation. Oldenburg queried his contacts for information that he could report to his readers. To one such letter, Auzout replied, "I must say a word about the plan we have here, since you express a desire to hear something about it ... We have been promised a fine observatory, furnished with all kinds of large instruments and a laboratory where all kinds of experiments can be performed; we are to do all sorts of anatomical dissections and, in general, all kinds of observations, both celestial and terrestrial."[25]

By the end of 1666, the foundations of the academy were reportedly in place, and we can turn attention to the development of the observatory plan. In Charles Wolf's *Histoire de l'observatoire de Paris, de sa fondation à 1793*,[26] Claude Perrault is again portrayed as the observatory's architect, yet with one important caveat: "The only passage of the *Procès-Verbaux* of the Academy of Sciences where there is a question about the plans of the Observatory was brought to my attention by Mr Ludovic Lalanne: '22 April 1667, Mr Auzout has given to Mr Perrault a plan for

Monsieur Auzout a donné a monsieur Perrault
un plan pour l'observatoire.

Ce 2 d'Avril Monsieur auzout a promis
de donner le devis de ce qu'il a proposé pour
la terrasse que l'on doit faire dans le lieu
destiné pour l'observatoire:

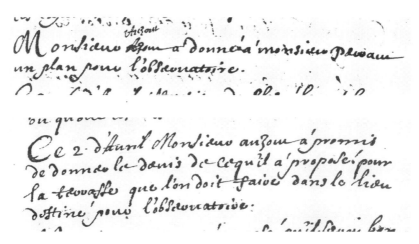

Fig. 6.5 Top "Monsieur Auzout a donné à Monsieur Perrault un plan pour l'Observatoire." Excerpt from the records of the Académie des sciences, *Procès-Verbaux*, Tome I (1667), 205.

Fig. 6.6 Bottom "Ce 2 d'Avril Monsieur auzout a promis de donner le devis de ce qu'il a proposé pour la terrasse que l'on doit faire dans le lieu destiné pour l'observatoire." Excerpt from the records of the Académie des sciences, *Procès-Verbaux*, Tome I (1667), 204.

the Observatory.' (*Procès-Verbaux*, Tome II, p. 205)."[27] The *Procès-Verbaux* are the recorded proceedings for each meeting of the academy. Note that Wolf does not claim to have seen this entry. Had he verified Lalanne's citation, he would have realized that it was incorrect. In fact, there was no academy meeting on 22 April, and there is no page 205 in Tome II. The entry *does* appear in the academy's minutes, however, but in the minutes of the meeting on 2 *April*, bound in *Tome I*.[28] This might seem to be a minor oversight; however, by not verifying this entry, Wolf and the many architectural historians who have since repeated his error – or worse, cited through him to a page that never existed – missed another important entry in the same minutes that substantiates Auzout's role in the origins of the observatory plans. Translated, it says, "This 2nd of April, Mr Auzout promised to give the *dévis* of what he has proposed for the terrace that must be in place, destined for the observatory."[29] Evidently, at the 2 April meeting, Auzout not only submitted a plan for the observatory but also promised a *dévis* for the work he proposed. A *dévis* would have been no small matter. In seventeenth-century construction parlance, a *dévis* was a set of detailed documents for an architectural project, the labour and materials needed for its construction, and perhaps even a cost estimate.[30] The information comprising a *dévis* would have been in the hands of only someone very close to the project.

A few months after presenting the plan and promising the *dévis* to his colleagues, there was another event that links Auzout to the origins of the observatory project. On the morning of the summer solstice, Auzout and four other astronomers from the academy met on the observatory's construction site.[31] In a ceremony described as something between a survey and a benediction, the five astronomers made a series of celestial observations. They scribed the corresponding lines and angles onto a large flat stone, then transferred them onto a plan for the observatory, establishing its astronomical geometry. Wolf quotes a passage from the *Histoire de l'Académie royale des sciences* that described the event:

If some kind of pomp and ceremony can count for something in these matters, nothing was more solemn than the observations that were made on 21 June 1667, the day of the solstice ... As this building had to be *tout savant*,[32] and was destined mainly for astronomical observations, it was wanted that it be put on a meridian line, and that all its angles respond to certain azimuths. So the mathematicians made their way to the site on June 21. They drew a meridian and azimuths with all the care that might inspire such particular divinations.[33] ... All these observations were the consecration of the site; the foundations of that edifice were also laid that year and a medal was pressed with these words: *Sic itur ad astra.*[34]

Summarizing briefly, there is evidence to show that, as Brown suggested, Auzout indeed was involved in the initial plans for the Paris Observatory. First, in a very public proposal, he effectively invented the project to establish the academy and build an observatory. Next, he presented a plan of the observatory to his colleagues and promised them a detailed description of the work. Ten weeks later, he was part of the group that determined the design's astronomical geometry and orientation on the site.

Up to this point – more than two years into the project – there has been no indication of Claude Perrault's involvement in the plans of the observatory. This claim might appear to contradict the reference in the *Procès-Verbaux*, in which Auzout presented the plan of the observatory to Monsieur Perrault.[35] As a member of that academy, Claude Perrault likely was present at the event, but I suggest that the "Monsieur Perrault" named in the *Procès-Verbaux* was not Claude but his brother Charles. Charles was the most familiar figure among the advisors surrounding Colbert, and in that situation, undoubtedly was the most familiar of the "Messieurs Perrault."[36] Charles was well known by the new academy members, likely having nominated several of them for their appointments. In contrast, Claude seems to have been entirely unaffiliated with the group prior to his appointment a few months earlier.[37]

Moreover, it is reasonable that drawings destined for the Bâtiments du Roi would have been given to Charles. For several years, he had been Colbert's closest assistant in architectural matters and a *contrôleur* in the Bâtiments du Roi. His involvement in the Louvre project and the unravelling of Bernini's schemes two years earlier is well known.[38] Furthermore, the 2 April meeting would have been within days of Charles's appointment as administrative secretary of the Petit Conseil, a new design subcommittee in the Bâtiments du Roi established by Colbert to focus on the architecture projects. This is not to suggest that Claude had no interest in the observatory project. On the contrary: beginning in April 1667 his involvement in architectural projects would greatly intensify.[39] What this does suggest is that, other than the line in Charles's memoirs, there is nothing so far that directly connects Claude to the observatory project.

FOLLOWING THE PLAN THROUGH THE
SCIENTIFIC CORRESPONDENCE

By the beginning of 1668, the construction was well underway and its progress was a frequent topic in the scientific correspondence of the time. Oldenburg's correspondence in April shows that he learned from Justel that "Mr Colbert has laid the first stone of the Paris Observatory, which will be magnificent. They are going to work there in good earnest."[40] In May, Justel writes about a recent eclipse, then adds news about the observatory: "The Observatory gets on well. It will be magnificent and there is nothing so fine in Europe. I shall try to get a plan of it which I shall send you as soon as possible."[41] A month later, Justel fulfilled that promise, opening his letter with these auspicious lines: "I send you the plan of the

Observatory, of which Mr Auzout makes you a present. The doorway, forecourt or antecourt, the laboratory, and garden are not marked, because that has not yet been decided upon." Further in the letter, Justel adds, "I beg you to show Mr Jeffreys the plan of the Observatory, since he has asked me for it. It will be easy for him to get it copied."[42]

It is significant that Justel credited Auzout as the source of the observatory plan. It had been fourteen months since Auzout submitted the plan to Charles and the academy, and three months after Colbert had laid the cornerstone, and he still was recognized as the author of the plan. It is also interesting that Justel mentions Edward Jeffreys, who was then a twenty-two-year-old medical student in England. His desire to see the observatory plan illustrates the breadth of interest in the project among Europe's scientific community. Justel's willingness to see the observatory plan copied and distributed is striking and likely betrays his true allegiances.[43]

The correspondence between the savants continued through the spring of 1668. In June, Auzout told Oldenburg that he was leaving on a *petit voyage* to Italy on scientific errands. The significance of this voyage will become apparent later in this study.[44] Later in June, Justel reported that the work of the observatory project "continues every day. It may be finished in two years."[45] Throughout the summer of 1668, Justel provided routine construction reports, mixed with news of scientific undertakings and political concerns. A letter dated 21 August 1668 is noteworthy. In part, it reads, "We eagerly await the secret of Mr Colbert's negotiation in England, and what will happen in Poland, in Crete, and in Switzerland. The King's claim to Condé and the counterscarp at Nieuwpoort might well disturb the public peace. It makes the Dutch anxious. The observatory makes good progress. A wooden model of it has been made. Mr Carcavy is to send its plan to England. Please do not let on that I have [already] sent it to you."[46]

It is the reference to Pierre Carcavy that makes this letter from Justel important. At sixty-seven, Carcavy was a generation older than the others in this story.[47] A respected mathematician and one of the first seven academy appointees, he was one of Colbert's two primary assistants in assembling the list of candidates for the academy.[48] Colbert entrusted Carcavy with many important projects, but undoubtedly the most important was to found and administer Colbert's private library, la bibliothèque Colbertine, his most prized possession.[49]

In short, a plan from Carcavy would have added legitimacy. Although there is no record that Oldenburg ever received the plan from Carcavy, this letter is significant. We can conclude from Justel's plea for discretion that he believed that the two plans – the one he had sent Oldenburg ten weeks earlier and the "official" plan from Carcavy – would be recognizable as essentially the same plan. This letter therefore links Auzout's observatory plan to Carcavy, and extends his connection with it through the summer of 1668 and after his departure from Paris.

Correspondence between Justel and Oldenburg continued through the fall of 1668, with periodic construction updates and no mention of changes or delays. During that time, the two men monitored Auzout and his activities in Italy. In October, Justel reported that Auzout had travelled to Bologna, where he met "several skilful mathematicians."[50] One was astronomer Giovanni Domenico Cassini, whose memoirs were mentioned above.[51] Cassini was the most celebrated mathematician and astronomer in Italy and had also submitted a theory on the 1664 comet. Auzout knew him well, at least by reputation. A few weeks later, Cassini reported that the two met again in Florence, where Auzout "brought me a letter from France and the plan of the Royal Observatory that the King of France was building for astronomical observations."[52] Cassini claims his overall disappointment with the design, complaining that the designers had not paid enough attention to how an observatory should function: "There had been at the very least as much respect paid to its magnificence as to its convenience for observations."[53] Cassini's criticism was directed toward the aspect of the design that the French may have considered most important: that it should strive to achieve glory for Louis and France.[54] As a fellow astronomer, did Auzout agree with Cassini's critique? Or as a Frenchman and someone who had been affiliated with the design for the past four years, did he attempt to defend it? Unfortunately, his reaction is unknown.

Within days of the Florence meeting, Cassini reported receiving a "pleasant surprise, that His Majesty Louis XIV wanted me to come to France."[55] Cassini's arrival in Paris on 4 April 1669 marks a new phase of the observatory project. Its stone walls were already up to the first floor and Claude Perrault was in charge. Auzout had taken residence in Rome, where he would remain almost continuously for the rest of his life. Two years after being named one of the first members of the

Académie des sciences, he had been replaced by Cassini as the premier astronomer in France. Four years after his appeal for the observatory, and two years after submitting plans to his academy colleagues, he is never again associated with the Paris Observatory in any of the Oldenburg correspondence.[56]

AUZOUT, *AMATEUR D'ARCHITECTURE*

With the exception of Charles's claim in his memoirs, all evidence points exclusively to Auzout as the primary author of the Paris Observatory design, but is there any reason to believe that he was qualified for the role? Harcourt Brown claimed that Auzout also made an exacting criticism of Perrault's translation of Vitruvius. That claim is certainly believable. Besides being a renowned mathematician, astronomer, and polymath who knew at least five languages,[57] Auzout apparently had a lifelong interest in Vitruvius and ancient architecture. Martin Lister, a London doctor, member of the Royal Society, and friend of Auzout, speculated that Auzout may have abandoned his position at the Academy and moved to Rome in part to pursue his interest in architecture and Roman ruins. Lister claimed that Auzout had studied Vitruvius "more than 40 years together, and much upon the place at Rome."[58] Lister writes about Auzout: "Monsieur d'Auzout was very curious and understanding in architecture; for which purpose he was 17 years in Italy by times; I do remember, when he was in England about 14 years ago, he showed me the design of several of our buildings drawn by himself; but of that of the Banqueting House at Whitehall, he expressed himself in very extraordinary terms, telling me it was the most regular and most finished piece of modern workmanship he had seen on this side of the Alps, that he could not enough praise it: That Inigo Jones, the Architect, had a true relish of what was Noble in that Art."[59]

In 1690 a friend of Lister returned from Rome with news of their friend Auzout: "He had about 80 difficult passages in Vitruvius [completed], which he had commented and explained; and the correction of a great number of errata in the text. Also that upon Julius Frontinus (though that was a much less book) he had much more to say, than he had upon Vitruvius."[60]

Auzout's translation of Vitruvius and his reconstruction of the lost volumes of Frontinus's *De aquaeductu*[61] were well known among his

THE ROYAL BANQUETING HOUSE IN WHITEHALL:

Fig. 6.7 Inigo Jones, Banqueting House, Whitehall, London (1619–22); drawing by Thomas Forster (1672–1722), Wikimedia.

science colleagues. Their preservation would become a serious concern after Auzout died in 1691. In a letter from Rome, friend and fellow mathematician Gottfried Leibniz wrote to Melchisédech Thévenot about his recent meeting with Auzout: "I found in Rome that Monsieur Auzout promises a new edition of Vitruvius, with which he probably could succeed since he had the means to see so many ancient ruins. He also claims that there are many passages where Mr Perrault has promoted his own thoughts rather than those of the author and ancients. But I find that Mr

Fig. 6.8 Giovanni Battista Piranesi, "Veduta dell'Arco di Settimio Severo," from *Vedute di Roma* (Rome, 1769), Rare Books and Special Collections, McGill University Library.

Auzout is too distracted, and as he does not want to release it in pieces, I fear this will completely deprive us of the fruit of his work."[62]

After Auzout's death, Leibniz was relieved to learn that his library had been turned over to someone whose name Leibniz recognized: "You have delighted me in saying that Father Nazari … is responsible for giving the public the fine points of Monsieur Auzout's Vitruvius and Frontinus … You know better, sir, that is, what will become of the books of Monsieur Auzout, among which there were many that are not easy to find and had a thousand curious remarks that had no relation to Vitruvius and Frontinus, he should also try to conserve."[63]

Unfortunately, Leibniz's earlier fears were justified, as Auzout's translation of Vitruvius indeed was lost; however, portions of it may have found their way to other parts of the world. In England, more than a century later, Auzout was still being quoted as an authority on Vitruvian theory. In *A Treatise on the Decorative Part of Civil Architecture* (1791), Sir William Chambers defers to Auzout's expertise on the origin of columns: "The first architects, says Mons. Auzoult [*sic*], probably made their columns in straight lines, in imitation of trees, so that their shaft was a frustum of the cone; but finding this form abrupt and disagreeable, they made use of some curve, which, springing from the extremities of the superior and inferior diameters of the column, swelled beyond the sides of the cone, and, by that means, gave a more pleasing figure to the outline."[64]

It is not surprising that Auzout found Frontinus interesting. In his later life, Auzout developed a broad fascination for Roman engineering projects, and became an "aqueduct hunter" who discovered and documented the ruins of lost aqueducts. He was "more keen-sighted than Lynceus himself or Argus," wrote his seventeenth-century colleague Raffaello Fabretti, "every bit of him an eye."[65] Fabretti credits Auzout with rediscovering the famous Aqua Alexandrina aqueduct and deciphering the cancelled line on the Arch of Septimius Severus in the Roman Forum.[66]

CONCLUSION: AUZOUT, PERRAULT, AND THE PLAN OF THE PARIS OBSERVATORY

There is no reason to doubt Cassini's assertion that, when he arrived in Paris in April 1669, Claude Perrault was managing the construction of the observatory, but how or when he became involved in the project should be a subject for speculation. Throughout the first two years of the observatory project, he was never named in association with it by the savants who were following the project with an intense curiosity. On the other hand, numerous sources connected Adrien Auzout with the design of the observatory – from its inception in January 1665 until November 1668, when he presented the plan to Cassini in Florence, and while the construction in Paris was well underway. Moreover, Auzout also seems to have been uniquely qualified for the assignment. Lister's claim that Auzout had studied Vitruvius for more than forty years suggests that his interest in architecture may have begun in the 1640s as a student in Rouen, twenty years before the first record of Claude's architectural interests.[67] Shown to be one of the premier astronomers in Europe, with an extensive background in architecture and involvement in establishing the original vision for the academy, it appears that Auzout would have been the more certain choice.

Despite decades of opportunities, and what may seem to be ample motivation, there is no record that Claude Perrault ever took credit for the design of the Paris Observatory.[68] This claim originated in a line from the personal memoirs of his brother Charles, a claim that is not corroborated by the findings of this study. The traditional portrayal of the origins of the Paris Observatory – that it begins with a design solely attributable to Claude Perrault – is improbable, and the doubts about his authorship in these projects may justifiably be expanded.

NOTES

1 See Robert Berger, *The Palace of the Sun: The Louvre of Louis XIV* (University Park: Pennsylvania State University Press, 1993), 83–6.

2 The Louvre and the observatory were among a group of projects initiated by Jean-Baptiste Colbert, the director of buildings for Louis XIV, in 1667. Design work on both began in earnest in early April. The observatory and the Louvre also shared *entrepreneurs* (general contractors) André Mazieres and Antoine Bergeron, and perhaps even the same site foreman. See Michael Petzet, *Claude Perrault und die Architektur des Sonnenkönigs der Louvre König Ludwigs XIV und das Werk Claude Perraults* (Munich: Deutscher Kunstverlag, 2000), 391–7.

3 Albert Laprade, *François d'Orbay 1634–1697* (Paris: [s.n.], 1954). See Appendix C, "Claude Perrault Preténdu Architecte ou Analyse Critique des Erreurs Accréditées Concernnant Le Louvre, l'Observatoire et l'Arch de Triomphe," 323–39.

4 This is mentioned by Antoine Picon: "Le nom de Claude Perrault s'impose tout naturellement à Colbert pour donner le dessin de l'Observatoire." Antoine Picon, *Claude Perrault, 1613–1688; ou, La curiosité d'un classique* (Paris: Picard, 1988), 197. It is also mentioned by Michael Petzet: "Scheint er von vornherein für die Planung des Observatoriums bestimmt." Michael Petzet, "Claude Perrault als Architekt des Pariser Observatoriums," *Zeitschrift fur Kunstgeschichte* 30, no. 1 (1967): 4.

5 Harcourt Brown, *Scientific Organizations in Seventeenth-Century France, 1620–1680* (New York: Russell & Russell, 1967), 138–40.

6 Brown cites *Lantiniana*, a manuscript collection from the papers of a lawyer from Dijon, and *Menagiana*, in the same collection. Bibliothèque nationale,

Fonds français, 23254, 218; *Lantiniana*, 355. For the citation, see Brown, *Scientific Organizations*, 138–9.

7 See the entry for Auzout in Thomas A. Hockey, Virginia Trimble, and Katherine Bracher, *The Biographical Encyclopedia of Astronomers*, 2 vol. (New York: Springer, 2007).

8 Charles Perrault and Claude Perrault, *Mémoires de ma vie. Écrits d'amateurs et d'artistes* (Paris: Renouard, 1909). Two earlier publications of the memoirs had made heavy alterations to the original text. The 1909 publication, edited by Paul Bonnefon, is said to be most true to Perrault's original manuscript. See Charles Perrault and Jeanne Morgan Zarucchi, *Charles Perrault: Memoirs of My Life* (Columbia: University of Missouri Press, 1989), 26–7.

9 Perrault and Zarucchi, *Charles Perrault*, 52. Charles told his children that many of the architectural ideas – including the famous paired colonnade of the Louvre – were his own, and that he had passed them along to Claude for development.

10 Jean-Dominique Cassini et al., *Mémoires pour servir a l'histoire des sciences* (Paris: Bleuet, 1810).

11 Cassini was quoted in Charles Joseph Étienne Wolf, *Histoire de l'observatoire de Paris de sa fondation à 1793* (Paris: Gauthier-Villars, 1902), 24–5. Cassini's word "conduite" would have been appropriate. The 1694 edition of the *Dictionnaire de l'Académie française* offers this definition for "conduite": "Avoir inspection sur un ouvrage, en avoir la direction, & en ce sens il se dit des ouvrages materiels. Conduire un bastiment. conduire un travail. conduire une tranchée. conduire un ouvrage."

12 The two others are the Louvre's east façade and the Arc de Triomphe for the Place du Trône.

13 Francis Bacon and Arthur Johnston, *The Advancement of Learning and New Atlantis* (Oxford: Clarendon Press, 1974), first published in Latin in 1624. Bacon imagined a state research institute that would gather and assemble knowledge through experiment and observation. In outlining his proposed working plan for the Académie des sciences, Christiaan Huygens wrote to Colbert that "the principal occupation of this Assembly and the most useful must be, in my opinion, to work in the natural history somewhat in the manner suggested by Verulam [Bacon]." Colbert scrawled "bon" in the margin next to this passage. Christiaan Huygens, *Oeuvres complètes* (The Hague: Nijhoff, 1888), 6:95–6.

14 Adrien Auzout, *L'ephéméride du nouveau comète* (Paris: Cusson, 1665).

15 Ibid., my emphasis.

16 Ibid.

17 Ibid.

18 Along with Christiaan Huygens, Pierre Petit, and others, Auzout was known to be a co-author of the plan for the Compagnie.

19 Auzout, *L'ephéméride*.

20 Ibid.

21 Royal Society, *Philosophical Transactions of the Royal Society of London* 1 (1665–66): 3–8.

22 Letter 526 (16 May 1666), Henry Oldenburg, *Correspondence*, 13 vol., ed. and trans. A. Rupert Hall and Marie Boas Hall (Madison: University of Wisconsin Press, 1965–86), 3:134.

23 See C.E. Engel, "Henri Justel," *XVIIe siècle* 61 (1963): 19–30.

24 It is difficult to know who were full members and who had a minor ranking. In a careful study, Academy historian David Sturdy lists twenty-two founding members. See D.J. Sturdy, *Science and Social Status: The Members of the Académie des sciences, 1666–1750* (Woodbridge, UK: Boydell Press, 1995), 78.

25 Letter 589 (22 Dec. 1666), Oldenburg, *Correspondence*, 3:296.

26 Charles Joseph Étienne Wolf, *Histoire de l'observatoire de Paris de sa fondation à 1793* (Paris: Gauthier-Villars, 1902).

27 Ibid., 20–1. Ludovic Lalanne was a colleague of Wolf.

28 At the very least, the date in Wolf's citation should have been evident as an error. The academy met only on Wednesdays and Saturdays; 22 April 1667 was a Friday. (In the Julian calendar, it was a Monday.) See Académie des sciences, *Procès-verbaux des séances de l'Académie*, 10 vol. (Hendaye: Impr. de l'Observatoire d'Abbadia, 1910–22), 1:205. Only Robert McKeon seems to have found the correct page in the correct volume. See Robert M. McKeon, *Etablissement de l'astronomie de prècision et oeuvre d'Adrien Auzout* (Paris: [s.n.], 1965), 2:303.

29 Académie des sciences, *Procès-verbaux*, 1:204.

30 "Devis, sign. aussi, Un memoire contenant le detail de certaines sortes d'ouvrage, & principalement d'Architecture & de la despense qu'il y faut faire. Devis exact. faire un devis. donner le devis d'une maison. le devis de l'Architecte ou du Maçon." *Dictionnaire de L'Académie française*, 1st ed. (1694), s.v. "dévis."

31 With Auzout were Jean Picard, Bernard Frenicle de Bessy, Jacques Buot, and Jean Richer.

32 Literally, "all knowing." What this phrase might have meant in this context is difficult to say.

33 "pouvaient inspirer des conjectures si particulieres …"

34 Académie royale des sciences, *Histoire de l'Académie royale des sciences* (Paris: Jean Boudot, 1702), 43. Wolf shortened the inscription from the full version: "Sic itur ad astra: turris siderum speculatoria anno MDCLXVII," or "Thus you shall go to the Stars: the Tower from which the stars are investigated, 1667." This phrase is rooted in Virgil and the *Aeneid*. For Wolf's quotation, see *Histoire de l'observatoire de Paris*, 11.

35 It is generally believed that this exchange between Auzout and Perrault was merely a "due diligence" procedure in which the astronomer passed along his ideas for the observatory to the architect.

36 Whenever confusion was possible, a modifier such as *le médecin* or *le frère* often would have been appended to Claude's *nom de famille*.

37 Historian David Sturdy considers Claude to be the least likely candidate among the founding members and would not have been admitted without the promotion of his younger brother. Claude's name does not appear in the decades of attendance lists of any of the science *cabinets* from which the rest of the academy members ascended. Sturdy, *Science and Social Status*, 86–7, 100.

38 Charles Perrault describes many scenes where his persistent questioning infuriated Bernini and undermined Colbert's confidence. See Perrault and Zarucchi, *Charles Perrault*, 53–79. Paul Fréart de Chantelou records nearly identical scenes in the daily journal he kept while hosting Bernini in Paris. For one example, see Paul Fréart de Chantelou, *Journal du voyage du Cavalier Bernin en France* (Paris: Gazette des Beaux-Arts, 1885), 205–6.

39 Like his brother, Claude was named to the Petit Conseil by Colbert, but as one of three principal design consultants. As a member of the Petit Conseil, he would also become associated with other architecture projects for the Bâtiments du Roi, including the east façade of the Louvre, the Arc de Triomphe du Trône, and the Paris Observatory. He would also be ordered by Colbert to begin the translation of Vitruvius at about the same time.

40 Letter 839 (15 Apr. 1668), Oldenburg, *Correspondence*, 4:323.

41 Letter 865 (20 May 1668), ibid., 4:416.

42 Letter 886 (10 June 1668), ibid., 4:461. At present, Justel's written description of the plan is all that remains of it. The various plans mentioned here are assumed to have been lost. This is undoubtedly the letter that Harcourt Brown mentioned.

43 In a February letter, Justel had already promised a plan meant for Jeffreys. Letter 770 (8 Feb. 1668), ibid., 4:155.

44 Letter 888 (16 June 1668), ibid., 4:465. Auzout likely was not aware of the significance of his trip. For reasons that have never been clear, he would not return to Paris permanently for the rest of his life.

45 Letter 894 (27 June 1668), ibid., 4:477. An estimate of four years for construction was wildly optimistic. The project would not be complete for more than a decade.

46 Letter 945 (21 Aug. 1668), ibid., 5:20. This would not have been Jean-Baptiste Colbert but his younger brother Charles, the Marquis de Croissy, a diplomat and Louis's ambassador to London. The model mentioned by Justel is the one Brown mentioned earlier. Until now, that model has been associated with a design authored by Perrault.

47 Both Colbert and Oldenburg were forty-eight years old. Justel and Auzout were a year younger. Claude was fifty-four and Charles was thirty-nine.

48 Colbert solicited advice from many sources, but it is likely that Carcavy and poet Jean Chapelain were given the lead roles in assembling candidates for the academy.

49 "The pleasure of forming my library is almost the only one I allow myself amid all the work placed on me by my duties to the king." Colbert to A.M. de Marle, 29 Nov. 1672; Jean Baptiste Colbert, Pierre Clément, and Pierre de Brotonne, *Lettres, instructions et mémoires de Colbert* (Paris: Impr. impériale, 1861), 7:68.

50 Letter 791 (3 Oct. 1668), Oldenburg, *Correspondence*, 5:76.

51 After moving to France, he became Jean-Dominique Cassini.

52 M.J.F.S. Devic, *Histoire de la vie et des travaux scientifiques et littéraires de J.-D. Cassini IV* (Clermont: Daix, 1851), 286. Note Cassini's assertion that the observatory was intended solely for astronomical observations, rather than its original, more comprehensive program.

53 Cassini et al., *Mémoires*, 286–7.

54 In 1669, Colbert created a list of his current architecture projects, and at the end added his expectations: "Le Louvre, à continuer. Arc de triomphe pour les conquests de terre. Observatoire pour les cieux. Pyramide; difficulté à

l'exécution. *Grandeur et magnificence.*" See Colbert, "4 – État des manu-
factures," *Lettres* 7:287–90.

55 Cassini et al., *Mémoires*, 287.

56 The archive of Oldenburg's correspondence extends to May 1677. There is
no other letter, either to or from Oldenburg, that associates Auzout with the
Paris Observatory.

57 He had mastered French, Italian, Latin, Hebrew, and Arabic, and his Eng-
lish must have been passable. See Anthony Gerbino and François Blondel,
*François Blondel: Architecture, Erudition, and the Scientific Revolution: The
Classical Tradition in Architecture* (London: Routledge, 2010), 275n60.

58 Martin Lister, *A Journey to Paris in the Year 1698* (London: Tonson, 1699),
30. Lister admired Auzout and dedicated a book to him, posthumously.

59 Ibid., 102.

60 Ibid., 101.

61 Sextus Julius Frontinus was a first-century Roman senator. Auzout was interested in Frontinus as the author of *De aquaeductu*, a two-volume record
of the status of the aqueducts of Rome, published at the end of the first century.

62 G.W. Leibniz, cited in André Robinet, *G.W. Leibniz: Iter Italicum (mars
1689–mars 1690): La dynamique de la république des lettres: Nombreux
textes inédits* (Florence: Olschki, 1988), 144.

63 Ibid., 145. The correspondent was l'abbé Claude Nicaise. The quotation is
from 5 June 1692, cited in C.I. Gerhardt, *Die philosophischen Schriften
von Gottfried Wilhelm Leibniz* (Berlin: Weidmann, 1875–90), 2:533.

64 William Chambers, *A Treatise on the Decorative Part of Civil Architecture*
(London: Taylor, 1836), 124.

65 See Harry B. Evans, *Aqueduct Hunting in the Seventeenth Century: Raffaello Fabretti's De aquis et aquaeductibus veteris Romae* (Ann Arbor: University of Michigan Press, 2002), 20.

66 Harry B. Evans, "Aqueduct Hunting without Frontinus," in *Rome and Her
Monuments: Essays on the City and Literature of Rome in Honor of
Katherine A. Geffcken*, ed. Katherine A. Geffcken, Sheila K. Dickison, and
Judith P. Hallett (Wauconda, IL: Bolchazy-Carducci, 2000), 251n29. Evans's
reference to the "cancelled line on the Arch of Septimius Severus" may refer
to the fifth line of text being damaged during the subsequent installation of
bronze letters.

67 Claude is credited with the design of an obelisk that, according to biographer

Wolfgang Herrmann, he made "a few days after his election to the Academy of Sciences." Perrault was named to the academy in October 1666. See Wolfgang Herrmann, *The Theory of Claude Perrault: Studies in Architecture* (London: A. Zwemmer, 1973), 18.

68 The periods of Perrault's architectural practice were intense but short-lived. In contrast, his work as a scientist never waned through his professional life. He would often distance himself from his architectural work. Leibniz wrote that he was told by Perrault that "he was not an architect by profession, neither did he wish to give up everything for the sake of architecture." It seems that architecture may have been interesting for Perrault when it melded with his scientific life. Gottfried Wilhelm Leibniz, *Journal général de l'Instruction Publique* (1857) 26:235n51, quoted in Herrmann, *Theory of Claude Perrault*, 30.

Constructing Architectural History in the Joseon Industrial Exhibition of 1915

Yoonchun Jung

Chora

INTRODUCTION

THIS ESSAY DISCUSSES the Joseon Industrial Exhibition in Seoul in 1915 and how modern Japan developed its "historical" intentions by incorporating Korean architectural traditions. Constructing its history was an important part of Japan's attempt to achieve a political status on par with the West. In this sense, "Japan as a modern state cannot be found outside the West ... Criticism of Japan includes that of the West."[1] In other words, modern Japan – as well as Korea and other modern Asian nations – cannot be considered without recognizing Western influence.

This relationship between Asia and the West underlies the nationalistic characteristics of modern Asian architecture. It also questions the common belief that modern Japanese architecture, especially from the beginning of the Meiji era (1868) to the end of the Second World War (1945), was merely a derivative of Western architectural forms and building methods. A closer examination will reveal its "hybrid nature,"[2] not in its architectural forms, but in its historical intentions, affirming that "the visible does not always tell you the whole story."[3]

THE ARCHITECTURE OF THE JOSEON INDUSTRIAL
EXHIBITION OF 1915

On 11 September 1915, the first Japanese governor-general of Korea,[4] Masatake Terauchi, announced the opening of the Joseon Industrial Exhibition at Geunjeongjeon,[5] the throne hall of Gyeongbok Palace in Seoul. This exhibition was the first official Japanese governmental event in colonized Korea, five years after Korea was annexed by Japan in 1910. The event was intended to both commemorate and legitimize Japanese colonial rule in Korea, responding to international criticism of its occupation. Accordingly, the exhibition emphasized material achievements in Korea during the past five years. To make this first event more symbolic and accessible, the exhibition committee decided to locate the exhibition in Gyeongbok Palace, the iconic seat of the Joseon dynasty (1392–1897), opening the palace to visitors for the first time in Korean history.[6]

The Joseon Industrial Exhibition was an important event, not only for the Government-General but also for the Japanese empire. On 1 October 1915, a member of the Japanese imperial family represented the emperor at a special event to commemorate the establishment of the Japanese

（共一）　場式會開會進共
フ賜チ旨御下殿宮院閣

（共二）　　上　同

共進會々場

1. Gwanghwamun
2. Entry Plaza
3. Exhibition Hall No. 1
4. Geunjeongjeon
5. Railway Hall
6. Art Museum

Fig. 7.1 Top The opening ceremony of the Joseon Industrial Exhibition of 1915, held at Geunjeongjeon, Gyeongbok Palace, Seoul, Korea; from *Keijokyousangkaihokoku*.

Fig. 7.2 Bottom Buildings in the Joseon Industrial Exhibition, illustrated in the exhibition guide; from *Maeilsinbo*, 3 September 1915.

Government-General of Korea. Both governments promoted the exhibition heavily, and more than one million people (mainly from Japan and Korea, but also from China and the West) travelled to Seoul to see it.[7] The exhibition lasted fifty days, with the closing ceremony celebrating the Japanese emperor's birthday on 31 October 1915.

It is generally accepted that the main purpose of the Joseon Industrial Exhibition was to legitimize Japan's colonization of Korea. To show how Korea had developed during its first five years of colonial rule, the exhibition displays used graphics, statistics, photos, and models to present a wide range of topics, from agricultural products to social systems. It has also been argued that Japan used the exhibition to reinforce its political presence in Gyeongbok Palace by creating deliberate contrasts between traditional (Korean) architecture and modern (Japanese) architecture.[8] Most of the palace's traditional buildings were demolished for the exhibition, leaving only a few to contrast the new Western-style pavilions. This architectural contrast was illustrated in the official exhibition poster, which juxtaposed the palace's traditional buildings and the modern Exhibition Hall No. 1.

Many art and architecture historians have argued that the Government-General intentionally placed Exhibition Hall No. 1 (Ilhogwan, the largest new pavilion in the exhibition) directly in front of Geunjeongjeon (the most iconic traditional palace building) in order to "beautify" the occupation. They claimed that this stark visual contrast showed visitors the core idea of Japanese colonial propaganda: that the modern is superior to the traditional.

They also claimed that the new, monumental Railway Hall (Cheoldogwan) was situated so that it would overwhelm Gwanghwamun, the main south gate of Gyeongbok Palace. Railway Hall's bright appearance also contrasted visually with the much darker Gwanghwamun.

The architecture of the Joseon Industrial Exhibition has been interpreted only as an attempt by Japan to legitimize its colonization of Korea. Most existing scholarship on the subject asserts that the new Western-style pavilions were intended only to create visual contrasts with the Korean palace architecture, showing that the modern is superior to the traditional. This Orientalist perspective implies that the traditional is old and decayed (i.e., inferior), and therefore should be devalued or rejected; however, other intentions in the architectural and urban design of this

Fig. 7.3 The official poster for the Joseon Industrial Exhibition; from *Keijokyousangkaihokoku*. This image is commonly used to support the proposition that the modern buildings were intended to appear superior to the traditional buildings.

Fig. 7.4 Below Postcard showing Exhibition Hall No. 1 (Ilhogwan, centre) and Geunjeongjeon (far right); reprint courtesy of Publishing Company Minsokwon.

Fig. 7.5 Postcard showing Railway Hall (Cheoldogwan, centre) and Gwanghwamun (right); reprint courtesy of Publishing Company Minsokwon.

1915 exhibition become evident if we consider the concurrent efforts by Japan to construct its own history[9] (*toyoshi*[10]) by incorporating Asian and Korean traditions. These efforts began during the early Meiji period (mid-nineteenth century) and were intended to confront the West. Before then, Japan's concept of history was conservative rather than progressive. Japan was content to record accomplishments, without interpreting them as signs of progress. To advance Japanese culture on the world stage, the Meiji government had to construct a progressive Japanese history from its earlier traditions. During the second half of the nineteenth century, the Japanese began to look for their ethnic origins in Asia and to construct their own historical narratives, emulating Western history. The efforts of Shogoro Tsuboi, the first Japanese anthropologist, were notable during this period.[11] To discern the origins of Japanese architecture, Japanese historians started exploring Asian (mainly Chinese Buddhist) architectural traditions, not only to construct Japanese architectural history but also to define Japanese architecture in the late nineteenth century.

Japanese interest in traditional Asian Buddhist architecture had been extended to the Korean peninsula before Japan annexed Korea in 1910. In the early 1900s, ancient Korean art and architectural traditions were studied, classified, and even celebrated by major Japanese architectural historians. Their efforts continued during the colonial period, with support from the Japanese Government-General of Korea.

Consequently, traditional Korean architecture should be understood not only from an Orientalist perspective, as the opposite of "modern," but also as part of a larger Japanese historical narrative in which "the traditional" plays an important role in the development of modernity.[12] As I will show, the modern potential of "the traditional" is evident in the architecture of the Joseon Industrial Exhibition. To understand this, it is important to recognize one of Japan's major architectural historians, Tadashi Sekino, and his research in the Korean peninsula, which began in the early twentieth century.

TADASHI SEKINO AND KOREAN ARCHITECTURAL TRADITIONS

Tadashi Sekino (1867–1935) was an assistant professor at Tokyo Imperial University. For many years, he had worked for the Japanese government as a promising architectural historian. Beginning in 1901, Sekino collaborated with his colleague Chuta Ito (1867–1954)[13] to do research on Asian (mainly Chinese Buddhist) architectural traditions, to discern the historical origins of Japanese architecture. Sekino's collaboration with Ito continued throughout his life, including architectural exhibits for the Japan-British Exhibition in London in 1910, which promoted Japanese architecture to an English audience.

Sekino also had a close relationship with Kakuzo Okakura (1862–1913). After training as an art historian under Ernest Fenollosa,[14] Okakura contributed to the historicism of traditional Japanese art and architecture; however, his research was even more ambitious, declaring that "Japan is a receptor of all phases of Asiatic civilization."[15] The nationalistic sensation caused by Okakura's historicism prompted his ideas to be used in major Japanese art displays in the West at the end of the nineteenth century, particularly in the art exhibition in the Phoenix Hall at the 1893 World's Columbian Exposition and in the Japanese art history book, *Histoire de l'art du Japon.*[16]

Okakura was a major figure in Japanese academic circles, especially in the Tokyo School of Fine Arts (Tokyo Bijutsu Gakko), the first Japanese fine arts academy. His historical perspective influenced Sekino and Ito's research on the origins and developments of Japanese architecture, including

Sekino's scholarship on Chinese Buddhist architectural traditions and the architecture of the ancient Korean (Buddhist) dynasties.

In 1902, Kingo Tatsuno, the architecture department head of Tokyo Imperial University, assigned Sekino to investigate ancient Korean art and architectural traditions. This was Sekino's first architectural study in Korea. Tatsuno asked him to cover as much of Korea as possible in a short amount of time. Sekino chose to focus on several ancient cities with many remains and relics, such as Kyungju (the seat of the Shilla dynasty, 57 BCE–935 CE), Gaesung (the seat of the Koryo dynasty, 918–1392), and Seoul (the seat of the Joseon dynasty, 1392–1897). Sekino completed his mission in sixty-two days, and in 1904 he published his report, *Joseon Kenchiku Chosa Hokoku* (Report on Korean Architecture).

After completing this first on-site research, Sekino was hired in 1909 by the Japanese resident-general of Korea to continue exploring Korean "ancient structures."[17] He published his results in two journals: *Karamomiji* (December 1909) and *Joseon Geijutsuno Genkyu* (Study on Korean Art) (August 1910). Following the Japanese annexation of Korea in 1910, Sekino continued his investigations there with the full support of the Government-General. Starting in 1916, Sekino also participated in the preservation of ancient Korean remains and relics, a project commissioned by the Government-General, and worked with professors from Tokyo Imperial University and Kyoto Imperial University. Sekino's efforts under the Government-General were consolidated in the fifteen volumes of *Joseon Koseki Zifu* (Album of Korean Ancient Remains), published between 1914 and 1935. In 1932, Sekino published the first history book on Korean art and architecture, *Joseon Bijutsu-Shi* (The History of Korean Art), summarizing his entire research career in Korea since the early 1900s.

Sekino's last publication, *Joseon Bijutsu-Shi* (1932), includes a very interesting diagram that demonstrates his understanding of ancient Korean remains and relics. This diagram shows Asian art flowing from Greece to Japan, via Persia, India, China, and Korea. It recalls an earlier idea about culture flowing from the West to the East, which Chuta Ito (Sekino's previous collaborator) had presented in *Horyuji Kenchikuron* (Discourse on the Architecture of Horyuji), the first historical paper on Japanese architecture. Sekino's historical perspective had much in common with Ito's; his interest in Korea was driven by the same desire to trace Asian origins of Japanese architecture. This intention was stated

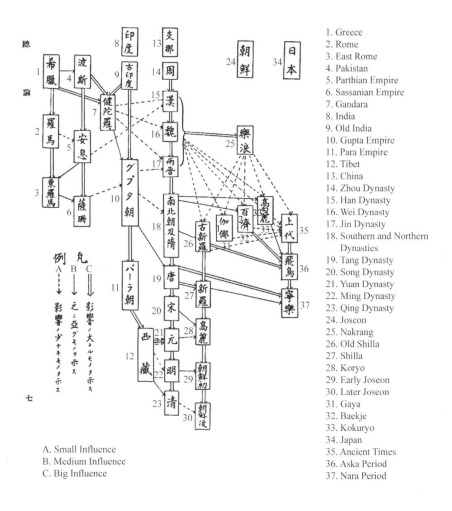

1. Greece
2. Rome
3. East Rome
4. Pakistan
5. Parthian Empire
6. Sassanian Empire
7. Gandara
8. India
9. Old India
10. Gupta Empire
11. Para Empire
12. Tibet
13. China
14. Zhou Dynasty
15. Han Dynasty
16. Wei Dynasty
17. Jin Dynasty
18. Southern and Northern Dynasties
19. Tang Dynasty
20. Song Dynasty
21. Yuan Dynasty
22. Ming Dynasty
23. Qing Dynasty
24. Joseon
25. Nakrang
26. Old Shilla
27. Shilla
28. Koryo
29. Early Joseon
30. Later Joseon
31. Gaya
32. Baekje
33. Kokuryo
34. Japan
35. Ancient Times
36. Aska Period
37. Nara Period

A. Small Influence
B. Medium Influence
C. Big Influence

Fig. 7.6 Diagram showing directions of artistic influence from Greece to Japan, via Persia, India, China, and Korea (with English legend added); from Tadashi Sekino, *Joseon Bijutsu-Shi* (1932), 7.

also in the conclusion of Sekino's first publication, *Joseon Kenchiku Chosa Hokoku* (Report on Korean Architecture), which discusses architectural relationships among Japan, Korea, and China. The contents of *Joseon Bijutsu-Shi* (1932) are almost the same as those of *Joseon Kenchiku Chosa Hokoku* (1904), showing that Sekino's primary intentions remained consistent throughout his research career in Korea. Arguing that Japanese architecture was a development from Greek architecture, as Ito had claimed with his famous image from 1893, Sekino also wanted to assert Japan's superiority over the West.

In constructing his history of Asian architecture in both *Joseon Kenchiku Chosa Hokoku* and *Joseon Bijutsu-Shi*, Sekino devoted considerable attention to the early Buddhist art and architecture of the Shilla period (57 BCE–935 CE) and especially the Unified Shilla period (668–935). He argued that the most prestigious Buddhist civilization was developed during these two periods under the consecutive influences of the Han, Northern, Southern, and Tang dynasties in China.[18] Noting that cultural connections among China, Korea, and Japan occurred frequently during these periods, he suggested that the eighth-century Bulguksa temple in Korea was the most developed Buddhist architecture from the Unified Shilla period: "The temple formation (arrangements) of Bulguk-sa imitated that of the Tang dynasty and it is also very similar to the temples in the Japanese Nara period."[19]

Sekino's observations of later art and architecture during the Joseon dynasty included comparisons not only to the previous Korean Buddhist

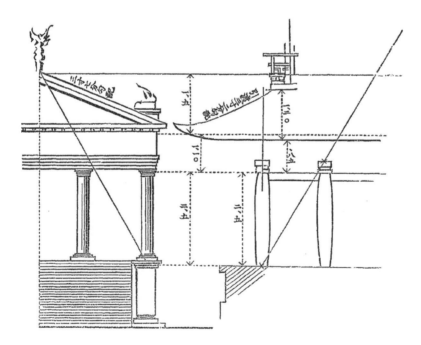

Fig. 7.7 Chuta Ito's comparison of Horyuji (Japan) and an Etruscan temple; from *Kenchiku Zassi* 83 (November 1893): 326.

施装 ノ 門大南

Fig. 7.8 Namdaemun (a city gate in Seoul), decorated to become part of the urban procession to the exhibition; from *Shiseigonenkinen Chosen butsankyoushinkai houkokusho* (The 1915 Exhibition Official Report), vol. 3. Visitors from other cities followed the route from Seoul Railway Station to Namdaemun, then to the main entry boulevard leading to the exhibition.

dynasties, but also to the Chinese dynasties.[20] He commented that early Joseon art and architecture was influenced by the Ming dynasty in China (1368–1644) but later declined as the Chinese influence diminished.[21] Sekino noted some formal similarities – but no direct cultural relation – between Joseon architecture and concurrent Japanese architecture.[22] In the architecture of the early Joseon period, Sekino most admired Seoul's Namdaemun and Gaesung's Namdaemun (fourteenth-century city gates), believing that the architecture of the time clearly showed the Joseon period's historical links not only to Koryo, the previous Korean period, but also to the Kamakura and Muromachi eras in Japan and the Song and Yuan periods in China.[23]

Sekino also admired Joseon palace architecture, comparing it to Japanese palace architecture and to the Tang and Song archetypes.[24] He compared the architecture of Gyeongbok Palace (where the Joseon Industrial Exhibition of 1915 later would be located) to Koryo Palace in Gaesung, the Forbidden City in Beijing, and Daminggong in Changan.[25] Sekino also complimented the beauty of individual buildings in Gyeongbok Palace, mainly Gwanghwamun (the south gate) and Geunjeongjoen (the throne hall). He declared that "Gwanghwamun is the most out-standing architecture among the hundreds of buildings in Gyeongbok Palace and it has the highest quality and is very beautiful."[26] However, his assessment of Geunjeongjeon was mixed: he praised its form, colour, balance, and harmony, but criticized its building methods and techniques.[27]

Sekino's study of Namdaemun, Gwanghwamun, and Geunjeongjeon as part of a series of architectural developments from China via Korea to Japan appears also in *Toyo Kenchiku* (Asian Architecture), which he published with Chuta Ito in 1925. This publication categorizes various Asian architectural traditions into several groups, based on their formal similarities. Here, Joseon architecture is included in the category of Chinese architecture, which in turn influenced the development of Japanese architecture. Sekino understood early Joseon architecture not just as a local Korean architecture but as part of a larger Asian historical context.

THE HISTORICAL DISPLAY OF KOREAN ARCHITECTURAL TRADITIONS IN THE JOSEON INDUSTRIAL EXHIBITION OF 1915

Tadashi Sekino's extensive research on Korean art and architectural traditions contributed a great deal to the development of the Japanese Government-General Museum. The museum was proposed by the first resident-general, Hirobumi Ito, and initiated by the first governor-general, Masatake Terauchi, as the Art Museum (Misulgwan) for the 1915 exhibition. An enthusiastic lover of Korean art and architecture, Terauchi wanted not only a permanent exhibition space for artifacts, but also a research institute to conduct future archeological investigations in Korea. He also purchased many ancient Korean artworks for the museum's collection.

The Art Museum built for the 1915 exhibition was the first step in establishing a more permanent Government-General Museum, which opened on 1 December the same year.[28] To prepare for the opening of the Art Museum, many Korean artifacts from various periods were transported to the museum and exhibited both inside and outside. The entire exhibition grounds were used as exhibition space.[29] Sekino's historical perspective guided the organization of the exhibits inside Art Museum, as well as the outdoor displays throughout the exhibition grounds, amidst the historically important Joseon palace architecture. Many Buddhist

Fig. 7.9 Top Geunjeongjeon (the throne hall) in the exhibition grounds; from the 1915 Exhibition Official Report, vol. 3.

Fig. 7.10 Bottom Postcard showing Art Museum (Misulgwan), built for the Joseon Industrial Exhibition; from the 1915 Exhibition Official Report, vol. 3.

artifacts (mainly from the Shilla and the Unified Shilla dynasties) were displayed in chronological order inside the museum, while relocated Buddhist statues and pagodas were arranged in its front garden. The organization of these displays implied that Japan and Korea shared ancient origins. This was an important part of Japan's political attempt to legitimize its colonial rule in Korea.[30] It is easy to see here that Sekino's historical perspective (his tracing of historical developments from China to Japan via Korea) was applied by taking into account the limited developments of Korean (Buddhist) art and architectural traditions (with their cultural decline during the Joseon period) and their shared culture with Japan in ancient times.

The 1915 exhibition included an axial procession that incorporated elements of the existing palace into a larger historical narrative. New, oversized models of ancient Buddhist pagodas were placed along the boulevard leading to Gwanghwamun, the main palace gate. According to Sekino, Gwanghwamun is one of the most important examples of Joseon palace architecture. Sekino celebrated the architecture of the palace for its historical connections to other palaces from previous Korean dynasties, as well as earlier Chinese and Japanese periods. The boulevard continued through Gwanghwamun, the main gate, to the entry plaza inside the exhibition grounds. This plaza was designed as a modern square with a splendid fountain in the middle. Two modern Western-style pavilions, Exhibition Hall No. 1 and Railway Hall, stood nearby, the latter with an observation deck and an obelisk on top. This urban procession, beginning with Buddhist pagodas, proceeding through the Gwanghwamun palace gate, and arriving at modern Western architecture, symbolized the shared architectural history of Korea and Japan, as well as their current shared position under the Japanese rule of Korea.

The procession from Gwanghwamun (the south gate) to Exhibition Hall No. 1 and then Geunjeongjeon (the throne hall) was intended as an urban sequence, not a visual contrast. In the Official Report on the 1915 Exhibition, these intentions were clearly laid out: "Circulation was suggested from Gwanghwamun to Geunjeongjeon through ... Exhibition Hall No. 1, and the architectural form of ... Exhibition Hall No. 1 was designed to accommodate it."[31]

Exhibition Hall No. 1 was the first building that visitors saw after entering the exhibition grounds. With Exhibition Hall No. 1 in the foreground and Geunjeongjeon in the background, blending the new with the

景　全　ノ　門　化　光

Light d "Ka uga" Lant rns i lumined at the "Kōkwa Gate."
(行發社信河見朝)

光化門外春日燈籠の夜景

Fig. 7.11 Top Postcard showing the Buddhist pagoda models along the main boulevard leading to the Exhibition; reprint courtesy of Publishing Company Minsokwon.

Fig. 7.12 Bottom Postcard showing the Buddhist pagoda models and Gwanghwamun (palace gate) at night; reprint courtesy of Publishing Company Minsokwon.

The "Kokwa Gate" and Special Hall building for Emperial Railway.   館設特道鐵と門化光
［朝鮮寫眞通信社發行］

Fig. 7.13 Postcard showing the entry plaza, with a fountain in the middle, Railway Hall
on the left, and Gwanghwamun (south gate) on the right; reprint courtesy of Publishing
Company Minsokwon.

Fig. 7.15 Below The urban procession from the entry boulevard (far right) through
Gwanghwamun (south gate, right) to Exhibition Hall No. 1 (middle) and the forecourt
of Geunjeongjeon (the throne hall, left); from the 1915 Exhibition Official Report, vol. 3.

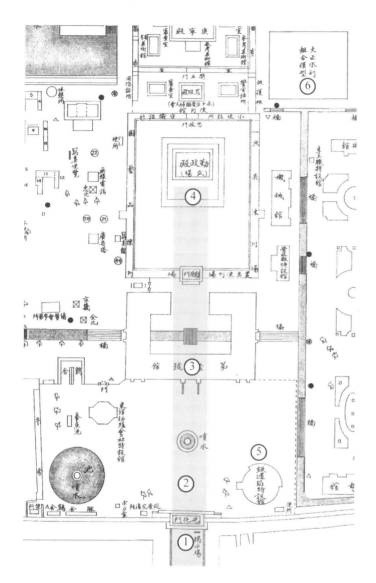

Fig. 7.14 Plan showing the urban procession from Gwanghwamun (south gate) across the entry plaza, and through Exhibition Hall No. 1 to Geunjeongjeon (the throne hall), with graphics added; from the 1915 Exhibition Official Report, vol. 1.

Legend:
1 Gwanghwamun; 2 Main Entry Plaza; 3 Exhibition Hall No. 1; 4 Geunjeongjeon; 5 Railway Hall; 6 Art Museum

Fig. 7.16 Exhibition Hall No. 1, with Geunjeongjeon (the throne hall) behind, showing how the two building forms are related; from *Chosen Ihou* (October 1915).

old, this architectural juxtaposition could be seen from the observation deck of Gwanghwamun, as well as from the outdoor terrace of Railway Hall. Together, they symbolized a shared future for Korea and Japan.

The arrival sequence leading to the exhibition, from the entry boulevard to the main gate and into the plaza, is evident also in the cover image of the Official Report on the 1915 Exhibition, published soon after it closed. Framed by Western-style columns that seem to be from the Art Museum, this layered image arranges three objects in chronological order but at different scales: the traditional Korean window frame in front, the flying Bicheon (Buddhist angels) in the middle, and Exhibition Hall No. 1 at the back. The image presents a historical progression that is evident in the urban procession to the exhibition, as well as the historical exhibitions in the Art Museum.

It is not enough to say that the architecture of the 1915 Joseon Industrial Exhibition was intended to produce a dramatic visual contrast between Western-style architecture and Korean palace architecture, as suggested by recent scholarship. The ancient Korean artifacts and the new exhibition pavilions also were carefully placed in relation to the Joseon architecture of Gyeongbok Palace to create an integrated historical composition. The architecture of the 1915 exhibition symbolized Japan's political intention to incorporate Korean art and architectural traditions into a new colonial history.

Fig. 7.17 Cover image from the 1915 Exhibition Official Report, vol. 1.

NOTES

1 Naoki Sakai, *Sa-san-doe-neun Il-bon-eo, Il-bon-in* (The Stillbirth of Japanese Language / People), trans. Deuk-Jae Lee (Seoul: Moon-hwa-gwa-hak-sa, 2003), 61.

2 Ibid., 191.

3 Alberto Pérez-Gómez, "Architecture as Embodied Knowledge," *Journal of Architectural Education* 40, no. 2 (1987): 57–8.

4 Japan's regional government ruled the entire Korean peninsula from 1910 until the end of the Second World War in 1945.

5 Geunjeongjeon, located on the north–south axis of Gyeongbok Palace, had symbolized the authority of the Joseon king. By choosing Geunjeongjeon as the site for the opening ceremony of the exhibition, Japan reinforced its occupation of Korea.

6 During the entire colonial period, there were three Joseon Government-General–sponsored exhibitions in Seoul: the Joseon Industrial Exhibition of 1915, the Joseon Exposition of 1929, and the Joseon Grand Exposition of 1940. The first two were held in Gyeongbok Palace and the last one was held on the outskirts of Seoul.

7 The number of visitors was reported in the Government-General–sponsored newspaper, *Maeilsinbo*, on 1 November 1915. See also *Shiseigonenkinen Chosen butsankyoushinkai houkokusho* (The 1915 Exhibition Official Report) (Keijo: Chosen Shotokufu, 1916), 1:271–3.

8 The following studies take this approach: Kal Hong, "Modeling the West, Returning to Asia: Shifting Politics of Representation in Japanese Colonial Expositions in Korea," *Comparative Studies in Society and History* 47, no. 3 (2005): 507–31; and Kal Hong, *Aesthetic Constructions of Korean Nationalism: Spectacle, Politics, and History* (New York: Routledge, 2011), 18.

9 Here I use the concept of history in the pragmatic sense described by Hannah Arendt: "a 'subjective' factor is introduced into the 'objective' processes of nature." Hannah Arendt, *Between Past and Future* (New York: Penguin, 1977), 48. "For us, on the other hand, history stands and falls on the assumption that the process in its very secularity tells a story of its own and that, strictly speaking, repetitions cannot occur." Ibid., 67.

10 *Toyoshi* literally means "the eastern-sea history."

11 On Japanese anthropological efforts to overcome the West, see Oguma Eiji,

A Genealogy of 'Japanese' Self-images, trans. David Askew (Melbourne: Trans-Pacific Press, 2002), chap. 1.

12 According to Octavio Paz, "modernity is never itself. It is always the other. The modern is characterized not only by novelty but by otherness." *Children of the Mire: Modern Poetry from Romanticism to the Avant-Garde* (Cambridge, MA: Harvard University Press, 1974), 1. In this sense, architectural modernity may be characterized as ceaseless change, without being fixed in a particular form or style.

13 "Ito Chuta's work on Horyuji, *Horyuji Kenchikuron* (1898), is generally regarded as the first Japanese architectural history paper." Akira Nakanishi, "Han-gook-geon-chook-cho-sa-bo-go-seo-e Bo-i-neun Sekino Tadashi eui Han-gook-geon-chook-gwan" (On Sekino Tadashi's Viewpoints of Korean Architecture in the 'Research Report on the Korean Architecture'), *Geon-chook-yok-sa-yon-gu* 13, no. 37 (2004): 22.

14 Ernest Fenollosa went to Japan in 1878 to teach philosophy (including Descartes and Hegel) and political science; however, he became very interested in traditional Japanese arts. For more information, please see Kojin Karatani, "Japan as Museum: Okakura Tenshin and Ernest Fenollosa," trans. Sabu Kohso, in *Japanese Art After 1945: Scream Against the Sky* (New York: Harry N. Abrams, 1994), 33–9.

15 Okakura Kakuzo, *The Ideals of the East* (London: J. Murray, 1903), 12.

16 Yoshio Ki et al., *Histoire de l'art du Japon: ouvrage publié par la Commission impériale du Japon à l'Exposition universelle de Paris, 1900* (Paris: M. de Brunoff, 1900).

17 Tadashi Sekino later summarized his Korean studies in *Ancient Remains and Relics in Korea: Efforts Toward Research and Preservation* (Tokyo: The Japan Council of the Institute of Pacific Relations, 1931).

18 Tadashi Sekino, *Joseon Mi-sul-sa* (Korean Art History), trans. Woosung Shim (Seoul: Dong-moon-sa, 2003), 144.

19 Ibid., 170.

20 See Tadashi Sekino, *Han-kook-eui Geon-chook-gwa Ye-sul* (Korean Architecture and Art), trans. Bongjin Kang (Seoul: Weol-gan Geon-chook-moon-hwa, 1990), 470.

21 Sekino, *Joseon Mi-sul-sa* (Korean Art History), 278.

22 Sekino, *Han-kook-eui Geon-chook-gwa Ye-sul* (Korean Architecture and Art), 469.

23 Ibid., 468.

24 Ibid., 469.

25 Ibid., 316.

26 Ibid., 293–4.

27 Ibid., 307.

28 "Many temporary pavilions were constructed for the 1915 Exhibition, however only Art Museum was built as a permanent structure ... In December, it was re-opened as the Government-General Museum with the collections gathered for the Exhibition." Seong-Si Lee, *Man-deul-eo-jin Go-dae* (An Invention of the Ancient: East Asian Story of Modern Nation-State) (Seoul: Sa-min, 2001), 278–9.

29 Lee, *Man-deul-eo-jin Go-dae* (An Invention of the Ancient), 278–9.

30 Although this anthropological idea about a shared origin was used by Japan to legitimize its occupation of Korea in 1910, this idea was developed earlier, around the end of the nineteenth century.

31 *Shiseigonenkinen Chosen butsankyoushinkai houkokusho* (The 1915 Exhibition Official Report), 1:54.

Silence and Communal Ritual in an Athonian Coenobitic Monastery

Christos Kakalis

Chora

THIS ESSAY STUDIES conditions of silence in the Gregoriou monastery at Mount Athos, a mountainous peninsula in northeastern Greece, a UNESCO World Heritage Site since 1988, and one of the most important contemporary pilgrimage sites. My fieldwork there in 2010–12, supported by secondary sources, notes how the community faces challenges to preserve the silence that is needed for its ascetic meditation.[1] The entire monastery is not silent at all times. Rituals performed by the eighty monks sometimes occur in the open spaces, temporarily breaking the silence with planned religious messages. Meanwhile, visitors often intrude on the monastery's religious atmosphere. This essay studies the choreography of these various conditions.

SILENCE, COMMUNAL RITUALS, AND HESYCHAST INHABITATION

All of the Athonian coenobitic monasteries share architectural characteristics that date back to their origin in the fourth century, during the Byzantine era.[2] A row of buildings around the perimeter encloses courtyards in which the main church (*katholikon*) is placed. The refectory is usually in the west part of the monastery, near the main entrance of the church, as these two spaces are linked liturgically in daily rituals.[3] The monks' cells are distributed around the perimeter in buildings called *kordes*.[4] Although the elements of the Athonian monasteries are similar, their layouts were adapted to the irregular topography of the mountainous peninsula. This is evident in the Gregoriou monastery, built on top of a hill on the west side of Mount Athos.

The Gregoriou monastery is not just an assembly of built and natural spaces but also a narrative that coordinates various groups and activities, including silent meditation, communal rituals, and the movement of strangers.[5] Its more public spaces accommodate communal actions, whereas the more private ones shelter the personal *ascesis* of the monks. Throughout the monastery, there is a reciprocity between the communal and the individual. This is evident in the spatio-temporal relation between the monastery and the monk's cell, between the church and the monk's stall, and between the refectory and the monk's seat. This essay focuses on the first pair: the monastery and the monk's cell. It also examines how outsiders are governed by rules that were set out in Byzantine foundational documents and continue to guide the life of the community.

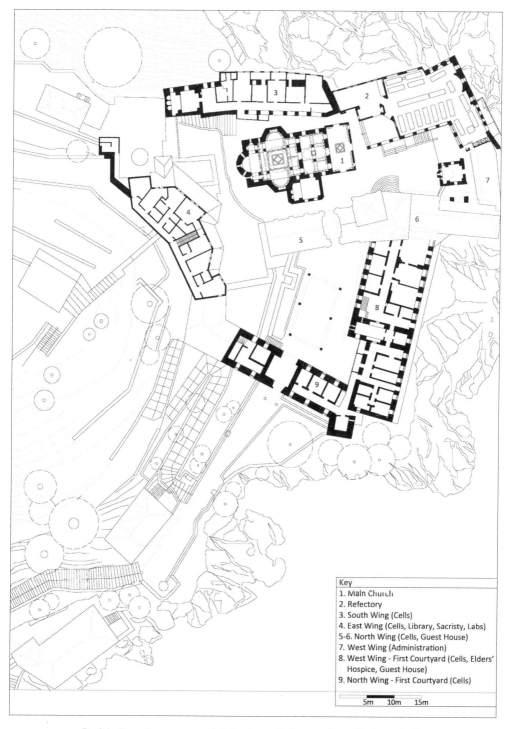

Key
1. Main Church
2. Refectory
3. South Wing (Cells)
4. East Wing (Cells, Library, Sacristy, Labs)
5-6. North Wing (Cells, Guest House)
7. West Wing (Administration)
8. West Wing - First Courtyard (Cells, Elders'
   Hospice, Guest House)
9. North Wing - First Courtyard (Cells)

5m   10m   15m

Fig. 8.1 Gregoriou monastery (all drawings and photographs are by the author).

Fig. 8.2 Gregoriou monastery.

The shared realm of the monastery can be understood as an "atmosphere."[6] According to philosopher Gernot Böhme, an "atmosphere ... is the reality of the perceived as the sphere of its presence and the reality of the perceiver, insofar as in sensing the atmosphere s/he is bodily present in a certain way."[7] Communal rituals, silent meditation, and the journey of the outsider engage a sacred site and its "atmosphere" through liminality ("limen" means threshold).[8] At this threshold, the monks and the visitors also encounter one another in an atmosphere that includes sounds, light, wind, incense, material objects, and human movements. Dissonant "outside" entities that transgress this atmosphere may be either expelled or incorporated harmoniously. Athonian monks practice hesychasm, an ascetic way of life that includes both intense private meditation and communal rituals. Hesychasm involves the silent recitation of the Jesus prayer ("Lord Jesus Christ Have Mercy upon me the sinner"), as well as other activities in daily life. For hesychasts, silence includes not only the elimination of dissonant sounds but also the elimination of visual appearances that may disturb the prayer. Although silence is maintained at most times, the community also conducts collective rituals in its open and enclosed spaces at regular times during the day and the year. These choreographed rituals produce a temporary, multisensory atmosphere through movements, chanting, reading, incense, and music from instruments.

Silence normally prevails in the courtyards. Sounds occur either as "tricksters" or as pre-defined ritual choreography. The elimination of noise and the normal absence of monks create an intense "void" feeling. Whenever monks appear in the courtyards, they usually walk quickly and bow their heads when passing strangers, maintaining the dual hesychast silence, both audible and visible. Still, the "void" inside the monastery is never really empty, as silence is a form of communication for the monks and the visitors, as we shall see later.

In *The World of Silence*, theologian Max Picard discusses how the embodied phenomenon of silence can transmit messages of holiness, memory, and anticipation.[9] He notes that silence is associated with nature, the night, and the hallowed space of cathedrals and museums.[10] Written in 1948, Picard's book also warns that silence risks being "contaminated" by the noise of modern technology.[11] Today, with our pervasive "telesthetic" activities, an examination of the hesychast atmosphere of Mount Athos may contribute to this academic discourse.[12] Gernot Böhme distinguishes between two types of human attention to sounds: one is "listening as such"; the other is "listening to" a specific source.[13] For the monks, silence pertains to the wider acoustic context ("listening as such") that enables them to experience ascetic solitude and an open relation to the natural environment. Böhme says, "In a listening which does not leap over ... sounds to the sources where they might stem from, listeners will sense ... sounds as modification of their own space of being. Human beings who listen in this way are dangerously open: they release themselves into the world and can therefore be struck by acoustic events."[14] This atmosphere changes suddenly when particular sounds invite one to *listen to* them.

The predefined daily and annual rituals are part of the monastery's "aural-scape." These liturgical performances commemorate religious events along a specific path that links various parts of the monastery. In his

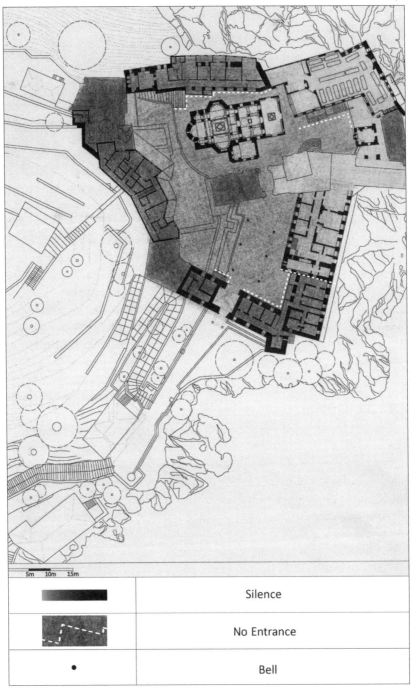

	Silence
	No Entrance
•	Bell

Fig. 8.3 Diagram of the "ideal" daytime soundscape of Gregoriou monastery. The wings with the monks' cells are the most silent parts of the monastery, insulated by additional layers of silence in the courtyard and by the exclusion of visitors who would disrupt the dual silence of sound and sight.

Fig. 8.4 Top The first courtyard of Gregoriou monastery.

Fig. 8.5 Bottom The second courtyard of Gregoriou monastery.

Fig. 8.6 The second courtyard of Gregoriou monastery.

discussion of atmospheres, Böhme mentions the staging of theatrical atmospheric phenomena with scenography and an attentive interaction of performers and observers;[15] however, this does not really apply to the processions in the Athonian monastery, as their rituals are not novel but thoroughly embedded in the community and the landscape. Instead, pauses or movements with different rhythms attract attention and participation.

Ritual processions were an intrinsic part of ancient Greek and Roman festivals, such as the Panathenaia, Dionysia, and Eleusinia. In forming a procession, a group of people distinguished themselves from the rest of the citizens.[16] By dancing, carrying objects, and singing hymns, their multisensory event ritualized the city by re-inscribing a particular route.[17] According to theologian John Baldovin, these processions expressed the urban character of Christian worship through stational liturgies that began during the early Christian period and are still evident in the liturgical practices of both Eastern and Western Christianity. According to him, a stational liturgy is "a service of worship at a designated church, shrine or public place in or near a city or town, on a designated feast, fast, or commemoration, which presides over by the bishop or his representative and intended as the local church's main liturgical celebration of the day."[18] Three litanies associated with Great Lent and Easter are held in Athonian monasteries each year: two are common in Eastern Christianity; the third (on Easter Monday) happens only on Mount Athos.

The first procession enacts the story of the Triumph of Orthodoxy. On the first Sunday of Great Lent, the Eastern Christian Church commemorates the victory of the iconodules over the iconoclasts with the decision of the Seventh Ecumenical Council. The restoration of the icons is celebrated throughout the day by a procession of priests, chanters, and faithful holding icons, flags, and lanterns. A similar ritual is conducted in the monastery on Mount Athos. It starts inside the church, at the opening in the screen (*iconostasis*) that divides the chancel from the nave. It proceeds out into the main courtyard of the monastery, follows a circular route around the church, and makes four stops along the way, one on each side of the building, where supplications are said. Finally, the procession returns inside the church to the *iconostasis*, symbolizing its importance in the liturgical life of the community.[19]

The second procession is conducted during the evening services on Good Friday, when the epitaph of Jesus Christ is held. *Epitaph* is a Greek word that means "on the grave" and refers to the lamentations during

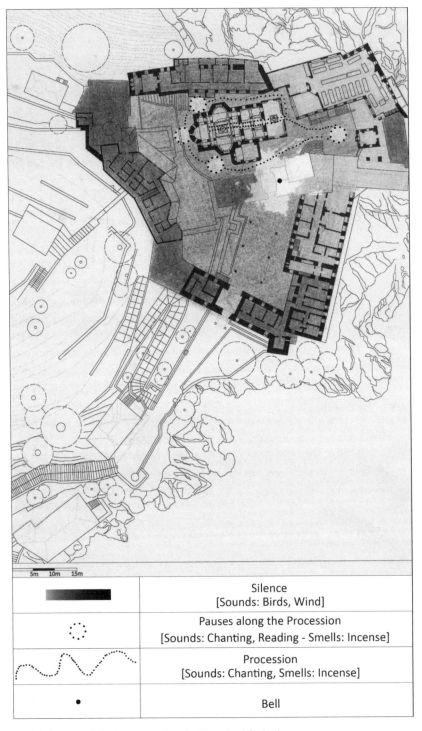

![gradient]	Silence [Sounds: Birds, Wind]
⋰⋱	Pauses along the Procession [Sounds: Chanting, Reading - Smells: Incense]
⋯⋯⋯	Procession [Sounds: Chanting, Smells: Incense]
●	Bell

Fig. 8.7 Diagram of the first procession, the Triumph of Orthodoxy.

the burial of a dead person. In the middle of the church, under the main dome, a bier symbolizes Christ's grave. On it is placed the epitaph: a richly embroidered cloth that represents the dead body of Christ.[20] After the "Lamentation upon the Grave" is chanted, the epitaph is lifted up by monks who are also priests, and a procession commemorates the burial of Christ and his movement towards Hades.[21] Monks carrying banners, lanterns, and metal depictions of cherubim are followed by the priest-monks (all dressed in liturgical uniform, with some carrying the epitaph) and chanters. They are followed by the rest of the monks and the laymen. This litany is held in both courtyards and includes four stops where supplications are said: for all of the dead monks of the monastery (in front of the south wing); for all Christians (in front of the north wing); for the political authorities (in the first courtyard); and for the donors of the monastery (in the chapel of Saint Anastasia). When the epitaph reaches the closed door of the church, the priest symbolically asks Hades to open the doors of the underworld for Christ to enter. The procession stops once more, in the narthex, where prayers are said for all the monasteries of the world. The epitaph is then held above the threshold so that the participants can pass under it, symbolizing Christians following Jesus's example. During this ritual, the bell rings in a funeral toll.

The third procession is a litany held in all monasteries on Mount Athos on either Easter Monday or Easter Tuesday to liturgically unite various places around the monastery.[22] At the end of the morning liturgy, the congregation exits the main church of Gregoriou monastery. Their order is similar to that in the epitaph procession, following the hierarchy of monastic roles. Holy relics, icons, banners, and candles are carried while psalms about the Resurrection are chanted. They depart through the main entrance of the monastery and ascend the footpath that leads to the cave of the founder of the monastery, St Gregory. They stop at the house of the vineyard (just above the monastery) and gather under a pergola to conduct the blessing of the waters, then return to the monastery and the main church. This blessed water is spread over the gardens, symbolizing both the regeneration of nature in spring and the spiritual regeneration of Christians celebrating Christ's resurrection. During the litany, the Canon of the Easter[23] is chanted and six stops are made to read supplications: for the dead monks of the monastery; for all the Christians of the world; for the participants of the litany; for the dead of the world; for the monks who live in the monastic structures that belong to the

![gradient bar]	Silence [Sounds: Birds, Wind]
⋰⋱	Pauses along the Procession [Sounds: Chanting, Reading - Smells: Incense]
∿∿∿	Procession [Sounds: Chanting - Smells: Incense]
●	Bell

5m   10m   15m

Fig. 8.8 Diagram of the second procession, on Good Friday.

monastery (*metochia*); and for the people (monks and laymen) who serve the monastery. The locations of these stops are not prescribed; they depend on how the *tepikaris* (the monk in charge of the rituals) divides the distance into seven parts.

Relying on the archetype of a journey, these circular rituals embody religious movement from the earthly sphere to the divine and back again. Religious liminality is expressed not only in their movement through spatial thresholds (the entrance of the main church and chapels, the entrance of the monastery, etc.) but also in how they change the aural environment at the stops along the route through the open spaces of the monastery. Each location has its own aural character that changes temporarily during a short service with reading, chanting, and censing. The various sounds penetrate the surrounding buildings and may even be heard by people down at the waterfront and along the footpath that leads to the monastery, especially during the third procession. The ringing of the bell (in either a funeral toll or a joyful toll) extends well beyond the monastery, informing everyone of the progress of the procession. The monks participate actively in all of these events: as celebrants, chanters, or simply members of the procession.

In addition to these litanies on special days, a ritualized series of sounds each day marks the progress of the monastery's liturgical program and invites the monks to participate. In this sense, the monastic cell is not just a space of silence but also a space of aural communication, as these sounds carry through the perimeter wall of the courtyard and into the cells beyond. Through its openings, each monk's cell is connected to the rest of the community. The monk's personal prayer reflects community life, and vice versa. Silent meditation is an embodied language that is shared when the monks are in the church, in the refectory, and even in their individual cells. The whole monastery is effectively a field where silent discourse takes place.

In the cell, the monk conducts his daily silent prayer. Constant repetition of the Jesus Prayer is combined with the rhythms of breathing and the posture of the body. While praying, a monk may kneel and look to the sky or may be seated in a low stall and bow his head in a circular motion. Even if his body remains in the same place, an ascetic rhythmic pace promotes an embodied understanding of the divine. Rhythm and repetition of the prayer encourage an internal "listening as such."

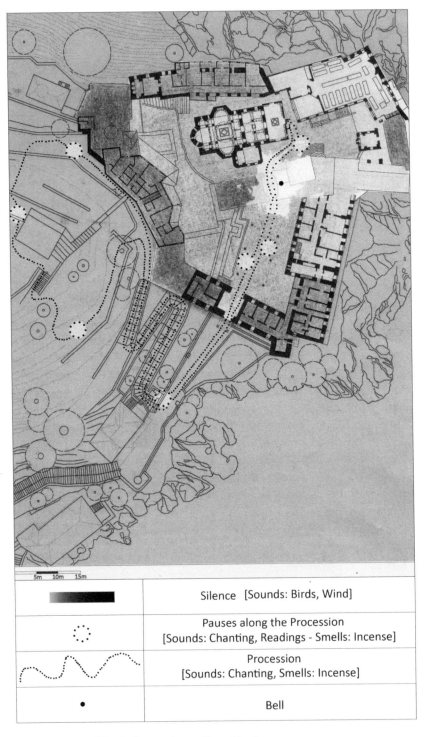

![gradient bar]	Silence [Sounds: Birds, Wind]
⋰⋱	Pauses along the Procession [Sounds: Chanting, Readings - Smells: Incense]
⌇⌇	Procession [Sounds: Chanting, Smells: Incense]
●	Bell

Fig. 8.9 Diagram of the third procession, on Easter Monday.

Each day, sounds in the courtyard inform the monks of communal rituals. They are made by four instruments that contribute dramatically to the liturgical life of the monastery: the *talanton* (τάλαντον), *semantron* (σήμαντρο), *kopanos* (κόπανος), and the bell.[24] One of the monks walks around the monastery, beating a *talanton* (a wooden board) with a wooden hammer to call the monks and visitors to attend a service. This symbolizes Noah's hammer: As "the noise made by Noah's carpentry reminded men of their danger from the flood," so the *talanton* calls monks to participate in the rituals in the church, the entrance to which will signal their possible salvation.[25] The beating usually follows the rhythmic repetition of the word *Adam*, reminding the monks of their fallen nature. A smaller metal *talanton*, called *semantron*, symbolizes the angel's trumpet that the "chosen ones" will hear on the Day of Judgment and also signals the monks to congregate, usually for Matins.

Fig. 8.10 The *kopanos* and the *semantron* of Gregoriou monastery.

At 03:30, the *talanton* and the *semantron* call the monks of Gregoriou monastery to the morning service that will begin in half an hour. Three *talanton* rites are held in the morning and the evening (before the Vespers): a circular movement in the two courtyards of the monastery; a circular movement around the main church; and a hammering of the *talanton* by the monk standing at the north side of the main church. The *talanton* defines its own thresholds, signalling the beginning and the different parts of the liturgies. Sound spreads throughout the whole monastery, conveying a certain message along a specific route around the main church. During the morning service the *talanton* also informs the devotees of the passing from the *Mesoniktiko* to Matins and from Matins to the Holy Mass, using sound to inscribe this liturgical form on the whole monastery. The movement of the monk and the sound creates an atmosphere that integrates different stories: the monastery and its surrounding landscape, the life of the monks, and the experience of the visitors.

According to Richard Coyne, repetitive sounds help demarcate a territory by creating a rhythmic sonic environment in which the individual can move and recognize its spatiality.[26] Monks in their cells listen to the repetitive sound of the *talanton* that becomes louder or softer, depending on where the monk with the *talanton* is walking. This sound reminds the monks of the service, as an alarm clock would do, but it also enables him to turn his attention acoustically towards the *katholikon* or the edges of the courtyard or to follow the progress of the liturgy, even if he is not in the church. The repetition gives him time to prepare for the service, while also being connected to the rest of the community that is hearing the sound. This repetition allows him to continue the silent recitation of his prayer, harmonizing his pace with the beatings of the *talanton*, together forming an atmospheric path that leads to the church. Bells also contribute to the soundscape of the monastery for both monks and visitors. They signal the different parts of the daily program for the monks by indicating the start of a ritual or a meal. Usually situated close to the church, the bell in the tower acoustically defines the sphere of the monastery by signalling the religious events taking place and by directing monks and visitors towards the church.[27] At dawn, in the twilight, one can see black figures of monks coming down from their cells, walking silently through the courtyards, and entering the church to find their "place" in the liturgy, in which their silent prayer will continue. Silence, their code of communication, defines boundaries that prohibit entry and loud speech.

	Silence
	No Entrance
••••••••••••••••	*Talanton* Route

5m   10m   15m

Fig. 8.11 The first *talanton* ritual.

	Silence
	No Entrance
••••••••••••••••	*Talanton* Route

Fig. 8.12 The second *talanton* ritual.

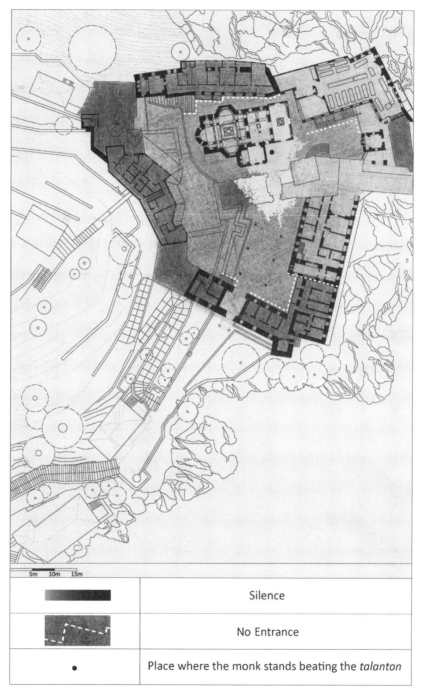

	Silence
	No Entrance
•	Place where the monk stands beating the *talanton*

Fig. 8.13 The third *talanton* ritual.

Sounds extend these boundaries outward, penetrating the built and nat-ural surroundings by inscribing a religious atmosphere onto them.

THE PRESENCE OF STRANGERS

Today, not all visitors to Mount Athos are pilgrims. People of different nationalities and religions visit this place with different motivations, departing temporarily from their everyday life. They are received by the Athonian community as potential pilgrims and are expected to abide by certain rules. At Gregoriou monastery the visitors stay at two guest hous-es: one above the monastery and one at the shore that was built during the 1990s to accommodate the increasing number of visitors.[28] During the summer, from sixty to a hundred visitors enter the monastery daily and are allowed to spend one night there. An extension is possible with the abbot's permission. The number falls to about twenty visitors per

Fig. 8.14 Right The water-front guest house of Gregoriou monastery.

Fig. 8.15 Opposite The upper guest house in the second courtyard of Gregoriou monastery.

day during the rest of the year. On the days of the monastery's main feasts, there are more than a hundred outsiders.[29] Orchestrating their presence is very important to avoid disturbing the hesychast life of the monastic community. Most visitors are allowed to attend services in the church, to dine in the refectory, and to visit the open spaces for a limited period of time.

Strangers have to keep silent while in the courtyards of the monastery. They are also not allowed to enter the open or enclosed spaces near the monks' cells. In some of the Athonian monasteries, non-Christian Orthodox visitors are refused admission to the main church during rituals. Instead, they can view the rituals from the exonarthex or stay outside. Signs are also used to forbid entry. In these ways, the audible and visible impact of strangers is controlled. Preserving the physical silence helps the monks conduct their silent meditation. Two kinds of silence are evident in the atmosphere of the coenobitic monastery: an imposed one ("being silenced") and a chosen one ("being silent"). The boundary between them sometimes acquires "border" characteristics.[30]

Visitors are allowed to attend communal rituals in the courtyards if they happen to be there. As observers of an unfamiliar performance, they can become either participants or audience. Pilgrims and religious tourists are more likely to participate in the religious processions, whereas cultural and recreational tourists usually remain distant, watching and listening aesthetically to the "picturesque" qualities of the procession.

In addition to the deliberate sounds that occur regularly in the monastery, the silence is sometimes interrupted by discussions between monks or visitors. This happens mainly during the summer, after the evening meal. The monks usually gather close to the main entrance or just outside it. The strangers also may sit on the benches in the first courtyard of the monastery. During the three years of my fieldwork, the noise at that time of day became more intense, changing the soundscape. The atmosphere also has been changed by communication devices such as mobile phones and the Internet, which are used by both visitors and monks. One of the monks who was allowed to have a mobile phone would "silently" text me during the afternoon to participate in an interview. Visitors also can send their observations of the monastery to the outside world. Although these actions do not break the silence of the monastery, they change how its space is perceived. This would become even more pronounced if the monks used mobile phones to communicate silently with one another or with the outside world. Changes in the perception of space that happened twenty years ago in the outside world are happening now on Mount Athos. Telecommunication is challenging the monastery's liminal zones and sacred atmosphere.

At 21:30 the bell rings, informing monks and visitors that sounds should stop in the monastery. The visitors return to their external guest house and the gate closes, restoring the silent canvas of the monastery that becomes even more intense at night. The only sounds are from the birds and the wind. Monks sometimes move silently through the courtyard to begin preparing meals for the next day or to finish another task. Darkness reinforces the silence of sound by introducing a "silence of sight." Together, they create an immaterial sphere of solitude in which the monks pray silently in their cells. Space and time become ambiguous in this nocturnal experience, as everything seems mysterious and remote.[31]

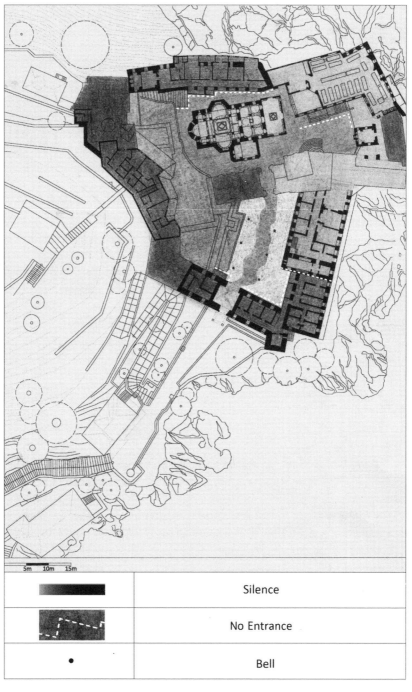

![silence gradient]	Silence
![no entrance]	No Entrance
●	Bell

5m 10m 15m

Fig. 8.16 Diagram of the soundscape of Gregoriou monastery after the evening Vespers (right), when monks and strangers spend time talking in the first courtyard and around the main entrance. This changes the usual soundscape, described in fig. 8.3.

The monk knows that this void is not empty but an ideal field for hesychast practice. Without vision, it is difficult for us to express ourselves through speech. We are inclined to whisper or to remain quiet and feel our surroundings through hearing, touch, and smell. The monks' nocturnal recitations of their prayer enable them to measure the passage from one day to the next, until the sound of the *talanton* invites them again to the morning liturgy.

NOTES

1 During fieldwork in August–September 2011 and September 2012, I observed how the monastery was used and experienced by monks and visitors. These observations were recorded in interviews, photographs, sketches, diagrams, video recordings, and sound recordings. Four archives provided drawings of the different building stages of the monastery.

2 See F.W. Hasluck, *Athos and its Monasteries* (London: Kegan Paul, Trench, Trubner, 1924), 92–114; and Patrick J. Quinn, "Drawing on Mount Athos: The Thousand-Year Lesson," *Places* 2, no. 1 (1985): 32–47.

3 The meals follow the daily services in the church.

4 *Korda* stems from the ancient Greek *chordè* (χορδή), a piece of string that joins the ends of an arc. It refers also to the perimeter buildings that surround the *katholikon*.

5 On narrative in Athonian topography, see Christos P. Kakalis, "Narrative and the Pilgrimage Topography of Mount Athos," in *Theoretical Currents II: Architecture and its Geographical Horizons* (conference proceedings, University of Lincoln, Lincoln, United Kingdom, April 2012), http://visit.lincoln.ac.uk/C18/C9/CDL/Document%20Library/Theoretical%20Currents%20II%20%20Full%20Paper%20-%20Christos%20Kakalis.pdf.

6 Gernot Böhme, "Atmosphere as the Fundamental Concept of a New Aesthetics," *Thesis Eleven* 36 (1993): 113–26.

7 Ibid., 122.

8 Victor and Edith Turner, *Image and Pilgrimage in Christian Culture* (New York: Columbia University Press, 1978). The authors connect liminality to pilgrimage procession. See also Arnold van Gennep, *The Rites of Passage* (London: Routledge, 1960).

9 Max Picard, *The World of Silence*, trans. Stanley Godman (London: Harvill Press, 1952), first published in German in 1948.

10 Ibid., 108, 141, 169.

11 Ibid., 198.

12 "Telesthetic" refers to the contemporary phenomenon of distant communication through media such as the Internet. See McKenzie Wark, *Telesthesia: Communication, Culture and Class* (Cambridge, UK: Polity Press, 2012), 25–38.

13 Gernot Böhme, "Acoustic Atmospheres: A Contribution to the Study of Ecological Aesthetics," *Soundscape: The Journal of Acoustic Ecology* 1, no. 1 (2000): 14–18.

14 Ibid., 18.

15 Gernot Böhme, "The Art of Stage Set as a Paradigm for an Aesthetics of Atmospheres," *Ambiances: International Journal of Sensory Environment, Architecture and Urban Space*, 19 Feb. 2013, paras. 12–14, http://ambiances. revues.org/315#text.

16 Walter Burkert, *Greek Religion: Archaic and Classical*, trans. John Raffan (Oxford: Basil Blackwell, 1985), 99. For the role of *pompe* in ancient Greek religion, see also Louise Bruit Zaidman and Pauline Schmitt Pantel, *Religion in the Ancient Greek City*, trans. Paul Cartledge (Cambridge: Cambridge University Press, 1992), 102–11.

17 Burkert, *Greek Religion*, 102.

18 John F. Baldovin, *The Urban Character of Christian Worship: The Origins, Development and Meaning of Stational Liturgy* (Rome: Pont. Institutum Studiorum Orientalium, 1987), 37.

19 The *iconostasis* is the most important boundary in the monastery, symbolizing the threshold between profane and sacred. This threshold is evident also in various rituals, especially the reception of the Holy Communion. The axis between the church entrance and the main door of the *iconostasis* also plays an important role in the procession.

20 Similar rituals are found in the Western Christian Church, such as the Anointing of the Body of Christ, held in South America (e.g., Vera Cruz).

21 The lamentations are included in the verses of Psalm 118. They are divided into three parts called *staseis* (stations). The first is signalled by censing. During the third, the priest sprinkles rose water and throws flower petals to recall the funeral procession.

22 The most important Easter Monday litany is held in the capital of Mount Athos, the small village-city of Karyes.

23 A collection of Easter psalms.

24 A *talanton* is a piece of wood about 2 metres long, 120 centimetres wide, and 30 millimetres thick. A *kopanos* is also a wooden instrument, about 3

metres long, 30 centimetres wide, and 15 centimetres thick. A *semantron* is a metal bar, usually placed next to the *kopanos*.

25 R.M. Dawkins, "Notes on Life in the Monasteries of Mount Athos," *Harvard Theological Review* 46, no. 4 (1953): 217–19.

26 Richard Coyne, *The Tuning of Place: Sociable Spaces and Pervasive Digital Media* (Cambridge, MA: MIT Press, 2010), 91–9.

27 For the acoustic perception of the bell, see Alain Corbin, "Auditory Markers of the Village," in *The Auditory Culture Reader*, ed. Michael Bull and Les Back (Oxford: Berg, 2004), 117–25.

28 "The Aim-Report for the Completion of the Onshore Guest House of the Holy Monastery of Gregoriou," Archives of K.E.D.A.K, 1987. This report confirms the increasing number of visitors in the monastery, especially during the summer (70 to 100 per day) and important feasts (200 on Saint Nicholas Day, 150 at Saint Anastasia Day, 150 on Easter Sunday, and 80 at Christmas). Despite the addition of the guest house, the situation is still quite difficult, with about 1,300 visitors per month during the summer, as recorded during my fieldwork there (around 35 to 45 per day).

29 This number was observed during fieldwork at Mount Athos in August–September 2011 and August 2012.

30 I often observed visitors being asked by the monks to stop talking the courtyards, as this annoyed some of them.

31 Walter Otto, *The Homeric Gods: The Spiritual Significance of Greek Religion*, trans. Moses Hadas (London: Thames & Hudson, 1979), 118–19, examines the role of Hermes as a nocturnal guide.

The Language of the Street:
A Vocabulary of Communal Space

Robert Nelson

Chora

THERE IS MUCH CONTENTION over the design and regulation of streets: what kind of buildings and businesses are allowed along them, how many vehicles and what type, how much their spaces afford cultural capital and create friendly pedestrian precincts, and what rights a citizen has to the space and even the sunlight.[1] There are also fervent environmental debates about the regulation of urban density, as sprawling automotive cities consume great amounts of fossil fuel. These debates consider what kinds of amenity or conservation should rise to priority, and therefore what kinds of streets a community will accept.[2]

Fig. 9.1 Samuel Halpert, *The Flatiron Building* (1919); The Metropolitan Museum of Art, Gift of Dr and Mrs Wesley Halpert, 1981 (1981.36).

Fig. 9.2 Canaletto, *Venice: Santa Maria della Salute* (ca 1750); The Metropolitan Museum of Art, Purchase, George T. Delacorte Jr. Gift, 1959 (59.38).

Whereas a building is largely the outcome of what its owner wants it to be, a street – especially one that is old and has been inherited after countless changes – is the result of dialectical compromise, often by people without an investment in it except as a highway. A street is regulated and conditioned largely by transitory stakeholders who use it to get somewhere else. Before the advent of mass transport, the pace and character of a street were decided by the people who built on it and lived there. Since then, many aspects of streets have been subordinated to the convenience of distant citizens, as the street has become owned by its traffic. Consequently, questions about what a street should look like and feel like, what it should express as well as serve, are conceptually fraught.[3]

This contentious situation can be traced to the obscure origins and chaotic history of concepts involving streets. To us, streets may seem to be a concrete reality, almost a timeless archetype, but the words used to describe them have been weak and fugitive, with few constants from epoch to epoch. Spatiality is seldom expressed accurately or evocatively in language, even though it is dialectical.[4] Without a meaningful vocabulary of spatial elements, it has become extremely challenging to analyze streets or to discuss how they might work better. It is ironic that we use the term "language of the street" when the street itself is so linguistically challenged, so pressed for expression (as I hope to show), and when its remote stakeholders have so little interest in its local ambience or meaning.

In this essay, I want to examine the historical gap in consciousness between what streets might mean to us and how we represent them pictorially and linguistically. Streets are among the most important areas of design for a community, yet the proverbial noise of the street bedevils our efforts to reflect on them in a cohesive way, unlike with buildings. Taking a somewhat archaeological view of the street, let us first consider the historical scarcity of streets in the visual arts.

Streets existed for many millennia before they were convincingly represented. The first evocative depictions of a street were made by Italian Renaissance artists in the late thirteenth century, such as Giotto. This quest for a stage set was continued by artists such as Masaccio, whose cycle of the *Miracles of St Peter* in the fifteenth century sets us firmly on the pavement.[5] In these masterful frescoes we can appreciate the measurements, lofty proportions, and spacious vistas of these urban façades.

Streets such as the ones that Masaccio depicted had existed long before his frescoes. We have archaeological remains of impressive streets in Greek and Roman times, but no pictorial record of what they looked like or felt like. Certain sculptures represent a procession of the people who walked on these streets, as in the Panathenaic frieze of the Parthenon and the senators and lictors on the Ara Pacis in Rome.[6] Although we recognize their urbane assembly along some imaginary urban corridor, the location is missing; only the actors are present in the abstract, shallow space of the relief sculptures.

A simple explanation might be that the necessary pictorial tools were not available because the art of perspective had not yet been invented. This technical reason seems credible in ancient Greece, where artists showed no interest in depicting space in either bas-relief or vase painting. The same cannot be said for ancient Rome, where painters created many views of interiors, as in the frescoes at Pompei. It seems strange that this spatial representation was not extended to streets, as Roman ruins retain evidence of elegant streets with neat paving and gentle layout.

Although the development of perspective promoted a recognition of streets in European visual art, the prior neglect of the street was due to a more fundamental weakness in the conceptualization of urban space. Streets had been depicted in paintings before the development of perspective, as in the *Allegory of Good Government* and *St Nicholas' Dowry* by Ambrogio Lorenzetti in the mid-fourteenth century.[7] It is likely that perspective was motivated by a desire to depict linear realities such as streets, rather than streets suddenly appearing in art because artists had developed perspective. The generations before Masaccio often depicted the external faces of buildings along a street, as in Duccio's *Jesus Opens the Eyes of a Man Born Blind* from his *Maestà*[8] and Giotto's *Homage of a Simple Man* in his St Francis cycle at Assisi. Both are from the early fourteenth century, antedating perspective by a century. The desire to represent the street anticipated the techniques for doing so systematically.

Despite the invention of perspective and the relative ease with which streets might have been depicted, streets are not very evident in the subsequent history of art. Outdoor scenes instead portrayed courtyards, gardens, and town squares. From the sixteenth century, even these fond locations were replaced by landscape scenes or indeterminate darkness. At the same time, architecture acquired great majesty, with the grand urban gestures of the Baroque celebrating their monarchies and the Church. Many European cities were stamped with impressive street patterns displaying grand symmetry.

Fig. 9.3 Canaletto, *Piazza San Marco* (ca 1728); The Metropolitan Museum of Art, Purchase, Mrs Charles Wrightsman Gift, 1988 (1988.162).

Although streets appeared in Dutch genre painting, their relative absence in Renaissance and Baroque painting shows that art and architecture responded to different cues. Earlier paintings, in the fourteenth century, had depicted streets mainly because their planes and perpendiculars added depth to their pictorial illusions. During the Renaissance, the challenge for painters was rather to portray an action in its own terms, often locating it in an imaginary and moody ruined antiquity. Illustrating a local or contemporary setting might have compromised the poetic ambition of the painter to evoke a holy or historical world beyond the present.

Eighteenth-century art introduced ancient and modern views, or *vedute*. With a growing attention to the cultural sights and wonders of the Mediterranean, Italy had become a favoured destination for travel, but its aristocratic tourist industry still did not produce a substantial corpus of streetscapes in painting. Insofar as urban spaces were depicted in any epoch before photography, they were typically expansive, comparable to the size of a town square. Venice became a popular subject for painting due to the generous horizontal disposition of water in front of its vertical façades, offering both compositional balance and pictorial depth.

The reluctance to paint streets might be related to what an artist once described to me as "the train problem."[9] From the front, a train appears as a very large and dominant locomotive, with a rapidly tapering perspective that sucks away all pictorial presence into a spatial funnel. The perspective might convey a sense of speed but it yields an ugly painting in which something very imposing slinks off into something unceremoniously diminished. An alternative is to view the train from afar, so that it resembles a distant snake, but this would lose the impressive experience of standing beside the train.

It was not until the late nineteenth century that streets became a vibrant subject for painters such as Monet and Pissarro. It was also a period of proliferation for photography, trains, and urban traffic. Ironically, the built-up street provided an ingenious aesthetic solution to the train problem, which may have been discovered by photographers such as Nadar before the Impressionist painters. Because the streets of most European cities are defined by two banks of four- to six-storey buildings, an upper balcony has a splendid view of the other side. The height and angle of the opposite bank slow the perspectival diminution, while the trees of the boulevard provide a felicitous fluffiness in atmospheric perspective.

Fig. 9.4 Camille Pissarro, *The Boulevard Montmartre on a Winter Morning* (1897); The Metropolitan Museum of Art, Gift of Katrin S. Vietor, in loving memory of Ernest G. Vietor, 1960 (60.174).

Rather than the far side of the street charging headlong toward the vanishing point, the wall of apartments recedes festively and disappears gradually into the distant haze.

With the advent of the automotive era, the photographic representation of streets grew exponentially, for two reasons. First, the camera enjoys the dramatically plunging perspectives from which painters resile; these dramatic angles, especially from high buildings, are themselves statements of modernity. Second, the skyscrapers and the narrow chasms between them are quintessentially modern. Influenced by documentary photography, we have come to expect a great profusion of activity in the streets, so that an advertisement for coffee beans or a film with urban content would be incomplete without a street scene. With some wonderful exceptions, such as Hopper and Balthus, twentieth-century painters tended to direct their attention away from daily life, leaving the street to amateurs whose work has become associated with tourist kitsch. The pictorial representation of streets thus has a patchy history: coincidental, fitful, oddly exiguous in periods of great architectural pride, and recently inconsequential in the ubiquitous backdrops of police dramas on TV.

Turning to the philological record, the representation of streets in words is not so different. Although we may assume that streets are a great constant in culture, they are relatively new. We have had streets for a much shorter time than we have had language or armies. Even the words by which we describe streets reveal uncertainty. In ancient Greek, for example, it is hard to think of a good word for street. We might think of "drome" (δρόμος), as in velodrome or aerodrome, but this word derives from the verb for running and was associated more with the course, the racetrack, and the hippodrome.[10] It could designate a street or colonnade, but always with the connotation of a run,[11] as in the Latin *cursus publicus*, which became the Italian *corso*, normally a large street with much hubbub.[12] Streets, in the customary sense of an urban corridor that connects dwellings, existed in the Mediterranean for aeons, but streets in the common Greek of antiquity were described using technical and metaphoric concepts such as "the widening" and "the broad flat" (πλατεία), a word that was carried into Latin and then Italian to become *piazza* and, in English, "place."[13] There is also the "way" (ρυμα), an inscrutable word that derives either from concepts of dragging or drawing along (perhaps inspired by carts pulled behind you) or, less likely, from a flow, as in a current of people.

These words appeared late in antiquity and were used interchangeably and somewhat arbitrarily, sometimes referring to corners.[14] "The broad flat" (πλατεία) might refer to a town square but perhaps not to a market (Greek αγορά; Latin *forum*), though it was definitely a place where one might teach, as we know from biblical passages in Luke.[15] There was also the road (οδός) that one might expect in the country.[16] But the road was for traversing, whereas the street was for standing, talking, being poor in – a context, a social and architectural nexus, a space for buildings to look at. In antiquity, the street – insofar as there was a word for it – did not connote movement or speed. It was above all a flat piece of land that existed to frame everything else and build a community. Conceiving a street as merely a thoroughfare seems modern.

However, the Latin *via*, by which Italian streets are still known, is the "way," the route: an action of traversing rather than a physical place. In

Fig. 9.5 Camille Pissarro, *Rue de l'Épicerie, Rouen* (1898); The Metropolitan Museum of Art, Purchase, Mr and Mrs Richard J. Bernhard Gift, 1960 (60.5).

Italian, the word *via* is also used as a preposition, as in "away," throwing away, *gettare via* and *buttare via*. Actually, it is the lowest snub in the gestural vernacular. Boccaccio, for example, deplored the hypocrisy of the church that gave to the poor what normally would be given to the pig or thrown away (*gittar via*).[17] As a preposition, it connotes disposability. *Via*, as both a noun and a preposition, and as both an item and a metaphor, added neither solidity nor dignity to the image of the street.

This lexical link between the street and disposability did not suggest that the street was conceived as a drain – though this may have been true in unplumbed towns – but that its primary function was passing by (*via*). The street as way (*via*) was philologically weaker than other, more robust nouns such as house, horse, door, and sword. Our own word *street*, like the German *Strasse* and the Italian *strada*, can mean either a road or a street. This word has a thoroughly physical origin, deriving from the layered foundation of pavements (*strata*). Despite this tangible origin, the

Fig. 9.6 Paul Signac, *Place de Clichy* (1888); The Metropolitan Museum of Art, Robert Lehman Collection, 1975 (1975.1.210).

word was used with surprisingly little physicality throughout the Renaissance. For example, in *Orlando furioso*, the epic of the Renaissance poet Ariosto, *strada* refers to a road or path through the countryside, where we cannot imagine it as a street with cobblestones or foundations. A hermit follows a lady in the woods "by many paths" (*per diversa strada*), like a canny dog snooting for the best chase.[18] The paths are chosen by scent, not signposts, suggesting tracks rather than a street. Ariosto even sings of others reaching their destination "in a little way" (*in poca strada*),[19] which is entirely metaphorical and has no concrete bearing, so to speak, on the pavement.

In most epochs the words for street, road, and path have been stronger as metaphors than as physical realities. This was already apparent in ancient Greek drama.[20] The sixteenth-century writer Baldassare Castiglione rarely used the word except as a metaphor: a "way" of doing things.[21] Metaphor is how we get words such as *method* (etymologically, a way or road by which you do things, μετα-οδός). Ideas of the non-physical "way" appeared in the sixteenth century, as when Bandello speaks of an opportunity: "You have opened the road to be able to speak of it."[22] Wrapped in metaphor, the street is nothing but an opening, a successful "avenue," a point of access, or a "route" to empowerment. *Avenue* simply means "coming toward."[23] It is a little like "alley," which derives from the French *aller*, "to go." The jejune utilitarian motif of either coming or going touches on our word "road," which derives from "ride." Again, this suggests movement along a strip of land rather than an architectural institution for communal and individual activities. By referring to where it leads, rather than what it is or what it contains, it is more open to metaphor. With all of this emphasis on transition, the street in its linguistic dress barely recognizes the activity of staying put, which is common to all the buildings along the street and, for the most part, the people inside them or taking coffee outside them.

Fig. 9.7 John Lewis Krimmel, *Nightlife in Philadelphia: An Oyster Barrow in Front of the Chestnut Street Theater* (181–ca 1813); The Metropolitan Museum of Art, Rogers Fund, 1942 (42.95.18).

The beloved French word for street (*rue*), like the Portuguese *rua*, has an obscure etymology that derives from the Latin for furrow or wrinkle (*ruga*), perhaps because people who walk on soft ground create a groove, or perhaps because the buildings on either side form the edges of a gully. The motif is hard to recognize as a physical reality but easier to use as a metaphor. This ambivalence of our vocabulary for streets may be due to the relatively late appearance of streets during the development of language.

The patchy pictorial history and ambivalent vocabulary of streets do not fully reflect their appearance or their diverse functions. Streets during the Renaissance, for example, were quite different from the metaphoric abstractions mentioned above. They were regarded as dangerous, and with reason.[24] Buildings emphasized fortification, with heavily rusticated ground floors punctured by small and high windows. They remind us that marauding gangs posed a threat in the streets. The very first story in Bandello's enormous collection of *Novelle* concerns a man who is stabbed in the street. Bandello also narrates the story of Romeo and Juliet, later taken up by Shakespeare, bringing severity to the family feud because of its impact on the streets of Verona.[25]

Danger exists whenever there are thugs, but from the earliest times, the street was regarded also as a place of belonging. The large collection of archaic texts in the Old Testament conveys a strong sense of community among individuals and their streets. The street was a symbol of parish, and therefore encouraged affection. References to biblical cities often mentioned their streets rather than their buildings.[26] The state of a city, including its economy, law and order, and public morale, was characterized by what happens in its streets, where there is always a telling mood.[27] One indication of a good city was "that there be no complaining in our streets."[28] If the streets are dead, the populace is demoralized,[29] as illustrated in Shakespeare's eerie line, "There is no stir or walking in the streets."[30]

To build or rebuild a biblical city, one would focus not on edifices but on streets: "Thou shalt make streets for thee in Damascus."[31] Two millennia later, in the Renaissance, pride in one's city was based not just on its buildings but on its streets. In *Book of the Courtier*, Baldassare Castiglione talks about persuading Francesco Gonzaga to make magnificent edifices, as Federico Gonzaga had done and as Pope Julius is now doing in St Peter's, and refers to "that street that goes from the palace to the

Fig. 9.8 Gustave Loiseau, *La Place de la Bastille* (1922); The Metropolitan Museum of Art, Robert Lehman Collection, 1975 (1975.1.190).

leisure spot of the Belvedere."[32] Castiglione means not just buildings but the whole street, even though he cannot name it.[33] The reason for using the street motif to describe the city is obvious. The grandiose individual buildings deserved pride from their patrons and acolytes, but the street was a symbol of community.[34] The town and its streets were an illustrious platform upon which monuments stand. Since antiquity, the street and the town square have been where important public and spiritual rituals take place, as mentioned in Nehemiah and Esther.[35] The quest for wisdom and community began in the street and the town square.[36] By symbolizing the public, they expressed something grand and solemn.[37]

The fourteenth-century paintings of Lorenzetti convey a great sense of density and complexity, with their cluttered rooftops and façades.[38] A contemporary writer, Boccaccio, filled in these spaces with people and actions. His streets were a stage for a disconsolate person realizing that he is the subject of a trick,[39] and for a practical joke (*beffa*) wrought by two shrewd men against a mystifying priest.[40] These streets were also the location of an attempted knifing.[41] In the sixteenth century, the street in Bandello's *Novelle* continued to be a place for action – including a courtship,[42] at least two escapes onto a street through a window,[43] and an assassination[44] – but it was described more evocatively with some carefully chosen verbs that suggest architectural conversations. A wall "responds above" or answers the street (*nel muro che rispondeva sovra la strada*) by displaying marble stones in a masterly fashion.[45] A jealous husband is keen for his wife not to go to any of the front windows; again, Bandello does not say that the windows "front onto the street" but "respond to the street" or "answer the street."[46] In another story, a big commotion breaks out in Paris as someone yells like a madman up high at "a window of the room which corresponds below to the public street."[47] A similar observation is made about a marchese who leans on a parapet of a wall that responds to the street.[48] We might say that the wall faces or overlooks the street, but in the high Renaissance one would say that the wall or window *answers* the street.

These literary expressions are from the same period as many grand civic projects in which urban orders suggest a lively conversation between buildings and the larger entity they meet, such as Michelangelo's project on the Capitoline Hill. Building and street were understood as interlocutors, just like the ladies and gentlemen who conducted courtship rituals across the right angle where the wall meets the pavement. This may also explain the Renaissance desire to revive ancient building ornamentation that would engage the street with a rhetorical language of moldings, flutes, dentils, and volutes.[49]

Renaissance paintings normally depicted august conversations, as in Raphael's *School of Athens*,[50] which was set appropriately in a grand hall rather than a chaotic street. They rarely showed streets as places of casual conversation, but popular literature again filled in the gap: for example, in a story by Bandello in which women speak across a street from their respective balconies, making fun of a gauche scholar who gets angry at them for thinking he is Jewish.[51] The street is itself a kind of theatre, with a scene below and houses or tenements on each side. One might speak of a house "on" the main road, but the Italians would say "above" the main road (*in su la strada maestra*).[52] You would be called "down" to the street, as we read in Castiglione, where a person knocks at a house and calls another down (*chiamandol giù*) from below (*da basso*).[53] The language reflects what we see throughout Europe: the street was always

Fig. 9.9 Luca Carlevaris, *Piazza San Marco, Venice* (ca 1709); The Metropolitan Museum of Art, Robert Lehman Collection, 1975 (1975.1.89).

conceived as below, with houses superintending it. The physical profile of all European cities was highly staged, with none of the buildings retiring from the street. In sixteenth-century *palazzi*, the earlier fortification of the ground level had eased off and a greater sense of urbanity and street theatre became evident.

Renaissance streets were engaging places, filled with noise and hub-bub. There were fights with police in the street.[54] There was fear of being tossed out onto the street.[55] There was even a rape[56] and a caning.[57] The street was a tragicomedy of intense carnality, without modern decorum.[58] The growth of comedy on the continent (and mixed genres in England) brought the street onto the stage. No street exists in the whole corpus of Racine the tragedian, but Shakespeare set some sixty scenes in the street. Baroque theatre often used the street as a backdrop for its entertainment. After going from the street into the theatre, audiences would see the curtain rise to reveal the street again, ready to present the outrages of accident, zeal, and humour that are still the masterpieces of Western literature. Shakespeare presented an even more significant historical development, in which the street became a political force: a receptacle for mass feeling, changes in civil fortunes, the power of the mob, and fear of the ruler – changes that would intensify in the more politically charged times of Hogarth.

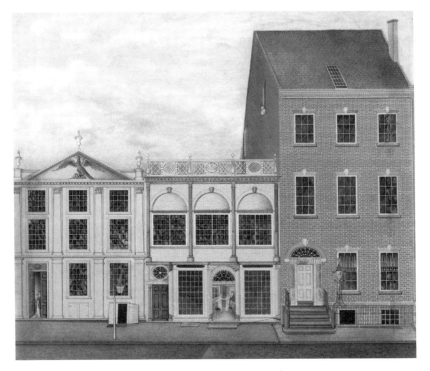

Fig. 9.10 Artist unknown, *The Shop and Warehouse of Duncan Phyfe, 168-172 Fulton Street, New York City* (ca 1816); The Metropolitan Museum of Art, Rogers Fund, 1922 (22.28.1).

The street was the first telecommunications network and, in matters of state, was a dangerous one: "This I have oft heard whispered among / patricians as they walk the streets of Rome: / that Caesar be the cause of all their faults, / and that he seeketh more to kill. But, soft!"[59] Noise in the street was hemmed by a conspiratorial hush. As a receptacle of crowds, the street had an enormous and unholy energy, threatening and deadly, where the pressure of people made it impossible either to act as an individual or to moderate group behaviour.[60]

The great difference between the theatre with stalls and the street with houses is that actors on a street are also the audience, and vice versa. On the stage of the street, people act theatrically but not to a script. They risk being upstaged or remaining unheard; conversely, a person who would rather remain inconspicuous at the periphery may be forced to take centre stage alongside the most pompous exhibitionist. According to La Bruyère, the ones we notice most are those who are happy to sing of the rage of Orlando in a laneway.[61] Others become identities in the city simply by haunting the streets and corners every night.[62]

Streets are also associated with different social status. According to La Bruyère, those who seek upward social mobility should not mention certain streets or even know their names. They should mention only the Louvre and the Place Royale. If they do mention lesser streets, they should grapple with the names and disfigure the pronunciation.[63]

The most famous invention of the eighteenth century was the encyclopaedia, but coffee had a greater impact on the street because it reinforced the idea of taking a walk to enjoy a conversation. Celebrated even

Fig. 9.11 Jean Michelin, *The Baker's Cart* (1656); The Metropolitan Museum of Art, Fletcher Fund, 1927 (27.59).

by the serious Bach, coffee was an ideal supplement to conversation and intimacy. Coffee encouraged the middle classes to spend time for leisure and restoration. The most common site was the coffee house, as portrayed in the *largo* in Goldoni's play *La bottega del caffè*. Coffee, though undoubtedly a drug, was not taken for intoxication, nor was it taken to reduce thirst, as water would have assuaged thirst more efficiently. The business of the coffee house was not simply to sell coffee but to attract customers from the street into an entertaining atmosphere created by a jolly waiter who knew how to play the buffoon.[64]

With the advent of the coffee house, the eighteenth century figuratively opened its doors to the street. Even with only one or two in a neighbourhood, the coffee shop told you that the street has nooks. Though clearly part of a building, the coffee shop augmented social engagement in the street. In Goldoni's plays the street is a place of action and idleness, encounters and conversations, like a living room for the whole community, served by permeable locales such as the coffee shop that offered free movement for leisure and conversation. The eighteenth-century street had a gentle complexion that continues to inform certain prestigious streets in our cities today.

Amid this urban prestige, discussed by Richard Florida,[65] the city became redefined during the Industrial Revolution, leading the stage-sets of Goldoni's plays to acquire unprecedented volumes of people and traffic. London, Vienna, Berlin, and Paris retained their six-storey tenement buildings with shops below, preserving the festivity of the street with large flows of traffic in the boulevard that provided spectacular subjects for Impressionist painters.

The poet of the street *par excellence* was Baudelaire, who recognized the new "teeming city, city full of dreams," where "mysteries flow like sap everywhere in the narrow channels of the mighty giant." To speak of the street as a channel recalls the etymology of *rue* as a groove, but the nineteenth-century channel was teeming, mighty, and unsettled, with unwholesome volumes surging through it. "One morning in the gloomy street ... the houses whose height the fog stretched upward, simulated the two banks of a swollen river." The imagery is threatening and morbid: "a dirty yellow fog inundated the whole space"; the "suburb was shaken by heavy trucks."[66] As Paris interacts with nature, its streets become traumatic.

Fig. 9.12 Eugène Atget, *Café, Avenue de la Grande-Armée* (1924–25); The Metropolitan Museum of Art, Gilman Collection, Purchase, Ann Tenenbaum and Thomas H. Lee Gift, 2005 (2005.100.133).

Paris the tourist attraction, with the names of its legendary streets embedded in songs and commercial products, does not echo Baudelaire's pessimism.[67] But then, his subject matter was social malaise and inner corruption rather than architecture. His remarks about architecture instead describe metamorphosis, as in his celebrated line "Paris is changing."[68] Perhaps his greatest statement of disappointment over the Parisian streetscape is the poem "Sunset," in which even the treasures of natural landscape are made cruel by modernity: "the charming evening" is a "friend of the criminal; it comes like an accomplice, with the footsteps of a wolf." The streets of Paris are ravaged by conditions of life: "unhealthy demons in the atmosphere wake up heavily, like business people, and knock against the shutters and awnings while flying. Through the lamps that the wind torments, prostitution lights up in the streets; like a swarm it opens its doors."[69]

While Baudelaire's street lamps struggled against the intemperate wind and the city's putrid sex life, they also enabled the city to gain many extra hours of nightlife and urban prestige. In former ages, nightfall meant great danger, and no one in his or her right mind would sally forth.[70] In the nineteenth century, citizens gained almost another city: the street life of the evening. In spite of Baudelaire's horror, Paris became known as the city of lights. Late nineteenth-century painters such as Monet and Pissarro portrayed streets full of vitality, capturing the unprecedented vibrations of the beautiful boulevard from the novel perspective of a balcony. The street continued to find modern apologists, such as the Orphists and at times the German Expressionists.

The story that began with equivocation over the very words for *street* ends fatefully with the weak reality of streets in contemporary suburbs, as if those lexical insecurities re-emerged in practice. With the advent of the automobile, streets with isolated houses could be stretched horizontally across former farmlands to become expansive, low-rise suburbs.[71] Suburban houses sit luxuriously behind a generous periphery of land, rather than forming vertical banks of urban configurations that had been common throughout Europe and that still exist with even greater density in large cities such as New York and Hong Kong. Instead of occupying the full footprint of a block, suburban buildings retreat behind a garden, returning the street to the wooded pathway described by the Renaissance poet Ariosto, which one traverses like a snooting dog. Even high-rise buildings have peripheral gardens, figuratively withdrawing from the street and aspiring to suburban autonomy.

Although the history of ideas has recorded the vivacity of streets and the theatricality of their architecture, it has not explained what makes them adorable. Evidence from the automotive age indicates that faith in the street as a symbol of community – a place for conversations and urban theatre – is exceedingly weak.[72] In the garden city and the suburb, the buildings, streets, and greenery promote withdrawal rather than a sense of belonging.[73] Against the corrosive spatial effect of the car, the lexical archaeology of the street has never provided a robust archetype that we can easily recognize. The street has been difficult to name, difficult to see, difficult to picture, difficult to understand, and difficult to love. Without the classical tradition of ceremony and ornament that once animated streets with architectural festivity, the street seems conceptually fragile, and risks becoming a built-up gully traversed by others: a disowned symbol of community that few but poets and playwrights can admire.

Finally, the street has existed in Western language more as a metaphor than as a reality. This has predisposed us to think of the street in relation to something else or as horrifically alienating in its own right. In European literature, the strength of its metaphors, combined with the weakness of

Fig. 9.13 Eugène Atget, *Shopfront of Courone d'or, Quai Bourbon* (1922); The Metropolitan Museum of Art, David Hunter McAlpin Fund, 1962 (62.548).

Fig. 9.14 Charles Caleb Ward, *Coming Events Cast Their Shadows Before* (1871); The Metropolitan Museum of Art, Bequest of Susan Vanderpoel Clark, 1967 (67.155.2).

its physical and social role, has allowed streets to be stigmatized as undesirable places where a car is needed for security. We see the street as a place where one might get killed (for which, ironically, we can thank the cars that are taken for safety). We assume that the street is the antithesis of privacy and safety; so if privilege and opportunity permit, we find ourselves a leafy haven as far away from the street as possible.

Caught between ancient metaphors of transit and contemporary preferences for gardens over masonry – and especially for free-standing architecture over engaged buildings[74] – the densely socialized street has few apologists and many refugees. But streets are more than the sum of their buildings. To reinvent streets and recreate street life, architects might re-examine the diverse pictorial images and etymological premises with which we have conceived the street from antiquity to now. In this project, it helps to interrogate our inherited assumptions about what a street is, what it has meant historically, and, figuratively speaking, where it is heading.

NOTES

1 See Sheila Foster, "The City as an Ecological Space: Social Capital and Urban Land Use," *Notre Dame Law Review* 82, no. 2 (Dec. 2006): 527–82, which identifies social costs – especially social capital – that remain obscured from regulatory frameworks.

2 Jane Jacobs, *The Death and Life of Great American Cities* (New York: Random House, 1961). See also Zeynep Çelik, Diane G. Favro, and Richard Ingersoll, *Streets: Critical Perspectives on Public Space* (Berkeley: University of California Press, 1994).

3 See John Mixon, "Jane Jacobs and the Law: Zoning for Diversity Examined," *Northwestern University Law Review* 62, no. 3 (1967–68): 314–56.

4 As in the spatial dialectics in Henri Lefebvre, *The Production of Space*, trans. Donald Nicholson-Smith (1974) (Oxford: Blackwell, 1991).

5 In the Brancacci Chapel in Florence.

6 Located, respectively, in the British Museum in London and Richard Meier's pavilion for the Altar of Peace in Rome.

7 The top right corner panel from *Four Stories from the Life of Saint Nicholas* (ca 1330), Uffizi, tempera on wood, 96 x 35 cm.

8 (1308–11), tempera on panel, 44 x 45 cm, now in the National Gallery, London.

9 Geoffrey Dupree, whose conversations helped me greatly with my book *The Visual Language of Painting: An Aesthetic Analysis of Representational Technique* (Melbourne: Australian Scholarly Publishing, 2010).

10 Starting with a cattle run in Homer, *Odyssey*, 4.605; see also Herodotus, 6.126 and Euripides, *Andromache*, 599.

11 Plato, *Theaetetus*, 144c; even a cloister, Plato, *Euthydemos*, 273a.

12 See the violence that occurred in Bandello's tale of Romeo and Juliet: "su il Corso vicino a la porta dei Borsari verso Castelvecchio." Matteo Bandello, *Novelle* (Lucca, 1554), 2.9.

13 For the Roman origins of urban spaces, see Joseph Rykwert, *The Idea of a Town: The Anthropology of Urban Form in Rome, Italy and the Ancient World* (1976) (Cambridge, MA: MIT Press, 1988), especially "Square and Cross" (72–96), "Guardians of Centre, Guardians of Boundaries" (97–162), and "Boundary and Centre: Mundus and Terminus" (117–26).

14 "εν ταις γωνίαις των πλατείων." Matthew 6:5–6.

15 "Then shall ye begin to say, We have eaten and drunk in thy presence, and thou hast taught in our streets (εν ταίς πλατειαις)." Luke 13:26.

16 "Go out into the highways and hedges (εις τας όδους και φραγμούς), and compel them to come in." Luke 14:23; in *Vulgate*: "in vias et sepes."

17 "E per ciò, come che ben facesse il valente uomo che lo inquisitore della ipocrita carità de' frati, che quel lo danno a' poveri che converrebbe loro dare al porco o gittar via." Giovanni Boccaccio, *Decameron* (ca 1353), 1.7.

18 Ludovico Ariosto, *Orlando furioso* (Milan, 1532), 8.33.7; also, "seeking the shadows of the darkest path" (5.48.6) and "Per mezzo il bosco appar sol una strada" (12.37.1).

19 9.80.5; cf. "per quella strada che più breve porta" (8.91.6). Also, see Bandello: "conosco quanto strabocchevolmente fuor di strada l'appetito mio disordinato mi tiri, e non so né posso ritrarmi e sul vero calle ritornare ed a questi folli pensieri volger le spalle! Dico 'non posso' e dir deverei 'non voglio.'" *Novelle*, 2.37.

20 Sophocles, *Ajax*, 889, or Aeschylus, *Persians*, 207.

21 E.g., "come chi camina per le tenebre senza lume e però spesso erra la strada." Baldassare Castiglione, *Il libro del cortegiano* (Venice, 1545), 1.30; or "fanno far strada a tutti" (2.25); cf. "Vederete ben molte volte alcuni, che non hanno paura né di morte né d'altro, né con tutto ciò si possono chia-

mare arditi, perché non conoscono il periculo e vanno come insensati dove vedeno la strada e non pensano più; e questo procede da una certa grossezza di spiriti ottusi." Bandello, *Novelle*, 3.18.

22 "Ora che voi m'avete aperta la strada di poterne parlare, non resterò che io non vi dica il parer moi." Ibid., 1.21.

23 Cf. "boulevard," which has technical origins in old battlements (German *Bollwerk* or bulwark) that can be reclaimed for genteel promenades by civic culture.

24 Especially in times of persecution: "They hunt our steps, that we cannot go in our streets." Lamentations 4:18; cf. "I do not without danger walk these streets." Shakespeare, *Twelfth Night*, 3.3.25.

25 "Three civil brawls, bred of an airy word, / By thee, old Capulet, and Montague, / Have thrice disturb'd the quiet of our streets, / And made Verona's ancient citizens / Cast by their grave beseeming ornaments, / To wield old partisans, in hands as old, / Canker'd with peace, to part your canker'd hate: / If ever you disturb our streets again, / Your lives shall pay the forfeit of the peace." *Romeo and Juliet*, 1.1.98–103.

26 "Tell it not in Gath, publish it not in the streets of Askelon." 2 Samuel 1:20.

27 "Wickedness is in the midst thereof: deceit and guile depart not from her streets." Psalms 55:11.

28 Psalms 144:13–14.

29 "There is a crying for wine in the streets; all joy is darkened, the mirth of the land is gone." Isaiah 24:11.

30 *Julius Caesar*, 1.3. See also "Then will I cause to cease from the cities of Judah, and from the streets of Jerusalem, the voice of mirth, and the voice of gladness, the voice of the bridegroom, and the voice of the bride: for the land shall be desolate." Jeremiah 7:34.

31 1 Kings 20:34.

32 "quella strada che va da Palazzo al diporto di Belvedere e molti altri edifici, come faceano ancora gli antichi Romani." Castiglione, *Il libro del cortegiano*, 4.36.

33 You might expect this with a little, nameless lane, e.g., "that narrow laneway that runs to the piazza," in Bandello: "per quella vietta stretta che conduce in piazza, verso la bottega de le bollette." *Novelle*, 4.22.

34 As Shakespeare says, "Are not the streets as free for me as for you?" *Taming of the Shrew*, 1.2.233.

35 Nehemiah 8:1; Esther 6:9.

36 Song of Solomon 3:2.

37 Proverbs 1:20–21.

38 Richard Ingersoll has invoked Lorenzetti in his *Sprawltown: Looking for the City on its Edges* (New York: Princeton Architectural Press, 2006), as he clearly distinguishes city and country agricultural lands (*contado*) and contrasts them today: "With the recent jumps in scale and segregation of functions and classes, city centers have been hollowed out and fields overrun by development" (4).

39 Boccaccio, *Decameron*, 2.5.

40 Ibid., 6.10.

41 Ibid., 7.6.

42 Bandello, *Novelle*, 1.11.

43 "essendo a la finestra vide il paggio che tutto solo per la strada veniva" (1.23). See also "con l'amante animosamente giú da una finestra saltò ne la strada e insieme con lui via se n'andò senza aversi fatto male." Ibid., 1.59.

44 Ibid., 1.1.

45 "nel muro che rispondeva sovra la strada, e tutto era di pietre di marmo maestrevolmente acconcie." Ibid., 1.25.

46 "Fa che io ti veggia piú a finestra nessuna di quelle che rispondeno su la strada." Ibid., 2.28.

47 "fuor del letto e, mal consegliata, aperse la finestra de la camera che rispondeva suso una strada publica, e cominciò come forsennata quanto piú poteva a gridare e chiamar i vicini e far levar quelli di casa." Ibid., 3.6.

48 "Il marchese con licenza de la compagnia si ritirò in un canto del seggio, e affacciatosi al parapetto del muro che su la strada risponde, attese ciò che il messo voleva dire." Ibid., 2.22.

49 See Joseph Rykwert, *The Necessity of Artifice: Ideas in Architecture* (New York: Rizzoli, 1982), which pays special attention to the street.

50 Also known as *Philosophy*. Stanza della Segnatura, Vatican.

51 "che per iscontro l'una a l'altra a dui balconi stavano a pigliar fresco e ragionare." Bandello, *Novelle*, 3.38.

52 "Egli aveva il palagio in su la strada maestra, di modo che era necessario passargli innanzi la porta." Ibid., 1.26.

53 Ibid., 2.75.

54 With "uno sbirro." Ibid., 3.24.

55 "confessando che in effetto ebbe una grandissima paura di non esser su la strada come un cane gittato," Ibid., 3.34.

56 Ibid., 4.11.

57 A Spanish prostitute is caned for her temerity in defying the law. Ibid., 4.16; cf. "This man shall be punished in the streets of the city, and where he suspecteth not he shall be taken." *Wisdom of Sirach*, 23.21.

58 Some of our concerns for erotic decorum in the street would have been familiar in earlier centuries. For example, in Shakespeare, *Taming of the Shrew*, 5.1.149, Petruchio asks Kate to kiss him. She replies, "What! In the midst of the street?" He asks if she is ashamed of him, to which she replies, "No ... but ashamed to kiss."

59 *Julius Caesar*, 2.2; cf. "Heard you of nothing strange about the streets?" *Antony and Cleopatra*, 5.1.16.

60 *Julius Caesar*, 2.4.33.

61 Jean de La Bruyère, "De la ville," I3 (V), in *Les caractères* (Paris, 1688).

62 La Bruyère, "De l'homme," I25 (VIII), in *Les caractères*.

63 La Bruyère, "De la société et de la conversation," 69 (IV), in *Les caractères*.

64 "in quelle botteghe, dove vi è qualcheduno, che sappia fare il buffone, tutti corrono." Carlo Goldoni, *La bottega del caffè* (Venice, 1744), 1.1.

65 Richard Florida, *Cities and the Creative Class* (New York: Routledge, 2005).

66 Charles Baudelaire, "Les sept vieillards," in *Les fleurs du mal* (Paris, 1861), 90.

67 The high sociability of the rue de Castiglione in Paris, designed in 1802 by Charles Percier and Pierre Fontaine, is evoked by Alain de Botton, *The Architecture of Happiness* (New York: Pantheon, 2006), 178.

68 Baudelaire, "Le cygne," in *Les fleurs du mal*, 89.

69 Baudelaire, "Le crépuscule du soir," in *Les fleurs du mal*, 95.

70 "La notte sará buia, e nessuno a quella ora va per la strada." Bandello, *Novelle*, 4.27. And Shakespeare: "I have walk'd about the streets, / Submitting me unto the perilous night." *Julius Caesar*, 1.3.46.

71 For the development of suburbs, see the eloquent study of Joseph Rykwert, *The Seduction of Place: The History and Future of the City* (Oxford: Oxford University Press, 2000), especially 160–88. See also Ebenezer Howard, *Garden Cities of Tomorrow* (London: S. Sonnenschein, 1902).

72 See, among many efforts to understand streets in social contexts, Jon Lang, *Urban Design: The American Experience* (New York: Wiley, 1994), with its sociogenic emphasis; Jill Grant, *Planning the Good Community: New Urbanism in Theory and Practice* (New York: Routledge, 2006); and Ali

Madanipour, *Design of Urban Space: An Inquiry into a Socio-Spatial Process* (Chichester and New York: Wiley, 1996).

73 See Robert Nelson, *The Space Wasters: The Architecture of Australian Misanthropy* (Melbourne: Planning Institute of Australia, 2011).

74 This distinction is explored as alpha-architecture versus E-type or engaged architecture in "Alphatecture: Architecture against the Street," ibid., 28–40.

The Laughing Girls

Marc J Neveu

Chora

THOUGH VERY LITTLE has been written about Douglas Darden, he is well known for his exquisite pencil drawings, displayed in various exhibitions, and for his book *Condemned Building*, published in 1993.[1] *Condemned Building* describes ten acts of building. Each begins with a canonical statement and the overturning of that canon. The act of turning over is a tactic often used and represented by Darden. Two details on the left side of the frontispiece of *Condemned Building*, for example, show the turning over of a turtle to reveal its underbelly.[2] Turning over was considered by Darden to be an architectural trope; indeed, the word *trope* comes from the Greek τρόπος, "to turn." Each of the projects in *Condemned Building* relies on this turning over to reveal what Darden referred to as the "underbelly" of architecture.[3]

This essay will describe and begin to unpack another project that Darden had been working on for at least five years prior to his death in 1996. It was named in various ways, but most often as *The Laughing Girls*.[4] Much bigger in scope than the ten short stories in *Condemned Building*, a 150-page graphic novel was planned in addition to at least forty objects to be made. The first dated material is from 1990, and at that time was already described as "an architectural novel." *The Laughing Girls* remains unfinished and has never been published.

Though similar themes and tactics are present, *The Laughing Girls* is a very different project than *Condemned Building*. First, it was always intended as a graphic novel and not as a monograph or collection of projects. Darden did not produce any large-scale pencil drawings for the project. The representations rely more heavily on collage than on architectural drawing conventions such as plan and section. While narrative was an integral component in his earlier work, the importance of storytelling in *The Laughing Girls* is much more evident. In an application for scholar-in-residence at the California College of the Arts and Crafts in 1994, Darden explained the intention of the work: "The purpose of this project is to establish a new approach toward communicating the relationship between the evolution of design and its results. This design project proposes an innovative form of communication, the architectural novel, which examines the relationships between story-telling, the process of design, and the designed environment."[5]

Darden was critical of the marginalization of the arts (and architecture in particular) and the alienation of architecture from the public. He attributed this marginalization to the fact that designers and artists rarely share

Fig. 10.1 Frontispiece from Douglas Darden, *Condemned Building: An Architect's Pre-text* (New York: Princeton Architectural Press, 1993). The frontispiece refers to the work of Marcel Duchamp, Giambattista Piranesi, and, perhaps most directly, Jean-Jacques Lequeu. Reproduced by permission of Princeton Architectural Press and Douglas Darden Estate, courtesy of Allison Collins.

their design process with the public, or even with each other. The intention of *The Laughing Girls* was to overcome that alienation through storytelling. This project, however, was not the voice of a sole author. It was intentionally collaborative and interdisciplinary. In an undated portfolio titled "The Graphic Novel: An Investigation of the Interdisciplinary Design Process," Darden lists the following participants: Kelton Osborn (print making), Jeff Dawson (urban design), James Trewitt (furniture design), Virginia Grote (ceramics), Andrew Grote (cartooning and illustration), Marty Hammond (computer graphics), Mark Wilkerson (industrial design), and Douglas Darden, program director (architecture). The format of the graphic novel, according to Darden, allowed for collaboration among all of the disciplines represented on the team.

The first iteration of *The Laughing Girls* was for an architectural competition. Over the next five years, the project and story would change dramatically. By 1994 a series of short drafts had been constructed, as well as a series of artifacts that included two laughs modelled in foam, Helen's cane, a juicer, and at least two tattoos.[6] The text in the following ten figures is from a pamphlet produced in 1994 that Darden sent to several journals.[7]

The Laughing Girls was intended to take place in parts and in at least three sites. An early proposal by the "Dardanus Design Consortium" shows a site in Troy, New York; Troy, Greece; and a future Troy.[8] A later version situates the project temporally, spatially, and physically. Part One takes place in Troy, New York. Objects designed in this section relate to the feet and the knees, and the design strategy was to work with fragments. Parts are identified without establishing a full connection to other parts. Part Two takes place in transit. This section includes objects that relate to the upper legs and torso. The design process is iterative but does not achieve completion. Part Three takes place in Troy, Greece and is the full embodiment of laughter. Individual designs in this section exist only in relation to other parts; each affects the others at all scales. Each part would take place over the course of nine days, with a final day (the 28th) acting as a postscript that returns the novel to the beginning. Each part is nine days long; the three nines plus one give the year 1999. The twenty-eight-day calendar is based on lunar and menstrual cycles. In many ways, this project is an affirmation of life, unlike Darden's meditation on dying in the Oxygen House in *Condemned Building*.

Two stories inform *The Laughing Girls*; one is fictional, the other is not. The first is a curious case of mass hysteria reported on 30 January 1962 in Kashasha, Tanzania. An epidemic of contagious laughter broke out at a mission-run girls' school and continued for six months. Ninety-five of the 159 students were affected; however, laboratory tests found no infectious or toxic evidence. Three girls later came forward and claimed to be the instigators of the laughter. This case is the only fully

Fig. 10.2 Douglas Darden, *The Laughing Girls*, page 1. Figures 2–12, 14–20 reproduced by permission of Douglas Darden Estate, courtesy of Allison Collins.

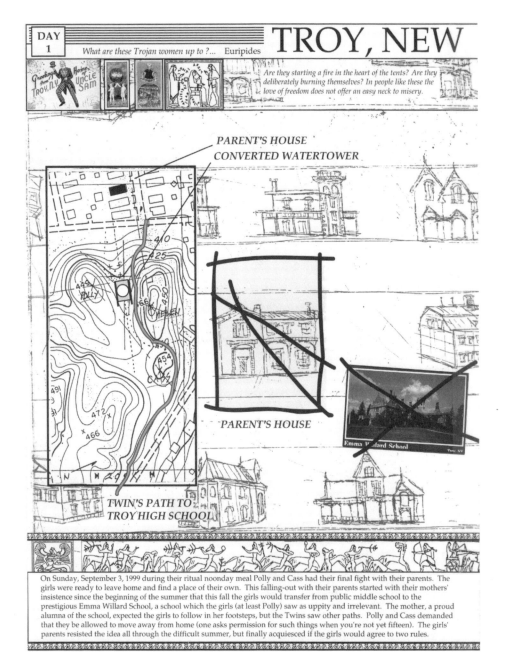

Greetings from TROY, N.Y. *Uncle Sam*

Are they starting a fire in the heart of the tents? Are they deliberately burning themselves? In people like these the love of freedom does not offer an easy neck to misery.

PARENT'S HOUSE
CONVERTED WATERTOWER

PARENT'S HOUSE

Emma Willard School

TWIN'S PATH TO
TROY HIGH SCHOOL

On Sunday, September 3, 1999 during their ritual noonday meal Polly and Cass had their final fight with their parents. The girls were ready to leave home and find a place of their own. This falling-out with their parents started with their mothers' insistence since the beginning of the summer that this fall the girls would transfer from public middle school to the prestigious Emma Willard School, a school which the girls (at least Polly) saw as uppity and irrelevant. The mother, a proud alumna of the school, expected the girls to follow in her footsteps, but the Twins saw other paths. Polly and Cass demanded that they be allowed to move away from home (one asks permission for such things when you're not yet fifteen). The girls' parents resisted the idea all through the difficult summer, but finally acquiesced if the girls would agree to two rules.

Fig. 10.3 *The Laughing Girls*, page 2.

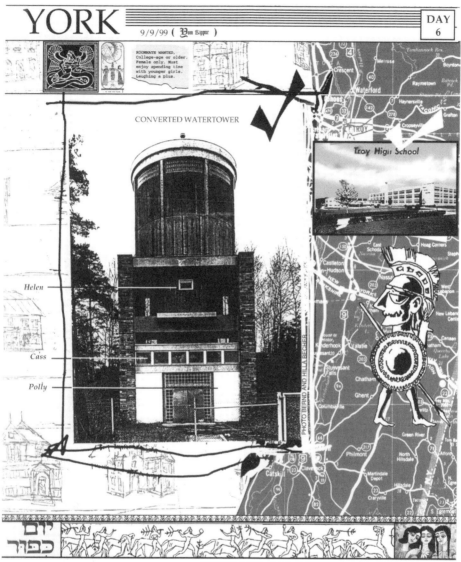

ROOMMATE WANTED. College-age or older. Female only. Must enjoy spending time with younger girls. Laughing a plus.

CONVERTED WATERTOWER

Troy High School

Helen

Cass

Polly

PHOTO BERND AND HILLA BECHER

יום כפור

RULE NO. 1 *"Get a Guardian"*; RULE NO. 2 *"Find a place close to HOME"*

The Watertower was a radical departure from the parent's suburban home, brazen and straightforward. Somehow it also was settled, it straddled two hillocks and nested into the land. It was totally a part of the forest path they took to school. The want-ad placed by the twins in the *Troy Guardian* was answered by a scholarship student named Helen, who attended R.P.I in downtown Troy. Helen was a studious classics major, whom the twins perceived as having a *wild* side. HELEN WAS OLD ENOUGH FOR RULE NO. 1 THE WATERTOWER WAS CLOSE ENOUGH TO HOME FOR RULE NO. 2

Almost immediatly Helen became the unadulterated leader of the girls.

Fig. 10.4 *The Laughing Girls*, page 3.

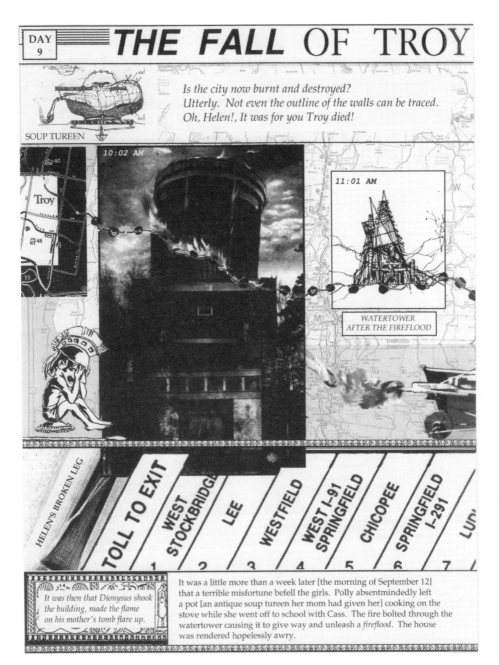

THE FALL OF TROY

SOUP TUREEN

Is the city now burnt and destroyed?
Utterly. Not even the outline of the walls can be traced.
Oh, Helen!, It was for you Troy died!

10:02 AM

Troy

11:01 AM

WATERTOWER
AFTER THE FIREFLOOD

HELEN'S BROKEN LEG

TOLL TO EXIT

WEST STOCKBRIDGE 1
LEE 2
WESTFIELD 3
WEST I-91 SPRINGFIELD 4
CHICOPEE 5
SPRINGFIELD I-291 6
7

It was then that Dionysus shook the building, made the flame on his mother's tomb flare up.

It was a little more than a week later [the morning of September 12] that a terrible misfortune befell the girls. Polly absentmindedly left a pot [an antique soup tureen her mom had given her] cooking on the stove while she went off to school with Cass. The fire bolted through the watertower causing it to give way and unleash a *fireflood*. The house was rendered hopelessly awry.

Fig. 10.5 *The Laughing Girls*, page 4.

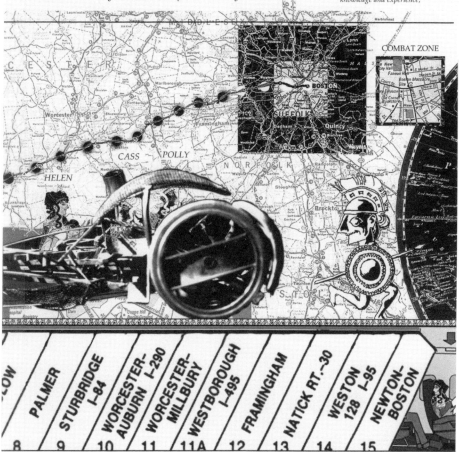

Pentheus: *This Bacchic arrogance advances on
us like a spreading fire.*

*You who thought you were living in the shadow
of Mount Ida, behind the sad battlements of Troy.
Helen, how did you steal home from that day?*

Dionysus: *My Bacchic worship is a
matter as yet beyond her
knowledge and experience;*

COMBAT ZONE

BOSTON

CASS   POLLY

HELEN

OW	PALMER	STURBRIDGE I-84	WORCESTER-AUBURN I-290	WORCESTER-MILLBURY	WESTBOROUGH I-495	FRAMINGHAM	NATICK RT.-30	WESTON 128 I-95	NEWTON-BOSTON
8	9	10	11	11A	12	13	14	15	

Helen had been sleeping-in [from a previous late night of debauchery] on the morning of the fire. She had jumped off the tower like it was a berserk horse, only to break her leg. Unlike the distraught twins. Helen saw the "misfortune"-like she viewed everything-as an opportunity. Helen's lifelong dreams began to commandeer the girl's destinies. Since Helen was a small girl, she had always dreamed of living in Greece. Her classical studies had only confirmed her desires. Now that the fire had consumed the watertower, Helen conceived that they had nothing left to lose. The three girls should go to the other Troy, to Troy, Greece. Helen would lead the way, broken leg and all.

Fig. 10.6 *The Laughing Girls*, page 5.

Fig. 10.7 *The Laughing Girls*, page 6.

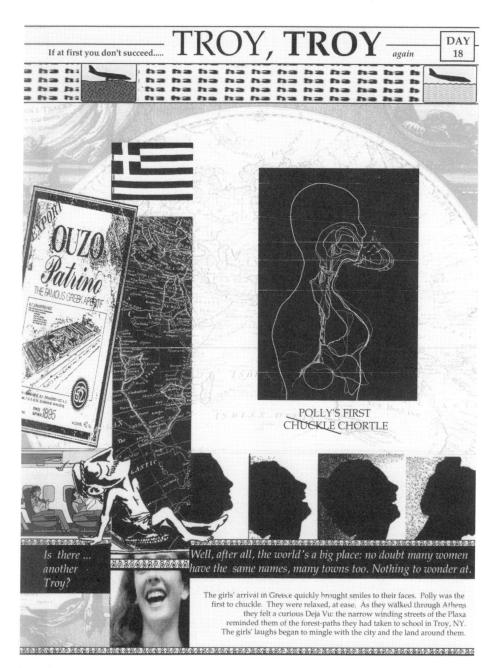

Fig. 10.8 *The Laughing Girls*, page 7.

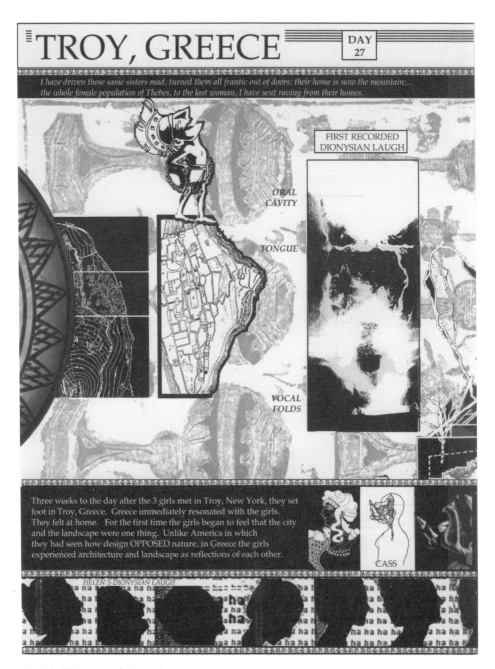

TROY, GREECE

I have driven those same sisters mad, turned them all frantic out of doors; their home is now the mountain;...
the whole female population of Thebes, to the last woman, I have sent raving from their homes.

FIRST RECORDED
DIONYSIAN LAUGH

ORAL
CAVITY

TONGUE

VOCAL
FOLDS

Three weeks to the day after the 3 girls met in Troy, New York, they set
foot in Troy, Greece. Greece immediately resonated with the girls.
They felt at home. For the first time the girls began to feel that the city
and the landscape were one thing. Unlike America in which
they had seen how design OPPOSED nature, in Greece the girls
experienced architecture and landscape as reflections of each other.

CASS

HELEN'S DIONYSIAN LAUGH

Fig. 10.9 *The Laughing Girls*, page 8.

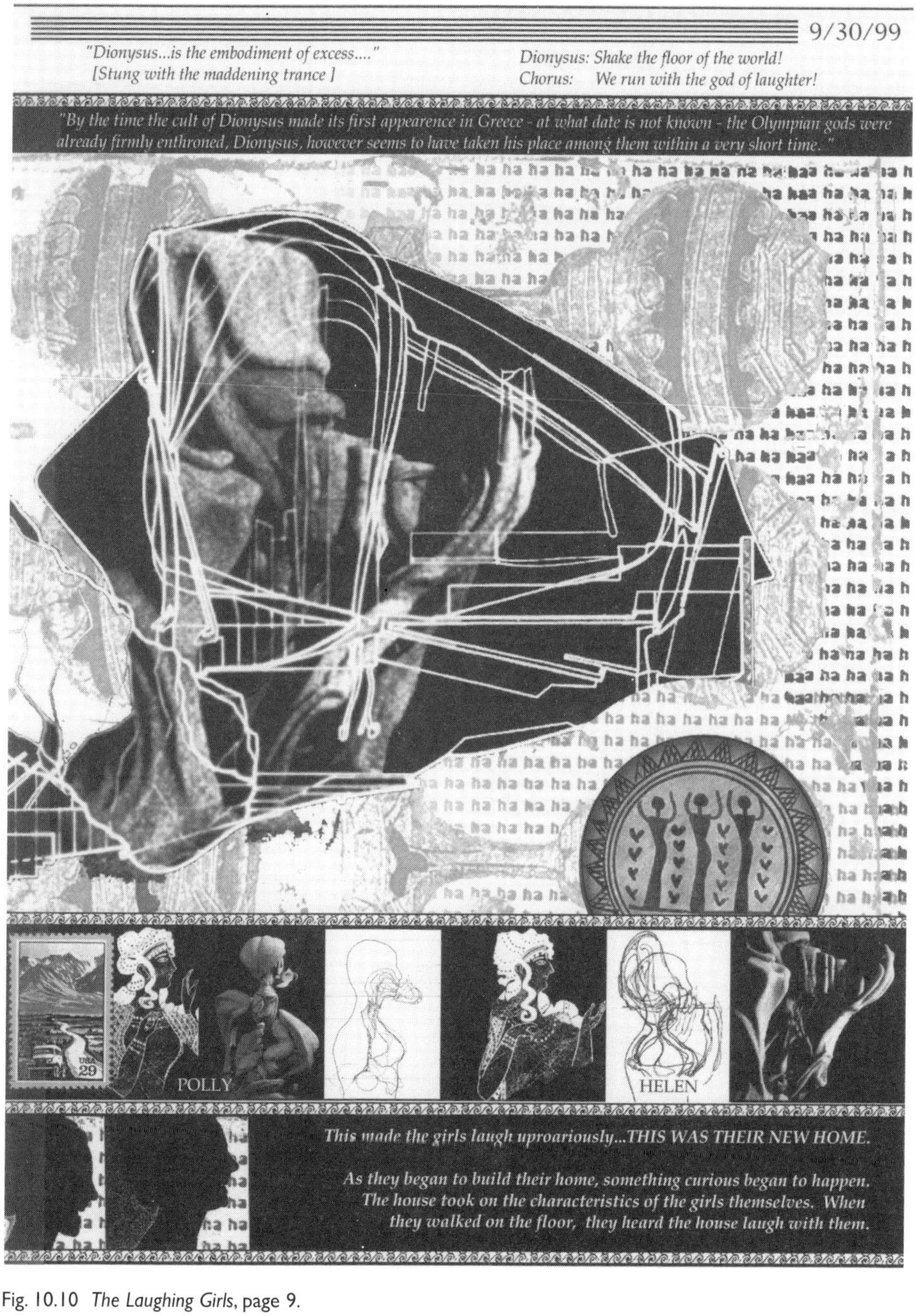

"Dionysus...is the embodiment of excess...."
[Stung with the maddening trance]

Dionysus: Shake the floor of the world!
Chorus: We run with the god of laughter!

"By the time the cult of Dionysus made its first appearance in Greece - at what date is not known - the Olympian gods were already firmly enthroned, Dionysus, however seems to have taken his place among them within a very short time."

POLLY

HELEN

This made the girls laugh uproariously...THIS WAS THEIR NEW HOME.

As they began to build their home, something curious began to happen.
The house took on the characteristics of the girls themselves. When
they walked on the floor, they heard the house laugh with them.

Fig. 10.10 *The Laughing Girls*, page 9.

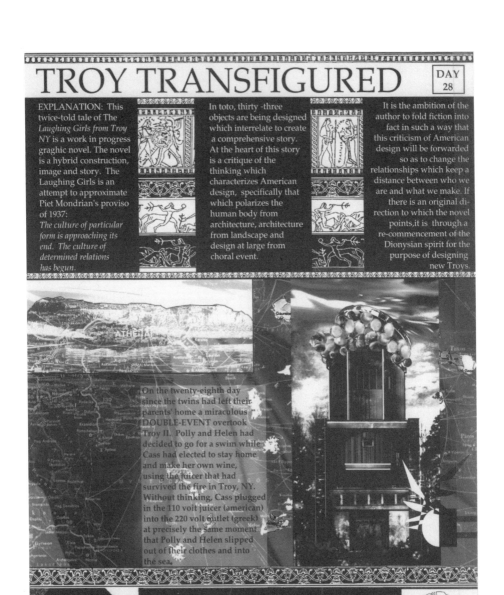

TROY TRANSFIGURED

DAY 28

EXPLANATION: This twice-told tale of The *Laughing Girls from Troy NY* is a work in progress graphic novel. The novel is a hybrid construction, image and story. The Laughing Girls is an attempt to approximate Piet Mondrian's proviso of 1937:
The culture of particular form is approaching its end. The culture of determined relations has begun.

In toto, thirty-three objects are being designed which interrelate to create a comprehensive story. At the heart of this story is a critique of the thinking which characterizes American design, specifically that which polarizes the human body from architecture, architecture from landscape and design at large from choral event.

It is the ambition of the author to fold fiction into fact in such a way that this criticism of American design will be forwarded so as to change the relationships which keep a distance between who we are and what we make. If there is an original direction to which the novel points, it is through a re-commencement of the Dionysian spirit for the purpose of designing new Troys.

On the twenty-eighth day since the twins had left their parents' home a miraculous DOUBLE-EVENT overtook Troy II. Polly and Helen had decided to go for a swim while Cass had elected to stay home and make her own wine, using the juicer that had survived the fire in Troy, NY. Without thinking, Cass plugged in the 110 volt juicer (american) into the 220 volt outlet (greek) at precisely the same moment that Polly and Helen slipped out of their clothes and into the sea.

A huge spark leaped out of the house while Polly and Helen - still laughing - leaped into the sea. Perhaps the girls' laughs combined with the spark - no one knows - but when Helen and Polly rose to the surface of the sea, they saw a whole new array of bright islands. . . The islands were all transfigured pieces of Troy, New York. Cass got the last laugh.

Fig. 10.11 *The Laughing Girls*, page 10.

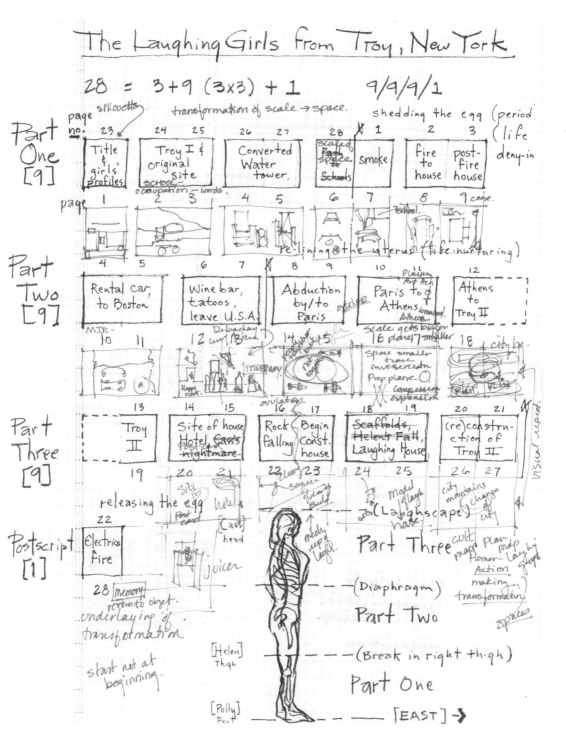

Fig. 10.12 Storyboard from *The Laughing Girls*.

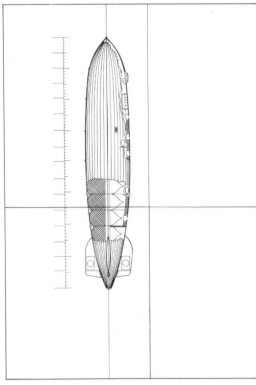

documented account of such mass hysteria in the twentieth century. The second story is Euripides's classical drama, *The Trojan Women*. Three girls – Helen, Polyxena, and Cassandra – are involved in the play. In the notes around *The Laughing Girls*, Darden makes frequent reference to Nietzsche's *Birth of Tragedy*, in which Nietzsche blames Euripides's moralizing tone for the decline of Greek tragedy. Darden sees a similar decline in contemporary design thinking. *The Laughing Girls* may be interpreted as a rewriting of Euripides's *The Trojan Women* to promote the Dionysian rather than the Apollonian spirit.

Darden's archive is full of clippings, postcards, handwritten notes, sketches, and marked-up essays. For each of his projects, Darden collected materials in files and boxes. For each of the ten acts of condemned building, he included a discontinuous genealogy: four images collaged together to guide the form of each building. For example, the images collected for the Oxygen House – an American Civil War engraving, a caboose water cooler and basin, a Westinghouse train brake, and the Hindenburg Zeppelin – are combined to form a composite ideogram that resembles the final form of the Oxygen House, as well as a graphic disclosure of the project intentions. The collages act as a visual metaphor

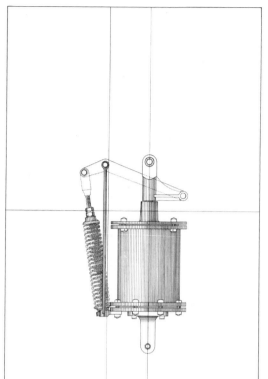

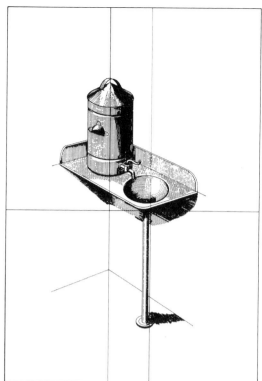

Fig. 10.13a–e Discontinuous genealogy of the Oxygen House, from *Condemned Building*. Reproduced by permission of Princeton Architectural Press and Douglas Darden Estate, courtesy of Allison Collins.

and follow Aristotle's understanding of the trope: "the right use of metaphor means an eye for resemblances."[9] Similar to his discontinuous genealogies in *Condemned Building*, Darden plays with the latent potential of found objects in *The Laughing Girls*. Each object in a context carries a certain meaning. When the object is removed, perhaps fragmented, and then inserted into a new context, a new meaning emerges. The original meaning, however, is never wholly lost. Marcel Duchamp and Paul Ricoeur proposed that all discourse overflows with a surplus of meaning.[10] Each object in *The Laughing Girls* does the same. This surplus of meaning is at the root of both metaphor and fiction.

For example, Darden sets a photograph of a water tower in Germany into the site plan of Troy, New York and manipulates it to become a house for the three girls. Maps of Troy, New York become a template for a cane. Maps of Ancient Troy give form to ankle tattoos. As noted above, the three main characters are based on three characters in Euripides's play *The Trojan Women*. Polly is the namesake of Polyxena, the most beautiful daughter of Priam, who was sacrificed on the tomb of Achilles. Cass, or Cassandra, the twin to Polyxena, could see the future, but was cursed because no one would believe her. Helen is the doppelgänger for the other Helen who may have caused the Trojan War.

The part that Darden seems to have studied most was the "found object" of laughter. In 1992 he claimed to have recorded twenty-seven young girls laughing. Three were chosen and named Polly, Cass, and Helen. I have not yet uncovered twenty-seven distinct laughs, but there is evidence of at least one girl laughing. Anna Saporito, the daughter of an architect in Denver, is referenced in Darden's notes for the project. Polaroid photographs of Anna laughing were taken and used in various collages. Other visual records include fluoroscopic images and x-rays that were produced while the subject was "chuckling" and "laughing robustly." These "laughs" were then modelled in foam. Auditory analysis of the laughing led to "temporal sections" for each of the laughs. These section cuts were translated into three-dimensional form that Darden referred to as "topographies." While there is no direct mapping of projects onto the laugh track, Darden does describe the plan of a city in terms similar to laughing. He also relates laughter to the making of a room. Beginning with the body and emanating outward, a hearty laugh fills a room. According to Darden, "Laughter starts with the space of the body, moves outward to affect

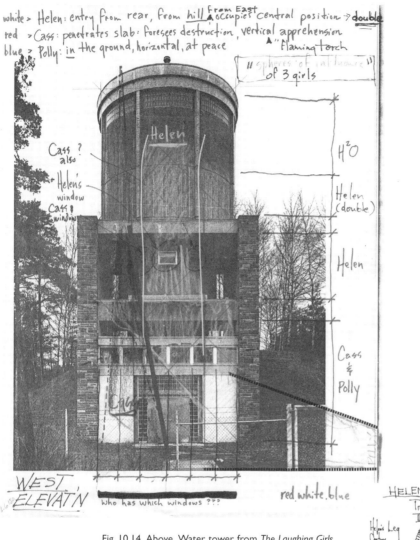

white > Helen: entry from rear, from hill. *From East* occupies central position → ~~double~~
red > Cass: penetrates slab: foresees destruction, vertical apprehension
blue > Polly: *in* the ground, horizontal, at peace

"flaming torch"

"spheres of influence"
of 3 girls

H²O

Helen
(double)

Helen

Cass
&
Polly

Cass?
also

Helen's
window
Cass's
window

Helen

Cass

WEST
ELEVAT'N

who has which windows ???

red.white.blue

Fig. 10.14 Above Water tower from *The Laughing Girls*.

Fig. 10.15 Right Helen's cane.

HELEN'S CANE

Helen's Leg
Contour

Tray
I

Tray I
[Hudson
River]

Helen's
X-Ray

Handle

[Polly]

[Cass]

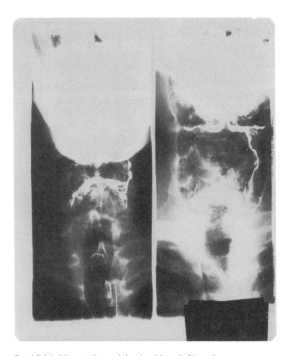

Fig. 10.16 X-ray taken while chuckling (left) and
laughing robustly (right).

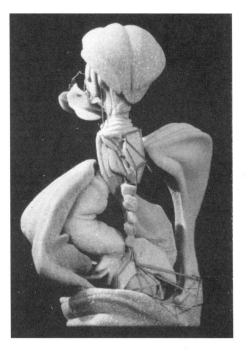

Fig. 10.17 Foam model of laughter.

a structure, and creates a site for an event." Indeed, the space of laughter informs the section of the girls' house in Troy.

Many, if not all, of the projects in *Condemned Building* are autobiographical. In many ways, *The Laughing Girls* may be the most autobiographical. Darden spent the 1988–89 academic year at the American Academy in Rome. While there, he experienced bouts of exhaustion. Returning to Denver after his fellowship, he was diagnosed with leukemia. A friend, Norman Cousins, recommended a book on curing cancer through laughter. Although Darden relied on medical treatment, this book was influential. Darden claimed that "the theme of the girl's laughter was chosen

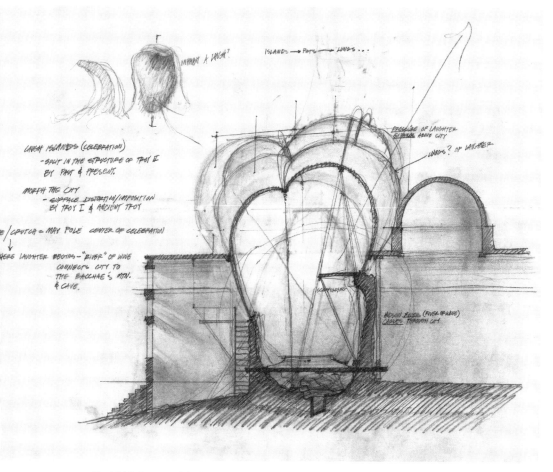

Fig. 10.18 Section of the laughing girls' house in Troy II. In the drawing Darden asks if it possible to "inhabit a laugh."

because nothing else makes me proceed in this world with a greater sense of hopeful lightness." Unbearably light, given the context.

Darden's heritage was Greek. He travelled to Greece in 1982, and *The Laughing Girls* project took him there again in 1992. On his first trip to Greece, he travelled to Monemvasia, where he met two women: Christiane Gollek, who had renamed herself Sophia on her first trip from Germany to Greece, and another woman named Janice, who referred to herself as the Greek Janus. These two women were quite close and even thought they might be twins. According to Sophia, "It was as if we were each other's shadows – not in a bad way, but positive,

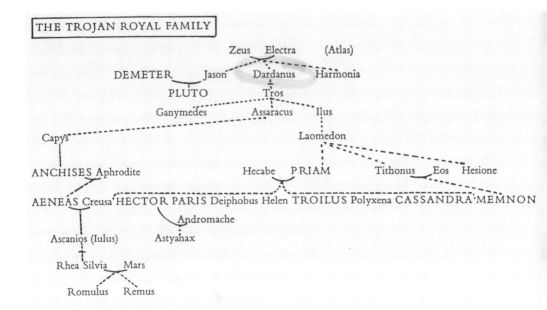

Fig. 10.19 The Trojan family tree.

like in a dream ... we were sharing each other's dreams."[11] Darden remained in touch with both women and visited Monemvasia again a decade later, this time with James Trevitt, a colleague who was working with him on *The Laughing Girls*.

Darden's family name is derived from Dardanus, who was the son of Zeus and Electra. His grandson, Tros, gave his name to the city and land over which he ruled. Dardania thus became Troy. The strait just north of Troy is known as the Dardanelles, a name Darden had fun with in postcards to himself. Priam, the great-grandson of Tros, was the last king of Troy. Among his many children were, of course, Helen, Cassandra, and Polyxena, the namesakes of Darden's three laughing girls. In an interesting twist, Robert Graves relates the Greek δάρδανος (Varvanos) "burned up" (from the verb δαρδάπτω, *dardapto*, "to wear, to slay, to burn up") to the name Dardanus.[12] Fire is, of course, a key element in the story of *The Laughing Girls*.

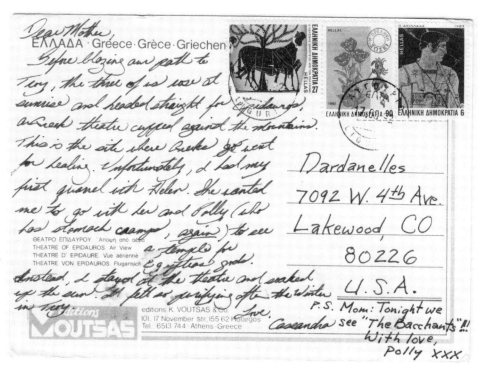

Fig. 10.20 A postcard of the Theatre of Epidaurus from "Cassandra" to the "Dardanelles." The postcard, addressed to "Mother," explains that this site is where "Greeks ~~go~~ went for healing." The address was Darden's house in Denver.

In his proposal for scholar-in-residence at the California College of the Arts and Crafts in 1994, Darden makes a specific connection between narrative and identity:

The new work on the architectural novel is based on my belief in the necessity of making architecture by folding other disciplines into its inquiry. Through this seemingly circumspect approach the architect can more cogently seek a recommencement with origins. It is through a recommencement with origins that architecture establishes resonant cultural identities. A key component of this recommencement is acknowledging that each of us has a life story, an inner narrative that we construct and which is our identity; that is, the narrative constructs us. To assert the human subject at the center of architectural practice, it is crucial to deepen the correspondence between personal, cultural, and architectural narratives. The study of myths and stories as part of the act of designing is necessary for the mooring of architecture to our culture. This mooring is further realized by envisaging buildings and designed objects as having the capacity to tell stories about the inhabitants and the places where they reside.[13]

Richard Kearney reminds us that "every act of storytelling involves someone (a teller) telling something (a story) to someone (a listener) about something (a real or imaginary world)."[14] This interplay of agencies not only affords a potentially rich and grounded reading of work, it also provides a particular experience of selfhood and, by extension, identity. When one makes architecture, it is always for another. It is an eminently social act, just like storytelling. This recognition of "the other" is also inherently ethical, leading to a sense of identity and selfhood that is essential to any sense of responsibility. It is clear that Darden understood this to be not only the potential but also the obligation of building. Although Darden is no longer with us, the story continues …

NOTES

1 After graduating magna cum laude with degrees in English and psychology from the University of Denver in 1974, Darden spent two years at Parsons in New York, then from 1979 to 1983 at the Harvard Graduate School of Design (GSD) in Cambridge. Although he graduated from the GSD with distinction, his time there was not particularly rewarding, except for a studio with Stanley Tigerman in his final year. Darden was inspired by Tigerman's witty critique of architectural agency, evident in Tigerman's *Versus: An American Architect's Alternatives* (1982), written while Darden was Tigerman's student. Darden dedicated *Condemned Building* to his parents and Tigerman. After graduation, he taught at several universities and spent time in Rome as a fellow at the American Academy. He returned to the United States in 1989 and began work at the University of Colorado at Denver, where he taught until his untimely death in 1996.

2 The act of turning over the turtle refers to the film *Blade Runner*. In an early scene, Holden is interrogating Leon to determine if he is a "replicant" and therefore not human. Holden proposes a hypothetical situation in which a turtle has been overturned and is lying on its back, baking in the sun, then asks Leon why he does not help the turtle by turning it over. Visibly shaken, Leon then shoots Holden and escapes.

3 "Underbelly" is a word that Darden often used to refer to his architecture. It is discussed at length in *Looking after the Underbelly*, a film made by architect and professor Rob Miller in 1992. In the introduction to *Condemned Building*, a certain Dweller by the Dark Stream claimed, "I am inclined while watching the turtle to turn it over and study its underbelly. From this unnatural position I see how this platonically solid creature makes its way through the world."

4 All of the sources for this essay are from a private archive of Darden's work that is currently held by Ben Ledbetter, a close friend and fellow member of the self-titled "unholy triumvirate" that somehow made it through the GSD in the early 1980s. Ledbetter graciously allowed me and a group of students from the Wentworth Institute of Technology to study the materials in the archive.

5 Unpublished application for scholar-in-residence at the California College of the Arts and Crafts, 1994.

6 Drawings of the cane and the tattoos are in the archive. The locations of the juicer and the modelled laughs are not known at this time.

7 In almost all of his grant applications, Darden states that *The Laughing Girls* was intended to be published in a forthcoming volume of *Chora*; however, it remained unfinished and was never published. With the publication of this essay, Darden may get the last laugh.

8 In other iterations of the project, the three sections are named variously as "passage one," "passage two," "passage three"; and "Troy, NY," "Troy, Greece," and "future Troy."

9 Aristotle, *The Poetics*, trans. W. Hamilton Fyfe, in *Aristotle: The Poetics; Longinus: On the Sublime; and Demetrius: On Style* (London: William Heinemann, 1932), 22.9. The translator further explains that the use of metaphor implies "the power of detecting 'identity in difference.'" This last phrase is often translated as the "similarities of dissimilars."

10 Paul Ricoeur describes surplus of meaning as the residue of literal interpretation. He discusses this idea, as well as the issue of metaphor and symbol, in *Interpretation Theory: Discourse and the Surplus of Meaning* (Fort Worth: Texas Christian University Press, 1976). The rationale for, and defense of, Duchamp's most famous readymade, *Fountain*, was presented in the second volume of the surrealist journal *The Blind Man* (May 1917). In an article entitled "The Richard Mutt Case," the anonymous author explains, "Whether Mr. Mutt with his own hands made the fountain or not

has no importance. He CHOSE it. He took an ordinary article of life, placed it so that its useful significance disappeared under a new title and point of view – created a new thought for that object." Most scholars agree that Duchamp was indeed the author. Both Ricoeur and Duchamp are referenced by Darden.

11 From an unpublished letter.

12 Robert Graves, *The Greek Myths* (London: Penguin Books, 1955), 1:89n2.

13 Unpublished application for scholar-in-residence at the California College of the Arts and Crafts, 1994.

14 Richard Kearney, *On Stories* (London: Routledge, 2002), 150.

Filarete's Sforzinda: The Ideal City as a Poetic and Rhetorical Construction

Alberto Pérez-Gómez

Chora

THE ARCHITECT ANTONIO DI PIERO AVERLINO (ca 1400–1469) characterized his life's work rhetorically by adopting the pseudonym Il Filarete, coupling the Greek words *philia* and *areté* to refer to himself as a lover of virtue. In the mid-fifteenth century he became the first "modern" to design an ideal city in its totality, founded from scratch in a natural site without history. This ideal city, named Sforzinda after his patron Francesco Sforza, is the central topic of his *Trattato di architettura*.[1] Although the operation that Filarete describes has been interpreted generally as a precursor of rational planning, it is actually a product of *disegno*, generated from geometric *lineamenti* that originated in the architect's mind's eye (fig. 11.1).

In Filarete's manuscript, the city is presented as a series of drawings in the margins, following medieval custom. The design is meant to be comprehensive. It has an outer wall in the form of an eight-pointed star, circumscribed by a circle. Inside there are many institutional buildings in the latest "style." These drawings are accompanied by descriptions of the geometric operations that generated the forms, with dimensions (mostly in *braccia*) of the main parts of the buildings. Although Filarete does not provide detailed working drawings, material specifications, or precise cost estimates – as might be expected from a modern architect or planner – he has full confidence in the capacity of a designer to carry out such a complex building operation.

I wish to show how Filarete's project is rich with ambiguities and possible implications for contemporary urban design. This early Renaissance project is indeed modern in important ways: Filarete imagines building an entire city through the force of human will, using politics to establish order. The success of his enterprise requires "marrying" the architect's imagination to the political power of an earthly prince. This resonates with Machiavelli's well-known premise that human politics is independent from divine will: a good prince (with an equally good architect) should be able to found a meaningful order without relying on ancestral authority, even using violence when necessary.[2]

Although the geometry of Sforzinda resembles earlier ideal cities in the Western tradition – Plato's, for example, as well as medieval representations of Heavenly Jerusalem inscribed in squares or circles – its horizon of meaning is radically different. Medieval images described an otherworldly reality that divine will would create for humanity at the end of time (fig. 11.2). Filarete's design is for an earthly world where the

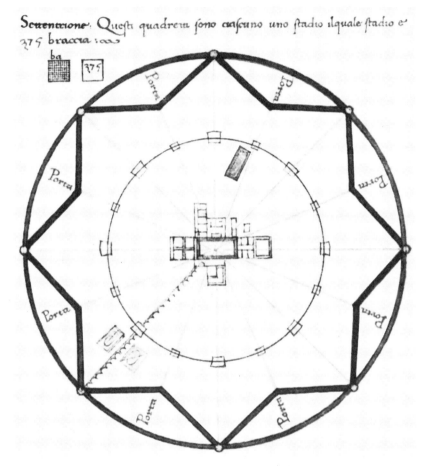

Fig. 11.1 Filarete's design for Sforzinda, showing the perimeter wall, gateways, radial streets, aqueduct, main square, and secondary public spaces. From *Trattato*, fol. 43r.

human imagination promotes a happy life "down below." His urban project for a real Italian prince does not maintain the medieval belief that God is the architect, with human masons acting merely as His hands. While acknowledging this important change, I will argue that a crucial rhetorical dimension grounds Filarete's project in its lived world and its history – dimensions that are often neglected by modern architects and planners, despite the good intentions articulated in discourses such as regionalism and sustainability.

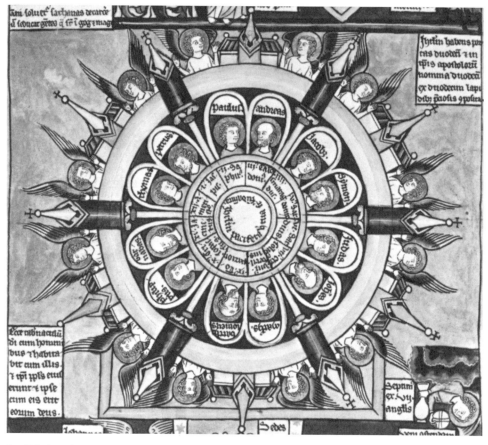

Fig. 11.2 A medieval image of Heavenly Jerusalem. From *Liber Floridus*, ms. Lat. 8865 (ca 1260). Bibliothèque Nationale de France.

The geometric form of Filarete's ideal city is based on operations and meanings that must be unpacked (fig. 11.3). During the Renaissance, the Neoplatonic tradition of Marsilio Ficino and Leon Battista Alberti proposed that an architect first shapes a building in the soul, rather than in matter. As Ficino explains in *De amore*, architecture seduces and inflames us with love, through the Idea embodied in *lineamenti*. Paraphrasing Plotinus, he writes,

In the beginning the architect develops a Reason or Idea, as it were, of the building in his soul. Then he builds, as nearly as possible, the kind of house he has conceived. Who will deny that the house is a body and that it is very much like the architect's incorporeal Idea, in the likeness of which it was built? Furthermore, it must be judged as being like the architect, more on

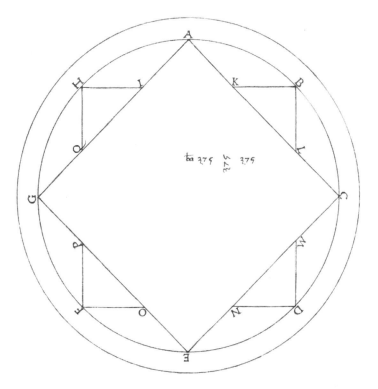

Fig. 11.3 Generative geometries for the schematic perimeter of Sforzinda.
From *Trattato*, fol. 13v.

account of a certain incorporeal design than on account of its matter. Therefore go ahead; subtract its matter if you can (and you can subtract it mentally), but leave the design. Nothing of body, nothing of matter will remain to
you. On the contrary, the design which came from the artist and the design
which remains in the artist will be completely identical.[3]

Geometric *lineamenti* ensure the splendour of form, enabling observers and inhabitants to commune with incorporeal beauty through
the incorporeal light that comes into our eyes.[4] Alberti adds, "All the
intent and purpose of lineaments lies in finding the correct, infallible way
of joining and fitting together (the) lines and angles (of a projected building)."[5] Thus, the visible artifact seduces us, and through physical love
we may realize that the source of all beauty is beyond matter – and is
also truth.

Although geometry is the epitome of rationality (representing the Greek *mathemata*, that which is immutable), it is crucial to recognize its *poetic* dimension in Filarete's project. Filarete would have understood this from Vitruvius's *Ten Books* (ca 25 BCE). In the opening paragraphs of his second book, Vitruvius provides the earliest theoretical account of the origins of Western architecture as a clearing in the forest, the first "public space." The story involves the simultaneous inception of language and culture,[6] signalling the separation of humanity from the animal world. According to Vitruvius, early humans discover they can maintain a fire that was initiated by lightning during a storm (fig. 11.4). The domestication of fire brings humans together. They recognize others, begin to speak, and eventually build. The fire is not stolen from the gods. It is a gift, a heavenly spark carried by the wind that Vitruvius still interprets as the breath of nature, an invisible force that lights up human desire in our hearts and is responsible for our capacity to create and reproduce, for our health and well-being. The first humans open up a clearing: a place for dwelling, where limits and mortality are acknowledged. Architecture is poetic, and its origins coincide with the origins of language and culture.

Vitruvius's architectural clearing is also a space of communication where the miracle of language happens. Both language and architecture reveal and frame human reality. Vitruvius shows how architecture embodies political and ritual action, reinforcing promises and establishing bonds. Human culture relies on domestication and domesticity; *domus* is the Latin word for home, but also for the heavenly vault. According to the wise fox in Saint-Exupéry's *Little Prince*, this is also a condition for true human knowledge. Vitruvius then describes how he imagines the first human dwellings. Walking not prone but upright, looking at the magnificent universe and its stars, humans used their hands and imitated nature in their construction of primitive huts. The geometric nature of these constructions is reinforced by Vitruvius's retelling of the story of Aristippus's shipwreck. Stranded on the shore of Rhodes, this philosopher noticed geometric diagrams that had been drawn in the sand and exclaimed, "Let's hope for the best, I see human footprints."[7] Vitruvius thus identifies the origin of architecture with the geometric construction of human dwelling, unlike later accounts that associated it with the particular typological form of a private home or a funerary monument.

In the classical tradition, the human encounter with nature was not reduced to an exploitation of natural resources, nor to an archaic ritual

Fig. 11.4 Illustration of the origin of architecture according to Vitruvius. From Vitruvius, *De architectura,* trans. Cesare di Lorenzo Cesariano (1521), xxxi.

communion with the elements. The place of human dwelling was a space of mediation that had to retain its boundaries in order to be fully partic-ipatory. This geometry of architecture "takes the measure of the earth," yet acknowledges that nature is alive and finite, often menacing, and always transforming. It is hard to recognize this oneiric space in our tech-nological, isotropic, and homogeneous world. Occasionally we grasp it through intuition and dreams. It is the space of *geo-metria,* discovered

by Aristippus after his shipwreck. It is also the space of imagination and
desire in modern literary works such as Lewis Carroll's *Alice in Wonder-
land* and Alain Robbe-Grillet's *In the Labyrinth*.

Very much part of the Vitruvian tradition, Filarete's Sforzinda is a
form of geometric augury. It is not a literal picture of a future city, but its
seed. The image of Sforzinda is to a real city as a seed is to a full-grown
tree. The working metaphor is alchemical, and Filarete elaborates on this
in his treatise.[8]

To appreciate its modernity, we can consider differences and similarities between Sforzinda and the more traditional reconstruction of Ezekiel's
Heavenly Temple by the Jesuit Juan Bautista Villalpando over a century
later (fig. 11.5).[9] Villalpando believed that the vision of Ezekiel, a Jewish
prophet, was a "perspective" induced by God's light and presented to
humanity. This power of imagining, learned through the Jesuit spiritual
exercises, was Villalpando's way to align human will and divine will. The
human architect, like the prophet, is then called upon to transform the
graphic projections of this vision into a real building of stone. Villalpando argues that this new form of worldly production is called for by Christ's
incarnation: the *propaganda fide* that must be pursued by all Catholic mis-
sionaries after the Counter-Reformation. Rather than remaining "otherworldly," the City of God on Earth now must be built by humans, so Philip
II of Spain assumed responsibility for its incarnation in the Escorial, which
also became a symbol of his absolute political power.[10]

Filarete's ideal city also was conceived as the manifestation of a
prince's will, but his augural geometry belongs to a very different, less
reductive architectural process. The treatise that describes the project is
a didactic text to educate the benevolent leader of an Italian city-state.
Filarete is explicit: his words are intended to be read aloud to this princely patron, to teach him "the modes and measures of building."[11] His text
is both a traditional tract for princely education and an expression of the
new humanist rhetoric. It was dedicated first to Cosimo de' Medici in
1464, and later to Francesco Sforza.

In a few revealing paragraphs, Filarete explains that the architect is
like a mother who needs a father (the client/prince) for procreating and
generating a building.[12] This is a serious matter for Filarete. This "loving
relationship" is not just a figure of speech; their mutual responsibilities are
a crucial condition for the success of the project. The patron is fecund
and provides the seed (which, in traditional Platonic genetics, is also the

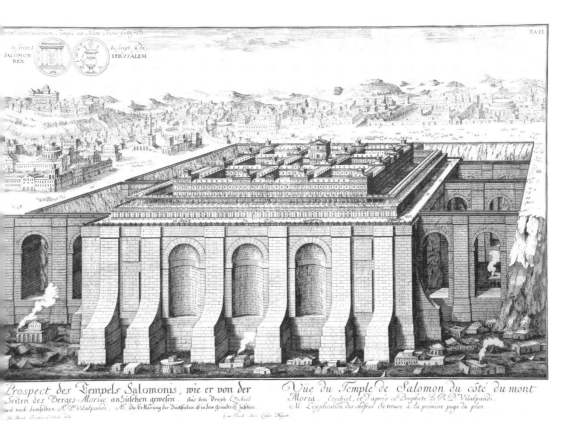

Fig. 11.5 Perspective view of Solomon's Temple, based on Juan Bautista Villalpando's reconstruction (1596–1604). From J.B. Fischer von Erlach, *Entwurff einer historischen Architektur* (1721), plate II.

concept). The architect then "carries" the building/city/child for nine months, taking care to contemplate beautiful things during this time, and eventually gives birth to the design/idea, the initial image that is the basic intellectual product of the architect. The building is a living organism. It breathes and must be cared for by its parents, or else it may die.

The text is a narrative written in Italian, rather than a Latin treatise such as Alberti's *De re aedificatoria*. As an oral and vernacular discourse, its form represents a significant innovation in architectural theory. The setting is a hunt, a typical princely activity, accompanied by a series of banquets and celebrations, with descriptions of buildings and bewildering archaeological discoveries. The narrative is hardly linear, as it is punctuated by sensuous encounters with nature, erotic events, poetic descriptions of paintings (in the tradition of *ekphrasis*), and revelations about architecture. Amidst its delightful wanderings is a clear pedagogical program for architecture that describes its meanings, appropriate ways of building, justifications, proportions, and qualities associated with measurement – all derived from architecture's primordial origins and aligned with a mythologized classical antiquity. Filarete's principles are founded on reason, authority (mostly Christian and classical precedents), and example. Drawing (*disegno*) and proportion (*misura*) are the central issues for architectural production. This convergence is much more evident here than in the humanist writings of Alberti.

Filarete traces the source of architectural meaning to the relationship between the body of Adam (the first of God's creations) and the circle and the square (as cosmic geometric figures). He states that God produced "in perfection" the body, the soul, the intellect, and the mind. These four constitutive elements of human consciousness were all "organized and measured," and allowed to produce each other "as seen in nature," while differences among individuals are caused by different positions of constellations and planets, revealing Filarete's belief in astrological influences.[13] Filarete sought to reconcile the origins of architecture with Christian scripture: God made Adam, the first architect, who covered his head to protect himself from rain after being expelled from Paradise. "Constrained by necessity," Adam had to find both food and shelter, and eventually "made some sort of shelter of branches."[14] Created with perfect proportions by the Christian God, Adam thus became the model for architecture. Columns then were proportioned according to the foot or the head. Despite the differences between Filarete's Judeo-Christian account and Vitruvius's pagan story, both presented an architecture that is traced to an origin, is ruled by measure and geometry, imitates the cosmos, and contributes to human health and happiness.

Filarete describes the building of a whole city, from foundations to inauguration. Although stories in his text refer to the territory and cities around Milan and to real historical events – particularly the exploits of the Sforza family – the site for Filarete's new city is not a real location in Sforza's duchy, but a literary *topos*. Later we learn that this city is not a new creation, but a historical re-enactment of an ancient mythical foundation, described in a golden book that was part of a treasure exhumed during the excavation of a port.

The architect is ready to start drawing the city. "I shall call the drawing Averliano" (a reference to himself) "and the city Sforzinda" (named after the client prince).[15] The geometric diagram is almost self-referential, yet Filarete indulges in a long description of the site's topography, beauty, and healthy attributes. Following Vitruvius's advice, it is protected from bad winds, exposed to favourable ones, nestled by mountains, and located near the beneficial waters of a river. We also learn that there is already a hermitage nearby – the hermit venerates "Our Lord and Our Lady" – suggesting that the place already has been found favourable.[16] The sites of cities and temples in classical antiquity had been found propitious on the basis of natural attributes and auspices that revealed a cosmic orientation.[17] Filarete relies instead on the agency of human narrative to consecrate nature, following the Christian tradition. One could even argue that the site is actually made auspicious through this agency. Human naming now takes precedence over the recognition of *topos* as a significant natural place. To Filarete, space is neither a topographic revelation of cosmic order nor a modern, isotropic Cartesian space.

Sforzinda's "new order" is strictly formal. It does not imply a social or political critique, as in Thomas More's *Utopia* in the sixteenth century, nor does it presume the Greek concept of *isonomia*, in which all citizens are politically equal. Instead, it manifests the powerful alliance of the prince and the architect. In the history of Renaissance utopias, Filarete's Sforzinda most closely resembles a much later text by Tommaso Campanella – *The City of the Sun*, which displays hermetic and magical interests.[18]

Sforzinda is a centralized city surrounded by a wall in the form of an eight-pointed star (fig. 11.1). Its geometry was generated by superposing two squares, then rotating one forty-five degrees (a well-known method in medieval *ad quadratum* building operations). By reconciling the square (symbolizing masculine *virtú*) and the circle (symbolizing feminine forces of destiny, associated with the circle of the horizon), this propitious form resonated with the cosmos and promoted a good life in human affairs, working literally as an amulet. During the Renaissance, it was still believed that formal transformations were also substantial – a principle of magic that is quite remote from modern science. A perfect geometry, *coincidentia oppositorum*, would guarantee the highest meanings and permit a healthy and happy life.

These beliefs are evident also in Filarete's description of the foundation ceremonies for the city and its buildings.[19] Once the architect ascertains that "a good constellation and moment will begin to reign during a week," the ceremony can take place. A marble cornerstone is inscribed with the date, the name of the prince, the name of the reigning pope, and the name of the architect. The architect and his divinely sanctioned patron thus are recorded as the metaphorical foundation of the work. The architect also might place a bronze-covered book in a marble box under the cornerstone, "containing a record of the age and the deeds of worthy men" (including the architect's own accomplishments!). As this first stone is laid, accompanied by music and witnessed by the bishop and the architect, an assembly of notable men makes offerings to the prince and his sons. Filarete shows a keen awareness of the ephemeral nature of all things human, believing that works of architecture must not challenge this ephemeral condition but be reconciled with it. Architecture is memory; it stabilizes meanings in the flux of historical time. Indeed, in the same box he suggests placing "an earthen vase full of grain," a simile of both the human body and the city. This vase "should be full of all that gives life to man," and on it "nothing is written but Life and Death."[20] The ceremony acknowledges the finitude of the city and its buildings. This new structure is sanctioned by a symbolic copulation of the sun and the moon. The earth is opened to receive seminal liquids such as blood, milk, honey, oil, and wine. A ritual sacrifice ensures the survival of the foundations, recalling medieval practices in which the master mason had to immolate his wife (or at least her shadow) and bury her in the foundations. In Filarete's account, a workman digging the foundations discovers a "beautiful serpent" that attacks and strangles him. Filarete also emphasizes the importance of continuing to "feed" the completed building so that it stays alive. This contrasts with the more limited responsibility of the modern architect, which is expected to end once the building has been "delivered."

Filarete clearly believes in the importance of foundation rituals and their association with Christianity, but he also speculates on their "true" rational significance.[21] His design for a city is comprehensive: it includes "infrastructure" such as roads and a water supply, as well as mysterious vents dug into the ground to help the city breathe and to minimize the impact of earthquakes. Although the city is built quickly, its construction follows a particular rhythm based on harmony and faith. Filarete's story is filled with fascinating, even perplexing features. Everything makes reference to something else, including ancient precedents. He often uses anagrams to demonstrate a relation between ancient sites and buildings and their counterparts in the present: for example, Nomila (an ancient city) becomes Milano, and Zogalia (an ancient prince) becomes Galeazzo (Sforza).[22] As in Ficino's hermetic writings, ancient practices are reconciled with Christian traditions to authorize present acts and artifacts.

Filarete's architect is a charismatic hero and a magician. His genius enables him to conceive the city's *disegno* in his mind and then carry it to completion. Filarete describes the building of Sforzinda as a massive operation that is carried out in a short period of time by thousands of workers. The architect is responsible for the entire building operation. With the support of his patron, he handles all administrative matters, including finding the best craftsmen and minimizing the cost of building.[23] He does this without using his own hands to build. Although Filarete privileges the image, the *disegno*, he states that its germ must transmute as it grows into its full embodiment. Unlike Alberti's more "modern" plea for the builder to "preserve the architect's music"[24] by precisely following the forms and proportions in the architect's drawing, Filarete welcomed changes and improvisation during the construction process. Although he himself was an excellent craftsman, his treatise portrays the architect as a detached leader and coordinator who upholds faith in the operation, like a secular version of a medieval priest in charge of building a cathedral.

Filarete often used a grid in his drawings – not as an instrument for efficient building nor to construe architecture as a spatial matrix, but to explain issues of scale to the prince. He tells the prince to imagine himself as a very small man and then project his image into the drawing to understand the architect's ideas.[25] This new way of conceiving architecture was unknown to medieval master masons. Although Filarete recognized a difference between sketches and scaled drawings, measurement during this period was imprecise, without the systematic precision that is implied in Cartesian geometry. Indeed, there are often significant discrepancies between plans and elevations of the same project. Filarete's drawings must be understood not as literal prescriptions, but as generative ideas that develop gradually into the final building. To elaborate on these drawings and develop the design, Filarete advises using models. He calls them *quadro*, literally a "square" or "squaring." This follows the Lombard tradition of building *ad quadratum*, but also implies cubic forms that evoke the generative power of the square and other mathematical entities.

Although Filarete recognizes that human works are finite, he exhorts his prince to build for glory and to create a longstanding reputation for himself and his architect. Together, they are capable of generating *arche*: origins and new foundations without precedent. This wholly new consciousness anticipates the modern technological project, but must be qualified in Filarete's time. According to Machiavelli, the most glorious government starts from nothing, as epitomized by the *condottiere* Sforza, who developed his political power in Milan not from aristocratic blood, but through sheer "force" (thus his name Sforza). In Sforzinda, Filarete (the "lover of virtue") seems to promote this highest form of *virtú*, yet his ultimate aim was to align this new city within its larger transcendental order. Machiavelli also recognized that the prince must seduce *fortuna* – tempestuous, unpredictable Nature – whose enigmatic forces greatly influence one's chances of success.

Despite the obvious symbolism of the city's external geometry, most of Filarete's treatise describes the institutions within its walls. Their particular building forms recall Florentine precedents and Milanese building practices, including Lombard Gothic details that are rich in texture and colour. Filarete respected the material history of Milan, including its local myths and Oriental sources. Although Sforzinda was "ideal," its architecture integrated those cultural sources into its narrative.

Filarete also relies on a Neoplatonic hierarchy to carry *disegno*, the initial poetic image, down through a series of levels: from numbers to figures, to line drawings, to models, and eventually to buildings. Like a magus, the architect operates throughout this range, at each level seeking the appropriate proportions and qualities to align the architecture with divine grace. Every step in the process is understood as an opportunity to enrich the outcome through successive interpretations. Filarete's text emphasizes the symbolism of numbers. All of the churches proposed in Sforzinda have four towers that celebrate the four evangelists, with a cruciform plan that symbolizes the cross of Christ. There are 365 windows in the castle (one for every day of the year) and seven radial rooms below grade (one for each deadly sin) in the House of Virtue and Vice.

The House of Virtue and Vice warrants special attention. This building is a predominantly circular structure on a square plinth, topped with an enigmatic emblem perched precariously on a pyramid (fig. 11.6). It is presented as a theatre of memory that epitomizes the meaning of the city.[26] Virtue is gained as one ascends toward knowledge, passing through rooms defined by the twenty-three letters of the Latin alphabet, culminating in astrology: "a science that puts everything in its place." This recalls the great medieval accomplishments of Hugh of St Victor's "index" system as an art of memory, but transposed into a Renaissance context that integrates classical, Christian, and secular knowledge.[27] This is a new architectural program with no precedent in antiquity or the Middle Ages.

Fig. 11.6 Sectional view of the House of Vice and Virtue. From *Trattato*, fol. 144r.

The central location of this House in Sforzinda's marketplace suggests that it is as important as the city's religious buildings – and perhaps superior. Its program for virtue and vice also invokes the architect's pseudonym. In European architecture, this is perhaps the first instance of a "theoretical project," in which the architect invents a new building program rather than relying on existing institutions. This attitude eventually would come to fruition in the late eighteenth-century work of Ledoux. In Filarete's imaginary city, human life is not merely a step on the medieval path to the eternal beyond, nor has it yet been reduced to a rational material process to be accommodated by modern planning; in this Renaissance context, life itself is sacred.

Filarete recognized that his architectural inventions needed to be integrated into the existing socio-cultural order. This is particularly evident in his drawings of urban marketplaces (fig. 11.7). Surrounded by orthogonal, well-proportioned buildings, these urban spaces present a rich social life. The purpose of these drawings is not mentioned in his text, but he probably intended to portray the "real" character of the squares in his ideal city. There is nothing rational or functional in these designs. Markets of all kinds line the rectilinear canals, crossed by bridges that evoke St Petersburg much later. The city has an ideal geometric order, yet its public spaces are real: framed not only by churches and palaces, but also by taverns and brothels, "temples to Bacchus and Venus." As was customary in medieval cities, these various aspects of urban life are situated in close proximity.

In this light, let me conclude by emphasizing the rhetorical dimension of Filarete's early modern imaginary city. Rhetoric, with its roots in spoken language, carries the values of a given culture. The great poet Dante had identified four characteristics of genuine language in *De vulgari eloquentia* (On vernacular speech), probably written between 1303 and 1305.[28] He considered whether poetic images could be communicated in a more genuine way in vernacular language rather than scholarly Latin. Concluding that this was the case, Dante proposed that vernacular, emerging from poetic oral speech, was better prepared to convey a historical situation and thus articulate relevant truths. This language is primarily directive, revelatory, and metaphorical – not argumentative, deductive, or rational (like traditional philosophy in the manner of Plato and Aristotle).[29] It is my contention that Filarete, more than a century later, was aware of Dante's four characteristics and used them for both his theoretical discourse and his designs, to develop a novel yet appropriate architecture for his time that would be more genuine than medieval building practices.

Allow me to enumerate Dante's categories and incorporate them into my conclusion. First, both language and architecture should be *illustre*, displaying an "illuminating brilliance" from their powerful poetic creation. Genuine linguistic practices must emerge from the depths of human creativity, be directed to all aspects of humanity, and lead to spiritual and practical self-realization. This enables them to embrace and advance humanity's political life. The motivation here is not innovation for its own sake, but an ethical concern. Any "new" architecture likewise must maintain its rootedness in a given culture, seeking the common good.

Second, architecture and the language that represents it must be *cardinale*, recalling the *cardo* as a fundamental urban and celestial axis in antiquity. Vitruvius describes how a gnomon or shadow-tracer was used to project the cardinal directions from the heavens onto the ground, constituting the point of origin of all architectural operations, marking the *templum* at the centre of urban orders.[30] *Cardinale* is also what gives authority. In language, this authoritative virtue enables many different dialects to resonate in the poet's ideal model. The *cardo* stands for geometry, the most universal of languages. It allows particularity and universality to coexist: the real and the ideal, the historical and the future vision.

Dante's third virtue is *aulica*, which enables the people's language to find its way into the royal court. Filarete's words had to be sanctioned by the *aula* of the prince, the "father" of his architecture. This was truly important for Filarete, as his description of this new Renaissance architecture was presented in *volgare* rather than in Latin – a tactic that was almost unprecedented. Beyond his personal interests, this may have been his main objective in writing the manuscript.

Finally, Dante states that language must be *curiale*. The *curia* is where law is established and administered. This is Filarete's intention for his text and his city: to provide a space of cultural communication, both familiar and new. It is more enlightening to understand Filarete's ideal city in the tradition of Ciceronian humanism than as a variation on Plato's imaginary cities or as a step toward modern utopias. Although his philosophical and architectural propositions are imaginary, they are rooted in the

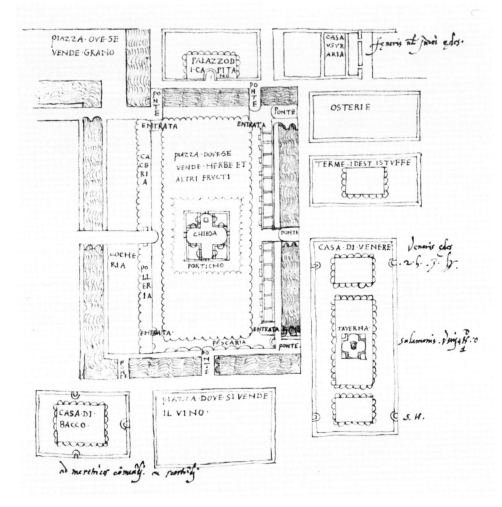

Fig. 11.7 Detail of a sketch plan for a public space in the city. Attached to the Codex Palatino version of *Trattato*.

social language of daily life. The origin of his city, like the origin of architecture in Vitruvius, is associated with the origin of language. His city and its architecture are generated by and for rhetoric; they are not products of scientific rationality or formal fancy.

NOTES

1 Filarete's manuscript was never published during his lifetime. Today there is an Italian edition, *Trattato di architettura*, 2 vols., ed. Anna Maria Finoli and Liliana Grassi, with introduction and notes by Liliana Grassi (Milan: Il Polifilo, 1972), and an English translation by John Spencer, *Filarete's Treatise on Architecture*, 2 vols. (New Haven: Yale University Press, 1965). For a sketch of the history of the manuscripts, see Spencer's introduction in *Filarete's Treatise*, 1:xvii–xviii.

2 Niccolo Machiavelli's *The Prince* was written in the early 1530s and published in 1532, almost a century after Filarete's writing.

3 Marsilio Ficino, *De amore* (1469); *Commentary on Plato's Symposium on Love*, trans. S. Jayne (Dallas: Spring Publications, 1985), 93.

4 Richard Krautheimer has unpacked the etymology of the Renaissance term *lineamenti*. The term has Latin origins and was used only figuratively during the Middle Ages. In Latin it referred to "lines" or even to the outline of a drawing. According to Krautheimer, during the early Renaissance, Lorenzo Ghiberti associated the term with "rules." This likely referred to geometric outlines illustrating rules that were then applied in drawing and making. *Lorenzo Ghiberti* (Princeton: Princeton University Press, 1970), 230.

5 Leon Battista Alberti, *On the Art of Building in Ten Books*, trans. J. Rykwert, R. Tavernor, and N. Leach (Cambridge, MA: MIT Press, 1988), 1.1.

6 Vitruvius, *Ten Books on Architecture*, ed. I.D. Rowland and T.N. Howe (Cambridge: Cambridge University Press, 2002), 2.1.

7 The story of Aristippus is told in Vitruvius, *Ten Books*, introduction to Book 6.

8 An alchemical imagination seems to be at work in several passages: for example, in the sections on foundation ceremonies (fol. 25v; *Filarete's Treatise*, 1:45).

9 Juan Bautista Villalpando, *In Ezechielem explanationes et apparatus urbis ac templi hierosolymitani* (Rome, 1596–1604). I have used the first Spanish translation by José Luis Oliver Domingo: *El Templo de Salomón*, 2 vols. (Madrid: Ediciones Siruela, 1991).

10 For greater elaboration, see Alberto Pérez-Gómez, "Juan Bautista Villalpando's Divine Model in Architectural Theory," in *Chora: Intervals in the Philosophy of Architecture*, vol. 3 (Montreal and Kingston: McGill-Queen's University Press, 1999), 125–56.

11 Filarete, fol. 1r; *Filarete's Treatise*, 1:3.

12 Filarete, fol. 7v–8r; *Filarete's Treatise*, 1:15–16.

13 Filarete, fol. 2v; *Filarete's Treatise*, 1:6.

14 Filarete, fol. 4v; *Filarete's Treatise*, 1:10.

15 Filarete, fol. 11v; *Filarete's Treatise*, 1:22.

16 Filarete, fol. 12v; *Filarete's Treatise*, 1:24.

17 The best-known study on this topic is Vincent Scully, *The Earth, the Temple and the Gods: Greek Sacred Architecture* (New Haven: Yale University Press, 1962).

18 Tommaso Campanella, *La città del sole: Dialogo poetico* (1602); *The City of the Sun: A Poetical Dialogue*, trans. D.J. Donno (Berkeley: University of California Press, 1981).

19 Filarete, fol. 25v–26v; *Filarete's Treatise*, 1: 45–7.

20 Ibid.

21 See, for example, Filarete, fol. 45r; *Filarete's Treatise*, 1:78.

22 Filarete, fol. 103v; *Filarete's Treatise*, 1:181.

23 Filarete, fol. 8v; *Filarete's Treatise*, 1:17.

24 Alberti's famous statement appears in a letter (dated 14 November 1454) concerning his church of S. Francesco in Rimini, addressed to the resident architect, Matteo de' Pasti.

25 Filarete, fol. 47r; *Filarete's Treatise*, 1:81–2.

26 Filarete, fol. 142v ff.; *Filarete's Treatise*, 1:245–9.

27 For an analysis of Hugh's contribution in this regard, see Ivan Illich, *In the Vineyard of the Text: A Commentary to Hugh's Didascalicon* (Chicago: University of Chicago Press, 1996).

28 The full Latin text can be found at www.interbooks.eu/poesia/duecento/dantealighieri/devulgarieloquentia.html.

29 For an analysis and brilliant contextualization of Dante's insight, see Ernesto Grassi, *Rhetoric as Philosophy: The Humanist Tradition* (Carbondale: Southern Illinois University Press, 1980), 80–3.

30 Vitruvius, *Ten Books*, 1:30.

Is the Endless a House?

Angeliki Sioli

Chora

ON THE NIGHT OF 16 June 1904, after spending a whole day in James Joyce's literary Dublin, Leopold Bloom returns home, bringing with him the drunken Stephen Dedalus. In the kitchen, Bloom begins to prepare coffee by turning the faucet and letting the water flow.

What in water did Bloom, waterlover, drawer of water, watercarrier returning to the range, admire?

    Its universality: its democratic equality and constancy to its nature in seeking its own level: ... the restlessness of its waves ... its hydrostatic quiescence in calm: its hydrokinetic turgidity in neap and spring tides: ... its capacity to dissolve and hold in solution all soluble substances including millions of tons of the most precious metals: its slow erosions of peninsulas and downward-tending promontories: ... its gradation of colours in the torrid and temperate and frigid zones: ... its violence in seaquakes, waterspouts, artesian wells, eruptions, torrents, eddies, freshets, spates, groundswells ... its healing virtues: ... its properties for cleansing, quenching thirst and fire, nourishing vegetation: its infallibility as paradigm and paragon: its metamorphoses as vapour, mist, cloud, rain, sleet, snow, hail: ... its variety of forms in loughs and bays and gulfs and bights and guts and lagoons and atolls and archipelagos and sounds and fjords and minches and tidal estuaries and arms of sea.[1]

An immense range of water's characteristics and qualities flow through the mind of Leopold Bloom, the dweller of a typical house in the Irish capital, as he simply turns the faucet. Did the architecture of his house contribute to these insightful perceptions;[2] or did they come solely from his creative imagination? Can we actually imagine a domestic environment that inspires thoughts so rich and intense? Can we envision and create an architecture that highlights our daily habits and conjures long-forgotten poetic features? And if this kind of architecture indeed can be created, could we actually live in it?

    The ambition to reveal meaning in everyday life motivated much of the art and literature of the twentieth century and especially work by Surrealist writers and artists. André Breton's essay "The Crisis of the Object" (1936) called for a creative relationship between the real and what exists beyond the real, by revealing the marvelous in everyday life.[3] Among architects, it was Frederick Kiesler (1890–1965) who pursued this ambition most vigorously, influenced by his association with the Surrealist group in New York during the 1940s.[4] Kiesler's life-long project of the

Endless House[5] shared some of the Surrealist intentions but evolved in new directions, seeking an architecture that could "shelter those 'continuous mutations' of life-force, which seem to be part of the 'practical' as well as of the magical," and could offer its inhabitants an exuberant life.[6] Whether Kiesler ever read Joyce's *Ulysses* is not a question this essay seeks to answer.[7] Nevertheless, forty years after *Ulysses* was published, Kiesler's book *Inside the Endless House; Art, People and Architecture: A Journal*[8] described water's presence in his Endless House in a quite similar way: "Every mechanical device must remain an event and constitute the inspiration for a specific ritual. Not even the faucet that brings water into your glass, into the teakettle, through your shower and into the bath – that turn of a handle and then the water flowing forth as from the rock touched by Moses in the desert, that sparkling event, released through the magic invention of man's mind, must always remain the surprise, the unprecedented, an event of pride and comfort."[9]

The Endless House was never built, but we can reconstruct its complex features from a mosaic of items: a few models, many sketches, drawings and plans, photographs from shows and exhibitions, and especially the notes in Kiesler's *Journal*, along with his manifestoes, theoretical essays, and poetic texts. To date, scholarship on the Endless House has focused mainly on its innovative form or its expression of Kiesler's theoretical beliefs; there has been little discussion of how its interior would be experienced. Meanwhile, there has been a vast amount of scholarship on Kiesler's work for theatre and art exhibitions,[10] which greatly influenced his architectural work.

This essay focuses on the intended lived experience of the Endless House and its implications for the history of modern architecture. Looking closely at Kiesler's own writings about the project enables the real potential of his drawings and models to be disclosed. Kiesler acknowledged that it would be difficult to imagine living in his Endless House without carefully considering these various modes of representation. He was relieved when his painter friend (and Breton's wife) Jacqueline Breton-Lamba finally understood the spatial quality of the Endless House:

How often have I tried (in 1942, '43, '44, '45, '46) to make clear to her with words, by molding spaces with my sculpting hands in free air, ... trying to form the spirit of the "Endless" for her, demonstrating, talking, silently inducing the feeling about it into her – no results! None. But now that she had a

Fig. 12.1 Frederick Kiesler with the model of the Endless House, New York, 1959. Photographer: Irving Penn. © 1960 (renewed 1988) Condé Nast. © 2013 Austrian Frederick and Lillian Kiesler Private Foundation, Vienna.

living experience by walking into the world of the Lascaux caves, her atheistic attitude toward my architecture vanished and she came back to my concept, although really never having been in it … now she got it. Yes, architecture cannot be experienced by plans, space planimetrically flattened out. Space, it seems, one gets only by walking, tramping through it. She did it now. Now, fifteen years later. Thank God! At least one who got it once.[11]

This entry in Kiesler's *Journal* is from 1961, when he was working on the third and final version of his project. This is also the version about which he wrote most, and on which my essay focuses.[12] The drawings and model of this version were presented in the exhibition "Visionary Architecture" at the Museum of Modern Art in New York in 1960.[13] I will examine how the spatial quality and architectural features of the House were intended to enrich the inhabitants' daily habits.

Kiesler believed that architecture should be based on the fullness of life, rather than on the reduced functionalism that was prevalent in his time. To him, functionalism was merely a standardization of routine activities. It enabled a foot to walk but not to dance; an eye to see but not to envision; a hand to grasp but not to create.[14] Instead, he sought a meaningful architecture through a thorough and careful observation of life itself, including things we tend to overlook or consider trivial. "Enmesh yourself in life forces and observe yourself. Every second is a universe ready to be discovered anew. Without your continuous observations you have nothing to feed your own brain. To get a fresh, independent look at familiar matter is a heroic undertaking; to bury your habits of thinking, feeling, and creating demands relentless, down-deep spade work."[15]

He sought an architecture that would challenge its inhabitants in an open and creative way, by manifesting their perceptions as actions, rather than adhering to the nineteenth-century premise that an inhabitant is a passive observer. He was apprehensive that humanity was settling into a "pre-equipped world" that would be seen, touched, and smelled in a standard, aesthetic way, with little emotional engagement.[16] "Make no mistake, architecture, particularly in housing, has too often become a gamble with people's standard habits and peace for the sake of fashions and fake-fame,"[17] he declared. "What price do we pay for our lack of resistance to conformity, whether in labor-saving devices or human relations? The answer to this question becomes more and more paramount for each of us, for our society and for the nation as a whole. Art and architecture can and must contribute to the clarification of this issue for us slaves of indirect living."[18] Consequently, he questioned even the most basic elements of domestic architecture. "In the 'Endless House' nothing can be taken for granted, either of the house itself, the floor, walls, ceiling, the coming of people or of light, the air with its warmth or coolness."[19] Let us enter these unconventional "actual conditions of life-space."[20]

THE ENTRANCE

Unlike the first version of the Endless House that rested on the ground, the third version is raised so that cars can drive underneath, as Kiesler explained in an interview with CBS in 1960.[21] Either by car or on foot, one arrives below the House's volume and is surrounded by three gigantic columns on which it rests. In the elevations and the model, the columns appear solid from outside, whereas the first floor plan shows that each column is hollow, with an entrance space and a staircase that leads to the

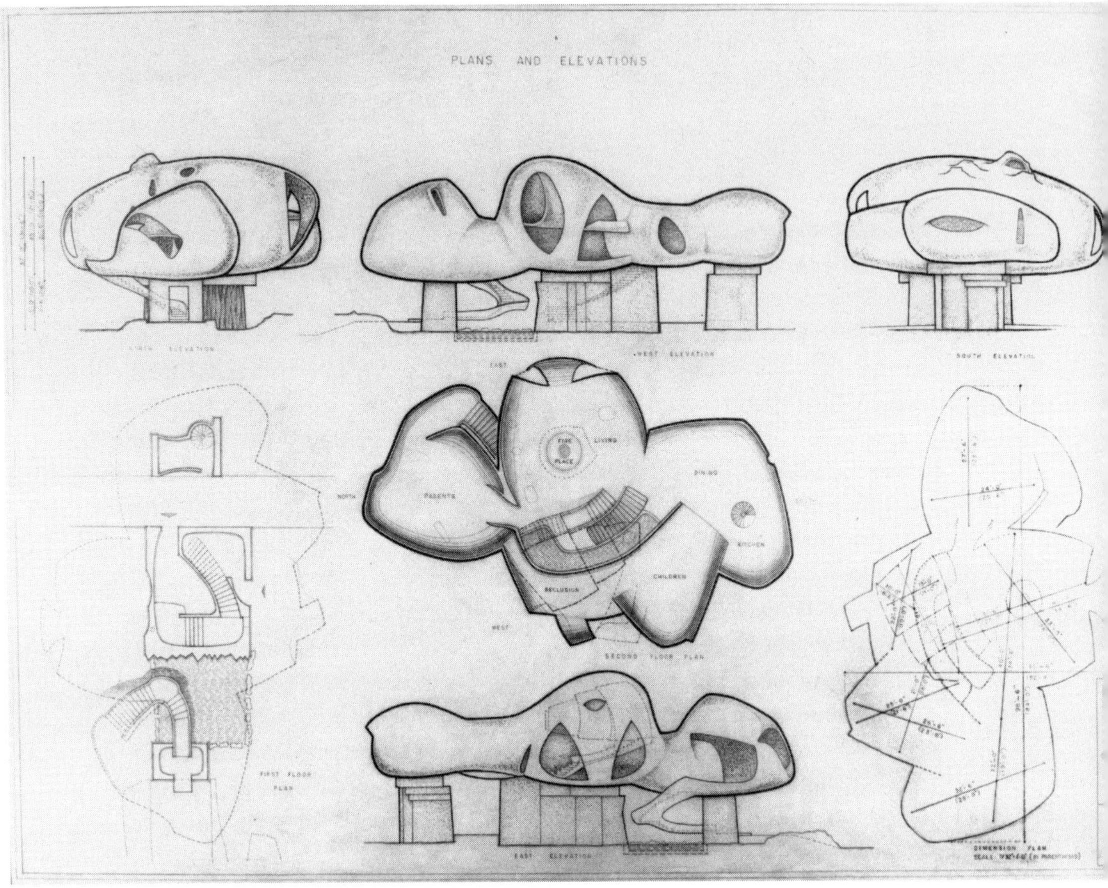

Fig. 12.2 Frederick Kiesler, Endless House presentation drawings, plans and elevations, pencil on transparent paper, New York, 1958/59. © 2013 Austrian Frederick and Lillian Kiesler Private Foundation, Vienna.

main floor. The middle staircase rises into the House's central area, indicated by the word "Living." The north staircase leads directly to the parents' area. The circular staircase inside the south column ascends into the kitchen. Of the three staircases, only the north one is visible as one walks towards the House. It emerges from an entry vestibule within the column, rises over a pool of water, and turns to penetrate the underside of the House. Both the north and south staircases seem to be reserved for private use by the inhabitants, as the ground floor plan shows an entrance arrow only to the larger staircase in the middle.

The architectural drawings convey only part of Kiesler's larger idea about the ritual of entry. On 14 May 1961, during a visit to Palm Beach, Florida, to examine a potential lot for the building, Kiesler explains to the lot's owner and prospective client:

268

Of course, you understand that no one can enter "The Endless House" with shoes on. Neither should men enter with their Huber e Bronner on or the Lady's (*sic*) with Acy's dresses on. That goes for the family as well as for guests ... To be specific, there will be dressing quarters close to the entrance of the House for men, women, and children with an exuberant wardrobe of capes, saris, panchos, in many colors, textures and weights, and sizes; to be worn loosely or tightened over the body ... It was interesting for me to hear of a silk and shoe manufacturer from Hong Kong, who offered at once to deliver, free of costs, slippers without soles, just covering the arch, made with many-colored feathers or silk, velvet or furs – because I made it clear to him that everyone's home is a sacred place, and a silent walk is imperative.[22]

No such dressing quarters are shown in the drawings, but the middle entrance room is spacious enough to accommodate them. The ritual of entering the House, barefoot and dressed in appropriate clothes, would prepare both inhabitants and visitors to leave behind the mundane world and emerge into a space that is understood as sacred.

THE FLOORS

The middle staircase leads to the living area, a double-height space. Moving around the living area challenges the very activity of walking, as one's "imperative silent walk" takes place on curvilinear floors with different slopes and levels. In the west and east elevations and the two longitudinal sections, we can discern at least four slightly different floor levels, but there are no stairs or ramps in the main floor plan. An entry in the *Journal* on 23 March 1961 clarifies Kiesler's intentions for the floors:

In the "Endless House," there was the concept of the floors which are treated in such a curvilinear way that they seem to be moving under your feet. They are not flat and, when you walk barefooted on them, the lifting and setting down of your body, plus moving at the same time, is like discovering your potentiality of flying. This is one example of reconditioning our reflexes; our life is conditioned by whatever we create around us. Just this one idea of a new floor would bring us much closer to truth within nature because we would be using our feet not to walk on shoes and through them on floors, but to walk on the very soil of the house. Not merely on the floor.[23]

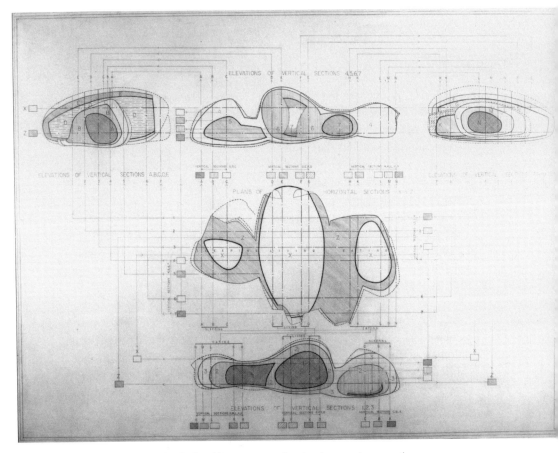

Fig. 12.3 Frederick Kiesler, Endless House presentation drawings, sections, pencil on transparent paper, New York, 1958/59. © 2013 Austrian Frederick and Lillian Kiesler Private Foundation, Vienna.

Walking inside the House requires a conscious adjustment of one's steps, especially in the steeper parts of the curvilinear floors. The drawings suggest that some effort would be needed to rise from the parents' area to the living area and then descend again to the concave part of the main floor. After waking up in the bedroom, one's path to the kitchen for a morning coffee would traverse four different slopes. Even the floor of the mezzanine level – in the plan, shown with dashed lines behind the main staircase – appears slightly inclined, following the slope of the staircase.

As part of his aim to evoke bodily sensations, Kiesler also envisioned different floor materials that would enrich the experience of walking. "The floors of the 'Endless' would, naturally, have many textures, such as pebbles, sand, rivulets, grass, planks, heated terra-cotta tiles; so that everyone can by touching the floor of the earth be stimulated by the touch ... We should learn to live not only on the floor but with the floor."²⁴ Unfortunately, he did not specify how the different materials would be distributed throughout the House.

THE WALLS AND THE CEILING

The walking experience that Kiesler created for the inhabitants was extended into a similar treatment of the walls and the ceiling. The first version of his project showed some typical interior walls, but as the design evolved, the undulating floors became sculpturally continuous with the external walls, while the interior walls disappeared to achieve spatial continuity. Kiesler had already mentioned this architectural idea in his "Manifesto on Correalism" (1947).²⁵ "It was during the years 1924–25 in a Vienna of Strauss Waltzes and a Paris of the Beaux-Arts, that I eliminated the idea of separation in the construction of the house, that is to say, the distinction between the floor, walls, and ceilings, and I created with the floor, walls, and ceiling a unique continuum."²⁶ In his work as an exhibition designer, he often removed the sharp edge between vertical and horizontal surfaces. "The house, that is, the walls, floors and ceilings, must not meet one another at sharp angles and be fused together artificially, but should flow into one another, uninterrupted by columns or beams."²⁷ Spatial continuity thus became a defining characteristic of the House.

The "Endless" is finite as to mechanics, and definite in its destruction of boundaries between areas of eating, sleeping, playing; between outside and inside, strangers and home folks. Privacy can be produced in any section of the "Endless" and continuity of space equally as well. Swinging wall sections, folding, rolling, fanning overhead or sidewise – that's a cinch in our ball-bearing age, space on pivots and time on coasters. Cubicles for the standard functions in our daily life (bathrooms, kitchens ...) are deadening experiments in the long run. If all spaces are kept open and free-flowing, and can be shut off at will, they are inspiring ... Life has a chance to become inventive. You, as the inhabitant, then become the real architect of your house ... We don't want cellophane between two pairs of lips; we want the naked touch.²⁸

Kiesler's drawings do not show partitions "folding, rolling, fanning overhead or sidewise," but his words evoke imaginative options for defining temporary spaces of different sizes and shapes. In this way, the interior form of the House would engage the changing realities of the inhabitant's life. "Space exists in slumber until we awaken it ... It is so fundamental to our being that we are not aware of it, as we are not aware of walking, breathing ... Space ... can only be perceived by inventions of our consciousness."[29]

Kiesler also envisioned that paintings would be incorporated into the walls of the House (and even the ceiling and floor), rather than being placed inside decorative frames. "While it is being built, the Endless House will grow its colors, in vast areas or in condensed compositions (fresco-like or paintings), into high or low reliefs, into the plasticity of full sculpture."[30] He believed that art should be not merely an afterthought, and that architecture should engage in a life-giving correlation with the plastic arts.[31]

THE FURNITURE

Kiesler planned for the House to be made of reinforced concrete: eleven inches thick at the floor, tapering to three-and-a-half inches thick at the ceiling.[32] Instead of relying on conventional chairs and couches, he envisioned the skin of the House providing its own furnishings, with the inhabitants resting on concave surfaces where floors turn into walls. A second shell added along certain parts of the exterior wall could provide storage space, especially in the dining area, the kitchen, and the sleeping quarters.[33] Kiesler also thought about alternative bed options in the sleeping quarters. During a trip to São Paulo, he wrote, "Just before entering the display grounds, an alley of high palm trees; between the trunks samples of woven hammocks in beautiful colors for sale at a shack in the forest beyond. Unable to stop and buy, which I wanted so much to do, particularly for Mrs. Regler who had told me back in New York, 'That is what you learn in Mexico, to sleep in a hammock. And in your "Endless House" you must not have beds, but hammocks.'"[34]

Throughout his life, Kiesler designed and manufactured many innovative pieces of furniture,[35] and probably had some of them in mind for the House. In an unpublished typescript from 1961, he provides some general instructions: "It is advisable not to transfer old furniture into the house, since furniture is an internal part of the concept of the house. The furniture designed for it is of more sculptural nature, in different materials, easily movable or built in."³⁶ No furniture is shown in his drawings of the House, but again the idea of sculptural continuity is evident in his written description.

THE LIGHT

In this sculpturally fluid space, the diffusion of light – both natural and artificial – should produce a unique effect: "Uninterrupted, overflowing, reflected on curving surfaces, the light multiplies itself, and even the minimal amount switched on only to enable us to see gives us physical information over a wider area."³⁷ The walls, floor, and ceiling were intended to carry lighting, using electric eyes to turn lights on and off automatically, accompanying the inhabitants wherever they walk in the House: brightening, dimming, or disappearing, depending on whether they stay or move on.³⁸ The lighting system of the Endless House also would include moving trolleys to provide light where it is needed, using relatively few light sources.³⁹

Kiesler was concerned also with natural lighting and fenestration. He believed that fenestration in a new building should not be determined by how the openings look from outside, but by how the light looks from inside. In his last article, "The Future: Notes on Architecture as Sculpture," he specifies that in the Endless "each area has vast openings in different shapes and forms, according to the orbit of the sun and prevailing winds; these are filled not with glass, but with molded reliefs in colored plastics of various thicknesses, so that the heat of the sun is refracted. In each of these larger or smaller openings (which during the evening, by the way, receive the same light from outside artificially) there are certain sections which are clear and translucent, affording a free view and visual connection to the outside environment."⁴⁰ The drawings show that some of the openings are small and directed towards the sky: for example, the one on the ceiling of the parents' area would enable them to watch the stars before falling asleep. Others, such as the central openings in the west elevation, are two storeys high. The larger ones not only bring diffused natural light into the House, but also seem to serve as external frames that exhibit blurred shadows of life inside. They are large enough to frame activities in various places, including the staircase to the mezzanine (as shown in the east elevation) and the mezzanine itself (as shown in the west elevation). There would be a theatrical quality in the shadows of the inhabitants' everyday activities, celebrating the real life that Kiesler valorized so deeply, "offering" it to the public as almost an art installation.

The first version of the Endless House included a special element: a colour clock. It was less prominent in the later versions, and Kiesler does not mention it in his *Journal*. Still, the south elevation of the final version shows a small, volumetric extrusion on the roof that resembles the colour clock in the previous versions. This device is described mainly in his article "Frederick J. Kiesler's Endless House and Its Psychological Lighting" (1950). The clock was intended to function as a window but offered no view outside, as reflecting mirrors obscured the view. It combined prismatic glass and mirrors that would receive light from the sun, divide it into spectral colours, then reflect it throughout the room. "Although it has rarely been done by architects, it is possible to send sunlight through a lens in order to concentrate it, and pass it through convex mirror reflex devices to diffuse it. The color clock of the endless house ... is designed to do these things, as well as to fill the interior with color and make the dweller organically aware of the continuity of time."[41]

The colour clock expresses the intense theatricality of the House. The inhabitants would be illuminated throughout the day by different colours chosen by the architect. According to Kiesler's drawing of the colour clock, the sunlight at dawn would be diffused by a deep yellow mirror, filling the interior of the House with a warm ochre light to revitalize the body. As the sun climbs higher in the sky, the light inside the House would change from an intense red to a darker brown, following the intensity of activities during the morning. At noon, the colour clock would create a smooth blue light: a cooling atmosphere during the lunch break. In the afternoon the interior of the House would be illuminated with a light turquoise light, then a green light that calms the eyes and prepares the body for the end of the cycle and the coming of night. At dusk the colour of the interior would return to deep yellow. Instead of relying on a mechanical clock that would splinter their day into minute divisions of time, the inhabitants would become aware of the continuity of time.[42] Although the colour clock is only minimally evident in the final version of the House, the interior nevertheless can be imagined as colourful and continually changing as time passes throughout the day.

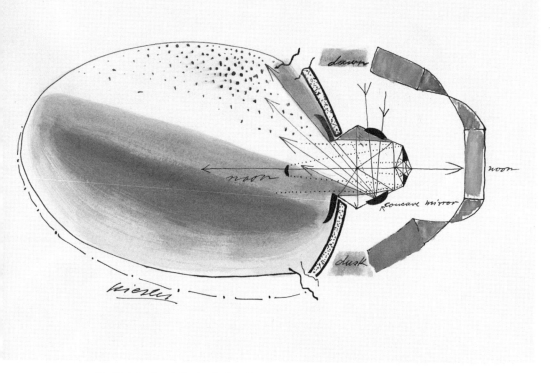

Fig. 12.4 Frederick Kiesler, Endless House project, study for color clock, 1951. Ink and gouache on paper, 14 ¾ x 18" (37.5 x 45.7 cm). Purchase. The Museum of Modern Art, New York. Digital image © The Museum of Modern Art / Licensed by SCALA / Art Resource, New York. © 2013 Austrian Frederick and Lillian Kiesler Private Foundation, Vienna.

THE ROOF

Kiesler conceived the surface of the roof as a private landscape of low hills and soft meadows, where the inhabitants could enjoy a break and rest under the sun, protected by the shadows of the roof's own volumes. In his *Journal* he states, "I always felt that there should be a way of getting onto the roof of the house, because it has such lovely valleys, where one can sit or lie in full form in delicious comfort, sheltered on its plains and inclinations."[43] His notes also describe how he developed this part of the design:

Some time ago I thought the only way to achieve [access to the roof] was to cut a trap door into the ceiling so that one could slip out onto the roof by using a short ladder, as it is often done in brownstone houses in New York. Yesterday, late in the evening, after a very hard and tiring day's work in which

I myself took a vigorous hand in finishing one half of the shell of the house in a rush of reaching the goal of completion ... I suddenly discovered a seemingly natural way to walk up and out on the roof by inserting a small platform into the mezzanine which offers the most logical and the most sustained way of three points of attachment to straight-out walking on an even level, to the meadows of the roof![44]

FIRE AND WATER

Kiesler's desire to immerse the House's inhabitants in natural elements was also expressed in the design of certain domestic features. On 25 July 1956, he noted,

Fire and water have always haunted me as sources of life, and I had placed both of them in the floor of my 'Endless House.' The question now was how to produce the fire, self-contained, independent of any outside source. I had often been fascinated by the smudge pots placed at night on the streets of New York to guard the open diggings of street repairmen. The flame of these smudge pots was just the type which presented itself in my vision, fluttering like a flag and giving off enough dark smoke to nighten the wooden sculpture above and around the flame. The idea was exciting and appeared irrevocable.[45]

Although he wrote nothing more about fire, we can imagine the House with a fire pit and a live fire at its very heart, spreading heat and light throughout the space.

With regards to water (and apart from the faucet), Kiesler envisioned a series of bathing pools instead of conventional bathtubs. The main floor plan shows a pool behind the main staircase that could be used for cleansing or even swimming, revealing the inhabitant's naked body as part of everyday life. He also imagined other pools within the House: "The white enameled coffins which are called bathtubs do not exist in any of the parts of the Endless House. Each of the space units has its own shape and style of indoor pool, surrounded by varying curtains of growing greenery. The water is renewed every minute, and the temperature remains constant once set on the dial. Since one cannot stretch out or sit or kneel in our tight bathroom coffins, the many pools in the many areas – for parents, children, or guests – are so designed that one can comfortably adjust to all the positions of relaxation."[46]

Earth, fire, and water are emphasized in the project: the earth that is the floor, the fire in the pit, and the water in the pools. The elements engage the flesh of the body. The Endless House seems to be a house of flesh and embodied consciousness, ultimately turning into the very "skin of the human body."[47] Contemplating how his project transcended conventional forms of dwelling, Kiesler concluded, "The house, freed from aesthetic tradition, became a living creature."[48]

IS THE ENDLESS A HOUSE?

The many features described above suggest how exhilarating it would be to live in the Endless House. Breaking from convention, every action by the inhabitants and every element in the House would promise new enlightenment. "You wander into habits thoughtlessly because they offer guidance to security. Insecurity, however, is what we search for,"[49] wrote Kiesler, advocating active engagement. However, wouldn't this deliberate insecurity make living sometimes difficult or even unbearable? Wouldn't it be hard to live in an environment that forbids complacency, where every breath is a new experience for the body, where the question of "being" is perpetually asked? Even if this kind of living were possible, wouldn't its inhabitants become accustomed to its novelty and stop being fascinated by the challenges it offers, eventually treating it in the same banal way as conventional architecture?

I would like to argue that interpreting the Endless House literally as a domestic environment does not align with Kiesler's broader theoretical positions. Two facts support this hypothesis. The first is Kiesler's statement in his CBS interview, when asked about the House's form. He explained that the form of the Endless "depends on the location, ... on the desire and size of the family, on the amount of money available and it should not be difficult for any imaginative designer to adopt that with an infinite variety."[50] In 1961 Kiesler designed a variation on the Endless House that would be built in Palm Beach for Mary Sisler, the client to whom he explained the idea of the dressing quarters, mentioned above. In his Sisler House project, he modified many domestic elements from the Endless House. The external form remained similar, but the drawings

Fig. 12.5 Frederick Kiesler, Mary Sisler House (sheet no. 2), brownprint, New York, 1961.
© 2013 Austrian Frederick and Lillian Kiesler Private Foundation, Vienna.

show internal changes: additional openings in the kitchen area, a different staircase in the same space, partitions for privacy in the washrooms, an open pool in the parents' area, built-in sculptural furniture and storage space, and no curved floors. Instead of adhering to the ideal design, Kiesler paid close attention to the client's personality, characteristics, and needs, as considerations that should be valued highly by an architect.[51] He adapted the Endless House so that it could become embodied in a particular place. This suggests that the Endless House was a poetic concept that had to be developed to permit active and conscious living. In its ideal form, it was a manifesto against the banal, functional boxes that other builders in his time were producing.

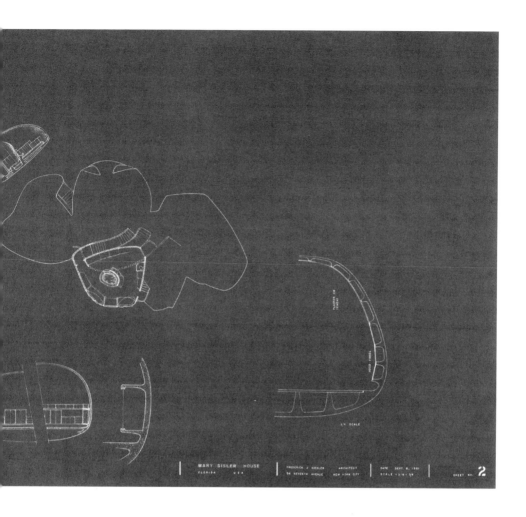

MARY SISLER HOUSE   FLORIDA   U.S.A.   FREDERICK J KIESLER   ARCHITECT   56 SEVENTH AVENUE   NEW YORK CITY   DATE SEPT. 6, 1961   SCALE 1 1/4"=34   SHEET NO. 2

The second fact supporting my hypothesis is that in 1958 Kiesler received a twelve-thousand-dollar grant to prepare preliminary plans to build the Endless House full scale in the garden of the Museum of Modern Art in New York. This project did not materialize because the museum decided to build a permanent exhibition wing in this very space;[52] otherwise, the Endless would have become a temporary exhibit for the museum's visitors, just like Kiesler's Space House in 1924.[53] The fact that Kiesler wanted the House to be exhibited in the museum reinforces the idea that it was a manifesto against the prevailing functionalism, enabling visitors to experience an environment in which basic functions are questioned. They could have walked on its curvilinear floors and imagined flying, sat on its curved walls and experienced the intimacy of their bodies with the flesh of the House, seen the changing colours in its interior and understood the passing of time, stepped on its roof and enjoyed the shadows of its volumes. This temporary architectural experience could have encouraged them to question mainstream architectural practices and cultivate new ideas about domestic living.

Theatrical qualities would also have been evident in the Endless House if it had been built for the museum exhibition. The continuous form of the project was a development of Kiesler's earlier design for the Endless Theater (1924),[54] and Kiesler had a lifelong involvement in theatre that included many stage designs and innovative stage sets that promoted audience participation. In the context of the museum, the Endless House would have operated as a stage, with visitors becoming both actors and spectators in an interactive plot with its environment. Like a theatrical performance, it would have transported the participants temporarily to another world – to consider certain questions of life and perhaps some cathartic solutions – then returned them to their previous reality, renewed and possibly enlightened. In this way, Kiesler's Endless House can be understood as a theatrical stage. In the museum, it would have inverted the traditional Western distinction between private and public, expressing Kiesler's desire for a meaningful architecture of active participation.

Until the early nineteenth century, the theatre was a paradigm for Western architecture, due to its "sacred" capacity to orient the participant through emotional involvement and self-understanding. If Giorgio Agamben is correct that we moderns must find meaning in our biological life,[55] rather than in theology or metaphysics, then the Endless House is indeed a modern sacred space, as Kiesler had envisioned. Its architecture manifests how our daily activities can point to something beyond themselves, to "give charm of novelty to things of every day, and excite a feeling analogous to the supernatural, by awakening the mind's attention from the lethargy of custom, and directing it to the wonders of the world before us."[56] In short, the Endless was designed as a collection of creative moments in order to reveal the divine meaning of life beyond our everyday actions. According to Kiesler, "The only question we still have to face is: What is the purpose of life? What is its content? Because 'that bit' of information is not given to us, we have to invent it."[57] "Architecture is striving, instead of for simple shelter, to be more than that, [but] it is striving persistently to be even more emotional, more than 'aesthetic,' thus urge is an unexplained dictate of faith in the unknown. Yet when buildings are less than all that, less we are too."[58]

NOTES

1 James Joyce, *Ulysses* (London: Penguin, 1992), 783–5.
2 Most details of Leopold Bloom's house are found in the fourth chapter of *Ulysses* but are insufficient to support such a hypothesis.
3 André Breton, *Surrealism and Painting* (New York: Harper & Row, 1972), 275–80.
4 Kiesler's direct involvement with Surrealism began in the 1940s, when André Breton, the central figure of the Surrealist group, lived in New York. In 1942, after meeting repeatedly with Breton and Peggy Guggenheim, he designed for the latter the gallery Art of This Century, where visitors were presented with innovative ways of viewing the paintings, using specially designed walls, appropriate furniture, and viewing devices. Kiesler participated in the Surrealist magazine *VVV*, and also designed (with Duchamp, Miró, Ernst, and Matta) "Kiesler's Hall of Superstitions" for the international Surrealist exhibition in Paris (1947). See Dalibor Vesely, "Surrealism, Myth and Modernity," *Architectural Design* 48 (1978): 93.
5 Kiesler was not consistent in how he wrote the term *Endless House* in his various articles, manifestoes, and books. In his book *Inside the Endless House; Art, People and Architecture: A Journal* (New York: Simon and Schuster, 1966), he typically uses double quotation marks and capitalizes the first letter of each word ("Endless House"). He also uses "Endless," "House," and sometimes just the word *house*. In his article, "Frederick J. Kiesler's Endless House and Its Psychological Lighting" (1950), he uses no quotation marks or capital letters (endless house). In his last article, "The Future: Notes on Architecture as Sculpture" (1966), he capitalizes the first letter of each word (Endless House). In this essay, I refer to the project as Endless House, Endless, or House, except in quotations by Kiesler where it is written differently.
6 Kiesler, *Inside the Endless House*, 568.
7 An entry in Kiesler's journal shows that he was familiar with Joyce's work. Ibid., 464.
8 The book, published posthumously, is a collection of Kiesler's thoughts, observations, ideas, descriptions of business and friendly meetings, travel memories, etc. from October 1955 to April 1964. Kiesler admits throughout the book that this documentation is scattered and not systematic.
9 Kiesler, *Inside the Endless House*, 568.

10 See R.L. Held, *Endless Innovations: Frederick Kiesler's Theory and Scenic Design* (Ann Arbor, MI: UMI, 1982).

11 Kiesler, *Inside the Endless House*, 511.

12 The Endless House began as a concept in the 1920s and became one of Kiesler's central preoccupations in the 1950s. In its first version (exhibited at the Kootz Gallery in New York in 1950) the House was ovoid in form. As Kiesler's concept for the House matured, the models developed a more flowing external skin with large cutouts. In the third and final version, the House rested on three gigantic columns and consisted of several perforated egg-shaped shells with uninterrupted, flowing spaces inside. This was the version publicized in articles in *Harper's Bazaar*, *Vogue*, *Art in America*, and *Time* (1959). It was also presented at the Museum of Modern Art in 1960 and at the Leo Castelli Gallery in January 1961. See Michael Wilk, "Affinity to Infinity: The Endlessness, Correalism and Galaxies of Frederick Kiesler" (MArch Post-prof. thesis, McGill University, 1999), 45.

13 Other participants in the exhibition included Bruno Taut, Frank Lloyd Wright, Buckminster Fuller, and Le Corbusier.

14 Frederick Kiesler, "Pseudo-Functionalism in Modern Architecture," in *Frederick Kiesler 1890–1965*, ed. Yehuda Safran (London: Architectural Association, 1989), 57.

15 Kiesler, *Inside the Endless House*, 381.

16 Marta Franco, "Towards a Correal Architecture: Reflections on Frederick Kiesler" (MArch Post-prof. thesis, McGill University, 1996), 1–2.

17 Kiesler, *Inside the Endless House*, 353.

18 Ibid., 309.

19 Ibid., 568.

20 Ibid., 63.

21 Frederick Kiesler, "Frederick Kiesler: The Endless House on Camera Three, CBS, 1960," in *Friedrich Kiesler: Endless House 1947–1961*, ed. Dieter Bogner (Ostfildern: Hatje Cantz, 2003), 85.

22 Kiesler, *Inside the Endless House*, 436–7.

23 Ibid., 412.

24 Ibid., 437, 272.

25 See Frederick Kiesler, "On Correalism and Biotechnique: A Definition and Test of a New Approach to Building Design," *Architectural Record* 86, no. 3 (1939): 60–75. According to this article, Correalism was a general law developed from what Kiesler called the "part-sciences," which included

disciplines such as chemistry, physics, and biology. He evaluated these part-sciences according to their effect on human health, then applied this new understanding to architectural design. Kiesler believed that good design must improve humanity. See Wilk, "Affinity to Infinity," 4.

26 Frederick Kiesler, "Manifesto of Correalism," in *Frederick J. Kiesler: Endless Space*, ed. Dieter Bogner and Peter Noever (Ostfildern: Hatje Cantz, 2001), 93. For more on how the cultural environment of Vienna influenced Kiesler's architectural development, see Yehuda Safran, "In the Shadow of Bucephalus," in *Frederick Kiesler 1890–1965*, ed. Safran, 6.

27 Kiesler, *Inside the Endless House*, 568–9.

28 Ibid., 308.

29 Ibid., 393.

30 Frederick Kiesler, "The Future: Notes on Architecture as Sculpture," *Art in America* 54, no. 3 (1966): 68.

31 Kiesler, *Inside the Endless House*, 155.

32 Kiesler, "Frederick Kiesler: The Endless House on Camera Three," 87.

33 Bogner, *Friedrich Kiesler: Endless House 1947–1961*, 94.

34 Kiesler, *Inside the Endless House*, 542.

35 For more on Kiesler's furniture, see Tulga Beyerle and Frederick Kiesler, *Friedrich Kiesler, Designer: Seating Furniture of the 30s and 40s* (Ostfildern: Hatje Cantz, 2005).

36 Bogner, *Friedrich Kiesler: Endless House 1947–1961*, 93.

37 Frederick Kiesler, "Frederick J. Kiesler's Endless House and Its Psychological Lighting," in *Friedrich Kiesler: Endless House 1947–1961*, 52.

38 Ibid., 56.

39 Ibid.

40 Kiesler, "The Future: Notes on Architecture as Sculpture," 68.

41 Kiesler, "Frederick J. Kiesler's Endless House and Its Psychological Lighting," 54.

42 Wilk, "Affinity to Infinity," 54.

43 Kiesler, *Inside the Endless House*, 234.

44 Ibid., 235.

45 Ibid., 25.

46 Kiesler, "The Future: Notes on Architecture as Sculpture," 68.

47 Kiesler, "Manifesto of Correalism," 92.

48 Bogner and Noever, *Frederick J. Kiesler: Endless Space*, 22.

49 Kiesler, *Inside the Endless House*, 395.

50 Frederick Kiesler, "Frederick Kiesler: The Endless House on Camera Three," 88.

51 Kiesler, *Inside the Endless House*, 376–7.

52 Ibid., 278.

53 In 1933, Kiesler worked on his Space House project as part of a larger commission for the Modernage Furniture Company in New York. He installed a full-size model of a family house as the centrepiece in the company's showroom. It was intended to raise interest in the thirty-three furnished rooms in the upper floors of the building. The house was one storey high, with an innovative lighting scheme and modern, built-in furniture. In fact, it was the only house that Kiesler ever built. Beatriz Colomina argues that Kiesler understood his Space House as theatre: "The model house is an exhibition space and theatrical space. The visitors are the actors." Beatriz Colomina, "Space House: The Psyche of Building," in *InterSections: Architectural Histories and Critical Theories*, ed. Iain Borden and Jane Rendell (London: Routledge, 2000), 59.

54 The "Endless Theater" was a concept Kiesler developed while still in Vienna in the 1920s. It was supposed to be an egg-shaped space, encased in a double shell of steel and opaque welded glass. The stage was conceived as an endless spiral and the various levels (stage, seating platforms, etc.) would be suspended and connected with elevator platforms. In this way, the drama would expand and develop freely in space. See Held, *Endless Innovations*, 24.

55 Giorgio Agamben, *Homo Sacer: Sovereign Power and Bare Life* (Stanford, CA: Stanford University Press, 1998).

56 Orhan Pamuk, *The Naïve and the Sentimental Novelist: Understanding What Happens When We Write and Read Novels*, trans. Nazim Dikbas (New York: Vintage, 2010), 177. Pamuk quotes Coleridge discussing Wordsworth's poetry.

57 Kiesler, *Inside the Endless House*, 135.

58 Ibid., 512.

The Juridical Character of
Alberti's Mind

Nikolaos-Ion Terzoglou

Chora

LEON BATTISTA ALBERTI: A RENAISSANCE CHAMELEON?

PICO DELLA MIRANDOLA, in *Oration on the Dignity of Man*, codified a new idea of the humanist subject in the early Renaissance, writing, "Who would not admire this our chameleon?"[1] Leon Battista Alberti seems to incarnate the ideal human type that Pico della Mirandola envisaged. This had been recognized already by Alberti's contemporaries; the striking versatility of his writings led Cristoforo Landino to characterize him as a "new chameleon" (*nuovo cameleonta*) in 1481.[2] A few years later, in 1486, Angelo Poliziano's preface to the first edition of *De re aedificatoria* for Lorenzo de' Medici noted the many-sidedness of this Italian humanist, describing Alberti as an "orator" and a "poet."[3] Is there a stable identity of Alberti? If not, the ambiguous nature of this Renaissance chameleon poses serious problems to the hermeneutical understanding of his ideas and writings. Jean-Marc Mandosio has analyzed the meaning and the epistemological implications of Alberti's "esprit du caméléon."[4]

One possible danger of the versatile character of Alberti's work is the tendency towards simplification and reduction: every epoch "constructs" its own Alberti using different intellectual eyeglasses, distorting the real meaning of his achievements. Jacob Burckhardt, in *The Civilization of the Renaissance in Italy*, read Alberti as a proof of the nascent individualism of modernity.[5] Sigfried Giedion recognized in Burckhardt's historiography not only an attempt to reveal "the origins of the man of today" but also the discovery of a whole era, namely the Renaissance.[6] Moreover, in Giedion's *Space, Time and Architecture*, Florence during Alberti's era stands out as the "workshop of the modern European spirit," which he characterizes as an "esprit nouveau," using an expression already employed by Le Corbusier.[7] According to Giedion, this new spirit inaugurated a new concept of space.[8] More recently, Alberti has been read through the lenses of structural linguistics (Choay), standardized formalism (Carpo), and even digital technologies of algorithmic design (Mitrović).[9] Obviously, these late interpretations are serious reductions. The problem of Alberti's identity is accentuated by the ongoing expansion and fragmentation of Albertian studies, which often leads to disagreements among scholars due to their philological specializations. Although specialization can illuminate neglected folds of Alberti's life and thought[10] – for example, the work of Mark Jarzombek on his "literary theories" and the research of Francesco Furlan on his dialogues and their successive reception[11] – it seems that something is missing: the coherence, the general character, and the unity of his thought and aspirations. In this way, Alberti still remains a "problem" for contemporary thought.[12]

The present essay is an attempt to formulate an alternate interpretation of Alberti's mind and its character that avoids reductionist fallacies and addresses the lack of unity noted above. It is based exclusively on *De re aedificatoria* and tries to interpret its structure from within the context of his own era and culture.

THE EARLY RENAISSANCE: *SAPIENTIA* (WISDOM) AND *ELOQUENTIA* (ELOQUENCE)

During the early Renaissance, philosophy and science were gradually emancipated from the established religious institutions to become rational and autonomous inquiries of the physical cosmos. This new "rationality," however, was not calculative or positivist in the modern sense – namely, as we understand the term *rationalism* after Descartes and Leibniz. Rather, it was part of a broader secular wisdom and effort to regulate the ethical life of civic society following the natural light of the intellect. Civic humanism attempted to synthesize the new moral subject with the open space of society and history, relying on Neoplatonic and Stoic thought. Humanism, as Paul Oskar Kristeller and Eugenio Garin have shown, originated from the *studia humanitatis*, the humanistic studies of the Italian schools that brought together the arts of discourse into a new moral education.[13]

In this context, the humanist Leon Battista Alberti relied on Stoic and Ciceronian moral ideals to unify the contemplative life (*vita contemplativa*) of the Renaissance subject with the exercise of wisdom (*sapientia*) in the public discourse (*eloquentia*) of the city.[14] In other words, Alberti sought an open dialectic between abstract reasoning and practical knowledge in a social space permeated by everyday experiences. One of the first texts to codify this relation between the individual and the Renaissance cosmos was Alberti's *De re aedificatoria*.[15] It is important not because it achieved its goal but because it revealed the difficulties of such a project. Few scholars still notice the inherent contradictions in Alberti's work in progress, which were noted by Manfredo Tafuri in 1969. Tafuri believed that *De re aedificatoria* expressed an "ambiguity resulting from tensions between thematic issues voluntarily placed in competition."[16] Those contradictions were evident in the relation between Alberti's theoretical discourse and his built work, as well as in the crisis of the Renaissance myth concerning the universal character of Classicism.[17]

The following analysis focuses on certain fundamental conceptual dualities and tensions in *De re aedificatoria*, the major text of architectural theory in the Renaissance. By focusing on these structural relationships, it attempts to understand the basic physiognomy and mentality of Alberti, or, as Michael Baxandall put it, "Alberti's cast of mind."[18]

ARCHITECT AND WORKMAN

In the Introduction to *De re aedificatoria*, Alberti defines the *ideal type* of the architect within the humanistic world view described above: "I should explain exactly whom I mean by an architect; for it is no carpenter that I would have you compare to the greatest exponents of other disciplines ... Him I consider the architect, who by sure and wonderful reason and method, knows both how to devise through his own mind and energy, and to realize by construction, whatever can be most beautifully fitted out for the noble needs of man."[19] In Book 9 he elaborates on this fundamental distinction between the architect and the workman: "Moreover, to make something that appears to be convenient for use, and that can without doubt be afforded and built as projected, is the job not of the architect so much as the workman. But to preconceive and to determine in the mind and with judgment something that will be perfect and complete in its every part is the achievement of such a mind as we seek."[20]

The verb *preconceive* (*praecogitasse*) describes a new power of the mind that differentiates the architect-humanist of the early Renaissance from the artisan of the Middle Ages. This power of judgment, this critical faculty of thought (*sinceroque iudicio*), can conceive a priori the totality of space and its relations. This led Alberti to define the task of the Renaissance architect according to a second fundamental dualism: architecture is divided into *conception* and *construction*.[21] In Book 1, he writes, "the whole matter of building is composed of lineaments and structure."[22]

LINEAMENTA AND MATTER

This second dualism is projected onto the object of architectural knowledge. Thus, Alberti holds that "the building is a form of body, which like any other consists of lineaments and matter, the one the product of thought, the other of Nature."[23] His concept of *lineamentum* presumes that architecture is generated as an ideal concept from the active mind of the Renaissance architect-creator. The spatial body of the building is produced later, when the workman moulds natural matter according to the architect's *lineamenta*. These definitions illustrate two more conceptual dualities that characterize Alberti's thought and spirit: the duality of mind and nature; and the more important duality of *lineamenta* and matter. This second duality underlies the content and structure of the first two books of Alberti's treatise. As a new understanding of the physiognomy of architecture and building, it distinguishes the architect from the workman and redefines their respective social positions. But what does *lineamentum* mean?

Scholars of Alberti have interpreted the term differently, showing its inherent complexity and ambiguity.[24] Most of them believe that *lineamenta* refer to the *design* and *drawing* of the architectural work: the lines and angles that represent the basic characteristics of the plan, the general geometrical structure, and the external form of the building.[25] Marco Frascari's imaginative interpretation of *lineamenta* as "denoting lines" goes even further, associating them with the physical plumb-lines and strings that were used to trace the geometry of a building on site.[26] These interpretations have certain shortcomings. First, they conflict with another term that Alberti uses to denote lines in architectural drawing: *lineas*.[27] Second, Alberti says explicitly, "Nor do lineaments have anything to do with material."[28] Moreover, he states, "It is quite possible to project (*praescribere*) whole forms in the mind without any recourse to the material."[29]

Recognizing that *lineamenta* are not the lines in a final drawing of the building, Alberti scholars have developed other hypotheses. One obvious solution was proposed by Françoise Choay, who interpreted *lineamenta* as the "form"[30] of construction or its "figure."[31] A similar reading was put forward recently by Branko Mitrović, who stated that *lineamenta* refer to the "shape" of a building – its visual, geometrically definable, and formal properties.[32] These formalistic, technical, and algorithmic interpretations of *lineamenta* disregard the historical context in which Alberti formulated this crucial concept. They simplify and misconstrue this richly layered term to suit postmodernism and the contemporary digital revolution. Caroline van Eck has argued convincingly that *lineamenta* designate a "mental activity of planning."[33] Dalibor Vesely has proposed the phrase "imaginary or ideal structure of design."[34] Those readings are far more consistent with the humanist culture of the early Renaissance. Stephen Parcell, in his systematic reading of Book 1, has rightly drawn attention to the mental, abstract, and ideal character of *lineamenta*: they do not refer to a physical building, but to "internal programmatic forces," rules of composition, or principles that are invisible.[35] I have argued elsewhere that *lineamenta* are concerned with the pure mental conception of the architectural work, *before* this process is codified into a graphic or digital representation.[36] This aligns with phrases by Alberti himself: for example, a *"lineamentum* is a certain, constant prescription (*praescriptio*), conceived in the mind."[37] Thus, a possible new interpretation of *lineamenta* is that they signify mental concepts and spatial characters that ascribe an ideal social purpose to an architectural project.

THE SOCIAL AND ETHICAL CHARACTER OF *LINEAMENTA*

Lineamenta establish an intellectual program for architectural praxis, schematizing the social and logical foundations of the whole architectural endeavor. Consequently, they are formed at the beginning of the process of architectural creation. *Lineamenta* are intimately associated with the new understanding of the architect as someone who can preconceive in his mind the entire work to be constructed. To distinguish the Renaissance architect from the medieval artisan, Alberti insists on this conceptual ability as though it was a natural predisposition: "But how congenial and instinctive the desire and thought for building may be to our minds is evident ... It often happens that we ourselves, although busy with completely different things, cannot prevent our minds and imagination from projecting some building or other."[38]

Because the human mind has a social character, the values of the architect-humanist help shape meaningful spaces for civic life. This social and political dimension is inherent in the moral humanism of the Renaissance architect, who will "gladly and willingly offer and broadcast his advice for general use, as if compelled to do so by nature."[39] By communicating their social and political purposes, the *lineamenta* enhance the honour and glory of the builder, the city, and human society as a whole. This humanist intention is essential to Alberti's architectural thinking. It prevents *lineamenta* from being merely a subjective image or an arbitrary form; on the contrary, they respond to collective needs, values, and ideals. *Lineamenta* attempt to establish a harmonious structure for the city and its social institutions. Carroll William Westfall has shown how Alberti's humanist values compelled him to try to connect architecture and society in an organic way.[40]

In Latin, *lineamentum* designates the character of the face or the soul. This ethical dimension is evident in Cicero's *De finibus bonorum et malorum*, which uses the same term (*animi liniamenta*) to refer to the soul's character.[41] John Onians has demonstrated the influence of Cicero's moral thought on Alberti's cast of mind.[42] The social and ethical dimension of *lineamenta* situates architectural thought, representation, and praxis in a broad cultural, philosophical, poetic, and moral *logos*. Acting with a sense of duty, the responsible architect-humanist participates in a civic discourse by addressing real social needs. In this way, *lineamenta* are the mental and social reasons for architectural creation. They link the factual exercise of wisdom (*sapientia*) to the public space and discourse of the city (*eloquentia*); however, this connection is not an easy task for the architect. Let us try to determine why this is so.

PRAESCRIPTIO / *PERSCRIPTIO*: THE MENTAL PARADIGM AND ITS MATERIAL TRACE

Relying on *praescribere*,[43] the mind's ability to "prescribe" – a term that seems to have a legal-juridical origin – the humanist-architect's ideal *lineamenta* become a stable, abstract structure or norm, associated with *praecogitasse* (to preconceive). Insofar as an architectural work is intended to be materialized for society,[44] its *lineamenta* need to be inscribed in a collective sphere of common values *before* its final construction. For this, Alberti relies on a process of *semeiosis* to produce *perscriptio*:[45] a registration that writes *lineamentum* (or *certa praescriptio*) into material space. Today we call this architectural representation: a system of signs that presents the idea and the spatial characters of an architectural work. According to Alberti, *lineamenta* can be inscribed into drawings and models that enable others in the public sphere to understand through sensible forms the social, scientific, and constructional qualities of the initial concepts-ideas.[46] In this way, the abstract mental creativity of the Renaissance architect can engage social institutions and their concrete historical, cultural, and natural conditions. Within the dualism of *lineamenta* and matter lies a less tangible duality between the *praescriptio* (the internal, abstract, intellectual concept or precept) and the *perscriptio* (the external, sensible inscription in drawing or model) that adapts it to the reality of social life in the Italian cities of the early Renaissance.[47]

AEDIFICATIO AND *AEDIFICIUM*

This duality is accompanied by another one that is similar. In his Introduction, Alberti associates the mental predisposition of the new humanist subject with the term *aedificatio*: "We ... cannot prevent our minds and imagination from projecting some building or other (*aedificationes*)."[48] Later, in his definition of the material building that is produced when *lineamenta* are brought to matter, Alberti uses a different term: *aedificium*.[49] *Aedificatio* (a structure or structuring) is the Renaissance architect's mental concept of the building; *aedificium* (edifice) is the material construction of the building in its place. These two dualities – between *praescriptio* and *perscriptio*, and between *aedificatio* and *aedificium* – reveal the double meaning of architecture as both structuring and edification, distinguishing also between idea and matter, mind and nature, and architect and workman. Alberti seems to suggest that the new Renaissance man has an innate, natural capacity for structuring, enabling the architect to create structures in his mind before they are realized physically in the public spaces of the city. Following Frascari's terms,[50] the differences between the mental edifice (*aedificatio*) and the actual edifice (*aedificium*) reveal the complexity of the architect's task. Architecture's double bind – both an abstract intellectual structure and a concrete material edifice – creates tensions and ambiguities that permeate and characterize Alberti's mind.

PRINCIPLES OF REASON AND VARIATIONS OF EXPERIENCE

Alberti was aware of the difficulties in reconciling unified, stable, and abstract *lineamenta* with the more complex, contingent, and variously changing social lifeworld.[51] He notes that the principles and parts of architecture are "very diverse in kind, infinite (almost) in number, admirable in nature, and marvelously useful."[52] He also wonders if it is possible to achieve a correspondence between the multiplicity of those infinite parts and the architect's unified intellectual idea: "Since buildings are set to different uses, it proved necessary to inquire whether the same order of lineaments could be used for several."[53] The issue cannot be settled easily.

This indicates a tension between a mathematical, unified, ethical discourse of reason and a concrete, differentiated, social reality. Alberti understands the importance of this tension, noting that the diverse functions of buildings are associated with different sources of beauty (*pulchritudo*).[54] In Book 6 and elsewhere, Alberti's thoughts vacillate between *unity* or *sameness* and *difference*: "The parts of a building may be classified in several different ways, but here we would prefer to draw the distinction between characteristics common to all buildings, rather than according to individual differences."[55]

Therefore, one fundamental conceptual structure that permeates both *De re aedificatoria* and his work *De iciarchia* (On ruling the household) is his distinction between the truth of reason (which is stable, unified, and immortal) and opinion or experience (which is unstable, ambiguous, and changeable over time).[56] It is evident also in distinctions between the abstract-general and the concrete-specific, between the common-universal and the individual-particular. In *De re aedificatoria* the tension between the unity of reason and the diversity of experience is related to other dualities: mind and nature, architect and workman, conception and construction, idea and matter, *aedificatio* and *aedificium*, *praescriptio* and *perscriptio*.

DE RE AEDIFICATORIA'S DUAL STRUCTURE: A POSSIBLE JURIDICAL ORIGIN

I would like to argue that these dichotomies underlie the organization of the whole treatise. The interpretations of the structure of Alberti's treatise are varied and complex. After Paul-Henri Michel and Richard Krautheimer suggested that *De re ædificatoria* imitated Vitruvius's *De architectura*, a tripartite division of Alberti's treatise became a standard assumption for scholarship. Krautheimer wrote, "The triad of *firmitas*, *utilitas* and *venustas* becomes for Alberti the organizing criterion of his book."[57] Choay adopted this argument but added a fourth part, suggesting that Books 1 to 3 are about necessity (*firmitas*), Books 4 and 5 are about commodity (*utilitas*), Books 6 to 9 are equivalent to the Vitruvian pleasure (*venustas*), and Book 10 alone is a fourth part on reparation.[58] This interpretation is problematic. Choay herself has eloquently demonstrated the huge difference between Vitruvius's "empiricism" and Alberti's "systematism,"[59] thus undermining her statement that these two treatises are structurally similar. Why would Alberti imitate the loose organization of *De architectura*? Other scholars have also dissociated Alberti from the influence of Vitruvius, tracing the assumed tripartite structure of his treatise instead to ancient texts on rhetoric and the "productive arts."[60]

A more credible interpretation of *De re aedificatoria* is John Onians's proposed two-part structure (Books 1 to 5 and Books 6 to 9) that corresponds to Cicero's distinction between utility (*utilitas*) and honour (*honestas*).[61] I would like to propose another two-part structure that is based on a different duality and origin. It also addresses the problem of Book 10 and suggests a wider framework for understanding Alberti's cast of mind.[62]

In the Introduction to his work, Alberti announces, "We have undertaken ... to inquire more fully into [the architect's] art and his business, as to the principles from which they are derived."[63] These principles, he tells us, define the field of a thorough knowledge (*absolutissima cognitio*) based on normative laws (*praecepta probatissima*).[64] However, contrary to what a modern rationalist would expect, these principles have a *dual* origin. In Book 6, Alberti writes, "These principles either direct every aspect of beauty and ornament throughout the building or relate individually to its various parts. The former are derived from philosophy, and are concerned with establishing the direction and limits to this art; the latter come from the experience of which we spoke, but are honed, so to speak, to the rule of philosophy and plot the course of this art."[65]

Alberti's distinction between universal principles (*universam*) and singular principles (*singulas*) corresponds to his distinction between the constant truths of reason known by the architect and the material accommodation of these truths in a fluid social and natural setting.[66] The same duality is evident in the relation between *aedificatio* and *aedificium*. The initial mental structures (*aedificationes*)[67] of the new architect-humanist are intended to be universal, but their material realization must be reconciled gradually with the various uses (*varii essent usus*)[68] and other local limitations. In return, difficulties during reconciliation can question or even distort the initial universal law that the *lineamenta* embodied. The complexity of this dialectic accounts for discrepancies that arise occasionally between the abstract, universal ideas and their concrete materialization, as Alberti acknowledges: "I have often conceived of projects in the mind that seemed quite commendable at the time; but when I translated them into drawings, I found several errors in the very parts that delighted me most, and quite serious ones."[69]

I argue that a similar dualistic and dialectic structure organizes the entire *De re aedificatoria* into two basic parts: Books 1 to 3 formulate *universal principles of structuring*: as abstract concepts of the mind, as a careful preparation of materials, and as the construction that brings together idea and matter; Books 4 to 10 then apply and specialize those normative principles to real edification, recognizing that adjustments and differentiations will be needed for functional needs, for various human characters and social classes, for appropriate ornamentation, and to compensate for mistakes and problems due to time, destruction, or war.[70]

This structural interpretation is illustrated in various parts of Alberti's treatise. For example, Book 1, on *lineamenta*, refers to normative laws, including a series of elements – *regio, area, partitio, paries, tectum*, and *apertio* – that are characterized as abstract principles (*principia*) or foundations (*fundamentis*).[71] These principles have no use or function that would associate them directly with the historical or social realm. At the end of Book 1, he also says, "We have said enough on the lineaments of buildings, drawing on observations that seem relevant to the work as a whole (*universum opus*)."[72]

These six principles remain as universals, as general laws of reason that are valid a priori. Alberti is fully aware of the dialectical tension between the universal and the particular, a tension that underlies *De re aedificatoria* as a whole. This is evident in statements such as this: "So as to keep the discussion general, we shall only deal with topics that we consider to be relevant."[73] This phrase appears in Book 1 after an argument about functional differences among built architectural works. In other words, for Alberti, those functional requirements cannot be discussed as a universal topic in the formation of *lineamenta*; instead, they belong to the second part of the treatise that deals with concrete factors affecting the art of building. The proposed conceptual structure that seems to under-lie Alberti's thought – namely, the distinction between universal laws of reason and their particular applications – is the only one that could make remarks as the above intelligible. At the end of Book 3, Alberti pauses to look back at the road travelled so far, then looks forward to the rest of the treatise: "Now that we have dealt with all the general characteristics of our subject matter, let us proceed to what remains to be considered in greater detail. First we shall deal with the various kinds of buildings, their differences and their individual requirements, then with the ornamenta-tion of buildings, and then finally with how to repair and restore their defects, whether they result from faulty workmanship or from damages inflicted by the weather."[74] This pause marks the main division in *De re aedificatoria*. The first part, Books 1 to 3, discusses intelligible, abstract, absolute principles of reason. The second part, Books 4 to 10, discusses how to reconcile those catholic laws with particular social, aesthetic, ethical, moral, historical, temporal, and topological circumstances.

One possible origin of this dual structure in the early Renaissance resides in the philosophy of law: the distinction between *natural law* (or *right*) and *positive law* (or *right*). Natural law (*lex naturalis*) is a univer-sal system of inherent, fundamental rights that are discoverable by human reason alone. On the other hand, positive law (*ius positum*) is a specific legislative act or decision, conditioned by history, which applies at a cer-tain time and place and is thus subject to continuous change. As Leo Strauss writes, "To reject natural right is tantamount to saying that all right is positive right, and this means that what is right is determined exclusively by the legislators and the courts of the various countries. Now it is obviously meaningful, and sometimes even necessary, to speak of 'unjust' laws or 'unjust' decisions. In passing such judgments we imply that there is a standard of right and wrong independent of positive right and higher than positive right: a standard with reference to which we are able to judge of positive right."[75] Strauss's succinct formulation of the philosophical conception of natural law as a rational standard by which positive law is criticized has a long history in European thought. Ada Neschke-Hentschke has traced its Platonic origins: "Plato develops a the-ory according to which every written law must align with the natural law (το φύσει δίκαιον). In modern terms: the positive law is subordinated to the imperative rules of natural law."[76] I argue that the distinction between natural law and positive or written law forms the central core of the "juridical" character of Alberti's mind. Alberti studied canon and civil law at the University of Bologna.[77] As Alberti's important text *De iure* (On law) shows, he was obviously quite aware of this philosophical distinction, as well as the tensions that can arise when their premises conflict.[78] He writes, "Possibly, most of the time, the law instituted by nature in the spirit of every honest man seems to be at variance with the written law (*scripto iure*) … the judge must therefore remember never to digress from the precepts of Nature (*nature preceptis*)."[79]

TOWARDS A DIALECTIC RATIONALITY

This juridical duality is clearly evident in Alberti's treatise, with its dialectical tension between universal ideas and precepts (natural law as *lineamentum*) and specific conditions in the social world and the city (positive law). Alberti was not a precursor of modern instrumental rationalism but a transitional figure of "juridical" humanism. His rationality included elements of contingency and rhetoric. Paul Oskar Kristeller has drawn up attention to the importance of rhetoric for Renaissance humanism and the related crucial role of the *secular public speech* (*ars arengandi*). Public disputations belong to this category.[80] Alberti recognized the importance of antagonistic viewpoints in architecture as public discourse or speech, trying to connect proto-rational concepts in the mind (θεωρία) to multifarious experiences in praxis. As Joseph Rykwert suggests, "His treatise (*De Re Aedificatoria*) is a rhetorical exercise, to be read as a literary text and it was much admired by his contemporaries as a stylistic masterpiece of modern Latin, to be set beside Cicero."[81] Alberti's rhetorical rationality is related to his design practice. The latter is understood as a spatial discourse that addresses the public sphere of the city, introducing theatrical statements that mould a new urban culture and atmosphere.[82] Alberti's "open," dialectic rationality was based on ideas about public speech, verbal communication and storytelling that transcend the modern monological ego. As Nicholas Temple suggests, the dialogue between "reflective and anticipatory realms"[83] demonstrates the interpretive character of Alberti's "reasonableness." To Alberti, the architect is not a technocrat who implements pre-given *formal* instructions, but an intellectual who narrates *ideas as arguments* and tests their moral validity through ongoing dialogue in the conflictive public space of the city.

ACKNOWLEDGMENTS

I would like to thank Professors Alberto Pérez-Gómez and Stephen Parcell for their insightful comments during the preparation of the first draft and for their careful editing of the second draft.

NOTES

1 Giovanni Pico della Mirandola, "Oration on the Dignity of Man," in *The Renaissance Philosophy of Man*, ed. Ernst Cassirer, Paul Oskar Kristeller, and John Herman Randall Jr. (Chicago: University of Chicago Press, 1948), 225.

2 Cristoforo Landino, *Scritti Critici e Teorici*, ed. Roberto Cardini (Rome: Bulzoni, 1974), 1:120.

3 Leon Battista Alberti, *On the Art of Building in Ten Books*, trans. Joseph Rykwert, Neil Leach, and Robert Tavernor (Cambridge, MA: MIT Press, 1988), 1 (hereafter cited as *OAB*); and Leon Battista Alberti, *L'architettura (De re aedificatoria)*, trans. Giovanni Orlandi (Milan: Edizioni Il Polifilo, 1966), 1:3 (hereafter cited as *DRA*).

4 Jean-Marc Mandosio, "Alberti ou l'esprit du caméléon," in *Alberti: Humaniste, architecte*, ed. Françoise Choay and Michel Paoli (Paris: Ecole Nationale Supérieure des Beaux-Arts, 2006), 129–41.

5 Jacob Burckhardt, *The Civilization of the Renaissance in Italy: An Essay* (London: Phaidon Press, 1965), 84–7.

6 Sigfried Giedion, *Space, Time and Architecture: The Growth of a New Tradition* (Cambridge, MA: Harvard University Press, 1941), 3–4.

7 Ibid., 30.

8 Ibid., 30–6, 45.

9 Françoise Choay, *La règle et le modèle: Sur la théorie de l'architecture et de l'urbanisme* (Paris: Éditions du Seuil, 1980); Mario Carpo, *Architecture in the Age of Printing: Orality, Writing, Typography, and Printed Images in the History of Architectural Theory*, trans. Sarah Benson (Cambridge, MA: MIT Press, 2001), 119–24; and Branko Mitrović, *Serene Greed of the Eye: Leon Battista Alberti and the Philosophical Foundations of Renaissance Architectural Theory* (Munich: Deutscher Kunstverlag, 2005), 101–25.

10 For a very good synopsis of contemporary research on Alberti, see Choay and Paoli, *Alberti: Humaniste, architecte*.

11 Mark Jarzombek, *On Leon Baptista Alberti: His Literary and Aesthetic Theories* (Cambridge, MA: MIT Press, 1989), ix–xvi; and Francesco Furlan, *Studia Albertiana: Lectures et lecteurs de L.B. Alberti* (Paris: J. Vrin, 2003), 7–11.

12 Ernst Cassirer, *The Philosophy of Symbolic Forms*, trans. Ralph Manheim (New Haven: Yale University Press, 1955), 1:73–5.

13 Paul Oskar Kristeller, "The Medieval Antecedents of Renaissance Humanism," in *Eight Philosophers of the Italian Renaissance* (Stanford, CA: Stanford University Press, 1964), 147–65; and Eugenio Garin, *Moyen Âge et Renaissance*, trans. Claude Carme (Paris: Éditions Gallimard, 1969), 8.

14 Cesare Vasoli, "The Renaissance Concept of Philosophy," in *The Cambridge History of Renaissance Philosophy*, ed. Charles B. Schmitt and Quentin Skinner (Cambridge: Cambridge University Press, 1988), 57–65; and Paul Oskar Kristeller, *Renaissance Thought and Its Sources* (New York: Columbia University Press, 1979), 213–59.

15 Ernst Cassirer, *The Individual and the Cosmos in Renaissance Philosophy* (Mineola, NY: Dover, 2000), 1–6, 24–36.

16 Manfredo Tafuri, *Architecture et humanisme: De la Renaissance aux réformes*, trans. H. Berghauer and O. Seyler (Paris: Dunod, 1981), 16, my translation.

17 Ibid., 14–19.

18 Michael Baxandall, "Alberti's Cast of Mind," in *Words for Pictures: Seven Papers on Renaissance Art and Criticism* (New Haven: Yale University Press, 2003), 27–38.

19 *OAB*, 3; *DRA*, 1:7.

20 *OAB*, 315; *DRA*, 2:855.

21 *OAB*, 2–6; *DRA*, 1:7–17.

22 *OAB*, 7; *DRA*, 1:19.

23 *OAB*, 5; *DRA*, 1:15.

24 For a discussion of the ambiguity of the concept of *lineamentum* and its resemblance to the Mannerist notion of *disegno interno*, see Dalibor Vesely, *Architecture in the Age of Divided Representation: The Question of Creativity in the Shadow of Production* (Cambridge, MA: MIT Press, 2004), 133–8. See also Leon Battista Alberti, *L'art d'édifier*, trans. Pierre Caye and Françoise Choay (Paris: Éditions du Seuil, 2004), 55n1.

25 *OAB*, 422–3; *DRA*, 1:18; and Susan Lang, "De lineamentis: L.B. Alberti's Use of a Technical Term," *Journal of the Warburg and Courtauld Institutes* 28 (1965): 331–5.

26 Marco Frascari, *Eleven Exercises in the Art of Architectural Drawing: Slow Food for the Architect's Imagination* (London: Routledge, 2011), 97–101.

27 *DRA*, 1:15–21.

28 *OAB*, 7; *DRA*, 1:19–21.

29 *OAB*, 7. The Latin text is: "Et licebit integras formas praescribere animo et mente seclusa omni materia." *DRA*, 1:21.

30 Choay, *La règle et le modèle*, 92–3.

31 Françoise Choay, *The Rule and the Model: On the Theory of Architecture and Urbanism*, ed. Denise Bratton (Cambridge, MA: MIT Press, 1997), 69, 72, 327n15.

32 Mitrović, *Serene Greed of the Eye*, 49–58.

33 Caroline van Eck, "The Structure of *De re aedificatoria* Reconsidered," *Journal of the Society of Architectural Historians* 57, no. 3 (1998): 295n15.

34 Vesely, *Architecture in the Age of Divided Representation*, 139.

35 Stephen Parcell, *Four Historical Definitions of Architecture* (Montreal and Kingston: McGill-Queen's University Press, 2012), 132–48.

36 Nikolaos-Ion Terzoglou, "The Human Mind and Design Creativity: Leon Battista Alberti and *Lineamenta*," in *The Humanities in Architectural Design: A Contemporary and Historical Perspective*, ed. Soumyen Bandyopadhyay, Jane Lomholt, Nicholas Temple, and Renée Tobe (London: Routledge, 2010), 136–46.

37 The translation is mine, from the Latin text: "ergo lineamentum certa constansque praescriptio concepta animo." *DRA*, 1:21.

38 *OAB*, 4; *DRA*, 1:11.

39 *OAB*, 4; *DRA*, 1:11.

40 Carroll William Westfall, "Society, Beauty, and the Humanist Architect in Alberti's *De re aedificatoria*," *Studies in the Renaissance* 16 (1969): 61–79.

41 Cicero, *De finibus bonorum et malorum*, with an English translation by H. Rackham (Cambridge, MA: Harvard University Press, 1914), 294–5.

42 John Onians, "Alberti and ΦΙΛΑΡΕΤΗ [Filarete]: A Study in their Sources," *Journal of the Warburg and Courtauld Institutes* 34 (1971): 96–114.

43 *DRA*, 1:21.

44 *DRA*, 1:2–17.

45 Ibid., 1:53.

46 Ibid., 1:97–9.

47 Choay and Caye render the term *perscriptio* as "trace." Alberti, *L'art d'édifier*, 73.

48 *OAB*, 4. The Latin text is: "nequeamus non facere, quin mente et animo aliquas aedificationes commentemur!" *DRA*, 1:11.

49 *DRA*, 1:15.

50 Marco Frascari, "The Tell-the-Tale Detail," in *Theorizing a New Agenda for Architecture: An Anthology of Architectural Theory, 1965–1995*, ed. Kate Nesbitt (New York: Princeton Architectural Press, 1996), 503.

51 *DRA*, 1:7–15.

52 *OAB*, 5; *DRA*, 1:15.

53 *OAB*, 5; *DRA*, 1:15.

54 *DRA*, 1:15.

55 *OAB*, 159; *DRA*, 2:459.

56 Mandosio, "Alberti ou l'esprit du caméléon," 129.

57 Richard Krautheimer, "Alberti and Vitruvius," in *Studies in Early Christian, Medieval, and Renaissance Art* (New York: New York University Press, 1969), 327.

58 Choay, *The Rule and the Model*, 71–2, 287.

59 Françoise Choay, "Alberti and Vitruvius," *Architectural Design* 49, no. 5–6 (1979): 26–9, 33.

60 Van Eck, "The Structure of *De re aedificatoria* Reconsidered," 285–94. For example, Veronica Biermann suggests that the tripartite division of the treatise (Books 1–2, 3–5, 6–9) corresponds to three distinct rhetorical stages for the preparation of a speech, namely *inventio, dispositio*, and *elocutio*.

61 Ibid., 289–90.

62 On this problem, see Pierre Caye, "La place du Livre X dans le *De re aedificatoria*," *Albertiana* 7 (2004): 23–40.

63 *OAB*, 5; *DRA*, 1:15.

64 *OAB*, 159; *DRA*, 2:457.

65 *OAB*, 159; *DRA*, 2:457.

66 *DRA*, 2:441.

67 Ibid., 1:11.

68 Ibid., 1:15.

69 *OAB*, 317; *DRA*, 2:861.

70 *OAB*, 320.

71 *DRA*, 1:23–5.

72 *OAB*, 32; *DRA*, 1:93.

73 *OAB*, 19; *DRA*, 1:53.

74 *OAB*, 91; *DRA*, 1:263.

75 Leo Strauss, *Natural Right and History* (Chicago: University of Chicago Press, 1965), 2.

76 Ada Neschke-Hentschke, *Platonisme politique et théorie du droit naturel: contributions à une archéologie de la culture politique européenne*, vol. 1: *Le platonisme politique dans l'antiquité* (Louvain: Éditions Peeters, 1995), ix, my translation. See also Strauss, *Natural Right and History*, 84–6.

77 Choay and Paoli, *Alberti: Humaniste, architecte*, 269.

78 Leonis Baptistae Alberti, *De iure (Du droit)*, trans. Pierre Caye, *Albertiana* 3 (2000): 157–91. On this subject, see Franco and Stefano Borsi, *Alberti: Une biographie intellectuelle* (Paris: Editions Hazan, 2006), 69–71.

79 Leonis Baptistae Alberti, *De iure (Du droit)*, 167, my translation.

80 Paul Oskar Kristeller, *Renaissance Thought and the Arts: Collected Essays* (Princeton: Princeton University Press, 1990), 228–41, 246.

81 Joseph Rykwert, "Theory as Rhetoric: Leon Battista Alberti in Theory and in Practice," in *Paper Palaces: The Rise of the Renaissance Architectural Treatise*, ed. Vaughan Hart with Peter Hicks (New Haven: Yale University Press, 1998), 38.

82 Ibid., 43–50.

83 Nicholas Temple, "Architecture and the Humanist Tradition," in *Four Faces: The Dynamics of Architectural Knowledge*, 20th EAAE Conference proceedings (Stockholm and Helsinki, 2003), 159–60.

The Architecture of Anselm Kiefer: La Ribaute and the Space of Dramatic Representation

Stephen Wischer

Chora

BECAUSE ART AND ARCHITECTURE since the eighteenth century typically have been understood as specialized and separate, elucidating relationships between the German artist Anselm Kiefer's creation at La Ribaute and modern architectural practice may seem precarious. Yet, having recently visited Kiefer's former home and studio, I will argue that his integration of painting, sculpture, photography, bookmaking, and construction at La Ribaute pursues the fundamental task of architecture. Kiefer's creations rely on a poetic form of making that disregards conventional art historical categories and reveals significant connections with architectural origins. It should not be surprising that an artist who is so concerned with ancient sources – from Egyptian and Mesopotamian myths and European gnosticism to the writings of Dionysus the Aeropagite and Sappho's poetry – would pursue the very beginnings of aesthetic experience and the ritual origins of Western art and architecture in the ancient Greek theatre.

The modern context has been influenced by dualistic tendencies popularized during the Enlightenment and cauterized in Bauhaus and Greenbergian aesthetics that emphasize separations between past and present, inside and outside, and objective and subjective realms. The "reversible" nature of Kiefer's work attempts to retrieve a non-dualistic practice that questions our assumptions regarding architectural form and space, our experience of time and, most emphatically, our relationship to history and its value to present thinking. By overlapping various media, scales, and potential meanings, Kiefer's work challenges the separation of the arts, demonstrates the relevance of ancient questions to contemporary culture, and discloses the importance of an active interpretation of history in the making and reading of a work. This essay examines Kiefer's work at La Ribaute in terms of its integrated modes of representation and its poetic and *dramatic* relationship between art and life. It explores how the act of creation and its potential meanings are embodied in work that gives form to life.[1]

THE ARCHITECTURE OF KIEFER

On a private piece of land just outside the small town of Barjac in southern France, Anselm Kiefer created La Ribaute: a home, studio, and living quarters for himself and his assistants, where he explored diverse cultural themes in a rigorously personal way for almost fifteen years. Myths,

Fig. 14.1 Anselm Kiefer, interior chamber with *Women of the Revolution* installation at La Ribaute; from Atelier Anselm Kiefer, photograph by Charles Duprat; © Anselm Kiefer, 2011.

stories, and legends involving both historical and contemporary subjects were folded backwards and forwards into works of painting, sculpture, and architecture. Established in 1993, his compound at La Ribaute occupies the site of an abandoned silkworm nursery. Today, the complex contains approximately forty-seven buildings, including an amphitheatre, the main studio, storage areas, a crypt, earthworks, tunnels, bridges, and pavilions that house works of painting, sculpture, and installation.[7]

Begun with an initial placement of rocks to mark out positions of buildings for his art making, it was in 2000 that Kiefer extended his artistic creation into an organic process of construction that left parts of the complex incomplete, on the verge of change, suggesting transformation. Amid chasm-like environments, collections of fragments, and elemental materials, many of the spaces at La Ribaute conjure atmospheres similar to Kiefer's paintings (fig. 14.1). Beyond the immediate "abstract expressionist musculature" of his paintings and the geological quality of spaces at the compound, his architecture, like his paintings, consists primarily of places to *re-create* stories.

What remains at La Ribaute has been described as both a *Gesamt-kunstwerk* (a total work of art) and its opposite, as the work, being constituted from fragments, can in no way be considered complete or total.[3] In its photography, painting, and bookmaking, its archaeological-like excavations and tower constructions, and even its giant sunflowers, Kiefer's work at La Ribaute may be understood as an attempt to re-create, albeit personally, a cosmology based on shared, but mostly forgotten, cultural memories.

As a place for the "permanent recycling" of subjects,[4] La Ribaute is impossible to categorize art historically or stylistically, as it is not limited to one discipline-specific type of making, nor is it reducible to one specific meaning. In fact, it is the opposite. Like his earliest performances, the all-encompassing environments at La Ribaute dramatize cultural themes with an inherent *ambivalence*, a parody of many acts or meanings. Kiefer's ways of working emulate various artisans, including medieval smiths who forged with fire and molten lead, and cubist painters who revealed multiple aspects of their subjects. Having "no era of his own," he fashioned La Ribaute with diverse materials and equipment, from traditional paint and palette to modern cranes, bulldozers, and excavators.[5] By using many instruments and playing many roles, Kiefer's work at the compound connects various eras by weaving times, places, and stories together.[6]

RUINS, MEMORY, AND LA RIBAUTE

The fusion of memory and experience at La Ribaute was anticipated by Kiefer's earlier work that conjured the dark historical legacies and mythical themes that led to Nazism, earning him worldwide acclaim and notoriety in artistic circles for years. Since Kiefer's *Occupations* performances in 1969, in which he enacted the Hitler salute (ironically) in front of European monuments and landscapes, each manifestation of his work has sought to transpose history into life by understanding it through the body.[7] Born in 1945 into the cultural amnesia that followed the Second World War, Kiefer has often introduced difficult themes from the past into our present reality. Since the mid-1980s, the broadening of Kiefer's themes to include theological, philosophical, and literary remnants has harkened back to ruins, inspired by his early childhood experiences of playing in the debris of German cities after the war. Kiefer maintained that "Art cannot live on itself. It has to draw on broader knowledge."[8] His creation at La Ribaute was inspired by the ambiguity and incompleteness of ruins, the feeling that they embody the past form of a present life and the possibility of recombination.

Exploring the compound, one gets the sense that memory was the primary motivation for building. This is accomplished through juxtapositions: between artworks of thick materials and complex themes enclosed within simple, light pavilions; between apertures that open to the sky or lead to dark chambers below. At La Ribaute everything has its opposite. Tunnel doors that are re-formed or left unfinished may lead to adjacent chambers or dissolve into cavities dug from the earth. The entire complex is formed equally above and below the ground. Material qualities from Kiefer's work – the thickness and brittleness of painted textures, coarse fragments of plant parts, and even the sound of brittle pages in his large books – are evident in the textures of walls and the petrified cultural remnants in the tunnels and chambers. In the delicate white painted glass of the greenhouses, the fragile balancing of the concrete towers, and the names, phrases, and markings on canvases, walls, and raw earth, complex narratives unfold through painting, installation, and architectural space.

As Danièle Cohn suggests, the compound contains "everything" – objects, pieces, plans, maps, early works, current ones, and the contours of future work – as if "Anselm Kiefer has never really left Germany, he has moved it, complete with its ruins, and set it up in the new studio."[9] Described as "a world within the world" and a "living archive," La Ribaute was the very centre of Kiefer's restorative acts. Here he could transform materials, objects, and themes so that "a particular work can be read in all of the others, just as all others can be read in a singular one ... [where] circularity guarantees the continuity of works."[10] This encompasses both the creation and the experience of work at La Ribaute, as memory gathers things together.[11]

Those who are familiar with Kiefer's work may associate the piles of hay stored in the amphitheatre (fig. 14.2) with his *Straw Cycle* paintings of the 1980s, in which straw associates the German landscape with the blond hair of an idealized Germanic beauty. The hay confined within a room that resembles a freight container is especially poignant, considering Kiefer's invocation of the Holocaust and the poetry of Paul Celan.

Fig. 14.2 Anselm Kiefer, chamber in the amphitheatre at La Ribaute; from Sophie Fiennes's film *Over Your Cities Grass Will Grow*; © Amoeba Films, 2011.

The field of wheat in his *Morgenthau Plan* installation (2012) in one of the pavilions re-emphasizes such themes, recalling the nightmarish ideologies of Nazism and the ludicrous plan by the Roosevelt administration to turn Germany agrarian after the war. Such connections renew our encounters with his previous works to recognize what has been forgotten and what may be lost.[12]

While the amphitheatre, main studio, library, and pavilions exist above ground, deeper layers of mythic history are invoked in the network of subterranean tunnels that are connected to the surface through crude vertical punctures or steep stairways that accentuate travelling up and down (fig. 14.3). Inspired by the Kabbalistic writings of Isaac Luria, this movement is a dominant theme in Kiefer's compound. Written in the fifteenth century, Luria's mystical theory describes movement between heaven and earth through a system of angelic forms based on Kabbalistic references to Jacob's ladder in Ezekiel's prophecy.[13] Like earlier works in history that describe passages between heaven and earth, Kiefer's tunnels and vertical passages emphasize transitions between dark and light. Such

Fig. 14.3 Anselm Kiefer, tunnels at La Ribaute; from Sophie Fiennes's film *Over Your Cities Grass Will Grow*; © Amoeba Films, 2011.

relationships are felt not only visually, but also through changes in temperature as one moves from cool tunnels to light-filled pavilions, atriums, and the amphitheatre. The moistness below becomes arid above as one rises into the amphitheatre. Silt turns to sand, and dust covers glass apertures, making them almost disappear into the concrete floor.

These bodily experiences are reinforced allegorically by the proximity of historical and mythical remnants. The painting *Shevirat Ha-Kelim*, for example (fig. 14.4), situated just above a pile of broken terracotta pottery in one of the tunnels, presents the emanation of God's light as a swash of paint that reverses dark light and white light, cascading between the symbols of *Tsimtsum* (the breaking of vessels) and *Tikkum* (the reconstitution of the bowls). In various forms at La Ribaute, this story points to a profound scheme of transformation in which the acts of man may attain a restorative function, bringing him closer to God and totality.[14]

At La Ribaute, Kabbalistic themes fuse with tenets from Platonic, Aristotelian, and other religious and theosophical schools that were concerned with the Great Chain of Being (between above and below), along which

Fig. 14.4 Anselm Kiefer, *Shevirat Ha-Kelim* in pavilion at La Ribaute; from Atelier Anselm Kiefer, photograph by Charles Duprat; © Anselm Kiefer, 2011.

various influences might pass.[15] There are propellers, books, wings, and airplanes made of lead, palettes, polyhedrons, and meteorites: all symbols of mankind's ongoing search for transcendence. These invoke ancient astrology, Kabbalistic and Old Testament references, Nordic creation myths, and Greek and Christian symbols that sought to pull heaven and earth together.[16] At the same time, these features recall particular episodes in recent human history and personal memory. This multilayered integration and tension of mythical and historical, universal and particular, formal and material, imparts a strange "otherly" quality to the complex at La Ribaute.

REVERSIBILITY: THE CRITICAL DIMENSION OF LA RIBAUTE

Since before Vitruvius, the ritual act of building relied on mimesis to associate the mutable realm on earth with the immutable realm of the heavens. Kiefer's creations continue this mimetic tradition, but in a *critical* way. He draws from archetypal constructions, both historical and mythical – towers, tunnels, and amphitheatres – and re-casts them to suggest meanings that are not fully accessible. The amphitheatre at La Ribaute is covered with modern steel trusses[17] (fig. 14.5); tunnels and chambers contain detritus; and precarious towers verge on devastation. Moreover, traditional symbols of ascendance are here made of lead: a Saturnine, melancholic, heavy material, impermeable to light and radiation, and often symbolizing wings that cannot fly. Archaic or modern remnants, as if buried under the destruction of world wars, are reminders of past worlds and previous beliefs that cannot simply be reclaimed.

The mystery of La Ribaute is this confusing, collapsed condition. Its paradoxes undermine traditional relationships, mix ancient and modern forms of knowledge, and confuse typical artistic and architectural production. Discussing Kiefer's painting practice, Thomas McEvilley recognizes how "the interconnected web of references in Kiefer's work, its intertextuality of traditions and images, reflects the idea of the interconnectedness of the universe on many levels simultaneously. Parallelisms intersect, become one another, separate, run parallel again for a while, then veer apart."[18] On another level, the work emphasizes the mutable, perishable, and perhaps diseased world that has changed from a world originally conceived through and through by correspondences and analogies to a world changed by mathematical regularity.[19]

Fig. 14.5 Anselm Kiefer, amphitheatre at La Ribaute; from Atelier Anselm Kiefer,
photograph by Charles Duprat; © Anselm Kiefer, 2011.

Kiefer's efforts to "turn meanings over" may seem like a response to
postmodern formalism, but his *weaving* of contradictory themes recalls
relations between art and construction at the very origins of language and
culture. As discussed by Maria Karvouni, the Greek word *tekton* – the
etymological root of *architekton* (chief builder) – refers to one who "cuts
and joins, divides and connects." Dividing and composing are also the
two main modes of a dual operation that underlies construction, philosophy, and the definition of art in general.[20] Kiefer's creations at La Ribaute both collate and displace meanings by pulling together various
references. This is echoed in his own account of the ambition of his practice: "to join together that which has been separated."[21]

Michael Auping notes the influence of Le Corbusier's monastery at La
Tourette on the "deliberately crude architectural elegies" at La Ribaute.[22]
Indeed, the dense, overlapping qualities at La Ribaute recall the mysterious spaces at La Tourette that are critical reinterpretations of traditional
rituals and types.[23] In visiting these places, it is evident that both rely on
disorientation to disengage the beholder from the everyday, rational world,
so that metaphors and references can arise from our memory. This enables

their respective spaces – the disorienting corridors of La Tourette and Kiefer's tunnels, as well as Le Corbusier's barely accessible cloister and Kiefer's doubly unreachable towers – to create tensions between history and myth, past and present, the individual and the universal, in ways both old and new.[24]

Kiefer's work at La Ribaute also conjures the embodied experience of the mythical labyrinth at the very origins of Western architecture. Daedalus's intertwined pattern of path and boundary has been re-interpreted for millennia in cities and buildings as a symbol of human existence, immersed in life and the world. Like all poetic works, it manifests both orientation and disorientation, revealing and concealing.

Unlike modern work by others who narrowly pursue an abstract "idea of space" or "idea of time,"[25] the labyrinthine depth of Kiefer's work at La Ribaute continues the traditional architectural desire for broad knowledge, together with a palpable encounter with our shared human history.

THE MATERIAL OF HISTORY

For Kiefer, historical and mythical themes are "lived through" in order to be realized. This is dramatically evident in his transformation of substances. Just as raising his arm during his *Occupations* performances made history palpable, Kiefer's use of many physical substances is likewise historical. For example, lead – much of which Kiefer acquired from the roof of the Cologne Cathedral – is his most widely used material, employed in various ways at La Ribaute, including in the creation of massive tomes, heated to a silver lustre and used like paint on canvases, and as the lining for a subterranean chamber (fig. 14.6). Taking lead from the roof of the tallest medieval structure in Germany, then melting, forging, and burying it beneath the earth, challenges religious meanings. As Auping suggests, lead is also associated with linings for coffins and boxes for the internment of hearts, and most notably with medieval alchemy. As the lowest and most impure metal in alchemy, lead was associated with *nigredo*, the base matter of transformation, as well as with air and the "highest" planet, Saturn. Being light and dark, a colour and a non-colour, lead is employed as both a liquid and a fossil-like material in his work, conveying ambivalence.[26] This is witnessed in the lead chamber, where tarnished, oxidizing lead and algae in the water of the sunken floor convey death, single cellular life, and transmutation.

Fig. 14.6 Top Anselm Kiefer, lead chamber at La Ribaute; from Atelier Anselm Kiefer, photograph by Charles Duprat; © Anselm Kiefer, 2011.

Fig. 14.7 Bottom Anselm Kiefer, the crypt at La Ribaute; from Atelier Anselm Kiefer, photograph by Charles Duprat; © Anselm Kiefer, 2011.

Kiefer's prolific use of concrete at La Ribaute also includes both fluid and brittle forms (fig. 14.7). In the crypt area at the compound, Kiefer bored holes into the earth and then filled them with concrete. When excavated, these liquid-like columnar forms appear imprinted with the weight of earth.[27] Kiefer also stacked concrete rooms into additive assemblies and pulverized concrete into fragments that suggest both modern and ancient ruins (fig. 14.8). The massive weight of concrete is contrasted by delicate glass greenhouses that seem to suspend a state of destruction by enclosing fragments resembling a lead warship, glass shards, broken concrete, and twisted steel.

The *act* of transforming both materials and themes is epitomized in Kiefer's use of fire. At La Ribaute, fire was applied directly to the surfaces of his art work – to melt lead onto earth and to form sculptures. It turned books into charred sculptural objects and generated piles of ash to be used on larger canvases. Used in medieval alchemy to convert lead into silver or gold, fire was associated with the Athanor furnace and the Magnum Opus. Like the capacity of fire to both separate and join substances,

Fig. 14.8 Anselm Kiefer, *Return to the Grand Palais*, in the greenhouse at La Ribaute; from Atelier Anselm Kiefer, photograph by Charles Duprat; © Anselm Kiefer, 2011.

Fig. 14.9 Anselm Kiefer, towers at La Ribaute; from Atelier Anselm Kiefer, photograph by Charles Duprat; © Anselm Kiefer, 2011.

Kiefer's work transforms one theme into another through both creation and destruction.

When asked what it means to burn, Kiefer says, "Everything all together, everything all together. When a painting is good, it means that it's seemingly simple, but if we look closer, it has many ties: an apparent simplicity behind which, however, there lies a complex, rich structure."[28] The same may be said of his compound at La Ribaute. At first, it is experienced as nothing but fragments: various forms, impure mixtures of materials, distal words, and diverse references. These fragments gradually encourage the visitor to uncover connections, reconstitute pieces, and recognize intersecting narratives.

In a field behind a cluster of trees, concrete towers emerge from the ground (fig. 14.9). Rubble and twisted steel around the bases of these towers anticipate their collapse. Appearing purposefully stacked, they seem like archaized spires, temples, and ruins from wars. Each of the towers consists of broken geometric forms that rotate around a hollowed-out column of space. Their stacked forms are offset and slightly angled, with corners projecting over edges below. This accentuates the teetering of the towers and creates fluctuating patterns of light and shadow on the interiors for those walking beneath. Gigantic lead books crushed under the towers symbolize the inaccessibility of ancient wisdom. The "liquid" property of these compressed lead books, supporting massive yet fragile concrete forms, expresses both monumentality and instability. Immense concrete stairs, laid on the hillside and in the field by the towers, imply movement between earth and sky but lead nowhere, continuing Kiefer's pervasive use of irony.

These towers of concrete "rooms," shaped and stacked like modern shipping containers, symbolize both industrial and spiritual transport. The verticality of the towers was inspired by the story of the Merkaba in the *Sefer Hechaloth*, which refers to the crossing of seven buildings towards Heaven.[29] In Ezekiel, the Merkaba are described as winged creatures that move in "any of the four directions."[30] Kiefer's towers suggest a similar "omnidirectional" movement, somewhere between traditional and modern, mythical and rational, simulated and real.

Expressing both creation and destruction – rubble and ruins, barbicans from Nazi camps, and stacked tombs – the towers suggest a reconstructive cycle in which ends become beginnings and beginnings become ends. Everything at La Ribaute teeters between what is there and not there. Everything is a signal of something hidden, and everything unfolds into something else. All of this relies on the visitor's motivation to follow combinations of materials and themes that form Kiefer's hermeneutic paths.

THE SPACE OF DRAMATIC REPRESENTATION

One of the most compelling lessons that Kiefer's work provides for architecture is how the provocations at La Ribaute rely on both the circumstances in which the work was produced and the visitor's engagement with the work. Its meanings were not conceived beforehand and then transcribed to the work, nor can meanings be easily recuperated here.[31]

Cohn reminds us that, for Kiefer, "It is because the superposition of layers of an often distant past with the present is random that it is productive."[32] This extends to the task of reading the work, where memories and themes are created anew each time they are discovered.[33] Just as Kiefer's earlier *Occupations* performances enabled him to internalize history and partially "understand the madness," the images that emerge from the thick materiality and thematic networks at La Ribaute strike a similar chord within our bodies.

At La Ribaute this relies on a weaving of time, memory, vision, and tactility to incite a tense communion between the world and the body. A pipeline that punctures vertically to bring light underground is contrasted with its horizontal counterpart, buried in the earth (fig. 14.10). The unevenness of the ground on both sides, together with an offset doorway within a circle, imparts a curious imbalance. Hollow steel pipes alternate with solid concrete columns, which in turn recall the excavations into which the liquid concrete was poured, hardened, then revealed. Concrete, also used for the towers, tunnels, and amphitheatre, suggest alternately tension or compression, casting or breaking. Their residual acts of construction, signifying both presence and absence, are reinforced by the empty dresses and impressions of bodies in the vacant beds of Kiefer's sculptures.

At each juncture we encounter tensions between the world of the senses and the world of ideas. Moving among towers, through tunnels, and along interconnected platforms, we linger at fault lines between the familiar and the uncanny. Tilted pipelines, offset promenades, and irregular burrows of earth are conjoined with more refined structures of concrete or steel. These juxtapositions create uneasy tensions among their references: mechanical systems, botanical sciences, creation myths, biblical narratives, prehistoric caves, and geological sedimentation.

Walking through Kiefer's palimpsest of traces, we accumulate many different meanings but no conclusive answers. Between various places we discover one era, work, or theme in the next. This quasi-archaeological participation has a profound effect on our experience of time: a "retroaction," where, from the now of the work, we encounter a past that never stops changing its meaning.[34]

Our overall participation at La Ribaute profoundly connects Kiefer's work to the origins of Western art and architecture in the ancient Greek theatre, with its space of dramatic representation.[35] Following along with the performances, spectators of Greek tragedies created for themselves the movement of feelings inspired by the spectacle before them.[36] The ambivalence of Kiefer's creations provokes a similar movement by extending one's self-understanding into larger cultural contexts (*katharsis*).[37]

Fig. 14.10 Anselm Kiefer, interior chamber at La Ribaute; from Atelier Anselm Kiefer, photograph by Charles Duprat; © Anselm Kiefer, 2011.

Like Greek tragedies, laden with conflict and culturally important move-ments,[38] Kiefer's work elicits an emotional response that dramatizes col-lective knowledge.

Leaving the tunnels, we arrive close to where we began on the slope of the hill, amid simple pavilions. With no particular beginning or end, the organization of the compound at La Ribaute and its many themes encour-age reconciliation by the visitor. What results is a coming out of ourselves and an "increase of being" that occurs when our own horizon meets the horizon of the work.[39]

NOTES

1 Danièle Cohn, *Anselm Kiefer: Studios* (Paris: Flammarion, 2013), 51.

2 Kiefer's Barjac compound remains private, still part of his artistic practice. As a way station for his Croissy studio in Paris, it is used to store old and new works, stretchers for future paintings, and other materials. Kiefer has allowed access to the site by researchers and for installations by other artists. I visited the compound on 17 May 2014, in a small group that was guided through certain areas by one of Kiefer's assistants.

3 Catherine Strasser, *Chevirat Ha-Kelim* (Paris: Editions du Regard, 2000), 72–5.

4 Ibid., 72.

5 Cohn, *Anselm Kiefer*, 50.

6 Ibid., 46.

7 See the interview in Roberto Andreotti and Federico De Melis, "With His-tory under His Skin," in *Anselm Kiefer: Merkaba* (Milan: Edizioni Charta, 2006), 46.

8 Michael Auping, *Anselm Kiefer: Heaven and Earth* (Fort Worth, TX: Mod-ern Art Museum of Fort Worth, 2006), 171.

9 Cohn, *Anselm Kiefer*, 37.

10 Ibid., 245.

11 Ibid., 23.

12 Hans-Georg Gadamer, *Truth and Method* (London: Continuum, 1975), 14.

13 See Klaus Dermutz's interview with Anselm Kiefer in Sophie Fiennes's film *Over Your Cities Grass Will Grow* (2011).

14 Strasser, *Chevirat Ha-Kelim*. See also John Hutchinson, "Kiefer's Wager," in *Anselm Kiefer: Jason* (Stuttgart: Edition Cantz, 1990).

15 Thomas McEvilley, *Anselm Kiefer: Let a Thousand Flowers Bloom* (London: Anthony d'Offay, 2000), 13.

16 Auping, *Anselm Kiefer*, 24.

17 The amphitheatre at La Ribaute was designed by Kiefer as a stage set for the opera *Elektra* at the Teatro Real in Madrid (2011). Adjacent to its tiered levels is a backstage area that appears to be one of several studios at the compound that stores equipment and some enormous paintings.

18 Thomas McEvilley, *Anselm Kiefer: I Hold All Indias in My Hand* (London: Anthony d'Offay Gallery, 1996), 9.

19 Didier Ottinger, "Contemporary Cosmologies," in *Cosmos: From Romanticism to the Avant-garde*, ed. Jean Clair (Montreal: Montreal Museum of Fine Arts / Prestel Verlag, 1999), 282–4.

20 Maria Karvouni, "*Demas*: The Human Body as a Tectonic Construct," in *Chora: Intervals in the Philosophy of Architecture*, vol. 3, ed. Alberto Pérez-Gómez and Stephen Parcell (Montreal and Kingston: McGill-Queen's University Press, 1999), 106–7.

21 Cohn, *Anselm Kiefer*, 26.

22 Auping, *Anselm Kiefer*, 44.

23 Alberto Pérez-Gómez and Louise Pelletier, *Architectural Representation and the Perspective Hinge* (Cambridge, MA: MIT Press, 2000), 362–3.

24 Ibid., 362–6.

25 Maurice Merleau-Ponty, *Phenomenology of Perception*, trans. Colin Smith (New York: Routledge, 2006), 82.

26 Auping, *Anselm Kiefer*, 37–9.

27 These spaces resemble the geological formations in the nearby caves of Aven d'Orgnac: a "troglodytic cathedral," to use Kiefer's own words. See Danièle Cohn, *Anselm Kiefer: Studios*, 50.

28 Andreotti and De Melis, "With History under His Skin," 48.

29 Lia Rumma, "Foreword," in *Anselm Kiefer: Merkaba*, 15.

30 Ezekiel 1:4–26.

31 See Sophie Fiennes's commentary on the architectural construction of Kiefer's compound in her film *Over Your Cities Grass Will Grow* (2011).

32 Cohn, *Anselm Kiefer*, 240.

33 Gadamer, *Truth and Method*, 120–1.

34 Paul Ricoeur, *The Symbolism of Evil* (New York: Harper & Row, 1967), 22.

35 Alberto Pérez-Gómez, "Chora: The Space of Architectural Representation,"

in *Chora: Intervals in the Philosophy of Architecture*, vol. 1, ed. Alberto Pérez-Gómez and Stephen Parcell (Montreal and Kingston: McGill-Queen's University Press, 1999), 10–15.

36 Ruth Padel, *In and out of the Mind* (Princeton: Princeton University Press, 1992), 66.

37 Alberto Pérez-Gómez, *Built upon Love: Architectural Longing after Ethics and Aesthetics* (Cambridge, MA: MIT Press, 2006), 49–51.

38 Padel, *In and out of the Mind*, 66.

39 Gadamer, *Truth and Method*, 122–5.

Chōra before Plato: Architecture, Drama, and Receptivity

Lisa Landrum

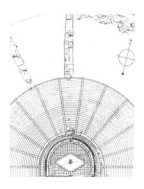

Hold back what would be ruinous to my *chōra*
Send forth what will benefit my city ...
–Athena to the chorus of Furies[1]

Stranger, in this *chōra* of fine horses you have come to
earth's fairest home ...
Here the nightingale, a constant guest,
trills her clear note under the trees of green glades, dwelling
amid the wine-dark ivy
and the god's inviolate foliage,
rich in berries and fruit, unvisited by sun, unvexed by the
wind of any storm.
Here the reveler Dionysus ever walks,
companion of the nymphs that nursed him ...
Nor have the *choroi* of the Muses shunned this [*chōra*]
nor Aphrodite of the golden rein ...
–A chorus of elders to Oedipus[2]

THIS ESSAY INITIATES a new approach to the architectural interpretation of *chōra* by considering the pre-philosophical meanings of *chōra* as an inhabited "region" or "land," and by drawing attention to certain situationally transformative scenes from Athenian drama in which *chōra* appears in the script. Through this approach, I intend to reveal the relatively ordinary meanings of *chōra* from the time just before Plato recast it, in *Timaeus*, as a highly enigmatic entity fundamental to cosmological formation and human making. Unfortunately, Jacques Derrida, whose philosophy of deconstruction influenced architectural theory in the 1980s and 1990s, generally ignored and even dismissed the "ordinary" meanings and contexts of *chōra*, in favour of its more abstract "paradoxes and aporias."[3] This essay counters that tendency with a hermeneutic approach. By taking a fresh look at primary sources, I aim to recover an understanding of the common, yet complex, world in which *chōra* originally came into being as a philosophically and architecturally suggestive concept. I believe this approach can help us recognize not only where Plato's notion of *chōra* was coming from, but also how *chōra* may remain relevant for present-day architects striving, amid politically and ecologically vexed circumstances, to engage and engender meaningful change.

By dipping into pre-Platonic sources, I also aim to reinforce some of the links between *chōra* (χώρα) and *choros* (χορός): between a broadly integrative yet regionally grounded understanding of space, place, and human situations (*chōra*) and the performative medium of collective dance, poetic speech, music, and song (*choros*, plural *choroi*) which, for the Greeks, involved the chorus (the group of dancers accompanying the principal actors in tragedy, comedy, and satyr plays) as well as the full institution, social practice, and setting of drama.[4] In examining these links between *chōra* and *choros* (words with different etymological roots),[5] the following observations build on crucial insights of Alberto Pérez-Gómez and Dalibor Vesely. In their respective studies of architectural representation, these scholars have postulated a situational and experiential resonance between *chōra* and *choros*, while seeking to recover the cultural and symbolic unity of place and event.[6] The present study adds to this work, less by extending their arguments than by uncovering significant details beneath them.

As a further preliminary, I must briefly consider the pre-philosophical meaning of *hypodochē*, the name Plato first gives to *chōra* (*Timaeus*, 49a). In the context of Plato's discussion of *chōra*, *hypodochē* is usually translated as "receptacle." Elsewhere, however, *hypodochē* refers to a social occasion: a hospitable and festive "reception" held in honour of gods and guests. To offer the most pertinent example, the City Dionysia, during which most of the extant Greek plays were performed, was understood as an elaborate "reception" for Dionysus.[7]

The City Dionysia was a reception in several interrelated ways. At the start of this annual festival, Dionysus himself (in the form of a statue) was ceremoniously received into the theatre in a grand procession that recalled the original reception of the god into Athens.[8] Just as importantly, this festival was a reception in the sense that the city of Athens physically received and actively hosted thousands of people (including citizens, immigrant-metics, slaves, released prisoners, male children, and arguably women, as well as foreign visitors and ambassadors) for collective feasting, revelry, and reflection on their shared (and contested) customs, stories, and concerns. During this week-long event in early spring, the theatre's *orchēstra*, the level "dancing ground," further received a great variety of official participants (priests, generals, diplomats, and soldiers, as well as some twenty-eight poets, twenty-eight producers, twenty-four masked actors representing a range of mortals and gods, more than

Fig. 15.1 Dionysus aboard a ship cart, escorted by aulos-playing satyrs, as depicted on a skyphos from Acrai Sicily, British Museum, B 79. Ludwig Deubner, *Attische Feste* (Hildesheim: Georg Olms Verlagsbuchhandlung, 1932; reprinted 1966), plate 14.2.

a thousand well-rehearsed and elaborately attired dancers, and dozens of musicians), together with their diverse performances: preliminary processions, inaugural rites, public announcements (declaring honours to deserving citizens and the names of freed slaves), civic displays (of troops and tributes), dithyrambic dance contests, up to seventeen plays staged in competition (three tragic trilogies, each followed by a satyr play, plus five comedies), culminating revelry, and a closing political meeting (to ratify pending peace treaties, and to issue fines to those who had misbehaved during the festival).[9] This diversely comprehensive receptivity of the festival was further intensified by the theatre's representational mutability, as it would become a plethora of places during the staging of many different plays. For the three days of Tragedy, the orchestra would momentarily become a variety of exceptional places from the mythic past: the sacred grounds before a temple, the sovereign grounds around a palace, the battlegrounds outside a city, or the burial grounds of a king. With the afterpiece of a satyr play, which culminated each day of Tragedy, the orchestra would become a series of liminal places eccentric to human society: a distant seashore, a wild mountainside, a mysterious grove, or a volcanic island and cave (as in the land of the Cyclops). On the last day of the Dionysian festival, the day of Comedy, the very same performance area that previously had represented exceptional and liminal places became a variety of contemporaneous common places: the open area of the agora (the Athenian market-place), the democratic area of the Pnyx (where the Assembly met), the public area just outside the Propylaea (the gateway to the Acropolis), or an urban stretch of street before a citizen's home. Occasionally, the comedic orchestra did become more uncommon and otherworldly places: the dreaded underworld (in Aristophanes's *Frogs*), the nebulous region of the sky (in Aristophanes's *Birds*), and the heavenly halls of Zeus (in Aristophanes's *Peace*). However, even when such extraordinary settings were manifested (and regardless of genre), the festive orchestra always remained the very same place: the profoundly mutable and radically receptive Theatre of Dionysus. When viewing the archaeological remains and reconstructed plans of this ancient theatre, we must not forget the full interactive variety of life that it received.[10]

By considering the diversely inclusive and broadly shifting scope of such a festive "reception," via sources composed before Plato presented *chōra* as an "all-receiving" *hypodochē* (49a, 51a), this study intends to recover some of the sociopolitical and mythopoetic premises underlying Plato's thinking about these influential terms. In doing so, this study further suggests that these same premises (or variations of them) ought to remain fundamental to our thinking about architectural representation and architecture's receptivity.

Before delving into specific passages from the extant corpus of Athenian drama (ranging from Aeschylus's *Persians* of 472 BCE to Aristophanes's *Wealth* of 388 BCE), it is helpful to rehearse the discursive situation leading up to the point midway through *Timaeus* when the interlocutor who lends the dialogue its name digresses to introduce what has since become a notoriously enigmatic concept: *chōra*.

CHŌRA IN TIMAEUS

Plato's *Timaeus* begins with Socrates recalling and summarizing the topic of yesterday's discussion: the constitution of an ideal city (17c).[11] Socrates ends his summary by expressing his desire to see this city "alive" and in action, "engaged in some struggle or conflict," or else "to hear someone tell of our city [Athens] carrying on a struggle against her neighbors" (19b–c). In response to Socrates's desire, Critias recounts a "strange but true" story he remembers hearing in his youth about the Athenians "of old" engaging in a "great and wondrous" conflict with invaders from the lost island city of Atlantis. Critias's story, a legend handed down through

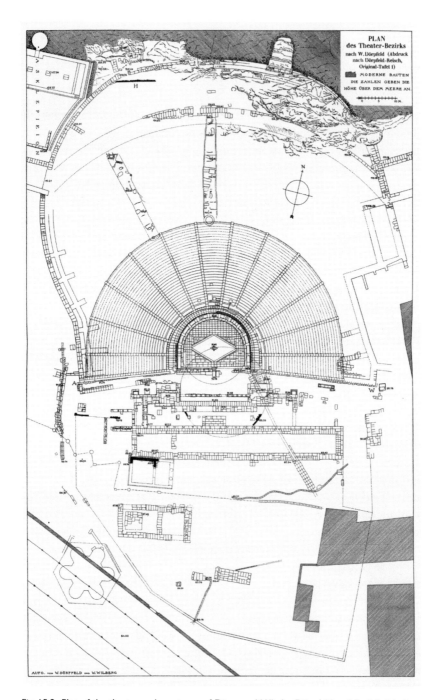

Fig. 15.2 Plan of the theatre and sanctuary of Dionysus. Wilhelm Dörpfeld and Emil Reich, *Das griechische Theater: Beiträge zur Geschichte des Dionysos-Theaters in Athen und anderer griechischer Theater* (Athens: Barth & von Hirst, 1898), plate 1; reprinted in Ernst Fiechter et al., *Das Dionysos-Theater in Athen*, vol. 1, *Die Ruine* (Stuttgart: Kohlhammer, 1935).

many generations (from Egyptian priests to Solon, to his great-grandfather, to his grandfather, then to Critias himself), tells of how Athens – due to the "greatness of her actions," the "magnanimity of her words," and the "fairness of her constitution" – defeated the Atlantic invaders, thereby liberating all of Europe, Libya, and Egypt from oppressive external rule (19c–26e). Socrates is pleased with this story of the exemplary beginnings of Athens. He also finds Critias's story to be most appropriate to the occasion that has brought the interlocutors together: a festival in honour of Athena.[12] Socrates and his companions then prepare to "receive" the next "feast of speech," to be offered by Timaeus (27b).

Whereas Critias relayed how Athena originally ordered Athens (24c), Timaeus discloses a prior ordering. Turning to a constitutive event well before the formation of cities, Timaeus describes the likely constitution of the cosmos: how a knowing creator or *demiurge* (literally, a "worker for the people") first fashioned the world by mingling fire, earth, air, and water in due measure and proportion, and by shaping all sensible things after timeless patterns. For this primordial event of making, Timaeus initially identifies two distinct realms: "being" and "becoming" (27d). According to Timaeus, the former, "being," is that which is eternal, unchangeable, and apprehended only by reason (the stable realm of ideas, from which the creator-demiurge draws ideal patterns), while the latter, "becoming," is that which is ephemeral, corruptible, and apprehended by imperfect opinion and sensation (the fluctuating realm of physical reality and human experience). However, in the midst of this story, Timaeus admits that these two kinds of reality, "being" and "becoming," are insufficient, so he begins again by positing a "third" that he initially calls the "receptacle" (*hypodochē*, 49a). This "receptacle," "reception," or situation of receptivity is presented as fundamental to every event of making, for it is "that in which all the elements are always coming to be, making their appearance, and again vanishing" (49e). Striving to explain this "reception," Timaeus likens it to an array of remarkably ordinary artifacts, agencies, and mediums: to a mirror, a mixing bowl, a mother, a winnowing fan, an odourless liquid, and a neutral plastic substance.[13] But such analogies and metaphors, it seems, can only ever approximate *chōra*, which, as Timaeus contends, remains highly ambiguous, "difficult," and "obscure." Whereas "being" is invisible and "becoming" is visible, this third kind of reality is only "dimly seen." Partaking of both the intelligible and the irrational, *chōra* must be apprehended by a "spurious reasoning ... as in a dream." Whereas "being" consists of immutable forms and "becoming" of variable copies, *chōra* is a formless open entity that receives, nurtures, and sustains all things and all change. This dream-like *chōra* is, according to Timaeus, "the nurse of all becoming," "the recipient of all impressions," and that which is "eternal and indestructible, providing a seat for all created things" (49a–52b).[14]

Having introduced *chōra* as fundamental to the making of the cosmos, Timaeus then describes in detail the constitution and workings of the human body, as well as many correspondences among the body, city, and cosmos. For the purposes of this essay, however, I must leave this summary of *Timaeus* here.

CHŌRA AS INHABITED LAND

Before *chōra* gained its uniquely mysterious philosophical definition in Plato's *Timaeus*, *chōra* served as a common term for an inhabited "region," "territory," or "land." *Chōra* first appears in this conventional sense in Homer's *Odyssey*, when the Phaeacian king implores Odysseus to share his stories of the diverse *chōras* experienced on his travels.[15] In the extant written records of the fifth and fourth centuries BCE, *chōra* as "land" appears hundreds of times: throughout the historical works of Herodotus, Thucydides, and Xenophon; in the speeches of Isocrates, Demosthenes, Lysias, Lycurgus, and Aeschines; and on official public inscriptions announcing diverse matters of common concern, such as political alliances, destinations of envoys, arrivals of foreign ambassadors, locations of international assemblies, sources of imported grain, and decrees concerning the collective "defense of the *chōra*."[16] *Chōra* also appears in its conventional sense in the Hippocratic texts,[17] in lyric poetry,[18] and throughout the extant dramas of Aeschylus, Sophocles, Euripides, and Aristophanes (as we shall see below). Though there are variations in detail,[19] it is *chōra*'s meaning as an inhabited "region," "territory," or "land" that is by far the most prevalent in classical Greek sources. Even Plato's own dialogues make frequent use of *chōra* in this most basic and common sense: as in *Timaeus*, when Critias explains how the tale of conflict between Athens and Atlantis had been preserved by the Egyptian *chōra* (22e).[20]

Where, then, is Plato's specialized cosmogonic concept of *chōra* coming from? Surely his appropriation of this term was neither arbitrary nor disconnected from its pre-philosophical meaning, for Plato easily could have chosen a more obscure word to name this most "difficult" and "obscure" kind of reality. Alternatively, he could have crafted a suggestive neologism, as he sometimes did for key terms in other dialogues.[21] Instead, Plato appropriated a well-known word with real-world geographical and sociopolitical connotations. It is necessary to investigate these everyday meanings of *chōra* before considering how the term figures in the performative and situational medium of *choros*.

Though *chōra* could imply any inhabited region, in the classical sources that have come down to us *chōra* frequently referred to the very "region" in which Plato lived: Attica, the roughly triangular peninsula extending south from the Parnes mountains, with the summit of Sounion at its tip and Athens at its core. This territory, which included a major political centre (Athens) and a topographically and demographically diverse countryside, constituted the geographic scope of the *polis*, the city-state. Indeed, the poets, historians, and orators noted above sometimes used *chōra* synonymously with *polis*, as both terms implied a cohesive human society: an entire political unit consisting of both towns (*astu*) and territory (*agros*), together with their overlapping and mutually sustaining defensive, agricultural, and ritual practices.[22] Yet, as scholars of the classical *polis* have argued, the town was not only territorially and culturally bound to its countryside; rather, "the whole political, social and religious structure of the Greek city was shaped by its countryside."[23] Mythically and historically, the unification of the *chōra* preceded the development of Athens as a prominent urban centre and was a necessary precondition for both the formation and perpetuation of democracy. According to Thucydides, when Theseus became King of Attica (a generation before the Trojan War) he "reordered the *chōra*," dissolving autonomous councils in the various towns and establishing in Athens a single council chamber (*bouleuterion*) and public hearth (*prytaneion*), where representatives from the outlying areas would gather periodically for collective deliberation and communal dining (2.15.2). This legendary founding of a cohesive community, by establishing shared institutions among otherwise disparate and dispersed people, was celebrated in an annual festival that aimed to perpetuate social order by regularly recalling

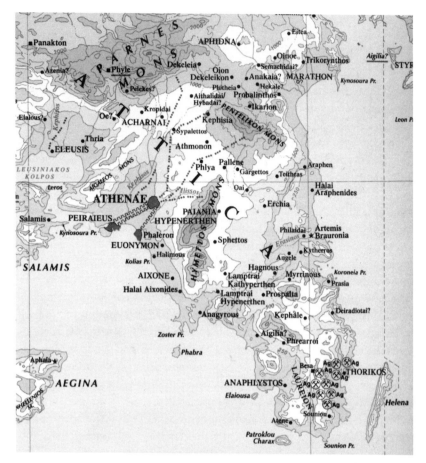

Fig. 15.3 Map of Attica. Richard J.A. Talbert, ed., *The Barrington Atlas of the Greek and Roman World* (Princeton: Princeton University Press, 2000), detail of plate 58; reprinted by permission of Princeton University Press.

its originary event.[24] Theseus's legendary unification of the *chōra* underlies the actions of later political reformers: notably, Solon, who made land ownership (instead of nobility) the basis of political involvement;[25] and Cleisthenes, who (in 507 BCE) further transformed the political landscape to promote the equality and comprehensive diversity of political involvement. As Aristotle tells us, Cleisthenes "divided the *chōra*" into 30 districts (*trittyes*), consisting of 139 communities (*dēmes*). These districts were assembled into 10 tribes (*phylai*), with each tribe having equal representation from the town, the coast, and the inlands. The intent was to "inter-mingle" the people, resisting oppressive tyranny by enabling more comprehensively representative and proportionate participation from the region's diverse districts and communities.[26]

Following the reforms of Cleisthenes, whom scholars have called an "architect of democracy,"[27] this more regionally articulated *chōra* became conspicuously manifest not only in democratic processes, as each of the ten tribes sent fifty members to participate in the Council of Five Hundred (the *Boulē*), but also in dramatic festivals, as each tribe sent two fifty-member choruses (one of boys, one of men) to perform dithyrambs at the City Dionysia.[28] During this same festival, the mixed political body of the *chōra* became manifest in a number of other ways: in the composition of the panel of dramatic judges (one from each tribe, selected by lot prior to performance); in the public displays of elected generals (one from each tribe), who poured inaugural libations; and through the configuration of spectators, who likely sat on the hillside arranged by tribe, with the Five Hundred councillors at the centre. Residents of other *chōras* from the greater Panhellenic region also had their place during the festival: seated on the extreme left and right sides of the assembly.[29] Thus, the distribution of people within the bowl of the theatre would have appeared as an ordered microcosm of the Athenian *polis* situated amid her regional allies: a lively social image, persuasively demonstrating an ideal (if propagandistic) synthesis of the mutable and heterogeneous *chōra*.[30]

When Plato composed *Timaeus* (sometime between 365 and 347 BCE) some of the symbolic and political aspects of the Dionysia had become diluted.[31] This erosion of the festival's cultural meaning and political efficacy reflected corresponding losses in the *chōra*. Over the course of several fractious decades, many of the crucial bonds between the town and countryside of Attica had been weakened to the point of mutual collapse. During the Peloponnesian War (431–404 BCE), Pericles's defensive strategy urged farmers to abandon their fields and take refuge in the walled city of Athens, while his offensive strategy focused on naval operations and foreign exploits. During this time, the neglected *chōra* suffered repeated invasions: fig trees, olive trees, and grape vines were mutilated, croplands scorched, homesteads plundered, and livestock and farm equipment stolen.[32] When the defeated, starving, and humiliated Athenians surrendered in 404, many displaced farmers, especially those of the "middle-class" – whom Aristotle would call *hoi mesoi*[33] – were ruined. "Middle" citizens who managed to re-cultivate their "fields," their *chōrion*,[34] found themselves marginalized by increasingly urban-based political practices, while others relinquished their former ways, joining state efforts to fortify the agonized countryside with defensive walls.[35] As a result of all this, the fertile *chōra*, which once had sustained an involved and vigorous population, waned; and the people of Attica grew increasingly dependent on foreign grain imported via the sea.[36] It has been argued that Plato and Aristotle were so troubled by this loss of agrarian livelihood and prosperity that they placed the "defense of the *chōra*" and "egalitarian landowning at the center of their reactionary philosophical utopias."[37]

This backstory of *chōra* helps us recognize both the appropriateness and the meaningfulness of *chōra* as a complex living metaphor and model in *Timaeus*. In the ears of classical Athenians, Plato's chosen term would have been far from neutral and abstract, recalling not only the political origins of Attica (including Theseus's original unification and Solon's and Cleisthenes's later transformations of the *chōra*), but also a more general premise: that regional cohesiveness, brought about by the proportional and reciprocal participation of disparate entities, remained crucial for both the constitution and the preservation of good cities. We must recall that Plato's *Timaeus*, though ostensibly concerned with the speculative origins of the cosmos and the corresponding formation of the human body, was both motivated by and framed by prior and anticipated discussions of the *polis*. As noted above, at the start of *Timaeus*, Socrates recalls that yesterday's discussion had concerned the composition of the best city and citizens (17c); and Critias promises that, after Timaeus speaks, he will continue their collective project to "transfer" (*metapherō*) the fictional city and citizens, fashioned yesterday in words, into reality (26d–27b). Timaeus's own middle discourse, with its digressive presentation of "being," *chōra*, and "becoming," must be taken as both advancing and preparing the way for these political discussions, while regrounding them in a strangely familiar arena that was both more fundamental and more cosmological. Accepting that these political (and metaphorically layered) premises frame and ground the dialogue of *Timaeus*, and acknowledging that Plato was writing in a politically charged time due to prior regional turmoil, it is likely that Plato modelled his cosmic *chōra* on a regional *chōra*, thereby appropriating what had been commonly accepted as the sociopolitical precondition for good cities and citizenry, and recasting this common *topos* as the originary ground for the human cosmos as a whole. In other words, the demiurge in *Timaeus* shapes the world in a pre-existing *chōra*, much as exemplary statesmen (Solon and Cleisthenes) had shaped Athens within a pre-given and pre-unified "region." Plato, of course, does not admit that this regional *chōra* was his model. Instead, he argues through *Timaeus* (and other dialogues) that the mimetic relation between divine and human realities operates more in the opposite direction: that the composition of cities and mortal selves ought to follow patterns and dynamic rhythms of the eternal cosmos (88d–e). Nevertheless, the everyday semantic context of *chōra* and the conflictual world in which Plato's *Timaeus* was composed cannot – or, rather, should not – be ignored.[38] For architectural interpreters, what matters most is neither the simple reversibility of these mimetic relations nor the apparent polarity of human and cosmic constructs, but rather their vital "fusion" and "reciprocal determination" within an ever-receptive and politically (and mythically) dynamic *chōra*.[39] Plato's *Timaeus* invites us to consider cosmic, social, and individual bodies as performing not in fixed binary and hierarchical relations but in complexly striving reciprocity: each part dynamically attuned to the other and to the whole, with *chōra* acting as the primary receptive milieu for bringing about, making apparent, and sustaining this full set of vital correspondences.

Plato's appropriation of the common *chōra*, together with its layered regional, sociopolitical, and mythic connotations, is significant for the history of ideas; however, this observation offers us only so much in our theoretical and disciplinary quest (somewhat like that of Socrates) to see *chōra* in action – namely, to regard *chōra*'s receptivity to situational transformation and architectural beginnings. To consider these more architecturally suggestive receptions we must turn to those dramatic scripts in which *chōra* appears, and thus to the links between *chōra* and *choros*. These scripts are relevant for us not simply because they provide evidence of the events that transpired in the theatre, but also because they attest to how the collective production of *choros* (which we may take as an intensified representation of life in all of its complexity) helped the people of Attica maintain meaningful participation with the many *chōras* that were active in shaping and sustaining both their cities and themselves.

CHŌRA IN ACTION IN ATHENIAN DRAMA

At first glance, *chōra* does not seem to bear any obviously charged conceptual significance in Athenian drama. When *chōra* figures into an actor's speech or a chorus's song it usually refers simply to a particular inhabited "region," "territory," or "land." For instance, in several tragedies, addresses are made to the king, lord, or ruler of this or that *chōra*. Such addresses serve partly to establish the specific narrative and politically charged setting of the play.[40] In each of these scenes, the ostensible geographic reference (to such-and-such a place, or to the land of so-and-so) is denotatively clear, yet significant ambiguities and tensions emerge when considered in dramatic context. First and foremost, we must recognize that when uttered in performance, *chōra* takes on layered and reflexive significance due to a basic situational duplicity inherent to dramatic representation. Performers often present the "land" in question as "*this* land," thereby implicating not simply the play's (often remote) geographical setting (Thebes, Delphi, Argos, Thrace, Troy, Susa, Egypt, etc.),[41] but also, somewhat paradoxically, the very land within and upon which the performers were acting: the beaten dirt floor of the orchestra at the foot of the Athenian Acropolis in the heart of Attica. Even in the absence of an actor's allusive gesture and emphatic "*this*," the surrounding *chōra* of Attica remained the primary, ever-present setting for each play staged in the festival, as the open hillside of the *theatron*, literally the "seeing place" of Dionysus, provided the assembled spectators with comprehensive (and immersive) views of Attica's natural and cultural topography. The spectators looked not only down at the orchestra, up to the shifting skies and around at one another, but also out over the full sanctuary of Dionysus and other familiar districts of southern Athens and, further still, toward the fortified port of Piraeus and the Sardonic Gulf, with the (then) rival Peloponnesian *chōra* perceived (however dimly) in the distance beyond. Each visible feature of the Attic *chōra* – the temples and sanctuaries, city walls and gates, river valleys and plains, delimiting mountain ranges and seacoast – bore layered significance for the people gathered in the theatre, as each feature was in some way tied to familiar myths, historical events, and common civic practices.[42] The extraordinary events dramatized in the orchestra were always viewed together with this relatively ordinary yet comparably storied terrain. In other words, the remote mythic *chōra* conjured during performance became meaningfully mixed with the local *chōra* of Attica, reinforcing their interdependence and their analogous potential for both persistence and change.

This comparative transference and layering of distant and local settings – through the performative interaction of *chōra* and *choros* – becomes most salient during significant arrivals and departures: when an actor addresses the *chōra* while crossing the perceived limits of the performance space to enter or exit the story. For instance, soon after arriving

Fig. 15.4 View south from the theatre of Dionysus, with Mount Hymettos to the far left and the Hill of the Muses rising to the right. The tree-covered sanctuary of Dionysus lies just behind the orchestra. Photograph: © Lisa Landrum 2011.

on the shore of the Cyclops at the beginning of Euripides's satyr play, Odysseus asks Silenus, "What is this *chōra* and who are its inhabitants?" (113).[43] Here the land of the Cyclops is instantly brought to Athens, just as the "inhabitants" of the theatre are all simultaneously delivered to the land of the Cyclops. With this situationally transformative question, the play's central ethical and existential problems – concerning the receptivity of a place and its people to others and to otherness – are brought forcefully to bear on both *chōras*. A reciprocal phenomenon can happen at the termination of a play. At the close of Sophocles's *Philoctetes*, as the eponymous hero leaves Lemnos, the deserted island that had harboured him during his ordeal, he bids farewell to "this *chōra*" (1452). Philoctetes's farewell to "this *chōra*" as he exits the orchestra brings closure to the theatrical event, but also renews attention to the representational function of the festival. As Philoctetes's story comes to an end, so too does the theatre's provisional presencing of Lemnos, but not without leaving a residual influence on the audience's understanding of their own situation. In this dramatically influential way, Philoctetes, with his descriptively detailed and surprisingly affectionate closing speech, returns the spectators' awareness to their own local situation in Attica, re-opening "this *chōra*" for renewed participation and interpretation, in light of the lingering tragedy of Lemnos.

Although meaningful and productive tensions between a represented *chōra* and a local *chōra* are readily apparent in any given play, other situations also can enter the mix, particularly when dramatized events resemble contemporaneous situations. In Euripides's *Trojan Women*, the Spartan island of Melos, though never mentioned in the play, is made tangibly present in the theatre. In this Euripidean tragedy, the defeated chorus of captive Trojan widows, having accepted their fate to be taken from their destroyed homeland as slaves, somehow manage to express hope that they at least might be taken away to Attica: to "the famous and blessed *chōra* of Theseus" (208–9). This longed-for "*chōra* of Theseus" stands in idealized contradistinction to the play's setting: the utterly destroyed and still smoldering city of Troy, which is vividly conjured through descriptive language at the start of the play by Athena and Poseidon – the very gods who built Troy, but then destroyed and abandoned it (1–97). Such stark juxtapositions of a venerated Attica and a desecrated Troy (and of the creative-destructive forces acting within and upon them) would have demanded critical reflection on the fate not only of the two named regions, but of other volatile situations familiar to the spectators: notably, to Melos. Just a few months prior to the staging of *Trojan Women* (in 415 BCE), the Athenians had ravaged the island of Melos over a dispute related to the ongoing Peloponnesian War. After refusing to accept the Melians' peace treaty, the Athenians executed the men, enslaved the women, and colonized the city.[44] With this fresh atrocity in mind, Euripides's audience may have been moved to view the suffering of the mythic Trojans in light of what the nearby Melians had actually endured; and further, to recognize in themselves the less than honourable victories won by the mythic and present-day Greeks. Since Euripides's plot reveals the ironic status of the mythic Greeks (ironic because, as Cassandra predicts, the ostensible victors are doomed to endure grave dangers when they return home),[45] the tragic poet may have been pressing his audience for a critical revaluation of such egregious actions as had just taken place at Melos, while questioning the extent to which even the well-founded – but neglected and war-torn – "*chōra* of Theseus" may yet suffer destruction, like Troy.

This subtle mixing of mythic and contemporaneous situations in *Trojan Women* points to an important basic function of Greek drama, whereby tragic poets treated ongoing regional conflicts indirectly, through the mimetic lens of dramatized mythic struggles.[46] This mixing of situations also demonstrates what Rush Rehm has called the "complicated inclusiveness of ancient Greek drama,"[47] whereby a great variety of real and imagined places were made tangibly present, less through changes of scenery (which were always minimal and typically negligible) and more by the performers' suggestive words and interactions. Aside from the basic duplicity of (re)presented *chōras* and the multiplicity of comparable situations drawn in by the power of self-reflexive allusion (as to Melos, in *Trojan Women*), other distant and concealed places were manifested through a diversity of dramatic means. For instance, the descriptive speeches of messengers brought forth the (frequently horrendous) events taking place out of sight: either at a remote location from which the messenger had just returned (another *chōra*, a nearby harbour, etc.) or within an interior space behind the wall of the *skēnē* (which might represent the threshold to a temple, palace, house, cave, or grove).[48] Alternately, the actors' formal manner of argument and debate could transform the theatre into a comparable democratic institution (such as the Pnyx or a court of law) while transforming the spectators into liable witnesses and judges.[49] More eccentrically, the chorus, through imagistic odes, might transport a willing audience to an idyllic "elsewhere" just before a moment of doom or project themselves into mythic and hypothetical situations – into "a far-off *chōra*" – sometime before or beyond the dramatized events.[50] Such comparative layering of partially present, partially obscured situations – dream-like situations always coming into being, appearing and vanishing in the persistently present theatre and *chōra* of Attica – would have been palpably experienced and remembered by a receptive audience, even if the meaning of such fleeting impressions and correspondences may have remained (like those of Plato's *chōra*) apprehensible only through a "spurious reasoning."[51]

As suggested above, the festive theatre "received" not only a variety of representative people and places but also a complex web of meaningful conflicts – which is precisely what Socrates wishes to see in *Timaeus* (19b–c). Much like Attica herself, each dramatized *chōra* was either caught in the midst of an ongoing crisis, verging on catastrophe, or anticipating an uncertain transformation due to dilemmas confronting not only representative leaders but the community as a whole, as typically represented by the collective body of the chorus.[52] The mutual well-being of both *chōra* and chorus was bound to the fate of their troubled leaders, usually exemplified by the protagonist. If a protagonist prospers, the *chōra* prospers and its inhabitants thrive. If the protagonist falters, the *chōra* withers and its inhabitants suffer. This comprehensively layered reciprocity – between striving individuals, communities, places, and plots – is implicit in several plays, both tragic and comic. In comedy, the actions of Aristophanes's heroes are often aimed at "saving the *chōra*" from basic dangers embedded within the community: from the bellicose behaviour of men,[53] from the ineffectual bickering of politicians,[54] and even from the bad poetry of Aristophanes's own rivals, which threatens to debase the audience, city, and *chōra* as a whole.[55] Such plots of comic salvation tend to culminate with a metatheatrical exit song with which the comedic chorus leads the rejuvenated performers (with spectators in tow) out of the orchestra and into a revived *chōra*.[56]

In tragedy, characters, choruses, and *chōras* reciprocally grapple with more mysteriously ironic and metaphysically intractable dilemmas that probe the very limits of intelligibility. Episodes from the life (and death) of Oedipus, as dramatized by Sophocles, exemplify this tragic bond. In *Oedipus Tyrannus*, the chorus recalls how Oedipus had been made King of Thebes for relieving the Theban *chōra* of a deadly plague, by out-smarting the Sphinx.[57] Ironically, the chorus remembers this positive bond a moment before Oedipus is stripped of his rule and banished from Thebes for afflicting the same *chōra* with barrenness, by his ill-fate and ignorance.[58] After wandering in exile for many years, Oedipus ultimately brings ruin to Thebes and prosperity to Attica by dying in a foretold place: a sacred grove in the *deme* of Colonus, just outside Athens (as described in the ode quoted at the beginning of this essay). In spite of his blindness, Oedipus recognizes this place as his "terminal *chōra*" (89), while the precise grove (and grave) where he will be "received" into the earth is an unseen "sacred *chōros*" (16, 37, etc.).[59] This mysterious dramatization of Oedipus's death, in Sophocles's *Oedipus at Colonus*, is saturated with symbolism concerning locality and involves *chōra* (and other cognate terms) more frequently than any other extant Greek play.[60] Together with the transfiguration of Oedipus (from an ill-fated exile to an honoured hero), his protracted "reception" into and by the *chōra* constitutes the primary agon of the drama. The chorus of elders, called the "guardians of this *chōra*" (145),[61] deliberates and ultimately chooses to "receive" Oedipus into their land in spite of his infamy. The chorus thus upholds Athenian traditions of welcoming strangers and integrating exiles. Their decision to incorporate Oedipus into their land – together with the remembrance of his troubling story – will keep their whole *chōra* safe, content, and free from sorrow, while causing tragic consequences for other *chōras* elsewhere.[62]

Whether explicitly named or not, conflicts involving a *chōra*'s receptivity are central to most tragic plots. Such conflicts are represented not only through situational arguments and interactions, but also through contrastingly peaceful imagery in which receptivity, the integration of difference, is described with images of elements mingling in dynamic strife.

Fig. 15.5 The "inviolate foliage" of Colonus, northwest of central Athens.
This is also the site where Plato founded his Academy in the early fourth century BCE.
Photograph: © Lisa Landrum 2009.

In Euripides's *Medea*, for instance, the distraught heroine who had been banished from Corinth implores King Aegeus of Athens to "receive me into your *chōra*" (813). The chorus then projects this potentially receptive *chōra* as animated: with sacred rivers, temperate breezes, and fragrant roses; with the Muses, Harmonia, Wisdom, and Love; but also with strong opposition to murderers such as Medea (835–48). In another tragedy of displacement, Aeschylus's *Suppliant Women*, a vulnerable chorus of refugees appeals directly to the *chōra* of Argos: "To what more friendly *chōra* than this could we come … receive as suppliants this female band, and may the *chōra* show them a spirit of respect" (19–30). Having been so "received" (however temporarily), they celebrate the receptive place in song, praising its "rivers that pour their tranquil waters through this *chōra* … propitiating the soil with their oil-smooth streams" (1025–9). In Sophocles's *Oedipus at Colonus*, when the chorus begins to acquiesce, agreeing to "receive" Oedipus into their land, they too describe their receptive *chōra* as complexly saturated with song, shade, foliage, revelry, and affection, but also with a formidable capability deterrent to enemies (668–703).[63] Finally, in Aeschylus's *Eumenides*, Athena persuades the chorus of vengeful Furies not to poison her *chōra* (479, 720, 787, 817) but instead to show "goodwill towards [her] *chōra*" and, once reformed, to be received into her land (968). Athena then portrays the anticipated prosperity that would follow their agreement with images of cooperative elemental agencies: earth, water, wind, and sunshine, mixed with mortal prowess in war (903–15).

More examples could be given, but these suffice to show how *chōra*'s receptivity to conflictual human affairs was often figured in dramatic poetry (as in Plato's *Timaeus*) with imagery of water, earth, air, and fire mingling in balanced tension. In the plays, such dynamic imagery would dramatize *chōra*'s fundamental vitality, mutability, and regenerative internal strife, as well as its periodic reciprocity with the changing seasons and the analogously animated cosmos: "the dance (*choreias*) of the stars," as Timaeus would put it (40c). Such imagery would also model corresponding ethical transformations underway within and among the potentially receptive people, who under the influence of persuasive language and reflective thought were in the midst of being moved, not just physically but emotionally and intellectually: either swayed, soothed, and softened or hardened, agitated, and enraged. This worldly and ethical imagery would further reflect Greek concepts of mortal health, which was understood as proportional negotiations among bodily fluids or humours. Believing that one's biological, emotional, and intellectual inner world was both part of and mimetic of the fluctuating outer world, the ancients perceived their individual and collective temperaments to be fatefully linked to the well-being of their inhabited milieu, their complexly shared *chōra*.[64] As important as these comprehensive correspondences between worldly and bodily elements would become to future architectural theories of proportion and symmetry (first articulated by Vitruvius),[65] we must also recognize that the transformative tempering of human situations already involved architectural beginnings in these early dramatic sources.

In Aeschylus's *Eumenides* (the final example mentioned above), Athena transforms the *chōra* from a fearful place of self-gratifying vengeance enacted behind closed doors to a more hopeful place of discursive debate and related democratic practices performed in the open.[66] She accomplishes this transformation, in part, by receiving into her *chōra* the reformed Furies, whom she redirects toward regenerative aims and renames the Eumenides (the "well-minded ones"). But Athena also brings about this transformation by founding an open-air homicidal court, the Areopagus, a public institution to serve as "a defense to keep *chōra* and city safe" (701). Athena further accommodates the Eumenides – and the remembrance of their vengeful story – in underground chambers directly beneath this newly founded court, where (as cited at the start of this essay) she bids them to "keep down below what would be ruinous to my *chōra*, and send up what will benefit my city" (1007–9). Thus, somewhat like an architect, and an "architect" of democracy (as described above), Athena, with the cooperation of the people, makes a new beginning for the city by reordering the *chōra*: by delineating a place within the preexisting milieu where inhabitants from the region can engage one another in ways that might lead to collective prosperity; by integrating into that place disparate, diverse, and even conflictual agencies; and by inaugurating human practices that cultivate collective memory and social consciousness.

CONCLUSION: RECEPTIVITY AT RISK

Throughout this essay, I have tried to demonstrate how a relatively ordinary yet politically and mythically potent *chōra*, as an inhabited "region," underlies Plato's cosmogonic *chōra* in *Timaeus*. I have also tried to show how Athenian drama reveals certain qualities and agencies of *chōra* that

Plato would later adapt and intensify: such as *chōra*'s receptivity to heterogeneity, its inherent mutability, and its harmonic reciprocity with human and worldly strife. If any doubt remains as to the influence of dramatic *choros* on the development of Plato's understanding of *chōra*, it should be enough to point out that Plato would have been a young man in his mid-twenties, and (in all likelihood) seated among the spectators at the Theatre of Dionysus during the performance of *Oedipus at Colonus* (in 401 BCE) – the play that, more than any other, featured *chōra* in both highly conventional and profoundly enigmatic ways.[67]

In addition to drawing out many layered correspondences between *chōra* as it appeared in dramatic *choros* and *chōra* as Plato later presented it, this essay has also uncovered at least one significant difference. In *Timaeus*, Plato presents *chōra* as "eternal" and "indestructible" (52a–b) and as having always existed, even "before the heavens" (52d). Plato's knowing demiurge neither makes nor remakes *chōra*, but rather works with and within the receptive (and resistive) preconditions of a found (if imperfectly perceived and unreasonably difficult) *chōra*: striving, therein, to bring about transformation through proportionate adjustments and interpretive mimesis. However, unlike Plato's projection of an eternally persistent *chōra*, every Athenian drama cited in this essay (whether tragic, comic, or satyric) shows *chōra* at risk: not timeless and indestructible, but profoundly vulnerable. Considered through Athenian drama (and, indeed, almost every classical source other than Plato's *Timaeus*), *chōra* appears as a precarious entity, rife with conflict. Susceptible to inexplicable ill-fate, intentional ill-will, and myriad erroneous judgments, *chōra*, the receptive precondition of human existence, must always be defended and, at times, even saved from internal and external threats. In some plays, a suffering *chōra* even appears personified, calling out for urgent attention. In *Prometheus Bound* (attributed to Aeschylus), the chorus hears "every *chōra* crying out in grief" over a situation of dire injustice (407); and in Aristophanes's *Peace*, the goddess Peace is portrayed as longing to return to her neglected and war-torn *chōra* of Attica (638). Somewhat like *Eumenides* and *Oedipus at Colonus*, *Peace* ends with the constitution of regional well-being: specifically, with a farmer-turned-architect "installing" Peace (as a statue) directly in the troubled *chōra*.

Uncovering this vulnerable *chōra* in dramatic poetry is no minor revelation – neither for our understanding of Plato's adaptation of the term, nor for our comprehension of how and why *chōra* remains relevant for architects today. As for Plato, we may interpret his transformation of *chōra* from vulnerable to indestructible as an expression of his optimistic desire that, no matter how troubling the geopolitical situation might become, the foundational premises of his ideal *polis* (such as the human valuation of justice and the universal truth of harmonic proportions) would always endure. With this transformation we may also recognize an inventive shift from geopolitical to philosophical premises as Plato's preferred grounds for cultivating the best cities and citizens. As for relevance to present-day architects, we may regard the dramatization of vulnerable *chōras* as a reminder that the regional preconditions essential for good cities (and good architecture) are not stable conditions that take care of themselves, but are precariously volatile ecological, geopolitical, and mythopoetic conditions, demanding continual reinterpretation, measured cooperation, and risky proportional adjustments. In other words, understanding architecture's tenuous bond to the vexed social and situational milieu that sustains it remains as urgent as ever.

To close on another front, it is necessary to re-engage a representative antagonist: Jacques Derrida. As mentioned at the start of this essay, Derrida (along with many of his architectural followers) consistently ignored and even dismissed the basic regional and sociopolitical meanings of *chōra*, which this essay has shown to underlie Plato's more enigmatic use of the term. However, at the close of an interview with Richard Kearney in New York on 16 October 2001 (soon after the tragic events of 9/11), Derrida admitted to his deferral: "At some point I am planning to examine the political consequences of the thought of *khōra* which I think are urgent today."[68] Derrida passed away in 2004 without (to my knowledge) having examined those political consequences beyond a few telling statements during this 2001 interview. In response to leading questions from Kearney, Derrida acknowledged the regional and reconciliatory possibilities of *chōra* by expressing a hope that "some *chōra*" (like Europe) – by its peculiar mutability, heterogeneity, and mediating agency – might enable what remains of a divided and increasingly polarized humanity to imagine, nurture, and sustain a situation of tolerance and reconciliation.[69] For architects interested in *chōra* as a metaphor and model for architectural making and representation, adhering to Derrida's unassimilable abstractions and deferrals is insufficient. Rather, re-engaging the basic troubled grounds of *chōra*, in its full geopolitical and mythopoetic scope, remains our crucial and timely task.

NOTES

1 Aeschylus, *Eumenides*, 1007–9 (458 BCE). This translation of Aeschylus, like others in this essay, is adapted from Alan H. Sommerstein, *Aeschylus*, 3 vols., Loeb Classical Library (Cambridge, MA: Harvard University Press, 2008).

2 Sophocles, *Oedipus at Colonus*, 668–93 (406/401 BCE), translation adapted from Richard C. Jebb, *Sophocles: Plays. Oedipus Colonoeus*, ed. P.E. Easterling (London: Bristol Classical Press, 2004; first published 1900). As Jebb notes at line 692, the last pronoun "this" (*nin*) refers back to the general region, i.e., *chōra*. Other translations of Sophocles in this essay are adapted from Hugh Lloyd Jones, *Sophocles*, 3 vols., Loeb Classical Library (Cambridge, MA: Harvard University Press, 1994; reprinted 1997).

3 Jacques Derrida, *On the Name* (Stanford, CA: Stanford University Press, 1995), 89–127, with note on 146; and *Paper Machine*, trans. Rachel Bowlby (Stanford, CA: Stanford University Press, 2005, first published as *Papier machine*, 2001), 77–8, see also 80, 83, 93–5. Derrida's influence on architectural theory took off after his recorded dialogues with Peter Eisenman in 1985. See Jeffrey Kipnis and Thomas Leeser, eds., *Chora L Works: Jacques Derrida and Peter Eisenman* (New York: Monacelli Press, 1997). In later correspondence and interviews, however, Derrida criticized Eisenman's interpretation of *chōra* and the vacuity and nihilism of his architecture of "absence," which Derrida deemed "facile." See "The Spatial Arts: An Interview with Jacques Derrida [1990]" in *Deconstruction and the Visual Arts*, ed. Peter Brunette and David Wills (Cambridge: Cambridge University Press, 1994), 9–32, esp. 27; and "Jacques Derrida: A Letter to Peter Eisenman [1989]," trans. Hilary P. Hanel, *Assemblage* 12 (1990): 6–13. A summary of the influence of Derrida's reading of *chōra* on architectural theory is provided by Anthony Vidler, "Nothing to Do with Architecture," *Grey Room* 21 (2005): 112–27. Vidler's summary, however, omits reference to this book series, *Chora*, and its affiliated scholarship, which opens lines of inquiry quite independent of deconstructivist theory.

4 From its earliest use, *choros* included the dance, dancers, and dancing ground (*Iliad*, 18.590–606; *Odyssey*, 8.260). As Steven H. Lonsdale emphasizes, "*choros* means, in addition to the choreographic activity, the group that performs it and the locus of performance, implying an indissoluble bond among the participants, the ritual act, and the sacred space." *Dance and Ritual Play in Greek Religion* (Baltimore: Johns Hopkins

University Press, 1993), 40. In the classical period (ca 480–338 BCE), the theatre's dancing ground was known as the *orchēstra*, while *choros* named the chorus, their choral performance, and institution. See Peter Wilson, *The Athenian Institution of the Khoregia: The Chorus, The City and the Stage* (Cambridge: Cambridge University Press, 2000), esp. 6.

5 The origins of these homophonic words have not been uncovered with certainty, but the spelling of *chōra* (χώρα), with a long "o" or "omega" (ώ), and of *choros* (χορός) with a short "o" or "omicron" (ο), suggest different semantic roots. *Chōra* has been linked to *cháos*: see Aristotle, *Physics*, 208b28–33, and Edward S. Casey, *The Fate of Place* (Berkeley: University of California Press, 1997), 7–11. *Choros* has been linked to *chara*, "joy"; *chairein*, "to rejoice"; and *cheir*, "hand," especially the expressive hand of a dancer, a chorus-leader, or one who votes "by show of hand." See Plato, *Laws*, 653e–654a; and Claude Calame, *Choruses of Young Women in Ancient Greece*, trans. Derek Collins and Janice Orion (Lanham, MD: Rowman & Littlefield, 2001), 19–20. See also Pierre Chantraine, *Diction-naire étymologique de la langue grecque: Histoire des mots* (Paris: Klinck-sieck, 1968–80), and H. Frisk, *Griechisches Etymologisches Wörterbuch*, vol. 2 (Heidelberg: Universitätsverlag, 1973).

6 Dalibor Vesely, "Architecture and the Poetics of Representation," *Daidalos* 25 (1987): 22–36. Here, Vesely emphasizes that "both *chorus* and *chōra* refer to the same symbolic situation of becoming, creating, and rebirth" (36). He elaborates on this correspondence in his discussion of "the mimetic nature of architecture" in *Architecture in the Age of Divided Representation* (Cambridge, MA: MIT Press, 2004), 370. Alberto Pérez-Gómez, in a seminal essay in this book series, has shown how the involved "distance" between spectators and actors in the theatre modelled the formative space between being and becoming in Plato's *Timaeus*, and further "enabled a participation in the wholeness of the universe." See "Chora: The Space of Architectural Representation," *Chora: Intervals in the Philosophy of Architecture*, vol. 1, ed. Alberto Pérez-Gómez and Stephen Parcell (Montreal and Kingston: McGill-Queen's University Press, 1994), 1–34. See also "*Chōra* as Erotic Space," in Alberto Pérez-Gómez, *Built upon Love: Architectural Longing after Ethics and Aesthetics* (Cambridge, MA: MIT Press, 2006), 44–51; and Alberto Pérez-Gómez and Louise Pelletier, "Vision and Depth," in *Archi-tectural Representation and the Perspectival Hinge* (Cambridge, MA: MIT Press, 1993), esp. 330–9, where the authors suggest correlations between Plato's philosophical *chōra* and Maurice Merleau-Ponty's phenomenological

"flesh." Pérez-Gómez's understanding of *chōra*, as a *choros*-like space of human creation and participation that is distanced from, yet reconciled with, the transcendent cosmos, underlies a primary argument of his book *Architecture and the Crisis of Modern Science* (Cambridge, MA: MIT Press, 1983): that toward the end of the eighteenth century, a "preconceptual spatiality" became obscured by a rationalized, demythologized, and homogenized notion of "geometrical space."

7 Aristophanes, *Peace*, 530. *Hypodochē* also can refer to a reception for returning troops (Herodotus, *Histories*, 1.119) or an intimate family reunion (Euripides, *Iphigenia at Aulis*, 1229). The noun derives from *dechomai* and *hypodechomai*, common verbs meaning "to receive" and "receive (from below)," especially by welcoming strangers into one's house (Homer, *Odyssey*, 16.70), foreigners into one's city or group (Euripides, *Bacchae*, 770, 1172), and suppliants into one's *chōra* (Euripides, *Children of Heracles*, 757). On the philosophical significance of "receptivity" to "the very reception of being," as Plato presents it, see John Sallis, *Chorology: On Beginning in Plato's Timaeus* (Bloomington: Indiana University Press, 1999), esp. 12. See also John Sallis, "Reception," in *Interrogating the Tradition: Hermeneutics and the History of Philosophy*, ed. Charles E. Scott and John Sallis (New York: State University of New York Press, 2000), 87–93, esp. 91.

8 According to myth, when a priest from Eleutherai first arrived in Athens with a statue of Dionysus, the god was not "received" with honour. Enraged by the cool reception, Dionysus afflicted all Athenian men with an erectile dysfunction. When the citizens consulted an oracle, a cure was pronounced: "introduce the god with all due honor." Dionysus's statue was brought back in a great procession, culminating with hospitality (feasting, wine drinking, and dramatic storytelling). Large phalluses were also fashioned and paraded by the Athenian men, in memory of the malady they had suffered. In light of this myth (known from the scholion to line 243 of Aristophanes's *Acharnians*), the Dionysian festival has been interpreted as a recurring enactment of atonement, providing Dionysus each year with the proper reception he was initially denied. In other words, the festival enacted the god's original reception as it ought to have occurred. For evidence and interpretations of this myth, see A.W. Pickard-Cambridge, *The Dramatic Festivals of Athens*, 2nd ed., revised by J. Gould and D. Lewis (Oxford: Oxford University Press, 1968), 57–8; Robert Garland, *Introducing New Gods: The Politics of Athenian Religion* (Ithaca, NY: Cornell University

Press, 1992), 159; and Christiane Sourvinou-Inwood, *Tragedy and Athenian Religion* (Lanham, MD: Lexington Books, 2003), 106–20.

9 On the spectators, performers, and order of events for the City Dionysia, see Pickard-Cambridge, *Dramatic Festivals*, 57–101, esp. 65–6; Jeffrey Henderson, "Drama and Democracy," in *The Age of Pericles*, ed. Loren J. Samons II (Cambridge: Cambridge University Press, 2007), 179–95, esp. 180; Rush Rehm, *The Play of Space: Spatial Transformation in Greek Tragedy* (Princeton: Princeton University Press, 2002), 48–54; and David Roselli, *Theater of the People: Spectators and Society in Ancient Athens* (Austin: University of Texas Press, 2011). On the significance of the various representative displays to Athenian democracy, see also Simon Goldhill, "The Great Dionysia and Civic Ideology," *Journal of Hellenic Studies* 107 (1987): 58–76, reprinted in John J. Winkler and Froma I. Zeitlin, eds., *Nothing to Do with Dionysus: Athenian Drama in Its Social Context* (Princeton: Princeton University Press, 1990), 97–129; and Simon Goldhill and Robin Osborne, eds., *Performance Culture and Athenian Democracy* (Cambridge: Cambridge University Press, 1999).

10 For recent scholarship on the configuration of the Theatre of Dionysus during the fifth century BCE, see Rehn, *Play of Space*, 37–41; Hans Rupprecht Goette, "An Archaeological Appendix," in *The Greek Theatre and Festivals: Documentary Studies*, ed. Peter Wilson (Oxford: Oxford University Press, 2007), 116–21; and Peter Meineck, "The Embodied Space: Performance and Visual Cognition at the Fifth Century Athenian Theatre," *New England Classical Journal* 39, no. 1 (2012): 2–46.

11 This is likely an allusion to Plato's earlier dialogue, the *Republic* (*Politeia*). See Sallis, *Chorology*, 14; and Eric Voegelin, *Order and History*, vol. 3, *Plato and Aristotle* (Baton Rouge: Louisiana State University Press, 1957), 171.

12 The dialogue takes place during a "general assembly" and "sacrifice" for "the goddess" (21a, 26e). For interpretations of the festival referred to here (perhaps the annual Lesser Panathenaea or Plynteria), see A.E. Taylor, *A Commentary on Plato's Timaeus* (Oxford: Clarendon Press, 1928), 45.

13 These metaphors provide tangible approximations of *chōra*'s receptivity: as a mirror that "receives likenesses of objects and gives back images of them" (71b, 46a); as a mixing bowl (*krater*) that receives the elements that the demiurge "mixes" (41d); as a mother who receives and nurtures the father's seed of their child (50d); as a winnowing fan that receives, shakes, separates, and disperses the grain (52e–53a); as an odourless liquid that receives

any scent for the making of perfume (50e); and as a neutral plastic substance such as wax that receives impressions (50d).

14 Unless otherwise noted, all translations of *Timaeus* are by Benjamin Jowett in *Plato: The Collected Dialogues*, ed. Edith Hamilton and Huntington Cairns, Bollingen Series 71 (New York: Pantheon, 1961).

15 "But come, tell me this and declare it truly: whither you have wandered and to what *chōras* of men you have come; tell me of the people and of their populous cities, both of those who are cruel and wild and unjust, and of those who are kind to strangers and fear the gods in their thoughts." *Odyssey*, 8.572–76, trans. A.T. Murray, revised by George E. Dimock (Cambridge, MA: Harvard University Press, 1995). This extended request shows places, people, and practices to be integral to *chōra*. Summarizing the various uses of *chōra* in Homer is beyond the scope of this paper. For an important study of this topic within architectural discourse, see Maria Theodorou, "Space as Experience," *AA Files* 34 (1997): 45–55.

16 See the entry for *chōra* in H.G. Liddell and R. Scott, *Greek-English Lexicon* (Oxford: Oxford University Press, 1996). On the "defense of the *chōra*," see Aristotle, *Athenian Constitution*, 43.4, with the appendix of inscriptions in P.J. Rhodes, *The Athenian Boule* (Oxford: Clarendon Press, 1972), 231–5. See also Aeschines, *On the Embassy*, 2.167, and Xenophon, *Ways and Means*, 4.52.

17 In *Airs, Waters and Places*, the Ionian form of *chōra* (*chōrē*) is used whenever the Hippocratic author describes how particular features and the climate of a "region" affect the constitution of one's disposition and health (1.8, 12.12, 13.8–15, 15.2–18, 18.24, 19.6–40, 24.7–54). A later work attributed to Aristotle, *Meteorologica*, similarly involves *chōra* in discussions of regional weather peculiarities such as variations in rainfall (360b).

18 Pindar offers a song "to glorify this *chōra* [of Aigina], where the myrmidons of old dwelled" (*Nemean*, 3.13). In another ode, Pindar calls on Apollo to "make this [land of Aitna] a *chōra* of brave men" (*Pythian*, 1.40). Elsewhere, Pindar tells his listeners to "follow my voice here [to Olympus] to a *chōra* shared by all" (*Olympian*, 6.63). In a Paean for Apollo, Bacchylides sings of how the god commanded Heracles to settle the people of Droypes in the *chōra* of Asine (Frag, 4.44).

19 In some instances, *chōra* can mean an occupied place or position at a more corporeal scale: in the *Odyssey*, Odysseus's bed is firmly rooted in its *chōrē* (23.186, cf. 21.366, 16.352); and in the *Iliad*, after rising to counsel his

son, Nestor sits back down, returning to his *chōrē* (23.349, cf. 6.516). At an even smaller scale, in the Hippocratic texts, *chōra* can refer to the socket cavity of bone joints (*On Fractures*, 9.7).

20 See also 23b–c, 19a. In its conventional sense, *chōra* appears most frequently (more than eighty times) in Plato's *Laws* (his last work), but also in the *Republic* and *Critias*: the two dialogues believed to have been composed either concurrently with *Timaeus* or immediately before and after.

21 On neologisms in Plato, see D.N. Sedley, *Plato's Cratylus* (Cambridge: Cambridge University Press, 2003), 69–73; and Lewis Campbell, *The Sophistes and Politicus of Plato* (Oxford: Oxford University Press, 1867), xxiv–xxviii.

22 Mogens Herman Hansen, *Polis: An Introduction to the Ancient Greek City-State* (Oxford: Oxford University Press, 2006), esp. 57; Mogens Herman Hansen, ed., *The Return of the Polis: The Use and Meanings of the Word Polis in Archaic and Classical Sources* (Stuttgart: Franz Stainer Verlag, 2007), 67–72.

23 Robin Osborne, *Classical Landscape with Figures: The Ancient Greek City and its Countryside* (Dobbs Ferry, NY: Sheridan House, 1987), 16. See also Victor Davis Hanson, *The Other Greeks: The Family Farm and the Agrarian Roots of Western Civilization* (New York: Free Press, 1995), 126. Hanson argues, "Agrarianism *defined* the nascent *polis* ... the Greek city-state was born as a rural institution and as an agrarian ideology" (his emphasis). These authors draw from François de Polignac, *Cults, Territory, and the Origins of the Greek City-State*, trans. Janet Lloyd (Chicago: University of Chicago Press, 1995, first published as *La naissance de la cité grecque*, 1984). Polignac argues for a "mutually fostering" relation between towns and their hinterland (154), forged largely through ritual processions moving periodically over the terrain – from a populated settlement out to a liminal sanctuary and back again – thus transforming the *chōra* into a great "stage" (40). For an architectural reading of Polignac's argument, see the section on the *polis* and "weaving the city" in Indra Kagis McEwen, *Socrates' Ancestor* (Cambridge, MA: MIT Press, 1993), esp. 79–91.

24 On the significance of this "unification" (*synoikismos*) and its festival (*synoikia*), see Rehm, *Play of Space*, 58–9, with further references.

25 Solon also made it easier for people to own land by cancelling their debt (Aristotle, *Athenian Constitution*, 12.1–5).

26 Aristotle *Athenian Constitution* 21.4; *Politics* 1319b23–7. See also Pierre

Lévêque and Pierre Vidal-Naquet, *Cleisthenes the Athenian: An Essay on the Representation of Space and Time in Greek Political Thought from the End of the Sixth Century to the Death of Plato*, trans. David Ames Curtis (Atlantic Highlands, NJ: Humanities Press, 1996).

27 Justina Gregory, *Euripides and the Instruction of the Athenians* (Ann Arbor: University of Michigan Press, 1997), 45.

28 Pickard-Cambridge, *Dramatic Festivals*, 74–9.

29 Ibid., 269–70. The area for spectators is believed to have been organized into thirteen pie-shaped sections fanning out across the hillside, with the middle section reserved for members of the Boulē, the five sections on each side for the ten *demes*, and the two sections at either end for foreign visitors.

30 John J. Winkler has similarly described the configuration in the theatre as "a kind of map of the civic corporation, with all its tensions and balances ... [a] map of the body politic." See "The Ephebes' Song: *Tragōidia* and *Polis*," in *Nothing to Do with Dionysus*, 20–62, esp. 39–42.

31 In Plato's *Timaeus*, Socrates laments that not even "the poets" could bring the ideal city to life (19d). Though the City Dionysia persisted throughout the fourth century BCE, its organization became more bureaucratic and self-serving than symbolic; see Wilson, *Athenian Institution of the Khoregia*, 269–70. On the popularity of theatrical festivals in Plato's lifetime (if not their crucial political and symbolic significance), see P.E. Easterling, "The End of an Era? Tragedy in the Early Fourth Century," in *Tragedy, Comedy and the Polis*, ed. Alan H. Sommerstein et al. (Bari: Levante Editori, 1993), 559–69. The loss of Athenian drama's political purpose also may be felt in Aristotle's later *Poetics*. Aristotle placed little value on the social, situational, and festive aspects of dramatic poetry; instead, he emphasized its influence on an individual's emotions and intellect. See Edith Hall, "Is There a *Polis* in Aristotle's *Poetics*?" in *Tragedy and the Tragic: Greek Theatre and Beyond*, ed. M.S. Silk (Oxford: Clarendon Press, 1996), 295–309.

32 Thucydides 2.13–17; 2.55–64; 7.27; see also Barry S. Strauss, *Athens After the Peloponnesian War: Class, Faction and Policy, 403–386 BC* (Ithaca, NY: Cornell University Press, 1986), 43–5. The psychological impact of the devastation may have been worse than the actual agricultural damage; see also Rehm, *Play of Space*, 60.

33 *Politics* 4.1295a36–1296a22; see also Hanson, *Other Greeks*, 132.

34 *Chōrion* (*chōra* in its diminutive form) denoted a plot of land, farm, or estate. Aristophanes depicts various rural characters longing to return to

their *chōrion* and doing everything they can to save it (*Peace*, 562, 1146, 1148; *Wasps*, 850; *Clouds*, 1123). *Chōrion* also may imply a small-scaled *chōra*. In Aristophanes's *Birds*, a student in Socrates's "Thinkery" shows off a novel representation: a map, the "*chōrion* of Attica" (209).

35 In his speech *On the Crown* (330 BCE) Demosthenes boasts of fortifying not just the port or the towns, but the "whole of the *chōra*" (18.299–300). On the "defensive mentality" and "deep fear of enemy invasion" that plagued Attica after the Peloponnesian War, see Josiah Ober, *Fortress Attica: Defense of the Athenian Land Frontier 404–322 B.C.* (Leiden: E.J. Brill, 1985).

36 Osborne, *Classical Landscape*, 161–4. Osborne argues that the separation of farmers from politics (and warfare) resulted in the Greek city's loss of its "essential identity."

37 Hanson, *Other Greeks*, 194, 408. In *Laws*, Plato provides a detailed strategy for protecting the *chōra* that involves not only building fortifications and performing regular perimeter patrols but also planning recreational and educational facilities for the troops and health-restoring settings for all citizens (6.670b–673b). See also Ober, *Fortress Attica*, 79–80. In his work on *Rhetoric*, Aristotle counts the "defense of the *chōra*" among the five most important topics for political deliberation (1359b19–22). In *Politics*, Aristotle contends that "the best material of democracy is an agricultural population" (6.1318b10–12) and recommends that a city maintain close ties with its *chōra* to retain self-sufficiency (7.1327a). Similarly, Xenophon enumerates the many geographical benefits and resources of Attica (its natural harbours, plentiful crops, honey, timber, silver mines, quarries, clay, etc.), all of which "are due to the *chōra* itself" (*Revenues* 2.1). See also Ober, *Fortress Attica*, 17–19.

38 Some scholars pass quickly over *chōra*'s meaning as "land" in their pursuit of more abstract definitions of "space." See Keimpe Algra, *Concepts of Space in Greek Thought* (Leiden: E.J. Brill, 1995), 33–4. More positively, John Sallis briefly speaks to *chōra*'s pre-philosophical meaning and discusses the inseparability of political and cosmological discourses for Plato: *Chorology*, 116–7; and "The Politics of the χώρα" in *Platonic Legacies* (New York: State University of New York Press, 2004), 27–45.

39 I use *fusion* here in the sense described by Hans-Georg Gadamer, *Truth and Method*, trans. Joel Weinsheimer and Donald G. Marshall (New York: Continuum, 1993), 306–7. For "reciprocal determination," I follow David

Leatherbarrow, "Leveling the Land, or How Topography is the Horizon of Horizons," in *Topographical Stories* (Philadelphia: University of Pennsylvania Press, 2004), 114–30.

40 In Euripides's *Iphigenia at Tauris*, a chorus of women refers to the Taurican leader Thoas as "lord of this *chōra*" (1294). In Euripides's *Children of Heracles*, a herald asks, "Who is the lord of this *chōra* and *polis* [*sc.* Demophon, son of Theseus]?" (114). In Euripides's *Archelaus*, the chorus addresses Cisseus of Thrace as "King of this fertile *chōra*" (Frag., 229). In Euripides's *Heracles*, Theseus fears that Lycus has "seized power of this *chōra* [*sc.* Thebes]" (1167). In Euripides's *Children of Heracles*, Iolaus explains that he has led Heracles's descendants to seek refuge in Marathon (a coastal town of Attica) because they have been "banished from all other *chōras* of Greece" (30). In Sophocles's *Antigone*, a chorus of Theban elders greets Creon as "King of this *chōra*" (155). In Sophocles's *Oedipus Tyrannus*, a Theban priest addresses Oedipus as "ruler of my *chōra*" (14); later, after Oedipus's decline, the chorus recognizes Creon as "guardian of the *chōra*" (1418). In Sophocles's *Oedipus at Colonus*, Oedipus asks a chorus of locals, "Where is the ruler of this *chōra* [*sc.* Theseus]?" (296); he later calls on Theseus as "lord of this *chōra*" (1476). In Aeschylus's *Eumenides*, the priestess of Delphi remembers Delphus as "lord and helmsman of this *chōra*" (16); and Orestes invokes Athena as "goddess of this *chōra* [of Attica]" (288). In Aeschylus's *Persians*, a chorus of Persian elders remembers how prosperous their land once was, when "god-like Darius ruled this *chōra*" (856). At the tragic end of Aeschylus's *Libation Bearers*, Orestes reveals his slain mother and her lover, saying, "behold the twin tyrants of this *chōra* [*sc.* Argos]" (973).

41 Of the thirty-two surviving tragedies, only one, Aeschylus's *Eumenides*, is set in Athens (though the opening scene takes place in Delphi), and just three are set in other parts of Attica: Sophocles's *Oedipus in Colonus* (just northwest of Athens); Euripides's *Suppliant Women* (in Eleusis); and Euripides's *Children of Heracles* (in Marathon).

42 For a more detailed description of what spectators would have seen from their places in the ancient theatre, see Rehm, *Play of Space*, 35–6.

43 Similarly, in Euripides's *Helen*, when Menelaus arrives on the shore of Egypt, he wonders aloud, "What is this *chōra*?" (459, see also 414). All translations of Euripides in this essay are adapted from David Kovacs, *Euripides*, 8 vols., Loeb Classical Library (Cambridge, MA: Harvard University Press, 1994–2008).

44 Thucydides, 5.84–116.

45 Agamemnon will be murdered by his wife, Clytemnestra; Odysseus, when he finally returns to Ithaca, will find his house threatened by suitors.

46 On Euripides's tendency to dramatize "contemporary public concerns while presenting a narrative from the 'mythic past,'" see Rehm, *Play of Space*, 37. See also Barbara Goff, *Euripides: Trojan Women* (London: Duckworth, 2009), 27–35.

47 Rehm, *Play of Space*, 272. See also 20–25, where Rehm defines six different kinds of spaces interacting in ancient drama: theatrical, scenic, extrascenic, distanced, self-referential (meta-theatrical), and reflexive.

48 On the revelatory function of the *skēnē*, as well as the "stage-machine" (*mēchanē*) that connected earth and heavens and the "rolling-out device" (*ekkyklēma*) that drew interior scenes out from behind the *skēnē* and into the orchestra, see Ruth Padel, "Making Space Speak," in *Nothing to Do with Dionysus*, 336–65.

49 In Aristophanes's *Peace*, Trygaeus, Hermes, and Peace chastise the audience for their political misconduct as if speaking directly to the Assembly (603–705). At the end of Euripides's *Trojan Women*, Helen defends her conduct as if standing trial in court (914ff). Such scenes attest to how ancient theatre cultivated political consciousness and served as an influential "forum for political action." See Oddone Longo, "Theater of the *Polis*," in *Nothing to Do with Dionysus*, 12–19, esp. 13.

50 Aristophanes, *Birds*, 1482. In general, see L.A. Swift, "The Symbolism of Space in Euripidean Choral Fantasy (*Hipp.* 732–75, *Med.* 824–65, *Bacch.* 370–433)," *Classical Quarterly* 59, no. 2 (2009): 364–82.

51 For important discussions of how this special kind of reasoning prevails in spite of (or because of) *chōra*'s irrationality, see Hans-Georg Gadamer, "Idea and Reality in Plato's *Timaeus*," in *Dialogue and Dialectic: Eight Hermeneutical Studies on Plato*, trans. P. Christopher Smith (New Haven: Yale University Press, 1980), 156–93, esp. 179; and Richard C. Palmer, ed., *The Gadamer Reader: A Bouquet of the Later Writings* (Evanston, IL: Northwestern University Press, 2007), 372–406, esp. 404.

52 On the complex identity of the chorus, including its overlapping representative, interpretive, and ritual functions, see Helene P. Foley, "Choral Identity in Greek Tragedy," *Classical Philology* 98, no. 1 (2003): 1–30; Claude Calame, "Choral Forms in Aristophanic Comedy: Musical Mimesis and Dramatic Performance in Classical Athens," in *Music and the Muses: The Culture of 'Mousikē' in the Classical Athenian City*, ed. Penelope

Murray and Peter Wilson (Oxford: Oxford University Press, 2004), 157–84; and Albert Henrichs, "'Why Should I Dance?': Choral Self-Referentiality in Greek Tragedy," *Arion* 3, no. 1 (1994/1995): 56–111.

53 In *Lysistrata*, the heroine asks, "Is there no one to help us, no savior in this *chōra*?" (524). Her own scheme ultimately restores "order and justice to *chōras*" torn apart by war (565–6).

54 In *Assembly Women*, as Praxagora initiates her scheme to save the city, she utters a prayer: "May the gods grant success to my plans! This *chōra* is dear to me" (173).

55 In *Wasps*, the chorus chastises the spectators for failing to appreciate Aristophanes's *Clouds* (which had placed third in the comic competition the previous year). They first praise their poet as "a bulwark against evil ... a purifier of the *chōra*"; then they blame the spectators for their lack of understanding, for "making fruitless" his "sown crop of brand-new ideas" (1042–5).

56 Calame, "Choral Forms in Aristophanic Comedy," esp. 175.

57 At the close of Sophocles's *Oedipus Tyrannus*, the chorus remembers Oedipus as having "destroyed the prophesying maiden with hooked talons, and for my *chōra* stood like a wall keeping off death" (1198–1201). See also Aeschylus, *Seven against Thebes*, where the chorus recalls how Oedipus had "removed from the *chōra* the man-snatching demon" (777).

58 At the beginning of *Oedipus Tyrannus*, the oracle of Apollo decrees that the Thebans must "drive out a pollution (*miasma*) from the *chōra*" (97). In the end, Oedipus realizes that he himself is the tainted one. Oedipus's downfall is brought about not simply because he had unknowingly acted against his own kin, but because he had failed to recognize his own responsibility in allowing a past crime of regicide to go unpunished. In the continued story, Oedipus's son, Polyneices, again puts the Theban *chōra* in danger; see also Aeschylus, *Seven against Thebes*, 1048; and Euripides, *Phoenician Women*, 246.

59 See also 1, 24, 38, 52, 54, 644, 1058, 1520, 1540. In Athenian drama *chōros* typically names a divinely communicative and portentous place, including sites of potential architectural significance. For instance, Athena orders a temple to be built in a certain *chōros* at the edge of Attica (Euripides, *Iphigenia at Tauris*, 1450; see also *Ion*, 283–5; *Hippolytus*, 1198; Sophocles, *Trackers*, 38; Aeschylus, *Eumenides*, 24; and *Libation Bearers*, 543). Similarly, in lyric poetry, Anchises promises to build Aphrodite an

altar in a "conspicuous *chōros*" (*Homeric Hymn to Aphrodite*, 100); and Apollo is said to have "built a temple" in the peaceful *chōros* of Telephousa (*Homeric Hymn to Apollo*, 244; see also 359, 413, 501, 521). *Chōros* (the masculine variation of *chōra*) has been shown to have close links to *choros*, based on the frequency with which *chōros* (a "place of contact between mortal and gods") becomes the site for *choros* (dance). See Deborah Dickmann Boedeker, "ΧΩΡΟΣ and ΧΟΡΟΣ," in *Aphrodite's Entry into Greek Epic* (Leiden: E.J. Brill, 1974), 85–91.

60 On this tragedy's preoccupation with locality, see Richard H. Allison, "'This Is the Place': Why is Oidipous at Kolonos?" *Prudentia* 16 (1984): 67–91. Colonus is particularly significant, as it was Sophocles's own home *deme* and the site of his birth. As *Oedipus at Colonus* was Sophocles's last play, composed just before he died at the age of ninety in 404/05 (staged posthumously in 401), Colonus also may have been the projected site of the poet's own grave. Colunus's significance is furthered by the fact that Plato founded his Academy there in 387 BCE.

61 This chorus is closely linked to *chōra* throughout the play, being qualified as "friends toward this *chōra*" (*prochōrōn xenōn*, 493), and "[men] of the *chōra*" (*egchōrioi*, 871).

62 Oedipus promises to bring "well-being" (*eudaimonia*) to "this *chōra*" (1553), providing "a protection stronger than many shields or spears" (1524–5, see also 72, 92, 459–60, 1764–5). This tragedy effectively dramatizes an aetiological myth, showing Oedipus's grave to be refounded as a hero shrine granting protective powers. See Eveline Krummen, "Athens and Attica: *Polis* and Countryside in Greek Tragedy," in *Tragedy, Comedy and the Polis*, ed. Alan H. Sommerstein et al. (Bari: Levante Editori, 1993), 191–217, esp. 200.

63 After singing the verses quoted at the start of this essay, the chorus of Sophocles's *Oedipus at Colonus* describe their *chōra*'s indestructable, self-renewing olive tree, which, as an emblem of Athena, instills terror in their enemies (695–703).

64 These links between inner and outer milieux made *chōra* an apt metaphor for one's internal seat of passions. For instance, in Aeschylus's *Agamemnon*, the chorus of old men compare their incapacity and unwillingness to wage battle to the weak drive of a child: "The immature marrow that rules in a child's breast is like that of an old man, there is no Ares in that *chōra*" (78).

65 For an important discussion of Vitruvius's concept of proportion and

symmetry in relation to humoral theory, see David Leatherbarrow, *Roots of Architectural Invention: Site, Enclosure, Materials* (Cambridge: Cambridge University Press, 1993), 82–92.

66 As *Eumenides* is the last tragedy of a trilogy, Athena's positive transformation extends back to the preceding plays: to *Agamemnon*, in which Clytemnestra murders her own husband inside the palace, bringing about the "pollution of this *chōra* and the gods who dwell in it" (1645); and to *Libation Bearers*, in which Electra swears an oath "to this *chōra*" to help Orestes avenge their father's murder (397) and Orestes ultimately kills his mother and her lover, "the twin tyrants of this *chōra*" (973).

67 In spite of Plato's rejection of dramatic poets from his ideal city in *Republic*, his indebtedness to drama has long been recognized and much discussed. See Hans-Georg Gadamer, "Plato and the Poets," in *Dialogue and Dialectic* (New Haven: Yale University Press, 1980), 39–72; and A.W. Nightingale, "The Philosopher at the Festival: Plato's Transformation of Traditional *Theoria*," in *Pilgrimage in Graeco-Roman and Early Christian Antiquity*, ed. Jas Elsner and Ian Rutherford (Oxford: Oxford University Press, 2005), 151–80. Nightingale's argument is elaborated in her *Spectacles of Truth in Classical Greek Philosophy: Theōria in its Cultural Context* (Cambridge: Cambridge University Press, 2004).

68 John P. Manoussakis, "Thinking at the Limits: Jacques Derrida and Jean-Luc Marion in Dialogue with Richard Kearney," *Philosophy Today* 48 (2004): 3–11, esp. 11.

69 Derrida specifically compared *chōra* to Europe, and to the mediating role it might play in the post-9/11 conflict. Ibid., 9.

About the Authors

Anne Bordeleau
Anne Bordeleau is an architect and associate professor in the School of Architecture at the University of Waterloo, where she teaches design studio and cultural history from medieval to modernity. She received a professional MArch degree and a post-professional MArch in architectural history and theory from McGill University, a PhD in architectural history from the Bartlett (University College London), and a postdoctoral fellowship from the Paul Mellon Centre for Studies in British Art. Her research gravitates around fundamental relations between architecture and time. Her writings on this subject have appeared in the *Journal of Architecture*, *Architectural History*, *Footprint*, and *Architectural Theory Review*. Her book, *Charles Robert Cockerell, Architect in Time: Reflections around Anachronistic Drawings* (Ashgate, 2014), studies how a nineteenth-century architect addressed shifting relations among architecture, time, and history.

Diana Cheng
Architect and historian Diana Cheng has an MArch degree from Carleton University and also studied with Jeff Wall, Mark Lewis, and Geoffrey Smedley at the University of British Columbia. She has a PhD in architectural history and theory from McGill University (2011) and is currently working on a book project, *The History of the Boudoir: A Room of Her Own*, based on her dissertation. Diana has taught at the Azrieli School of Architecture and Urbanism at Carleton University and at McGill University School of Architecture. Her most recent article, "Ordres architecturaux et expression chez Clément-Pierre Marillier," appears in *Imager la Romancie: Dessins de Clément-Pierre Marillier pour* Le Cabinet des fées *et* Les Voyages imaginaires *(1785–1789)*, ed. Aurélie Zygel-Basso (Hermann, 2013).

Negin Djavaherian
Negin Djavaherian has a professional MArch degree from Azad University in Tehran, where her architectural practice included residential and cultural buildings. She also has a post-professional MArch and PhD in architectural history and theory from McGill University. Her doctoral dissertation explored architectural potential and experience in the theatre of Peter Brook, during which she conducted personal interviews with Peter Brook, Jean-Claude Carrière, and Jean-Guy Lecat. Her

research focuses on theatre as a source of inspiration for architects: a ground for exploring the ethical and poetic dimensions of architecture. She was awarded a Canadian Centre for Architecture / McGill University research grant and has presented papers at international conferences. Her long-held interest in Persian mystical poetry and Sufi mysticism led her to become part of an award-winning design and research team at Safamanesh and Associates for a competition called House of Mawlānā.

Paul Emmons
Paul Emmons was born and raised in Wisconsin, just north of Taliesin. He received an MArch degree from the University of Minnesota in 1984, when Ralph Rapson was head of the school, and became a registered, practicing architect in Minneapolis while teaching part-time at the university. After moving his family to Swarthmore, he earned a PhD in architecture at the University of Pennsylvania in 2003. For the past fifteen years, he has been teaching at the Washington-Alexandria Architecture Center of Virginia Tech, where he is currently associate professor and director of the PhD program in Architecture + Design, founded by the late Marco Frascari. Emmons's research, published in many book chapters and articles, is devoted to understanding architectural practices: from why some architects sign their buildings to the role of pencil lead in design. He is currently writing a book, entitled *The Mirror of Design*, on how architects imagine architecture through embodied activities of drawing.

Paul Holmquist
Paul Holmquist studied painting and drawing at the University of California at Los Angeles before pursuing professional graduate studies in architecture at the Southern California Institute of Architecture. He has a post-professional MArch in architectural history and theory from McGill University and is continuing there as a PhD candidate, focusing on late eighteenth-century architectural and political theory in Claude-Nicolas Ledoux's ideal city of Chaux. He has taught architectural design and theory, with an emphasis on poetics, politics, and technology, at the SUNY College of Technology in Alfred, New York, Kansas State University, McGill University, and most recently at the Azrieli School of Architecture and Urbanism at Carleton University.

Ron Jelaco
Ron Jelaco was raised in a small town in southeast Idaho. He has
degrees in architecture from the University of Idaho and the University
of Pennsylvania, and studied also at the Architectural Association in
London. He has been a practicing architect in the western United States
and a professor of architectural design, history, and theory at several
universities in the United States and Canada. He now teaches in the
School of Architecture and the School of Environment at McGill University, where he is also a research fellow in architectural history and
theory. His research is developing an understanding of the structures of
contemporary life by focusing on their sources in seventeenth-century
France, currently in a project on the origins of the Paris Observatory.

Yoonchun Jung
Yoonchun Jung completed a PhD in architectural history and theory at
McGill University, with a dissertation entitled "Inventing the Identity
of Modern Korean Architecture During the Colonial Era, 1904–1929."
His research focuses on social, cultural, and political phenomena in
modern Asian cities. He is originally from South Korea and has worked
as an architect in Seoul, New York, Paris, and London. He taught at
Cornell University from 2004 to 2006, the State University of New
York at Buffalo from 2006 to 2008, and McGill University in 2010.
From 2012 to 2013, he conducted PhD research on Korean architectural modernity as a Japan Foundation fellow at Kyoto University.

Christos Kakalis
Christos Kakalis received a diploma in architecture from the University
of Thessaly in Volos and has practiced in Greece as an architect. He
also has an interdisciplinary MSc degree in design, space, and culture
from the National Technical University of Athens and a PhD in architecture from the University of Edinburgh, where he received the David
Willis Prize (2010) and a Richard Brown Scholarship (2011). His
research focuses on embodied experience in architecture and natural
landscape. He has participated, independently or as a collaborator, in
architectural and artistic exhibitions and competitions, and has published on the experience of architecture and architectural typology.
Since 2008 he has been teaching architectural design, history, and

theory at the National University of Athens and the University of Edinburgh. Funded by the Alexander S. Onassis Public Benefit Foundation, he will become a postdoctoral fellow at the School of Architecture at McGill University and the Edinburgh School of Architecture and Landscape Architecture.

Lisa Landrum

Lisa Landrum is an architect, artist, author, and educator, currently an associate professor in the Department of Architecture at the University of Manitoba. Her research on the dramatic agencies of architecture and architectural theory has been shared in international conferences and published in two books by Ashgate in 2013: *Architecture As a Performing Art*, ed. Marcia Feuerstein and Gray Read; and *Architecture and Justice: Judicial Meanings in the Public Realm*, ed. Jonathan Simon, Nicholas Temple, and René Tobe. Lisa holds a bachelor of architecture degree from Carleton University (1995), as well as a post-professional MArch (2003) and PhD (2011) in the history and theory of architecture from McGill University. Her dissertation, titled "Architectural Acts: Architect Figures in Athenian Drama and their Prefigurations," uncovered the poetic and ethical dimensions of "architecting" in early Greek plays. Lisa's creative research extends to the collaborative devising of award-winning Group Costumes for civic parades. Lisa is also a registered architect in New York State and the province of Manitoba.

Robert Nelson

Associate Professor Robert Nelson is Associate Director Student Experience at Monash University in Melbourne, Australia, and art critic for *The Age*. The focus of Robert's research is the link between the aesthetic and the moral in art, design, and architecture. His books include *The Spirit of Secular Art* (Monash University ePress, 2007), *The Jealousy of Ideas: Research Methods in the Creative Arts* (Ellikon and Writing Pad, 2009), *The Visual Language of Painting* (Australian Scholarly Publishing, 2010), *Moral Sustainability and Cycling: Toward an Ecology of Ambition for a Hyperactive Planet* (Ellikon, 2010), *The Space Wasters: The Architecture of Australian Misanthropy* (Planning Institute of Australia, 2011), and *Instruments of Contentment: Furniture and Poetic Sustainability* (Craft Victoria, 2014). He is the author of many articles in the refereed literature, plus one thousand newspaper reviews and articles. Robert is also a scene painter (polixenipapapetrou.net).

Marc J Neveu
After graduating with a professional architecture degree, Marc completed a post-professional MArch and PhD in architectural history and theory at McGill University. While working on his dissertation, he was awarded a Fulbright Fellowship to study in Venice, as well as a Collection Research Grant at the Canadian Centre for Architecture. He has taught history, theory, and studio at universities in the United States and Canada, and has published on architectural pedagogy in the Italian eighteenth century, as well as in our contemporary context. In 2014, he was appointed chair of the School of Architecture at Woodbury University in Los Angeles. He is also executive editor of the *Journal of Architectural Education.*

Alberto Pérez-Gómez
Alberto Pérez-Gómez was born in 1949 in Mexico City, where he studied and practiced architecture. In 1983, he became director of Carleton University's School of Architecture. Since January 1987, he has occupied the Bronfman Chair of Architectural History at McGill University, where he founded the History and Theory post-professional (master's and doctoral) programs. He has lectured extensively around the world and is the author of numerous articles published in major periodicals and books. His book *Architecture and the Crisis of Modern Science* (1983) won the Alice Davis Hitchcock Award in 1984. Later books include *Polyphilo or The Dark Forest Revisited* (1992), *Architectural Representation and the Perspective Hinge* (co-authored with Louise Pelletier, 1997), and most recently, *Built upon Love: Architectural Longing after Ethics and Aesthetics* (2006), which examines points of convergence between ethics and poetics in architectural history and philosophy.

Angeliki Sioli
Angeliki Sioli is originally from Greece. She obtained a professional diploma in architecture from the University of Thessaly in 2005, followed by a post-professional master's degree in architectural theory

from the National Technical University of Athens in 2008. She has worked as an architect on housing and office buildings, as well as small-scale objects and stage sets for dance performances. In 2015 she was awarded a PhD in architectural history and theory from McGill University. Her research seeks connections between architecture and literature in the public realm of the early twentieth-century European city, focusing on bodily spatial perception in the urban environment. She has presented her work in professional and interdisciplinary conferences and architectural publications. She has taught studio and history courses at McGill University and is currently a research professor at the Monterrey Institute of Technology and Higher Education in Puebla, Mexico.

Nikolaos-Ion Terzoglou
Nikolaos-Ion Terzoglou received a diploma in architecture (2000), a master of science (2001), and a PhD (2005) from the National Technical University of Athens. He also has a degree in painting from the Athens School of Fine Arts (2009). His PhD dissertation, "Conceptual Structures of Architectural Thought: Leon Battista Alberti, Étienne-Louis Boullée, Le Corbusier," was awarded the Second International ICAR-CORA Prize in 2007. He has published a monograph in Greek, *Ideas of Space in the 20th Century* (Nissos, 2009), based on his postdoctoral research in the Department of Humanities, Social Sciences, and Law of the National Technical University of Athens (2007–8). He has taught at the University of Patras, Greece (2007–10) and is currently a lecturer at the National Technical University of Athens, where he teaches Concepts and Theories for the Organization of Space.

Stephen Wischer
Stephen Wischer is currently an associate professor of architecture at North Dakota State University, where his architecture studios and seminars emphasize transdisciplinary relationships among art, architecture, history, and philosophy. Born in Edmonton, he received a bachelor of fine arts from the University of Alberta in 1998 and an MArch and master of fine arts from the University of Calgary in 2004. Since 2010, he has been working on a PhD in architectural history and theory at McGill University, focusing on the architectural significance of Anselm

Kiefer's situated art practice. His research on the relation between architectural representation and the fine arts has led to publications and presentations in various countries. As an exhibiting artist since 1994, his mixed media drawings, sculpture, and installations have been exhibited in museums and galleries in Canada and the United States.